The Cross of the Son of God

MARTIN HENGEL

The Cross of the Son of God

Containing

The Son of God
Crucifixion
The Atonement

SCM PRESS LTD

Translated by John Bowden from the German.

The Son of God, first published 1976 by SCM Press Ltd,
is a translation of *Der Sohn Gottes. Die Entstehung der
Christologie und die jüdisch-hellenistische Religionsgeschichte*,
published 1975 by J. C. B. Mohr (Paul Siebeck), Tübingen.

Crucifixion, first published 1977 by SCM Press Ltd, is
translated from '*Mors turpissima crucis*: Die Kreuzigung
in der antiken Welt und die "Torheit" des "Wortes vom Kreuz" ',
published in *Rechtfertigung. Festschrift für Ernst Käsemann
zum 70. Geburtstag*, ed. J. Friedrich, W. Pöhlmann and P. Stuhlmacher,
by J. C. B. Mohr (Paul Siebeck), Tübingen, and Vandenhoeck and
Ruprecht, Göttingen, 1976, with substantial later
additions by the author.

The Atonement, first published 1981 by SCM Press Ltd,
was originally an extended article, 'Der stellvertretende
Sühnetod Jesu. Ein Beitrag zur Entstehung des urchristlichen
Kerygmas', *Internationale katholische Zeitschrift* 9,
1980, 1–25, 135–47, with substantial additions by the author.

334 01963 x

This collection first published 1986 by
SCM Press Ltd,
26–30 Tottenham Road, London N1

Printed in Great Britain by
Richard Clay (The Chaucer Press) plc,
Bungay, Suffolk

Contents

CRUCIFIXION

THE ATONEMENT

Abbreviations

AAG	Abhandlungen der Akademie der Wissenschaften in Göttingen
AAMz	Abhandlungen der Akademie der Wissenschaften in Mainz
AGAJU/ AGJU	Arbeiten zur Geschichte des antiken Judentums und des Urchristentums, Leiden
AGSU	Arbeiten zur Geschichte des Spätjudentums und Urchristentums, Leiden
AJT	*American Journal of Theology*, Chicago
ALGHJ	Arbeiten zur Literatur und Geschichte des hellenistischen Judentums, Leiden
AnalBibl/ AnBib	Analecta Biblica, Rome
ANEP	*The Ancient Near East in Pictures*, ed. J. B. Pritchard, Princeton 1954
ANTJ	Arbeiten um Neuen Testament und Judentum
AOAT	Alter Orient und Altes Testament, Kevelaer
ARW	*Archiv für Religionswissenschaft*
ATANT	Abhandlungen zur Theologie des Alten und Neuen Testaments, Zürich
AzTh	Arbeiten zur Theologie
BBB	Bonner biblische Beiträge, Bonn
BEvTh	Beiträge zur evangelischen Theologie
BFCT	Beiträge zur Förderung christlicher Theologie
BGBE	Beiträge zur Geschichte biblischen Exegese, Tübingen
BGU	Ägyptische Urkunden aus den königlichen Museen zu Berlin: Griechische Urkunden I–VIII, 1895–1933
Bibl	*Biblica*, Rome
BJ	Josephus, *De Bello Judaico*
BWANT	Beiträge zur Wissenschaft vom Alten und Neuen Testament, Stuttgart

BZNW	Beihefte zur Zeitschrift für die neutestamentliche Wissenschaft, Berlin
CAH	*The Cambridge Ancient History*
CBQ	*Catholic Biblical Quarterly*
CC	Corpus Christianorum, Turnholt
CH	Corpus Hermeticum
CIL	Corpus inscriptionum Latinarum, Berlin
CRAI	Comptes rendus des séances de l'académie des inscriptions et belles lettres, Paris
CSEL	Corpus scriptorum ecclesiasticorum Latinorum, Vienna
DJDJ	Discoveries in the Judaean Desert of Jordan, Oxford 1955ff.
EKK	Evangelisch-katholischer Kommentar zum Neuen Testament, Neukirchen
ÉPROER	Études préliminaires aux religions orientales dans l'empire romain, Leiden
ET	English translation
ÉtBibl	Études bibliques, Paris
ETS	Erfurter theologische Studien
EvTh	*Evangelische Theologie*, Munich
FGH/ *FGrHist*	*Die Fragmente der Griechischen Historiker*, ed. F. Jacoby, Berlin 1923ff., reprinted Leiden 1957ff.
FRLANT	Forschungen zur Religion und Literatur des Alten und Neuen Testaments, Göttingen
GCS	Griechischen christlichen Schriftsteller der ersten drei Jahrhunderte, Berlin
GRBS	*Greek, Roman and Byzantine Studies*
HAT	Handbuch zum Alten Testament, Tübingen
HAW	Handbuch der Altertumswissenschaft
HNT	Handbuch zum Neuen Testament, Tübingen
HSCP	*Harvard Studies in Classical Philology*
HTK	Herders theologischer Kommentar zum Neuen Testament, Freiburg im Breisgau
HTR	*Harvard Theological Review*, Cambridge, Mass.
HUCA	*Hebrew Union College Annual*, Cincinnati
IEJ	*Israel Exploration Journal*, Jerusalem
JAOS	*Journal of the American Oriental Society*, Baltimore
JbAC	*Jahrbuch für Antike und Christentum*, Münster
JBL	*Journal of Biblical Literature*, Philadelphia

JJS	*Journal of Jewish Studies*, London
JSHRZ	*Jüdische Schriften aus hellenistisch-römischer Zeit*
JSJ	*Journal of the Study of Judaism in the Persian, Hellenistic and Roman Period*, Leiden
JTS	*Journal of Theological Studies*
KAT	Kommentar zum Alten Testament
KEK	Kritisch-exegetischer Kommentar über das Neue Testament, founded by Heinrich August Willhelm Meyer
KlT	Kleine Texte
LAB	Liber Antiquitatum Biblicarum (Pseudo-Philo)
LCL	Loeb Classical Library
LXX	Septuagint (Greek text)
M	Massoretic (Hebrew) text
MBT	Münsterische Beiträge zur Theologie
MBPF	Münchener Beiträge zur Papyrusforschung und antiken Rechtsgeschichte
MGWJ	*Monatsschrift für Geschichte und Wissenschaft des Judentums*, Breslau
MPL	J. P. Migne, *Patrologia, Series Latina*
MPT	*Monatsschrift für Pastoraltheologie*, Göttingen
MusHelv	*Museum Helveticum*, Basle
NF (NS)	Neue Folge (New Series)
NT	*Novum Testamentum*, Leiden
NTA	Neutestamentliche Abhandlungen
NTS	*New Testament Studies*, Cambridge
NT.S	*Novum Testamentum* Supplement
OBO	Orbis biblicus et Orientalis
OTS	*Oudtestamentische Studien*, Leiden
PCZ	*Zenon Papyri*, ed. C. C. Edgar, Vols. I–IV; ed. O. Guéraud and P. Jouguet, Vol. V, Cairo 1925–40
PFLUS	Publications de la faculté des lettres de l'université de Strasbourg
PG	Patrologia Graeca, ed. J. P. Migne, Paris
PGM	*Papyri Graecae Magicae: Die griechischen Zauberpapyri* I–III, ed. K. Preisendanz, 2nd ed. Stuttgart 1973f.
POxy	*The Oxyrhynchus Papyri*, ed. B. P. Grenfell, A. S. Hunt et al., London 1898ff.

PSI	Pubblicazioni della Società Italiana, Papiri Greci et Latini, Rome
PTA	Papyrologische Texte und Abhandlungen, Bonn
PW	*Paulys Realencyclopädie der classischen Altertums-wissenschaft* (2. R. = second row, beginning with R), Stuttgart
QD	Quaestiones disputatae
RAC	*Reallexikon für Antike und Christentum*, Stuttgart 1950ff.
RB	*Revue biblique*, Paris
RBPH	*Revue belge de philologie et d'histoire*
RdQ	*Revue de Qumran*, Paris
RÉG	*Revue des études grecques*, Paris
REJ	*Revue des études juives*
RGG	*Die Religion in Geschichte und Gegenwart*, Tübingen
RHDF	*Revue historique de droit français et étranger*, Paris
RhMus	*Rheinisches Museum für Philologie*
RM	Religionen der Menschheit
Roscher	W. H. Roscher, *Ausführliches Lexikon der griechischen und römischen Mythologie*, Leipzig 1884ff.
RSR	*Revue des Sciences Religieuses*
RVV	Religionsgeschichtliche Versuche und Vorarbeiten, Giessen
SAB	Sitzungsberichte der Deutschen (Preussischen) Akademie der Wissenschaften zu Berlin
SAH	Sitzungsberichte der Heidelberger Akademie der Wissenschaften
SANT	Studien zum Alten und Neuen Testament
SB	*Sammelbuch griechischer Urkunden aus Ägypten*, ed. F. Preisigke et al., Strassburg et al. 1915ff.
SBS	Stuttgarter Bibelstudien
SBT	Studies in Biblical Theology
SCHNT	Studia ad Corpus Hellenisticum Novi Testamenti
SIFC	*Studi Italiani di Filologia Classica*
SJ	Studia Judaica, Berlin
SNT/StNT	Studien zum Neuen Testament, Gütersloh
SNTS	Studiorum Novi Testamenti Societas
SNVAO.HF	Skrifter utgitt av det norske videnskaps-akademi i Oslo. Historisk-filosofisk klasse
StPB	Studia Post-biblica

SupplNT	Supplements to *Novum Testamentum*
SUNT	Studien zur Umwelt des Neuen Testaments, Göttingen
SVF	Stoicorum veterum fragmenta, Berlin
SVT	Supplements to *Vetus Testamentum*, Leiden
Syll.	W. Dittenberger, *Sylloge Inscriptionum Graecarum*, Leipzig
TBAW	Tübinger Beiträge zur Altertumswissenschaft
TBLNT	*Theologisches Begriffslexikon zum Neuen Testament*, Wuppertal 1967ff.
TDNT	G. Kittel and G. Friedrich, *Theological Dictionary of the New Testament*, Grand Rapids, Michigan
THAT	E. Jenni and C. Westermann, *Theologisches Handwörterbuch zum Alten Testament*, Munich
ThB	Theologisches Bücherei, Munich
ThLL	*Thesaurus Linguae Latinae*, Leipzig 1900ff.
ThViat	*Theologia Viatorum*, Berlin
TLZ	*Theologische Literaturzeitung*, Leipzig
TQ/ThQ	*Theologische Quartalschrift*, Tübingen
TU	Texte und Ubtersuchungen zur Geschichte der altchristlichen Literatur, Berlin
TZ	*Theologische Zeitschrift*, Basle
UNT	Untersuchungen zum Neuen Testament, Leipzig
VigChr	*Vigiliae Christianae*, Amsterdam
VT	*Vetus Testamentum*, Leiden
WdF	Wege der Forschung, Darmstadt
WF	Westfälische Forschungen, Münster
WMANT	Wissenschaftliche Monographien zum Alten und Neuen Testament, Neukirchen
WuD	*Wort und Dienst, Jahrbuch der theologischen Schule Bethel*, Bielefeld
WUNT	Wissenschaftliche Untersuchungen zum Neuen Testament, Tübingen
ZDPV	*Zeitschrift des deutschen Palästina-Vereins*, Wiesbaden
ZNW	*Zeitschrift für die neutestamentliche Wissenschaft*, Berlin
ZPapEp	*Zeitschrift für Papyrologie und Epigraphik*, Bonn
ZTK/ZThK	*Zeitschrift für Theologie und Kirche*, Tübingen

THE SON OF GOD

The Origin of Christology and the
History of Jewish-Hellenistic Religion

I

The Problem

At the feast of the Passover in the year 30, in Jerusalem, a Galilean Jew was nailed to the cross for claiming to be Messiah. About twenty-five years later, the former Pharisee Paul quotes a hymn about this crucified man in a letter which he writes to one of the communities of the messianic sect which he has founded in the Roman colony of Philippi:

> He was in the form of God,
> (but) did not count equality with God a thing to be grasped,
> but emptied himself,
> taking the form of a slave,
> being born in the likeness of man and found in human form.
> He humbled himself
> and became obedient unto death,
> even death on a cross (Phil. 2.6–8).

The discrepancy between the shameful death of a Jewish state criminal and the confession that depicts this executed man as a pre-existent divine figure who becomes man and humbles himself to a slave's death is, as far as I can see, without analogy in the ancient world. It also illuminates the riddle of the origin of the christology of the early church.[1] Paul founded the community in Philippi in

[1] Cf. M. Dibelius, *RGG*[2] 1, 1593, on the 'main problem of christology'. This is the question 'how the knowledge of the historical figure of Jesus changed so quickly into belief in the heavenly Son of God'. From the abundant literature on the Philippians hymn see J. Gnilka, *Der Philipperbrief*, HTK X, 3, 1968, 111–47; R. P. Martin, *Carmen Christi, Phil. II, 5–11 in Recent Interpretation* ..., SNTS Monograph Series 4, 1967, with an extensive bibliography; C.-H. Hunzinger, 'Zur Struktur der Christus-Hymnen in Phil. 2 und 1 Petrus 3', in *Der Ruf Jesu und die Antwort der Gemeinde, Festschrift für J. Jeremias*, 1970, 145–56; K. Wengst, *Christologische Formeln und Lieder des Urchristentums*, SNT 7, 1972, 144ff.; cf. C. Talbert, *JBL* 86, 1967, 141ff.; J. A. Sanders, *JBL* 88, 1969, 279ff.;

about the year AD 49, and in the letter which he wrote to the
believers there about six or seven years later he will have presented
the same Christ as in the preaching which brought the community
into being. This means that the 'apotheosis of the crucified Jesus'
must already have taken place in the forties, and one is tempted to
say *that more happened in this period of less than two decades than in
the whole of the next seven centuries, up to the time when the doctrine
of the early church was completed.* Indeed, one might even ask
whether the formation of doctrine in the early church was essentially more than a consistent development and completion of what
had already been unfolded in the primal event of the first two
decades, but in the language and thought-forms of Greek, which
was its necessary setting.[2]

J. T. Sanders, *The New Testament Christological Hymns*, SNTS Monograph Series 15, 1971, 9ff., 58ff. For special problems see J. G. Gibbs,
NT 12, 1970, 270ff.; P. Grelot, *Bibl* 53, 1972, 495ff.; 54, 1973, 25ff.,
169ff., who conjectures an origin from a bilingual milieu; J. Carmignac,
NTS 18, 1971/72, 131ff.; C. Spicq, *RB* 80, 1973, 37ff. I must refrain
from going further into the most recent and utterly reckless interpretation
by H.-W. Bartsch, 'Die konkrete Wahrheit und die Lüge der Spekulation',
Theologie und Wirklichkeit 1, 1974, in which the pre-existence of Christ
in the hymn is denied and the statements in the first part are related solely
to the man Jesus. This is no realization of historical truth, but a triumph
of ideologically motivated and utterly fantastic speculation. Bartsch's
study makes it clear what New Testament exegesis can expect if it follows
the newest political and theological fashions. See now O. Hofius, *Sklave
und Herr*, WUNT 17, 1976.
    [1] For the chronology see W. G. Kümmel, *Introduction to the New
Testament*, [2]1975, 252ff., 322ff.: founding of the community 48/49; p.
332: composition of the letter either between 53 and 55 in Ephesus or
between 56 and 58 in Caesarea. J. Gnilka, *Der Philipperbrief*, 1968, 3f.,
24, suggests that the year 50 is 'extremely probably' the year in which the
community was founded and that part A of the letter was written from
Ephesus in the years 55 and 56. One or two years' difference is of little
account here. The new publication of the Gallio inscription by A. Plassart,
Fouilles de Delphes Tome III, Epigraphie, Fascicule IV, Nos 276 à 350,
1970, No 286, pp. 26ff., seems to me rather to suggest an early date; cf.
id., *RÉG* 80, 1967, 372-8, and J. H. Olivier, *Hesperia* 40, 1971, 239f.
For the whole question see my study 'Christologie und neutestamentliche
Chronologie', in *Neues Testament und Geschichte, Festschrift für O.
Cullmann zum 70. Geburtstag*, 1972, 43-67.

2

Criticism

This, of course, is the point at which modern criticism begins. No less a scholar than Adolf von Harnack lamented the development 'as the history of the suppression of the historical Christ by the pre-existent Christ (the real Christ by the fictitious Christ) in dogmatics'. For 'this apparent enrichment of Christ amounted to an impoverishment, because it in fact obliterated the complete human personality of Christ'.[3] While he celebrated Paul as the founder of 'western and Christian civilization' in *What is Christianity?*,[4] he also saw a danger that 'under the influence of the Messianic dogmas, and led by the impression which Christ made, Paul became the author of the speculative idea that not only was God in Christ, but that Christ himself was possessed of a peculiar nature of a heavenly kind . . . Christ's *appearance* in itself, the entrance of a divine being into the world, came of necessity to rank as the chief fact, as itself the real redemption.' Of course that was not yet the case with Paul, since for him the cross and resurrection were the crucial facts and the incarnation could be interpreted in moral terms as 'an example for us to follow' (II Cor. 8.9). But the incarnation 'could not permanently occupy the second place; it was too large'. However, 'when moved into the first place it threatened the very existence of the Gospel, by drawing away men's thoughts and interests in another direction. When we look at the history of dogma, who can deny that this was what happened?'[5] But this

[3] A. von Harnack, *Lehrbuch der Dogmengeschichte* (unaltered reprint of fourth edition of 1909), 1964, I, 704f.
[4] A. von Harnack, *What is Christianity?*, 1901 reprinted 1957, 179.
[5] Harnack, op. cit., 185; cf. the reference to the 'dangers' of Pauline christology, among which he includes the doctrines of 'objective redemption', 183. On this see K. Barth/E. Thurneysen, *Briefwechsel, Vol. II, 1921–1930*, 1974, 36, 'as a result of which the two others (C. Stange and

means the dogmatic ossification of faith: 'The living faith seems to
be transformed into a creed to be believed; devotion to Christ, into
Christology.'[6] Thus Harnack's critical observations, which may be
regarded as characteristic of the christological thought of wider
circles of modern Protestantism. In contrast to 'speculative progress' there was a demand for a 'return' to the simple gospel of
Jesus,[7] unburdened by christological speculation, since – to use
Harnack's words once more: 'The Gospel, as Jesus proclaimed it,
has to do with the Father only and not with the Son.'[8]

Jewish scholars made the same kind of criticism. The Galilean
was rediscovered in modern Jewish scholarship and attempts were
made to 'bring him home' to Judaism. Apostasy from the faith of
the fathers began, rather, with Paul. As an example we may take
the picture of Paul drawn by the Erlangen philosopher of religion,
H. J. Schoeps: 'It was Paul who for the first time, reflecting on
the messianic figure (of Jesus), made out of a title of dignity an
ontological affirmation and raised it to a mythical level of thought.'[9]
His 'Christ has become a supernatural being and approximates to

---

E. Hirsch) once again suspect that I have a "physical doctrine of redemption", which in this generation is about the worst thing that you can say
about anyone'.

[6] Harnack, op. cit., 193.

[7] Cf. Harnack, *Lehrbuch der Dogmengeschichte*, 704f., and *What is
Christianity?*, 184: 'The formation of a correct theory of and about Christ
threatens to assume the position of chief importance, and to pervert the
majesty and simplicity of the Gospel' (the author puts this sentence in
italics). Harnack does not remember here that Pauline christology is
chronologically earlier than the synoptic gospels in their 'simplicity'.
Perhaps the 'original gospel', too, was not as 'simple' as Harnack would
have liked. Did not Jesus' own proclamation of the coming Son of Man
as judge of the world contain a quite 'speculative', apocalyptic messianology? Might not the first 'speculative' fall of early Christian theology be
already connected with this heavenly figure? It is understandable – at
least on apologetic grounds – that some of the most recent exegesis wants
to purge the original proclamation of Jesus of these apocalyptic shadows.
That will make it more modern, but not more authentic.

[8] A. von Harnack, *What is Christianity?*, 144 (the author puts this
sentence in italics).

[9] H. J. Schoeps, *Paul: The Theology of the Apostle in the Light of Jewish
History*, 1961, 150 (here as elsewhere the translation has been slightly
altered in the cause of accuracy).

gnostic heavenly beings ... This heavenly Christ seems to have wholly absorbed the earthly Jesus into himself ... The myth clearly represented here ... points to pagan spheres',[10] more specifically to the 'religious syncretism of Asia Minor'.[11] Schoeps' verdict is consistent and clear: 'Hence we see in the υἱὸς θεοῦ belief the sole, albeit decisive heathen premiss of Pauline thought. All that belongs to and flows from it ... is un-Jewish and akin to heathen ideas of the time.'[12] When Pauline christology and soteriology combined with this 'un-Jewish belief in the Son of God' and became 'the dogma of the Christian church, it burst the framework of Jewish belief once and for all'. Schoeps concludes with a reference to Harnack's verdict: 'The "acute Hellenization of Christianity", so much discussed in its day, takes place at this point.'[13]

It would be fascinating to trace further this *encounter between*

[10] Schoeps, op. cit., 153.

[11] Schoeps, op. cit., 158. In this connection Schoeps refers to the old hypothesis of influence from Sandan, the city-god of Tarsus, who in the Hellenistic period was worshipped as Heracles. For criticism see the excellent review by A. D. Nock, *Gnomon* 33, 1961, 583, n. 10 = *Essays on Religion and the Ancient World*, 1972, II, 930. The hypothesis that Sandan-Heracles was a dying and rising god is extremely questionable, see also H. Goldman, *JAOS* 60, 1940, 544ff., and *Hesperia* Suppl. 8, 1949, 164ff. Zwicker, 'Sandon', *PW*, 2R, I, 2, 1920, 2267, was already stressing 'our scanty knowledge of the nature of Sandan', which '(leads) to various uncertain interpretations'. Quite apart from this, according to Acts 22.3; 26.4; Phil. 3.5; Gal. 1.13f., we must take into account the possibility that Paul moved to Jerusalem at a very early age, as a child, and was brought up there. See W. C. van Unnik, *Sparsa Collecta* I, 1973, 259–327.

[12] Schoeps, op. cit., 158 (italicized by the author, though this is not indicated in the English translation).

[13] Schoeps, op. cit., 167. Cf. what he already wrote in *Aus frühchristlicher Zeit*, 1950, 229: 'In my view, no analogous speculations are capable of demonstrating that belief in the υἱὸς θεοῦ, alien to the Jewish-Christian primitive community, is Jewish.' As will be demonstrated, this argument is erroneous. Schoeps here begins from a normative concept of 'Judaism' which only developed out of Pharisaism in the post-Christian period in the constant controversy with Christianity, cf. G. Lindeskog, *Die Jesusfrage im neuzeitlichen Judentum*, 1938, 15. He completely fails to notice the phenomenon of *Jewish mysticism*, and like many Jewish historians suppresses it for apologetic reasons (see pp. 89f., n. 150 below). The article cited by Schoeps, A. Marmorstein, 'The Unity of God in Rabbinic Literature', in *Studies in Jewish Theology*, 1950, 101ff., cf. 93ff., does reflect this later controversy between Judaism and Christianity.

reformed Judaism and liberal Protestantism in their criticism of christological dogma,[14] but the responsible theologian, historian and exegete can no longer be satisfied with D. F. Strauss's much-repeated remark: 'The true criticism of dogma is its history.' He must attempt, rather, not only to analyse the historical derivation of the conceptions and terms created by early Christian belief but also to understand them and interpret them theologically.[15] This task always includes a critical examination of earlier criticism.

[14] The controversy over Paul runs parallel to the 'restoration of Jesus to Judaism'; cf. already the two works by Joseph Klausner, *Jesus of Nazareth*, 1925, and *From Jesus to Paul*, 1944, or the more recent studies by Schalom Ben-Chorin, *Bruder Jesus*, ³1970, and *Paulus*, 1970; cf. also L. Baeck, 'Romantische Religion' (1922), in *Aus drei Jahrtausenden*, 1958, 47ff., and more positively 'The Faith of Paul', *JJS* 3, 1952, 93–110, and M. Buber, *Two Types of Faith*, 1951, 79ff. See R. Mayer, 'Christentum und Judentum in der Schau Leo Baecks', *Studia Delitzschiana* 6, 1961, 58–64. In contrast to the books from Klausner to Schoeps, the simple booklet by Ben-Chorin, while preserving a Jewish standpoint, shows the most thorough understanding of Paul and recognizes above all the Jewish roots of Pauline thought: 'By way of a generalization one can say that, consciously or unconsciously, Paul took over the building material for his theological construction from Judaism. In this powerful edifice of Pauline theology there is hardly an element which is not Jewish. Sometimes it seems as if something quite different, new and strange, were appearing, but on closer inspection the Jewish background to Paul's thought appears, even where he seems to be in abrupt contrast to Judaism' (p. 181).

[15] K. Barth/E. Thurneysen, *Briefwechsel* (n. 5 above), 253f., on the doctrine of the Trinity in the early church: 'Men and brethren, what a mess! But don't think that it is all old rubbish; in the right light everything seems to make sense . . .'

3

The Testimony of Paul

Let us begin with *the earliest* primitive Christian *evidence that we have*, the authentic letters of Paul. Statistical evidence alone seems to contradict Schoeps' view that the title Son of God is of central significance for Paul. For Paul uses the two titles 'Lord' and 'Son of God', which describe Jesus in a special way as an exalted, heavenly figure, quite disproportionately. Whereas he uses '*Kyrios*' 184 times, we only find '*huios theou*' 15 times. The distribution of the two terms is also striking. 'Son of God' appears most frequently in the letters where the controversy with the Jewish tradition is at its height, in Romans and Galatians (7 and 4 times respectively), whereas the two letters addressed to the community in Corinth, which was now really threatened with 'acute Hellenization', contain 'Son of God' only 3 times. There was a danger there, in true Greek fashion, that the new message would be interpreted, not in gnostic terms, but – following a false interpretation of Paul's doctrine of freedom – as a doctrine of salvation along the lines of the cult of Dionysus and the mysteries.

Kramer, who has made the most recent analysis of the christological titles in Paul, comes to a quite different result from Schoeps on the basis of the 'statistical' evidence and form-critical analyses:

1. 'In Paul's view both the title Son of God and the ideas associated with it are of relatively minor importance.'

2. Paul usually employs the term in stereotyped formulas which he has taken over from earlier tradition, and 'the original meaning of the title has already faded'.[16]

Now this means that the alleged lapse into the speculative Hellenization of christology must already have taken place in the early church before the time of Paul!

[16] W. Kramer, *Christ, Lord, Son of God*, SBT 50, 1966, 189, 186.

Before we turn to the difficult question of the historical derivation of the title Son of God, we must therefore examine Kramer's
two arguments. Let us first turn to the significance of the title in
Paul.[17] This significance could depend not only on statistics, but
also on the context of the use of the title within Paul's letters. It is
striking that the title appears 3 times right at the beginning of
Romans, in the introduction, and that Paul uses it to describe the
content of his gospel (1.3, 4, 9). It occurs 3 times again at the
climax of the letter, in ch. 8, the point of which could be summed
up in a single sentence: The 'Son of God' makes us 'sons of God',
who are to participate in his heavenly *doxa* (8.3, 29, 32).[18] This
indicates that for Paul the *soteriological* rather than the speculative
significance of the term stands in the foreground. Galatians makes
the same impression. Here Son of God appears at the beginning
of the letter in connection with the radical change in the apostle's
way of life:

> But when he (God) who had set me apart before I was born, and had
> called me through his grace, was pleased to reveal his Son to me, in
> order that I might preach him among the Gentiles . . . (1.15f.).

Here Paul shows at the same time that Son of God is the real
content of his gospel.[19] We find the title also – just as in Rom. 8 – at
the climax of the letter:

---

[17] For what follows see E. Schweizer, υἱὸς θεοῦ, *TDNT* 8, 1972, 382ff.;
J. Blank, *Paulus und Jesus*, SANT 18, 1968, 249–303; W. Thüsing, *Per
Christum in Deum*, NTA NF 1, ²1969, 144–7.

[18] Above all Rom. 8.29f.; cf. Phil. 3.21. See J. Blank, op. cit., 287ff.;
H. R. Balz, *Heilsvertrauen und Welterfahrung*, BEvTh 59, 1971, 109ff.
For criticism of Kramer see 110, n. 246: he has 'made the framework
of the statements about the Son taken over by Paul too narrow'. Cf. also
W. Thüsing, op. cit., 121ff., and P. Siber, *Mit Christus leben*, ATANT 61,
1971, 152ff. Paul's terminology here is strongly moulded by tradition.

[19] J. Blank, op. cit., 222ff.: 'The "subject matter" of the revelation is
the "Son of God", Jesus Christ who is risen from the dead' (229, cf. 249,
255). Similarly H. Schlier, *Der Brief an die Galater*, KEK, ¹²1962, 55:
'The revelation of God to Paul has a personal object: God reveals to him
his Son. Here that means the exalted Lord.' P. Stuhlmacher, *Das paulinische Evangelium I. Vorgeschichte*, FRLANT 95, 1968, 81f., defines the
revelation of the Son as 'allowing the Risen One to be seen enthroned by
God and thus as the Son of God who is appointed ruler', cf. id., *ZTK* 67,
1970, 30. This could be a reference to the early confession of the Son of

But when the time had fully come, God sent forth his Son, born of woman, born under the law, to redeem those who were under the law, so that we might receive adoption as sons (Gal. 4.4f.).[20]

The point is again clearly soteriological: the 'Son of God' frees us to become 'sons of God'.

This finding is confirmed by a quite different text at the beginning of II Corinthians:

As surely as God is faithful, our word to you has not been Yes and No. For the Son of God, Jesus Christ, whom we preached among you . . . was not Yes and No; but in him it is always Yes (1.18f.).

Here too the content of the apostle's message is the Son of God. As Bachmann already observed in his commentary, the solemn use of the title 'Son' emphasizes that 'the Son belongs together with the Father'. In his incarnation, God's Yes is clearly spoken to abandoned man: 'For all the promises of God find their Yes in him' (1.20). And because through the Son, God's Yes has become reality for all men, the community can conclude and endorse its prayer to the glory of God 'through him' with the 'Yes' of the Amen.

In I Corinthians, too, the Son first appears at the beginning of the letter (1.9) and then again at a climax (I Cor. 15.28). At the end of all things, when even the last power, death, has been conquered by the parousia of Christ and the general resurrection, *'the Son* himself will also be subjected to him who put all things under him, that God may be everything to everyone'.[21] Thus Paul uses

---

God in Rom. 1.3f. For the dative understanding of *en emoi* see F. Mussner, *Der Galaterbrief*, HTK IX, 1974, 86f., n. 45.

[20] Cf. E. Schweizer, *TDNT* 8, 383f.; J. Blank, op. cit., 260–78; W. Thüsing, op. cit., 116f.; G. Eichholz, *Die Theologie des Paulus im Umriss*, 1972, 157ff.; F. Mussner, op. cit., 268ff.: 'The Son's destiny had a definite saving purpose' (270); 273: 'The Son is wholly Son for us.' Paul does not introduce the 'Son christology for speculative reasons . . . but out of soteriological concern'.

[21] For the history of the interpretation of this passage, which was so significant for the christology of the early church, see now E. Schendel, 'Herrschaft und Unterwerfung Christi. I Kor. 15, 24–28', in *Exegese und Theologie der Väter bis zum Ausgang des 4. Jhdts*, BGBE 12, 1971.

the term Son to describe as the content of his mission preaching
not only the pre-existent and incarnate redeemer of the world, but
also the perfecter of creation and history. He does the same thing
in his earliest writing, I Thess. 1.10, which speaks of the expectation of the Son coming from heaven, 'who delivers us from the
wrath to come'.[22]

It is also striking that in almost all his statements about the
Son of God, Paul uses the title *when he is speaking of the close bond
between Jesus Christ and God, that is, of his function as the mediator
of salvation* between God and man. We must therefore support the
old master of the history of religions school, W. Bousset, against
Kramer when he observes that while 'Son of God' – like the verb
'believe' – appears much more rarely in Paul than in the Johannine
literature, we do find it 'at the climactic points of the presentation'.
Here Bousset can even appeal to Luke: 'The only place where the
author of the book of Acts uses the title ὁ υἱὸς τοῦ θεοῦ occurs
in the summary of the Pauline preaching' (9.20).[23]

While we can follow Bousset and the history of religions school,
and also Harnack and Schoeps, in their stress on the significance of
the title 'Son' for Paul, Bousset's hypothesis that 'we have to do
with an independent creation of Paul'[24] is less convincing. Form-
critical and traditio-critical analysis has long shown that Paul took
over this title from earlier tradition. That is clear simply from the
fact that he connects it with the event of his call, which will have
taken place between AD 32 and 34.[25] In particular, there are two
formulations which the apostle could have taken over from the
church which came before him (or, more precisely, existed alongside him, presumably in Syria):

1. *The sending of the pre-existent Son into the world.* Here we

---

[22] Cf. G. Friedrich, *TZ* 21, 1965, 512ff., and E. Schweizer, *TDNT* 8,
371, 383, who refer to Rev. 2.18 and suggest that 'Son of God' here has
been introduced into a saying about the Son of Man. The only question
is where and when this substitution took place.

[23] W. Bousset, *Kyrios Christos*, ET 1970, 206. For criticism of Kramer's
theory see also J. Blank, op. cit., 283f.; cf. 300ff.

[24] W. Bousset, op. cit., 207.

[25] M. Hengel, 'Christologie und neutestamentliche Chronologie' (n. 2
above), 44, 61f. Here, too, the difference of a year or two is immaterial.

find the same syntactical pattern in Rom. 8.3 and Gal. 4.4: God
is the subject, followed by a verb of sending as predicate. The
object is the Son, followed by a final clause introduced by ἵνα,
which explains the soteriological significance of the sending. We
often find this statement formulated in the same way – independently of Pauline tradition – in the Johannine writings (John 3.17;
I John 4.9, 10, 14). On the other hand, the theological interpretation is typically Pauline: liberation from the power of sin and the
law and the appointment of the believer to the relationship of being
a son of God himself.[26]

2. *The giving up of the Son to death.* The apostle begins the
radiant conclusion of Rom. 8.32ff.:

> If God is for us, who is against us? He who did not spare his own
> Son but gave him up for us all, will he not also give us all things
> with him?

Here we have on the one hand echoes of the Old Testament
account of Isaac's sacrifice,[27] and in addition what is presumably
once again an established pattern which has also been written
down in a well-known verse of the Gospel of John:

---

[26] W. Kramer, op. cit., 111ff.; E. Schweizer, 'Zum religionsgeschicht-
lichen Hintergrund der "Sendungsformel", Gal 4.4f., Rö 8.3f., Joh
3.16f., 1 Joh 4.9', *ZNW* 57, 1966, 199–210 = *Beiträge zur Theologie des
Neuen Testaments*, Zürich 1970, 83–95; id., *TDNT* 8, 374ff., 386; id.,
Jesus, 1971, 81ff. The objections to the existence of a 'sending formula'
made by K. Wengst, *Christologische Formeln und Lieder des Urchristentums*, SNT 7, 1972, 59, n. 22, do not convince me. Even if we heed H. von
Campenhausen's warning, *ZNW* 63, 1972, 231, n. 124, that we should be
sparing with the use of the term 'formula', so that the 'voracious formula-
hydra' does not grow 'more rampant heads', the usage seems to me to be
legitimate. So too F. Mussner, *Galater*, 271ff.: 'a pre-Pauline pattern of
proclamation . . . filled with a variety of material' (272).

[27] ὅς γε τοῦ ἰδίου υἱοῦ οὐκ ἐφείσατο, cf. Gen. 22.12, 16: καὶ οὐκ ἐφείσω
τοῦ υἱοῦ σου τοῦ ἀγαπητοῦ δι' ἐμέ. Cf. further Ps.Philo 18.5; 32.2ff.
Literature in Blank, op. cit., 294ff., and E. Käsemann, *An die Römer*,
HNT 8a, 1973, 237. For the Jewish parallels and their relationship
to Rom. 8.32 see G. Vermes, *Scripture and Tradition in Judaism*,
²1973, 193–227 (218ff.); S. Spiegel, *The Last Trial. On the Legends and
Lore of the Command to Abraham to offer Isaac as a Sacrifice: The Akedah*,
New York 1969, 82ff. See there, 83, n. 26, the anti-Christian polemic of
R. Abin in the name of R. Hilkiah, Agg. Ber. c. 31, ed. Buber, 64.

God so loved the world that he gave his only-begotten Son . . . (3.16).

In Gal. 2.20 Paul no longer speaks of God, but of the Son as the subject of this action:

> The life I now live in the flesh I live by faith in the Son of God, who loved me and gave himself for me.

Here the title Son describes the uniqueness of the saving event, the magnitude of the sacrifice for our sake. Here again we have Johnnine parallels, though they do not use the title Son (10.11; 15.13; I John 3.16).[28] These formal statements about the Son of God, which therefore probably already existed in Paul's time, have two complementary focal points:

1. The sending of the pre-existent Son into the world.
2. His being given up to death on the cross.

The two themes recur in the Philippians hymn quoted at the beginning of this study, where the divine being of the pre-existent Christ and the slave's death of the incarnate Jesus are connected. The difference is that the title 'Son of God' does not appear there. Rather, in the final act of exaltation the crucified one is acclaimed as 'Kyrios', an indication of the close relationship in content between the titles 'Kyrios' and 'Son of God'.[29]

We must also look at Colossians, the authenticity of which is disputed. Here we find hymnic expressions where the subject is again the 'beloved Son' (1.13):

> He is the image of the invisible God, the first-born of all creation; for in him all things were created. . . . (1.15).

Even here the reference to death on the cross cannot be absent at the end (1.20). Here, however, it is not a self-emptying as in Philippians, but the work of an all-embracing reconciliation of the

---

[28] For the formulas of Rom. 8.32 and Gal. 2.20 see W. Kramer, op. cit., 116ff.; cf. also the criticism by W. Popkes, *Christus Traditus*, ATANT 49, 1967, 201ff., though in my view it does not meet the point; also E. Schweizer, *TDNT* 8, 384; J. Blank, op. cit., 298ff., and F. Mussner, *Galater*, 50f., 183, n. 77.

[29] We should not therefore assume two fundamentally different historical roots for them. Rather, they will both come from the same religious milieu.

world.[30] We will not go more closely into the many problems of the hymn at this point, as it seems to have a clearly post-Pauline character.[31] We shall keep to those features which we find again in Paul himself. First mention must be given to the *mediation* of Christ *at creation*. Paul alludes to it in a passage which seems like a formula:

> For us there is one God, the Father, from whom are all things and for whom we exist, and one Lord, Jesus Christ, through whom are all things and through whom we exist (I Cor. 8.6).

The Father is the primal ground and goal of creation, whereas Christ is the mediator.[32] At the same time, we can also see here the

[30] For more recent literature see W. Pöhlmann, *ZNW* 64, 1973, 53, n. 2: the various hypotheses do not lead to the construction of any original form that is at all certain. This is also true for the statement about atonement in 1.20b, which cannot definitely be shown to be an addition. At any rate, the hymn was Christian from the beginning. Pöhlmann gives a considered attempt at a reconstruction on p. 56. For the reconciling of the world cf. E. Schweizer, *Beiträge zur Theologie des Neuen Testaments*, 1970, 132ff., 139ff. For the parallel in Eph. 2.14–18 see P. Stuhlmacher in *Neues Testament und Kirche, Festschrift R. Schnackenburg*, 1974, 337–58.

[31] With E. Lohse, *Colossians and Philemon*, Hermeneia, 1971, 41ff., against W. G. Kümmel, *Introduction to the New Testament*, ²1975, 342ff. Colossians and Ephesians are, however, substantially earlier than the Pastoral Epistles. I do not think it impossible that they were written before AD 70.

[32] P. H. Langkammer, *NTS* 17, 1970/71, 193ff.: 'It cannot be doubted that there are the beginnings of a Son of God theology here' (194). This formula which Paul directs against the multiplicity of pagan gods and lords will have had predecessors in the theology of the Jewish mission, cf. e.g. Sib. 3.11; Fr. 1.7 (Geffcken, 227); also Fr. 3.3 (230); 3.629, 718; II Macc. 7.37; Dan. 3.45; Josephus, *Antt.* 4, 201, etc., cf. M. Hengel, *Die Zeloten*, AGSU 1, 1961, 101ff. The acclamatory form may correspond to the formula ʿΕΙΣ ΘΕΟΣ in pagan cults, although these formulas are almost always later, see E. Peterson, ʿΕΙΣ ΘΕΟΣ, FRLANT 41, 1926, 227ff., 253ff., 276ff., 304ff. At any rate, the connection with the idea of creation indicates a Jewish origin, cf. Aristeas 132. On the other hand, it is too fanciful to relate it to the fragmentary Orphic-Dionysic Gurob papyrus from the third century BC, as does K. Wengst, *Christologische Formeln und Lieder des Urchristentums*, SNT 7, 1972, 139. The riddle of this papyrus and the formula εἰς Διόνυσος which appears in it, in an obscure context, for the first time, is still unsolved, see M. P. Nilsson, *Geschichte der griechischen Religion*, ²1961, II, 244f., and O. Schütz, *RhMus* 87, 1938, 241ff., who attempts a very hypothetical reconstruction

close connection between the titles 'Lord' and 'Son of God'. The
fact that we have only this one statement about Christ's mediation
in creation – almost, one might say, by chance – merely shows how
little we know of the whole of Paul's theology. We only know the
tip of the iceberg, fascinating though that may be.

There remains the question why Paul could use the title 'Kyrios'
so much more frequently than 'Son of God', although the content
of the two titles is closely connected and they are in part interchangeable, because they both refer to the risen and exalted Christ.
While the much rarer 'Son of God' above all expressed the unique
relationship of the exalted Christ to God, the Father, the title
Kyrios, which could also be used as a form of address in prayer
and in acclamation, expressed above all the relation between the
exalted Christ and his community, or the individual believer. The
formula *Kyrios Iesous* (Rom. 10.9; I Cor. 12.3; Phil. 2.11) made
up the basic confession, reduced to its briefest form, by the community of the crucified and risen Jesus, who had been exalted by
God and would come again. Thus Kyrios became the current title
in worship and in the individual life of the believer, while *the form
'Son of God', with its more complicated language, was kept for
exceptional usage, at the climax of certain theological statements.*

In Paul Christ is also the *eikon*, the *'image of God'*, whose radi-
ance shines out in the proclamation of the gospel (II Cor. 4.4). In
this concept the idea of the mediator of revelation and that of the
mediator at creation are combined. The εἰκὼν θεοῦ has connections with the μορφὴ θεοῦ of the Philippians hymn; indeed, one
might ask whether the one term does not interpret the other.[33]

---

of the damaged papyrus. εἰς Διόνυσος here is not an acclamation (246,
line 23). For Christ as mediator at creation see H. F. Weiss, *Unter-
suchungen zur Kosmologie des hellenistischen und palästinischen Judentums*,
TU 97, 1966, 288, 301, 305ff.; H. Hegermann, *Die Vorstellung vom
Schöpfungsmittler im hellenistischen Judentum und Urchristentum*, TU 82,
1961, 88f., on Col. 1.15ff., and 111f., 135, 137, 200.
[33] F.-W. Eltester, *Eikon im Neuen Testament*, BZNW 23, 1958, 133;
R. P. Martin, *An Early Christian Confession: Philippians II.5–11 in
Recent Interpretation*, 1960; see also id., *Carmen Christi. Philippians
II.5–11 in Recent Interpretation and in the Setting of Early Christian
Worship*, 1967, 107ff. However, the two terms should not be over-
hastily identified with each other, see already J. Behm, μορφή, *TDNT* 4,

This designation, too, is concerned with the soteriological significance of Christ. In him, God's image – with E. Jüngel one might even say God's 'parable' – God's real being, his love, is made visible for believers (I John 4.8f.).

Paul's conception of the Son of God, which was certainly not his own creation but goes back to earlier community tradition before Paul's letters, thus proves to be quite unique. Jesus, the recently crucified Jew, whose physical brother James – the ἀδελφὸς τοῦ κυρίου – Paul himself had personally known well (Gal. 1.19; 2.9; cf. I Cor. 9.5), is not only the Messiah whom God has raised from the dead, but much more. He is identical with a divine being, before all time, mediator between God and his creatures. That is, at the same time he is mediator of God's saving revelation which, for example, accompanied Israel through the wilderness as a water-bearing rock (I Cor. 10.4). Born as man, he took the Jewish law upon him and died the most shameful death known to antiquity, death on a cross.

1967, 752, and more recently, with numerous linguistic examples, C. Spicq, *RB* 80, 1973, 37–45. Cf. Sib. 3,8: ἄνθρωποι θεόπλαστον ἔχοντες ἐν εἰκόνι μορφήν; CH 1, 12: περικαλλὴς γάρ, τὴν τοῦ πατρὸς εἰκόνα ἔχων· ὄντως γὰρ καὶ ὁ θεὸς ἠράσθη τῆς ἰδίας μορφῆς.

4

The Theory of the
History of Religions School

It is quite understandable that this new picture of Christ should be claimed to represent a *new 'Hellenistic Christianity'*.[34] R. Bultmann, who here emerges as to some extent the spokesman of the history of religions school, could describe it as 'basically a wholly new religion, in contrast to the original Palestinian Christianity'. Speculation of this kind must have seemed even further removed from the proclamation of Jesus as Bultmann described it, following Wellhausen: 'pure Judaism, pure prophetic teaching',[35] thus completing the return of Jesus to Judaism. At the same time the great Marburg scholar corrected Harnack's thesis of a 'Hellenizing of Christianity' along the lines of the history of religions school. He argued that the cause of this new form was not – as was still supposed in the nineteenth century, under the influence of F. C.

[34] W. Heitmüller, *ZNW* 13, 1912, 320–37 = K. H. Rengstorf (ed.), *Das Paulusbild in der neueren deutschen Forschung*, WF XXIV, 1964, 124–43; cf. also the Bonn dissertation by H. W. Boers, *The Diversity of New Testament Christological Concepts and the Confession of Faith*, 1962, 114ff., and M. Hengel, 'Christologie und neutestamentliche Chronologie' (n. 2 above), 47ff.

[35] R. Bultmann, *Faith and Understanding*, 1969, 271, 283. For Jesus see also id., *Jesus and the Word*, [2]1958, 48f., and *Theology of the New Testament*, I, 1952, 27, for the phrase 'prophet and rabbi'; see M. Hengel, *Nachfolge und Charisma*, BZNW 34, 1968, 46ff. See already J. Wellhausen, *Einleitung in die drei ersten Evangelien*, 1905, 113: 'Jesus was not a Christian, but a Jew. He did not proclaim a new faith but taught men to do the will of God.' On this see the controversy between R. Bultmann, 'The Primitive Christian Kerygma and the Historical Jesus', in Carl E. Braaten and Roy A. Harrisville (eds.), *The Historical Jesus and the Kerygmatic Christ*, 1964, 15–42, and E. Käsemann, *Essays on New Testament Themes*, SBT 41, 1964, 37; id., *New Testament Questions of Today*, 1969, 42f.

Baur – a speculative philosophical interest on the part of Greek Gentile Christians, but a new 'cultic piety',[36] moulded by the mystery religions. In his criticism of the christological confession of the World Council of Churches in 1950, Bultmann made this theory of the history of religions school more precise in connection with the 'Son of God':

> For the figure of a son-deity suffering and dying and raised again to life is also known to the mystery religions, and gnosticism above all is aware of the notion of the Son of God become man – of the heavenly redeemer become man.[37]

Bultmann, his teachers Bousset and Heitmüller, and his followers repeated this argument *ad nauseam* without verifying it adequately by the ancient sources. If they were right, then a few years after the death of Jesus an 'acute Hellenization', or more precisely *a syncretistic paganization of primitive Christianity*, must have come about among the spiritual leaders of Jewish Christianity like Barnabas, or the former scribe and Pharisee Paul. Moreover, this must have taken place either in Palestine itself or in neighbouring Syria, say in Damascus or Antioch. In that case, the criticism of Paul's christology by the Jewish philosopher of religion H. J. Schoeps would be quite justified. It is clear that such an extraordinary historical development would have been in radical and irreconcilable contradiction to the preaching of Jesus. In that case a decision would have to be made between Jesus and Paul.

In what follows, we shall attempt to illuminate the development of the title Son of God, moving back from Paul to the origins of Christian belief. In so doing, we shall consider whether there really was a fundamental breach in many respects in the rise of christology between Jesus and Paul, or whether it is not the case that – at least after the death of Jesus or the Easter event – it is possible to see an inner trend in christological thought which contradicts

---

[36] R. Bultmann, *Faith and Understanding*, 271f.

[37] R. Bultmann, *Essays*, 1955, 279. But see the embittered and at the same time knowledgeable protest against the speculative theories of the history of religions school in K. Holl, 'Urchristentum und Religionsgeschichte', *Gesammelte Aufsätze zur Kirchengeschichte* II, 1928, 1–32, esp. pp. 18ff. on Paul.

Herbert Braun's theory and shows that christology was not a
random 'variable' but *the consistent 'constant'*.[38]

[38] H. Braun, *Gesammelte Studien zum Neuen Testament und seiner
Umwelt*, [2]1967, 272. Cf. the early protest by E. Käsemann, *New Testament
Questions of Today*, 1969, 37f.

5

The Meaning of 'Son of God'
and the History of Religions

We must first – within the limits imposed here – attempt to discover the philological and religious significance of the term 'Son of God' in Semitic and in Greek contexts.[39] The meaning of the Greek *'huios'* is almost completely limited to physical descent, and a transferred meaning is only marginal. Its usage is further limited by the fact that it is often replaced by the 'more comprehensive expression' *pais* or *paides*, small boy, children.[40]

I.   *The Old Testament*

The Hebrew *'ben'* (Aramaic *bar*) is very different: 'It is the most common term of relation in the OT (some 4850 instances).'[41] In contrast to *'huios'* it not only (or even primarily) designates physical descent and relationship, but is a widespread expression of subordination, which could describe younger companions, pupils and members of a group, membership of a people or a profession, or a characteristic. In this extended sense it was also used in a number of ways in the Old Testament to *express belonging to God*. First of all were the *members of the heavenly court*, the angels, who are often

[39] For what follows see W. von Martitz/G. Fohrer, υἱός, *TDNT* 8, 1969, 335ff., 340ff. On the other hand, the study by Petr Pokorný, *Der Gottessohn*, Theologische Studien 109, 1971, a preliminary to an article in *RAC*, is of little help. For the Old Testament see also J. Kühlewein in E. Jenni/C. Westermann, *THAT* 1, 1971, 316–25; W. Schlisske, *Gottessöhne und Gottessohn im AT*, BWANT 97, 1973.

[40] W. von Martitz, *TDNT* 8, 335f.

[41] G. Fohrer, *TDNT* 8, 340.

called 'sons of the gods' in the Old Testament. These may originally have been depotentiated gods of the Canaanite pantheon, but this can no longer be detected in the Old Testament texts: as Yahweh's creatures they are quite subordinate to him.[42] In Daniel, which is near to the New Testament period, Nebuchadnezzar sees a fourth figure 'whose appearance is like a son of the gods' in the fire alongside the three Jewish confessors (3.25).[43] After Hippolytus this passage was interpreted by the church fathers with reference to Christ,[44] while a rabbi in the fourth century, in anti-Christian terms, affirmed that for this blasphemy God had delivered the king over to an angel of Satan who began to smite him because in fact only 'his angel' was written there.[45]

God's people, Israel, is addressed in a special way as 'sons' or even 'son of God', because it has been chosen by God and is the object of his care and love: 'And you shall say to Pharaoh, "Thus says Yahweh, Israel is my first-born son, and I say to you, 'Let my son go that he may serve me'; and if you refuse . . . I will slay your first-born son"' (Exod. 4.22f.).[46] Finally, *the Davidic king* could also be called 'son of God', following Egyptian models. This expressed the divine legitimation of the ruler. The interpretation of the relationship of God and king as that of father and son already appears in the oracle of Nathan, II Sam. 7.12–14; it is taken up

[42] G. Fohrer, *TDNT* 8, 347ff.: Gen. 6.2, 4; Job 1.6; 38.7; 2.1; Pss. 29.1; 89.7, cf. Ps. 82.6 and Deut. 32.8f. (LXX and 4QDeut^q). Cf. also W. Schlisske, op. cit., 15ff.: the Canaanite-Ugaritic parallels are the most interesting.

[43] *dāmeh l^{e}bar-^{e}lāhin*. Theodotion: ὁμοία υἱῷ θεοῦ. LXX: ὁμοίωμα ἀγγέλου θεοῦ. The statement is in remarkable contrast to 7.13: *k^{e}bar ^{e}nāš*.

[44] A. Bentzen, *Daniel*, HAT I, 19, ²1952, 37.

[45] Ex. R. 20.10 after R. Barachiah, c. AD 340, see Billerbeck I, 139. There are further examples of rabbinical polemic against the use of the designation 'Son of God' for angels in P. S. Alexander, 'The Targumim and Early Exegesis of the "Sons of God" in Genesis 6', *JJS* 23, 1972, 60–71. R. Simeon b. Johai cursed all those who called the angels 'sons of God': Gen. R. 26.5 (see ibid., 61).

[46] Cf. Jer. 31.9, 20; Hos. 11.1. God as father of Israel: Deut. 32.6, 18; Jer. 3.4; all Israel as sons (and daughters) of Yahweh: Deut. 14.1; 32.5, 19; Isa. 43.6; 45.11; Hos. 2.1 etc.; see G. Fohrer, op. cit., 351ff.; W. Schlisske, op. cit., 116–72.

and developed in Ps. 89.4ff. and I Chron. 17.13; 22.10 and 28.6.[47] Isa. 9.5 also belongs in this context. Ps. 2.7: 'He (Yahweh) said to me, "You are my son, today I have begotten you" ', probably also comes from the Jewish royal ritual. Scholars have rightly stressed that the 'today' excludes all physical concepts of begetting.[48] More precisely, H. Gese has stressed that 'you are my son' represents a realized promise of salvation which is further strengthened by the addition of the clause 'today I have begotten you'. 'That the house of David are sons of God is not foreign mythology, but the conception of the relationship with the *naḥᵃlā*-lord to be found in Israelite family law.' 'According to Ps. 2.7 and 110.3 ... the enthronement of the Davidic king on Zion is understood as birth and creation through God.'[49] The juridical concepts of adoption and legitimation are hardly adequate to describe this happening appropriately. It is certainly no coincidence that Psalms 2 and 110 become the most important pillars of the early church's christological argument from scripture.

II. *Greek and Hellenistic parallels*

The possibilities of developing the Old Testament statements about the Son of God thus appear to be remarkably varied. This

[47] For the Egyptian and Near Eastern background see H. Brunner, *Die Geburt des Gottkönigs*, 1964; K. H. Bernhardt, *Das Problem der altorientalischen Königsideologie im AT*, SVT 8, 1961; G. W. Ahlström, *Psalm 89. Eine Liturgie aus dem Ritual des leidenden Königs*, Lund 1959, 111f.; see 182ff. for II Sam. 7.14ff.; id., *VT* 11, 1961, 113ff.; H. Gese, 'Der Davidsbund und die Zionserwählung', *ZTK* 61, 1964, 10–26 = *Vom Sinai zum Zion*, BEvTh 64, 1974, 113–29; K. Seybold, *Das davidische Königtum im Zeugnis der Propheten*, FRLANT 107, 1972, 26ff.; W. Schlisske, op. cit., 78–115.

[48] G. Fohrer, op. cit., 351: an Egyptian ritual underlies that at Jerusalem. 'The Egyptian idea of physical sonship is changed into a legal one.' The question is whether the bare alternative 'physical or legal' really does justice to the act of election and new creation.

[49] 'Natus ex virgine', in *Probleme biblischer Theologie. Gerhard von Rad zum 70. Geburtstag*, 1971, 82 = *Vom Sinai zum Zion*, 139. For Ps. 110.3, see p. 81 (= *Sinai zum Zion*, 138): the text probably meant originally: 'On the holy mountain from your mother's womb, from the dawn of the morning I bore you.' The 'holy mountain' corresponds to Zion, the 'dawn of the new day is the pendant to the "today" of Ps. 2.7'. Cf. W. Schlisske, 100ff.

cannot so readily be said of the alleged Greek and Hellenistic parallels. Certainly the prolific *Zeus*, πατὴρ ἀνδρῶν τε θεῶν τε,[50] produced countless divine, semi-divine and mortal offspring, but there is no link between these παῖδες Διός of Hellenic nature religion and the early Christian confession of the *one* Son of the *one* God. And those who in enlightened fashion followed the Stoics in confessing that all men are by nature children of Zeus because they bear his seed in them by virtue of their reason, no longer need a 'son of God' as mediator and redeemer. Here the motto could only be: 'Become what you already are!'[51] When Luke makes Paul quote the famous verse of Aratus, 'We are his offspring', in the Areopagus speech (Acts 17.28),[52] he does so with bewildering inconsistency.

[50] *Iliad* 1, 544; *Odyssey* 1, 28; 20, 201, etc. We find πατήρ about 100 times out of the 300 or so passages in Homer where Zeus has an epithet: see M. P. Nilsson, 'Vater Zeus', in *Opuscula selecta*, 2, 710ff.: id., *Geschichte der griechischen Religion*, I, ³1967, 336f. See G. M. Calhoun, 'Zeus the Father in Homer', *Transactions and Proceedings of the American Philological Association* 66, 1935, 1–12.

[51] W. von Martitz, *TDNT* 8, 337: Chrysippus and Cleanthes already suggest divine sonship, but it appears in so many words in Epictetus: *Diss.* I, 3, 2; 13, 3; 19, 9; II, 16, 44 (Heracles) cf. 8, 11; III, 22, 82; 24, 15f. The use of 'Son of God' in the Christian-Pythagorean *Sentences of Sextus* has probably also been influenced by Stoicism: see H. Chadwick, *The Sentences of Sextus*, Cambridge 1959, nos. 58, 60, 135, 221 (Lat.), 376b: the wise man is 'God's son' and therefore 'godlike' (18f., 45, 48–50, 381, see p. 106). Cf. G. Delling, 'Zur Hellenisierung des Christentums in den "Sprüchen des Sextus" ', in *Studien zum NT und zur Patristik. E. Klostermann zum 90. Geburtstag dargebracht*, TU 77, 1961, 208–41, esp. 210f. There is also strong stress on kinship with God, indeed divine sonship, in the Olympian speech of Dio Chrysostom of Prusa (*Or.* 12.27–34, 42, 61, etc.). M. Pohlenz, *Stoa und Stoiker*, 1950, 341f., 382, conjectures dependence on Posidonius. Cf. above all Dio Chrysostom 12.28 with Acts 17.27 and on it K. Reinhardt, *PW* XXII, 1, 1953, 812f. In the discourse 'On the Law', the law is said to be 'of insuperable . . . might' with an allusion to Heracles – ὁ τοῦ Διὸς ὄντως υἱός (ch. 8).

[52] The Aratus quotation already appears in the earliest Jewish 'philosopher of religion' whom we can discover, Aristobulus, about the middle of the second century BC, see M. Hengel, *Judaism and Hellenism*, I, 1974, 165, from Eusebius, *PE* 13, 12, 5f.

II.(a)   *Mysteries, dying and rising sons of God and the ruler cult*

The constantly repeated view that the development of the Son of God christology is a typically Hellenistic phenomenon and represents a break in primitive Christianity hardly bears closer examination. The Hellenistic mysteries did not know of sons of God who died and rose again, nor did the mystic himself become a child of the god of the mysteries.[53] Dying vegetation deities like Phoenician Adonis, Phrygian Attis or Egyptian Osiris had no function as sons of God. In late antiquity they were often regarded as men from the mythical primal period, to whom – as to Heracles – immortality was given after their death. Of all the 'sons of Zeus' in Greek religion, *Heracles* might be most likely to provide analogies to christological ideas, but he never became a god of the mysteries: he only had a strong influence as a model for the ruler cult, i.e. on political religion, and on the religious views of popular philosophy. Even where, as e.g. in Ps-Seneca's Heracles dramas, he is represented as '*soter*', '*pacator orbis*' (*Her. oet.* 1990), and indeed as vanquisher of death, we in fact have no more than a poetic extension of the true, model ruler and wise man *par excellence*. He 'earned heaven by his deeds of valour', so he can ask his father for 'the world' (*Her. oet.* 97f.). His victory over death and chaos (*Her. fur.* 889ff.; *Her. oet.* 1947ff.) merely represents the victory of the Logos, divine reason, over all the powers that are hostile to reason. For this, *virtus in astra tendit, in mortem timor* (1971).[54] The Zagreus myth, in which

[53] M. P. Nilsson, *Geschichte*, II, ²1961, 688f.: 'In Christianity believers are often called children of God, but as far as I know the initiate is never called a child of the god in any of the mystery religions . . . Although mythology was familiar with a large number of children of deities, expedients had to be found for making the idea of divine sonship credible in the mysteries . . . The great contribution of Christianity was to understand the fatherhood of God in this sense (i.e. of trustful love), thus making man's divine sonship part of the essence of its belief.' The evidence adduced by R. Merkelbach, *ZPapEp* 11, 1973, 97, which is supposed to indicate that in the mysteries men 'experienced . . . that they were truly descended from a god or from a "king" ', on the other hand, quite misses the point. E.g. Heliodorus 2, 31, 2 is merely a theme that is widespread in folk-tales and comedies.

[54] G. Wagner, *Das religonsgeschichtliche Problem von Rö 6,1–11*, ATANT

39, 1962, 180ff. on Adonis; 124ff. on Osiris, and 219ff. on Attis. Adonis
was not a god of the mysteries at all, and was no more a god of salvation
than Attis. Osiris and his mysteries, which are first attested by Apuleius,
were quite overshadowed by those of Isis: initiation to Osiris was an
appendix to initiation to Isis, in which money played more than a small
part: Apuleius, *Met.* 11, 27ff.; cf. the fraud of the priests of Isis in Rome,
Josephus, *Antt.*, 18, 65ff. The concept of 'dying and rising gods' is being
questioned increasingly today, see C. Colpe, 'Zur mythologischen Struktur der Adonis-, Attis- und Osirisüberlieferungen', in *lišān mithurti,
Festschrift für W. Freiherr von Soden*, AOAT 1, 1969, 28–33, and W.
Schottroff, *ZDPV* 89, 1973, 99–104, especially 103f. For the function of
Adonis, Osiris and Attis in the Hellenistic period see also A. D. Nock,
Essays on Religion and the Ancient World, 1, 1972, 83: 'Attis, Adonis,
Osiris die, are mourned for, and return to life. Yet it is nowhere said that
soteria comes by their death.' None of the dying vegetation deities died
'for' other men, 2, 934: 'As for the "dying gods", Attis, Adonis and
Osiris, it is to be remembered that, in the traditional stories, they, like
most of the deities of popular religion, were deemed to have been born
on this earth and to have commenced their existence at that point in time;
they might descend into death, but they had not descended into life.' In
other words, the decisive theme of 'sending' is absent. Pre-existence and
sending are again absent with Heracles. His death and apotheosis have
only limited saving significance for mankind. His apotheosis is the reward for his primal superhuman virtue. He is therefore *soter* and *euergetes*
as typically understood by Hellenistic political religion from the time of
Alexander, as annihilator of evil-doers and bringer of political peace. Like
the Stoic wise man, the ruler must imitate him or reproduce his deeds in
his own; in other words, 'in accordance with' the great exemplar he must
make his salvation through his own virtue. For Epictetus, he is the symbol
that all men who are endowed with reason are sons of Zeus (*Diss.* II, 16,
44; III, 24, 16, cf. also his example as son of Zeus, III,26, 31). He is regarded 'as the best of all mankind, a godlike man and rightly to be considered a god' because in utter poverty he 'ruled earth and sea', had
'self-control and hardness, he wished to be powerful, not to enjoy luxury':
Ps. Lucian, *Cyn.* 13. In other words, his divinity or sonship consisted solely
in the realization of his *arete* (Cornutus, 31; Max. Tyr., 15, 6, 2). In my
view the orientalizing of Heracles in the dramas of Seneca by J. Kroll, *Gott
und Hölle*, 1932, reprinted 1963, 339–447, goes too far. W. Grundmann,
ZNW 38, 1939, 65ff., is quite senseless in seeking to attribute a 'Heracles
christology' to the Hellenists of Acts 6.1 because of the occurrence of the
terms '*Archegos*' and '*Soter*' in Acts 3.15; 4.12; 5.31. His role as a 'pro-
tective or apotropaic spirit' in ancient popular belief no more affects
christology than his identification with Melkart of Tyre. At best one could
indicate analogous complexes of thoughts and ideas which are generally
typical of the ancient world, see e.g. C. Schneider, *Geistesgeschichte des
antiken Christentums*, I, 1954, 53f., 57; H. Braun, *Gesammelte Studien*,
256ff.; M. Simon, *Hercule et le christianisme*, Paris 1955. Of course, in a

the child Dionysus is torn apart by the Titans, consumed and then reconstituted in miraculous fashion,[55] has even less to do with early Christian thought. It should also be remembered that we have more detailed accounts about the real 'oriental' mystery deities or their cults only from the second and third centuries AD. The mysteries were originally a typically Greek form of religious practice, which only had to be 'exported' to subject eastern territories in the Hellenistic period. More recent investigations of the most important oriental 'mystery religion' in the Greek-speaking East, the Isis cult, by F. Dunand, *Le culte d'Isis dans le bassin oriental de la Méditerranée* (ÉPROER 26, 1973, Vols. I–III), and L. Vidman, *Isis und Sarapis bei den Griechen und Römern* (RVV 29, 1970), say what has long been known, making it more precise by an abundance of evidence, with all the clarity that could be desired, and one can only hope that in the end it will also come to the notice of New Testament exegesis, so that the worn-out clichés which suppose crude dependence of earliest Christianity between AD 30 and AD 50 on the 'mysteries' may give way to a more pertinent and informed verdict: 'The great wave of the oriental mystery religions only begins in the time of the empire, above all in the second century, as we have stressed many times already. The struggle and at the same time the first beginnings of a synthesis of the most powerful oriental cults also begin in this century' (Vidman, 138). In the

---

structural comparison, the fundamental differences which are usually passed over in historical comparisons of religions (e.g. in the far too simple collection of quotations by Herbert Braun) would also emerge. But see E. Käsemann, *Das wandernde Gottesvolk*, FRLANT 37, 1939, 65 (against H. Windisch): 'But to use Heracles as an example or to talk of an adoptionist christology is to miss the real situation.'

[55] See W. Fauth, *PW*, 2R, IX, 2, 1967, 2221–83, cf. esp. 2279f. for alleged influence on early Christianity. The myth of Dionysus-Zagreus played a decisive role above all in dualistic Orphic speculations (cf. O. Schütz, *RhMus* 87, 1938, 251ff.); the mysteries of Dionysus at the time of the empire seem to have been less influenced by him. For the eucharist, W. Heitmüller, *RGG*¹ 1, 20f., points simultaneously to the aetiology of the Passover in Exod. 12 and the Zagreus myth, an example of the uncritical free association of the history of religions school. For the whole question see also M. P. Nilsson, op. cit., II, 364ff., and A. D. Nock, op. cit., 2, 795f.

second century AD, Christianity was already widespread and established; it was a strong competitor, but hardly the object of syncretistic alienation any longer. At this period syncretistic gnosticism was engaged in bitter struggles with Christianity. We can
hardly draw conclusions about the early period from it, and cannot
therefore simply transpose the conditions depicted by Apuleius or
even by the Christian fathers from the second century, like Justin,
Clement of Alexandria and Tertullian, to the time between AD 30
and AD 50 which is of particular interest to us. Moreover, we know
virtually nothing about the extent of the mystery cults in Syria in
the first half of the first century BC. There is no indication that they
were particularly widespread there at this early period or that they
had a strong religious influence. On the contrary, we should reckon
rather that there is strong Christian influence on the later evidence
of mysteries from the third and fourth centuries AD. Finally, we
must distinguish between the *real cults* and a widespread *'mystery
language'*. The latter certainly derives from the religious terminology of the specifically Greek mysteries of Eleusis and Dionysus,
but had long since gained complete independence. As the examples
of Artapanus, the Wisdom of Solomon and Philo show, it had also
been taken over by the synagogues of the diaspora. Evidence of it
in the New Testament still does not mean direct dependence on
the mystery cults proper. In his *Theology of the New Testament*,
Bultmann, to take one example, may postulate the dependence of
Paul on 'certain Gnostic groups organized as mystery-cults. In one
such group, for example, the mystery-god Attis had coalesced with
the Gnostic redeemer-figure.' But this is a pure figment of the
imagination which obscures, rather than illuminates, the religious
background of the early Syrian communities. On the other hand,
the Greek Corinthians do seem to have misunderstood Paul's
message in terms of the ecstatic mysteries of Dionysus, with which
they were probably familiar.[56] Furthermore, the designation υἱὸς

---

[56] Cf. Bultmann, *Theology of the New Testament*, I, 298, similarly 170f.
K. Holl, *Gesammelte Aufsätze*, II, 7, already referred to the question of
chronology: '*Certain* (author's italics) evidence for the great upsurge of
the mysteries is only available from the second century AD.' The cult of
Mithras from Ptolemaic Egypt in the third century BC which he mentions

is a survival from Persian rule and has nothing to do with the later mysteries, cf. Nilsson, op. cit., II, 36, n. 2; 669, n. 9. For the origin of the mysteries of Mithras and their treatment in Justin and Tertullian see now C. Colpe, in *Romanitas et Christianitas, Studia I. H. Waszink*, 1973, 29–43, esp. 37, n. 1. For the problem of the language of the mysteries see A. D. Nock, op. cit., 2, 796ff.: 'The terminology, as also the fact, of mystery and initiation acquired a generic quality and an almost universal appeal' (798). That is, the use of mystery language in no way signifies direct dependence on specific 'mysteries'. Even Judaism did not escape this influence, see 801ff.: Philo 'refers to pagan cult-mysteries with abhorrence but finds the philosophic metaphor of initiation congenial' (802). Similarly I, 459ff., 'The Question of Jewish Mysteries', and the discussion of Goodenough's theories which is associated with it: 'The metaphor of initiation was by its philosophic usage redeemed from any undue association with idolatry; it was particularly appropriate, inasmuch as it expressed the passive and receptive attitude of mind which Philo held to be necessary' (468). This is even more the case if one suggests that primitive Christianity or Paul are 'dependent' on the Hellenistic mysteries. In reality they are dependent on the Greek-speaking synagogue, which partly used the religious *koine* of its environment. Cf. A. D. Nock's review of Bultmann's *Primitive Christianity* in *Nuntius* 5, 1951, 35ff., and the protest there against his interpretation of the mysteries and of gnosticism. For a criticism of earlier research on the mysteries in relation to the New Testament see also H. Krämer, *Wort und Dienst, Jahrbuch der Kirchlichen Hochschule Bethel*, NF 12, 1973, 91–104. The most recent assertion by H.-W. Bartsch, 'Die konkrete Wahrheit' (n. 1 above), 120, that '*in the mystery cults, which spread out from Iran* (my italics), there opened up a possibility of overcoming humiliation in the ecstatic experience of the cult, despite the continuation of slavery', is quite unscientific, but not surprising in view of the knowledge of the Hellenistic environment to be found in German New Testament scholarship. The confusion of the mystery religions with the supposedly pre-Christian gnostic redeemer myth which becomes evident here and even more on pp. 26f. shows that the author still has not got beyond Reitzenstein's misleading theories. Even in classical times, slaves were allowed to be initiated into the earliest Greek mysteries of Eleusis, whereas the most important mysteries in Hellenistic-Roman times, those of Dionysus, were above all for the more exalted members of society. Here ecstasy traditionally played a part, but not slaves. The great inscription of Tusculum, according to which slaves were also admitted as long as they belonged to the *familia* of the noble mistress Agrippinilla is an exception. As in the time of the empire the *thiasoi* of Dionysus had largely become upper-class traditional associations (see e.g. the Io Bacchae in Athens in the second century AD, Ditt., *Syll.³*, 1109, lines 40–46), where ecstatic experience retreated into the background, this experience was sought in new cults like primitive Christianity. The nearest parallel to what went on in Corinth still seems to me to be Livy's account of the scandal of the θεοῦ, son of God, is relatively rare in the Hellenistic world and, with one exception, is never used as a title. The exception is the Greek translation of *divi filius*, son of the divinized, a title which Augustus took soon after the murder of Caesar and which is reproduced on Greek inscriptions as θεοῦ υἱός.[57] But this terminology too was no more a serious influence on the conceptuality of the earliest Christianity which was developing in Palestine and Syria than the title Kyrios used of the ruler, which had become more frequent since Claudius, or the εὐαγγέλια which appears on individual imperial inscriptions.[58] This official, secular state religion was at best a negative stimulus, not a model. The first conflicts only arose a generation or two later under Nero, in AD 64, and Domitian.

Bacchanalia in Rome in 186 BC (39, 85ff.). Pagan polemic kept transferring the charges made at that time to Christians, cf. W. Pöhlmann, *TLZ* 95, 1970, 43, certainly with no historical justification at a later date. However, there must have been points of contact in the Pauline communities which gave rise to an interpretation along the lines of the Greek *mysteries* because of their ecstatic experience of the spirit and their very lively worship. But all this still has very little to do with dualistic gnosticism; see p. 33, n. 66 below. For the whole question see F. Bömer, *Untersuchungen über die Religion der Sklaven in Griechenland und Rom*, 3: *Die wichtigsten Kulte der griechischen Welt*, AAMz 1961, 4, 351–96, and M. P. Nilsson, *The Dionysiac Mysteries of the Hellenistic and Roman Age*, 1957.

[57] A fundamental distinction must be drawn between the numerous παῖδες or υἱοὶ Διός and υἱὸς θεοῦ as a title. For this reason alone, the collection of parallels in H. Braun, *Gesammelte Studien*, 255ff., is extremely doubtful. Ὑὸς θεοῦ is *not* a widespread title in 'eastern religion', to which the 'Hellenistic community' resorted. For the ruler cult see P. Pokorný, *Der Gottessohn* (n. 39 above), 15ff.; W. von Martitz, *TDNT* 8, 336; F. Taeger, *Charisma*, 2, 1960, 98, and index, 708, s.v. 'Gotessohnidee'. For resistance from Augustus, Tiberius etc., see S. Lösch, *Deitas Jesu und antike Apotheose*, 1933, 47ff. Individual instances may be found in P. Bureth, *Les Titulatures impériales dans les papyrus, les ostraca et les inscriptions d'Égypte*, 1964, 24, 28. The title is not very frequent and rarely appears alone. After Claudius we find κύριος much more frequently. This 'son' terminology had a predecessor in the East in the designation of Ptolemaic kings as 'son of Helios' (i.e. of the sun-god Re) and of Alexander the Great as the son of Zeus Ammon.

[58] For the term εὐαγγέλιον see P. Stuhlmacher, *Das paulinische Evangelium, I. Vorgeschichte*, FRLANT 95, 1968, 196ff.

II.(b)   *Divine men*

The classical philologist Wülfing von Martitz has also shown that the title son of God should not be over-hastily associated with the type of the so-called θεῖος ἀνήρ, the divine man, especially as it is questionable how far one can speak at all of this as an established type in the first century AD. The sources to which Bieler refers in his well-known book[59] almost all come from Neo-Platonism and the church's hagiography.[60] Of course, from the heroes of the iron age onwards, Greece is familiar with the physical descent of great warriors and wise men from individual gods, and stories of miraculous births are associated with them as in the case of Pythagoras, Plato, Alexander, Augustus and Apollonius of Tyana. However, we do not find in this context the combination of pre-existence and sending into the world which is typical of Pauline christology – that is, apart from a few untypical exceptions to which we shall return later.[61] Consequently in his much-cited but presumably

---

[59] L. Bieler, ΘΕΙΟΣ ANHR. *Das Bild des "göttlichen Menschen" in Spätantike und Frühchristentum*, I/II, 1935/36 (reprinted 1967).

[60] W. von Martitz, *TDNT* 8, 337f., 339f.: θεῖος ἀνήρ is by no means a fixed expression, at least in the pre-Christian era . . . One cannot tell from the material even that such θεῖοι are usually sons of gods. When, therefore, divine sonship is associated with description as θεῖος this is quite accidental. The conceptual spheres of divine sonship and θεῖος may well be related, but the terminology does not support this association.' For legitimate criticism of the inflationary use of θεῖος ἀνήρ in more recent literature on the New Testament see O. Betz, 'The Concept of the So-called "Divine Man" in Mark's Christology', in *Festschrift Allen P. Wikgren*, SupplNT 33, 1972, 229–40; E. Schweizer, *EvTh* 33, 1973, 535ff.; J. Roloff, *TLZ* 98, 1973, 519, and for the miracle stories G. Theissen, *Urchristliche Wundergeschichten*, SNT 8, 1974, 262ff., cf. 279ff. The warning by K. Berger, *ZTK* 71, 1974, 6, is very appropriate: 'A collective abstract which is inappropriate for explaining individual cases and which should in any case only be used with the greatest care.'

[61] Even H. Braun has to concede this in his pretty row of supposed parallels to New Testament christology, see *Gesammelte Studien*, 258f. and n. 47. The possible variation in the different forms of divine descent can be seen in the case of the religious founder Alexander of Abonuteichus in the second century AD. He introduced the cult of the snake-god Glycon as the cult of the new Asclepius, son of Apollo and grandson of Zeus, claimed that he himself was descended from the divine miracle doctor Podaleirus, the son of Asclepius, and that he fathered his daughter by

little-read book on 'The Son of God',[62] G. P. Wetter was essentially able to refer only to sources which had been influenced by Christianity. He refers above all to those mysterious wandering beggar-prophets whom the Platonist Celsus will have encountered on his travels in Phoenicia and Palestine in the middle of the second century AD.[63] They proclaimed: 'I am God, or a son of God (θεοῦ παῖς), or a divine spirit. And I have come. For already the world is going to ruin, and you, O men, are to perish because of (your) iniquities.' The whole context, and the introduction with the Christian triad of God, Son and Spirit, shows that in his anti-Christian pastiche Celsus is not depicting real prophets, but is parodying the Christian missionaries and their founders, to unmask them as religious frauds. And when later Christian sources claim that individual figures like Simon Magus, the author of all heresies, or the mysterious Samaritan Dositheus, gave themselves out to be sons of God, we have polemical stylizations rather than historical accounts.[64] For the same reason, the Didache can say that the Anti-Christ will appear in person as the Son of God.[65]

Selene. In other words, he made himself a great-great-grandson of Zeus. There were countless variations on the theme, but it has very little to do with 'Son of God' in christology (see Lucian, *Alex.* 11, 14, 18, 35, 39f.). He himself is said to have been a pupil of a pupil of Apollonius of Tyana and also to have understood himself to be a second Pythagoras. At the celebration of the 'torchlight mysteries' there was a representation not only of the birth of Apollo and his son Asclepius, but also of the union of the mother of Alexander with Asclepius' son Podaleirus and of the goddess Selene with the founder of the mysteries himself, as a *'hieros gamos'* (38f.). His hate was directed especially against Christians and Epicureans, both of whom he regarded as *'atheoi'* (25, 38). For the whole question see O. Weinreich, *Ausgewählte Schriften*, Vol. 1, 1969, 520–51.

[62] G. P. Wetter, *Der Sohn Gottes*, FRLANT 26, 1916.

[63] Origen, *C. Cels.* 7, 9. Cf. the 'trinity' of Simon Magus according to Hippolytus, *Phil.* 6, 19, and Irenaeus, 1, 23, 1. D. Georgi, *Die Gegner des Paulus im 2. Korintherbrief*, WMANT 11, 1964, 118ff., is one example of the uncritical interpretation of this much-cited passage. He connects it with itinerant Jewish missionaries. O. Michel, *TZ* 24, 1968, 123f., draws attention to the parallel between ἥκω δέ and the prophetic appearance of Josephus before Vespasian (*BJ* 3, 400).

[64] Simon Magus: Ps. Clem., *Hom.* 18, 6, 7; *Passio Petri et Pauli* 26 (Lipsius/Bonnet 1, 142). Dositheus: Origen, *C. Cels.* 6, 11.

[65] 16.4: καὶ τότε φανήσεται ὁ κοσμοπλανὴς ὡς υἱὸς θεοῦ καὶ ποιήσει σημεῖα καὶ τέρατα.

II.(c)   *The gnostic redeemer myth*

There remains the hypothetical *gnostic myth of the sending of the Son of God into the world*. Here we have a typical example of a modern – one might almost say pseudo-scientific – development of a myth which either leaves the foundation of historical research, the chronology of sources, out of account, or manipulates it in an arbitrary fashion. There really should be an end to presenting Manichaean texts of the third century like the 'Song of the Pearl' in the *Acts of Thomas* as evidence of supposedly pre-Christian gnosticism and dating it back to the first century BC. In reality there is no gnostic redeemer myth in the sources which can be demonstrated chronologically to be pre-Christian. This state of affairs should not be confused with the real problem of a later gnosticism standing apart from Christianity, as we find it, e.g. in the Hermetica and in some of the Nag Hammadi writings.[66]

[66] It is to the credit of C. Colpe, *Die religionsgeschichtliche Schule*, FRLANT 78, 1961, that he brought this hypothetical construction crashing down. Typical examples of unhistorical and speculative work on gnosticism are: A. Adam, *Die Psalmen des Thomas und das Perlenlied als Zeugnisse vorchristlicher Gnosis*, BZNW 24, 1959, and W. Schmithals, *Die Gnosis in Korinth*, FRLANT 66, 1956, ³1969. The latter's reaction to Colpe's work from the second edition of 1965, 32–80, onwards only shows his complete inability to learn. J.-E. Menoud, *RSR* 42, 1968, 289–325, has clearly shown that the much-cited 'Song of the Pearl' from the *Acts of Thomas* certainly cannot be used as evidence for a pre-Christian redeemer myth. The present form is a Manichaean redaction; an earlier form could go back to Syrian Christianity, under Jewish-Christian influence. At any rate, it presupposes the Christian christological tradition. For the newest, utterly fanciful work by H.-W. Bartsch on supposed pre-Christian gnosticism see above p. 1, n. 1. Cf. the posthumously published article by A. D. Nock, 'Gnosticism', *Essays*, 2, 940–59 = *HTR* 57, 1964, 255–79, which is to some extent a 'last testament'; cf. also R. Bergmeier, 'Quellen vorchristlicher Gnosis?', in *Tradition und Glaube, Festgabe für K. G. Kuhn zum 65. Geburtstag*, 1971, 200–20; cf. id., *NT* 16, 1974, 58ff. and now the thorough investigation by K. Beyschlag, 'Zur Simon-Magus-Frage', *ZTK* 68, 1971, 395–426, and id., *Simon Magus und die christliche Gnosis*, WUNT 16, 1974, who demonstrate that even the Samaritan 'magus' Simon should not be regarded as a key witness for 'pre-Christian gnosticism'. One may hope that the 'gnostic fever' (G. Friedrich, *MPT* 48, 1959, 502), which has already died down in the meantime will completely disappear and make way for a more appropriate assessment of the phenomenon. It is remarkable how much influence it still has in popular theological literature, in theological colleges and in examination work.

Gnosticism itself is first visible as a spiritual movement at the end
of the first century AD at the earliest, and only develops fully in the
second century. Neither Jewish wisdom speculation nor Qumran
and Philo should be termed 'gnostic'. As chief witness here I can
appeal to one of the most significant specialists in ancient religion,
A. D. Nock, whose clear verdict, based on the sources, is far too
little known in Germany: 'Certainly it is an unsound proceeding
to take Manichaean and other texts, full of echoes of the New
Testament, and reconstruct from them something supposedly
lying back of the New Testament.'[67] Without going further into
the much disputed question of the origin of gnosticism, I would
only say that in addition to the combination of Jewish speculation
connected with wisdom and creation, together with apocalyptic, on
the one hand and a popular dualistic Platonism on the other, early
Christianity itself was a catalyst in the rise of the gnostic systems. To
quote A. D. Nock again: 'It was the emergence of Jesus and of the
belief that he was a supernatural being who had appeared on earth
which precipitated elements previously suspended in solution.'[68]

As far as I can see, there are only very few parallels in the
Graeco-Roman world to the sending of a pre-existent divine
redeemer figure into the world, and these are remote. First of all,
of course, we must make a clear distinction between these and the
view widespread in the ancient world that all human *souls* were
sent into the world from heaven and returned there. We must also
leave out of account the fact that these souls could be said to be
godlike in some way, or to be of divine origin.[69] We are not

[67] *Essays*, 2, 958.
[68] A. D. Nock, loc. cit. For the influence of Middle Platonism on
gnosticism see H. Langerbeck, *Aufsätze zur Gnosis*, AAG, 3 F. 69, 1967,
17ff., 38ff. and H. J. Krämer, *Der Ursprung der Geistmetaphysik*, 1964,
223ff.
[69] A. D. Nock, *Essays*, 2, 935f.; cf. E. Rohde, *Psyche*, ²1898, reprinted
1961, II, 165, n. 1; 269ff.; 304f.; 324f., n. 1. For the period up to Plato
see D. Roloff, *Gottähnlichkeit, Vergöttlichung und Erhöhung zu seligem
Leben*, 1970, 192ff.: in Empedocles; 203ff.: in Plato. The Orphic-
Pythagorean myth of the transmigration of souls favoured ideas of this
kind. The entry of the pre-existent soul into an earthly body could thus
be interpreted as a guilty fall (Empedocles), as the consequence of fatal
weakness (*Phaedrus* 246a, 6ff.), as a combination of choice and destiny
(*Republic* 617e–621b) or as divine will (*Timaeus* 41a, 7–44b, 7; 90d, 1f.).

concerned with this 'constant coming and going' of souls, which corresponds to a notion which was almost a matter of course in late antiquity and has nothing to do with gnostic speculation either, but with a unique, once-for-all happening, which is the consummation of history: 'When the time was fulfilled, God sent forth his Son.' This presupposes neither the gnostic myth, which is completely oriented towards protology, nor the timeless myth of Greek and oriental nature religion, but Jewish apocalyptic thought.

II.(d)   *The sending of the redeemer into the world and related conceptions*

We shall attempt to consider the Hellenistic 'analogies' rather more closely. Reference should first be made to the demythologizing interpretation of the doctrine of the Greek gods in the Stoic Cornutus: '*Hermes*, son of Zeus and Maia, is the Logos which the gods have sent us from heaven.' Of course this is not a sending into history, but a mythical expression for the fact that 'they created man as the only living being on earth who is endowed with reason'.

For the late Hellenistic and Roman period see A.-J. Festugière, *La Révélation d'Hermès Trismégiste*, III, *Les doctrines de l'âme*, 1953, 27ff., 63ff.; M. A. Elfrink, *La descente de l'âme d'après Macrobe*, Philosophia Antiqua 16, 1968. Numerous tomb inscriptions show that these views were popular: cf. e.g. W. Peek, *Griechische Grabgedichte*, 1960, no. 353, 2ff. (first/second century AD): '. . . But his immortal heart ascended to the blessed ones, for the soul is eternal, which gives life and came down from the godhead (καὶ θεόφιν κατέβη) . . . the body is only the garment of the soul, consider my divine part'; 465, 7ff. (second/third century AD): '. . . but the soul which came down from heaven entered the dwelling of the immortals. The corruptible body rests in the earth. But the soul which was given to me dwells in the heavenly home.' Cf. also the answer to the question 'Who are you? Where do you come from? I am a son of the earth and the starry heaven?', which appears often on the Orphic gold leaves, see Kern, *Orph. fragm.*, pp. 105ff., no. 32. The idea of the pre-existence of souls was also taken over by Judaism, Billerbeck, II, 341ff. Philo can interpret Jacob's ladder in Gen. 28.12 with the ascending and descending angels in terms of the ascent and descent of souls: *De somn.* 1, 133ff. H. Braun, *Gesammelte Studien*, 258f., nn. 46f., does not note this possibility in his parallels to 'pre-existence' or the 'descent of the divine being'.

Hermes is the *keryx* and *angelos* of the gods in so far as we know their will through the rational thoughts which are implanted in us. As the 'rational principle', of course, he has lost all personal features and, like the other gods, for Cornutus has become a mere symbol.[70] While there are perhaps certain contacts with the role of Jewish Wisdom,[71] the relationship to early christology is purely formal: the Stoic Logos doctrine is only taken up in Christian thought with the second-century apologists. The Logos of the prologue to the Gospel of John is not the abstract, divine 'world-reason', but the creative word of God's revelation. As such it is dependent on the Jewish Wisdom tradition and not on the Stoa (see below, pp. 48ff., 71ff).

I am indebted to A. D. Nock for three further instances.[72] The first is a late text from the Hermetica. Here, at the request of the elements, Osiris and Isis are sent into the world by the supreme God to bring order out of moral chaos. After they have created a civilized order on earth as *prōtoi heuretai*, i.e. as bringers of culture, they are recalled to heaven. According to Nock, this is 'perhaps a counterblast to Christian teaching, and meant to suggest, "Our gods had an incarnation long ago, in a manner not repugnant to philosophic reason." '[73]

The second instance concerns *Pythagoras*. He was identified by his followers with *Apollo Hyperboreios*,[74] and at a very early stage he was also said to be the offspring of Apollo. In addition, the biography of Iamblichus about AD 300 mentions various divine figures whose earthly manifestation he was thought to be. It was his task to bring men the blessings of philosophy. Of course, in his case it is hard to distinguish the idea of the transmigration of souls

[70] *Theol. graec.* 16 (Wendland, 113), cf. E. Schweizer, *Beiträge zur Theologie des Neuen Testaments*, 1970, 83f. = *ZNW* 57, 1966, 199f.; A. D. Nock, *Essays*, 2, 934.

[71] M. Hengel, *Judaism and Hellenism*, I, 162, cf. also pp. 48ff., 51ff. below.

[72] *Essays*, 2, 937f.; *Kore Kosmou*, Fr. 23, 62–69, ed. Nock/Festugière, CH 4, 20ff. For the Osiris-Isis aretalogy see H. D. Betz, *ZTK* 63, 1966, 182ff.

[73] A. D. Nock, *Essays*, 2, 937f.

[74] Aristotle, Fr. 191, pp. 154f. Rose, following Aelian, *Ver. hist.* 4, 17, and Iamblichus, *Vit. Pyth.* 31, 140ff.; Porphyry, *Vit. Pyth.* 2, 228 (18.31f. Nauck); cf. F. Taeger, *Charisma* I, 73f.

from the notion of the incarnation of a god. Alexander of Abonuteichus, the founder of a religion, therefore considered himself to
be the incarnation of the soul of Pythagoras and when two followers
asked whether 'he had the soul of Pythagoras . . . or another like
it', made his oracular god Glycon reply in hexameters: 'The soul
of Pythagoras waxes at one time and wanes at another; but that
(i.e. his own), with prophetic gifts, is a part of the divine spirit, and
the (divine) Father sent it to support good men. Then it will return
again to Zeus, smitten by Zeus' thunderbolt.'[75]

The third example comes from politico-religious poetry. In his
second ode, *Horace* asks whom Jupiter will choose to expiate the
past guilt of Caesar's murder. After a request to Apollo, Venus and
Mars, Octavian appears as the incarnation of Hermes/Mercury to
avenge Caesar and return once again to heaven. In this form of
political, poetic flattery, the poet is certainly saying no more than
that he regards Augustus as a ruler sent by the gods,[76] a view

---

[75] Iamblichus, *Vit. Pyth.* 30f.; but cf. chs. 7f.: Apollo did not beget
Pythagoras himself, 'no one will, of course, doubt that the soul of Pythagoras was under the guidance of Apollo, either as a companion or in some
other close relationship to this god, and in this way was sent down to men'.
Against H. Braun, *Gesammelte Studien*, 259, n. 47, this is not a question
of the pre-existence or descent of a god, but of the sending of a human
soul. According to Heracleides Ponticus he was said to be descended from
or closely connected to Hermes (Diog. Laert., 8, 4). For Alexander of
Abonuteichus see Lucian, *Alex.* 40, but see 4: Μυθαγόρα ὅμοιος εἶναι ἠξίου.

[76] *Carmina* I, 2, 29ff., cf. F. Taeger, *Charisma*, II, 166f., and E.
Fraenkel, *Horaz*, 1963, 287ff. He sees the identification of Mercury and
Augustus as 'an inspiration of the poet's' (294):

    Cui dabit partis scelus expiandi
    Iuppiter? Tandem venias, precamur
    Nube candentis umeros amictus
        Augur Apollo
    . . .
    Sive mutata iuvenem figura
    Ales in terris imitaris almae
    Filius Maiae, patiens vocari
        Caesaris ultor:
    Serus in caelum redeas diuque
    Laetus intersis popula Quirini
    Neve te nostris vitiis iniquum
        Ocior aura
    Tollat . . .

which we also find held about other ruler figures – e.g. Alexander – and above all in the luxuriant inscriptions in the Greek-speaking eastern part of the empire.[77]

The development of the *Romulus saga*[78] should probably also be understood against the background of this early ruler ideology. Some scholars look for parallels to New Testament christology above all in Romulus' miraculous ascension. The twins Romulus and Remus were seen as sons of Mars; but whereas Remus was killed by his brother Romulus, the saga told how Romulus, the founder of Rome, was caught up into heaven in a miraculous ascension. According to a more rationalistic interpretation, however, like Caesar he was murdered by senators. The development of the saga transformed the ascension into an apotheosis. Whereas Ennius[79] still produces an anonymous eyewitness, Cicero, Livy and later writers know his name; there are also reports of the identification of Romulus with the god Quirinius. In Livy, the glorified Romulus commands the eyewitness Proculus Julius: ' "Tell the Romans the will of Heaven that my Rome shall be the capital of the world . . . and let them know and teach their descendants that no human strength will be able to stand up against Roman arms." When he had said this, he departed on high.'[80]

---

[77] Plutarch, *De fort. aut virt. Alex.* 6 (329C): 'But he believed that he came as a heaven-sent governor to all and as a mediator for the whole world.' 8 (330D): 'But if the deity who had sent Alexander's soul here had not recalled him so quickly, there would (now) be one law over all men and they would look to one justice as a common source of light. But as it is, the part of the world which has not looked upon Alexander has remained without the sun.'

[79] Ennius, *Ann.* 1, 110ff. (ed. J. Vahlen). According to *Ann.* 1, 65, the divine plan which was seen to underlie the foundation of Rome also included Romulus' immortality.

[79] Ennius, *Ann.* 1, 110ff., V. According to *Ann.* 1, 65, V, the divine plan which was seen to underlie the foundation of Rome also included Romulus' immortality.

[80] Livy, 1, 16; see Cicero, *De re pub.* 2, 10, 2; Ovid, *Met.* 14, 805ff. Cf. also 848ff. on the ascension of Romulus' consort Hersilia, who becomes the goddess Hora. My colleague Herr Cancik points out that the title Augustus is connected with the '*augurium augustum*' (Enn., *Ann.* 502) of the saga of Romulus and Quirinius, see Carl Koch, *Religio*, 1960, 94–113 (= *Das Staatsdenken der Römer*, ed. R. Klein, 1966, 39–64).

There is a certain formal analogy here to the accounts of the appearances of the risen Christ in Matthew and Luke and to his ascension. The theme of sending appears in Plutarch: 'It was the will of the gods . . . that I should dwell among men only a short time, build a city destined to be the greatest on earth for power and fame, and then dwell again in the heavens whence I came.' One could read the sending of a pre-existent deity out of this. However, as in his writing on Alexander, Plutarch is only bringing his Middle-Platonic doctrine of souls into play. For he expressly attacks what he considers to be the primitive notion of a physical ascension and quotes Pindar: 'Every man's body is overwhelmed by death, and only his primordial image remains eternal, for that alone comes from the gods.' He adds: 'It comes thence and returns thither, not with the body, but when it has detached itself completely from the body and has become pure and unfleshed and clean.'[81] According to Iamblichus, the soul of Pythagoras was also sent to earth in similar fashion.

A fundamental distinction must be made between ideas of this kind about sending and the notion of '*hidden epiphany*' which we come across, say, in the legend of Philemon and Baucis or among the citizens of Lystra, who after a healing miracle revere Barnabas and Paul and say, 'The gods have come down to us in the likeness of men.'[82] The age-old theme of the visit of the gods in human form already appears in the *Odyssey* (17, 484ff.), where the young men chide one of the wooers who abuses the right of hospitality towards Odysseus in the form of a beggar.

> You are doomed, if he is some god come down from heaven.
> Yes, and the gods in the guise of strangers from afar
> put on all manner of shapes and visit the cities.

[81] Plutarch, *Romulus* 28, 2, 7–9.
[82] Ovid, *Met.* 8, 611ff.; *Fasti* 5, 495; Acts 14.11. Cf. also Themistius, 7, p. 90 (see Wettstein ad loc.): 'Pure and divine forces tread the earth for man's good. They descend from heaven, not in airy form, as Hesiod claims, but clothed with bodies like ours. They take upon themselves a life below their nature for community with us.' However, we may certainly assume that there is Christian influence on this Platonizing rhetorician of the fourth century AD. With Julian, he is concerned for a renewal of pagan religion. See also the Neo-Platonic *Vitae Sophistarum* of Eunapius, p. 468, with the quotation from the *Odyssey* 17, 485.

Philo refers to this example in order to explain the epiphanies of
God, or more correctly the forms of his intermediaries in Genesis
(cf. Gen. 18.1ff.), at the same time stressing that 'God is not like
man' (Num. 23.19), has no form and therefore could not assume
a body (*Somn.* 1, 232ff.). However, these examples do not mention
sending, nor does God take upon himself human fate and death.
True, the Greek gods are born and have human pleasures (sometimes even with human beings), but they can never die. Their bodily
form is only 'show', and their immortality distinguishes them even
more fundamentally from transitory 'mortals'. *All this gets us no
nearer to the mystery of the origin of christology.* Celsus, the enemy
of Christianity, does not idly keep reminding us that 'neither a God
nor a son of God (θεοῦ παῖς) has descended from heaven or will
descend. And if you are talking about angels, tell us what kind they
are, whether they are gods or have a different nature? You presumably mean some other kind – the demons.'[83] As A. D. Nock

---

[83] Origen, *C. Cels.* 5, 2, cf. 4, 2–23, see A. D. Nock, *Essays*, 2, 933,
where there is further evidence. In contrast to the gods, demons were partially 'earthbound' (8,60). The angels of Celsus correspond to the
δυνάμεις of Themistius. The 'scandal' of christology is clearly expressed
in pagan polemic against the peculiar – because without analogy – 'God'
of the Christians. See the pagan opponent in Minucius Felix, *Oct.* 10, 3:
'*Unde autem vel quis ille aut ibi deus unicus solitarius destitutus . . .?*'; 10,5:
'*At autem Christiani quanta monstra quae portenta confingunt . . . ?*' cf.
12,4, etc. According to a series of oracles reported by Porphyry (contained
in Augustine, *City of God*, 19, 23), Apollo gave the following answer to
the question of a man about how he could dissuade his wife from Christian faith: 'Let her go as she pleases, persisting in her vain delusions,
singing in lamentation for a god who died in delusions, who was condemned by right-thinking judges and killed in hideous fashion by the
worst of deaths, a death bound with iron.' It is striking that Porphyry
already attempts to play off the 'historical Jesus' in neo-Platonic interpretation against the folly of his supporters with their absurd doctrines.
Thus Hecate is said to have replied to the question whether Christ was
God with the words: 'The immortal soul goes on its way after it leaves the
body; whereas when it is cut off from wisdom it wanders for ever. That
soul belongs to a man of outstanding piety; this they worship because
truth is a stranger to them.' To the further question, 'Why then was he
condemned?', the goddess gave the oracular reply: 'The body indeed is
always liable to torments that sap its strength, but the souls of the pious
dwell in a heavenly abode. Now that soul of which we speak gave a fatal
gift to other souls . . . entanglement in error . . . For all that, he himself

rightly stresses, the incarnation of a divine figure and still more his shameful death on the cross was not a 'point of contact', but a 'scandal' and a 'stumbling block'. Celsus, the opponent of the Christians, therefore taunts them that the worship of Jesus is no different from the cult set up by Hadrian for his boy-friend Antinous, who was drowned in the Nile and whom the Egyptians would not identify with Apollo or Zeus at any price (Origen, *C. Celsum* 3, 36). This cult was scandalous and reprehensible even to pagans, and the Egyptians were only forced into it because they were afraid of the emperor (Justin, *Apol.* 1, 29, 4). At least he was so incomparably beautiful that he could be compared with Ganymede, whom Zeus put among the gods in Olympus (Clem. Al., *Protr.* 49, 2), whereas for educated or noble men of antiquity the crucified Jesus was only an expression of folly, shame and hatefulness. In the judgment of the younger Pliny, to worship him was a '*superstitio prava immodica*' and merited appropriate punishment (10, 96, 8). *The 'Hellenization' of Christianity thus necessarily had to lead to docetism.* The humanity and the death of Jesus were only tolerable as 'show'.

III.   *The Son of God in ancient Judaism*

After this entirely unsatisfactory result, we must return to the contemporary Jewish sources in which the traditional Old Testament conceptions of the son or sons of God were further developed in a number of ways. Here, of course, it should be noted that religious thought in the motherland and the diaspora after the exile, and even more after Alexander, was increasingly driven towards an encounter with the Greek spirit. We cannot have too much variety in an account of Jewish religious thought at the end of the first century BC. The unique intellectual endowment of the people

---

was devout, and, like other devout men, passed into heaven. And so you shall not slander him, but pity the insanity of men. From him comes for them a ready peril of headlong disaster' (translation by Henry Bettenson, 1972). One might almost suppose that some modern 'christological' outlines are nearer to this neo-Platonic oracle of Hecate than to the New Testament.

which made them able to assimilate new patterns of thought can already be seen in antiquity.[84] The sources for early Christian thinking are to be sought primarily here, and not directly in the pagan sphere.

III.(a) *Wise men, charismatics and the royal Messiah*

In addition to the collective designation of Israel as son or sons which we find down to the rabbinic writings, there is also an individual application of the term in Jewish wisdom to particular *wise* men and *righteous* men, when in earlier texts it was reserved for the Davidic king:

> Be like a father to orphans,
> and instead of a husband to their mother,
> then God will call you his son,
> will have mercy on you and save you from the grave (Sir. 4.10).

Significantly, the grandson of the writer of the proverb tones it down in the Greek translation and writes, 'and you will be like a son of the Most High' (καὶ ἔσῃ ὡς υἱὸς ὑψίστου). Finally, in later Talmudic texts the *charismatic wonder-worker* or even *the mystic who is transported to God* is often designated 'son' by God or addressed as 'my son'.[85] We find a further development in the

---

[84] M. Hengel, *Judaism and Hellenism*; id., 'Anonymität, Pseudepi-graphie und "Literarische Fälschung" in der jüdisch-hellenistischen Literatur', in *Pseudepigrapha*, I, Entretiens sur l'Antiquité Classique XVIII, 1972, 231–329.

[85] This fact is usually overlooked completely in discussions of the history of religions. But see D. Flusser, *Jesus*, 1968, 98ff.; G. Vermes, *Jesus the Jew*, 1973, 206ff., and *JJS* 24, 1973, 53f., who refers above all to Hanina b. Dosa as 'son of God': 'Day by day a *bat qol* was heard saying: "The whole universe is sustained on account of my son Hanina; but my son Hanina is satisfied with one kab of carob from one Sabbath eve to another" ' (Taan. 24b; cf. Ber. 17b; Hull. 86a). Cf. Taan. 25a: God appears to Eleazar ben Pedath in a dream: 'Eleazar, my son, is it right that I should begin the whole creation of the world anew . . . ?' Hag. 15b: God says: 'My son Meir said . . .' Cf. also the Midrash of Moses' Death, Jellinek, *Bet ha-Midrasch* (reprinted 1967), 1, middle of 121: 'The Holy One immediately began to soothe him and said to him: My son Moses . . .', cf. also 119: 'I am God and you are God' (Exod. 7.1). According to Ber. 7a the high priest Ishmael b. Elisha had a vision of Yahweh in the

Wisdom of Solomon, which comes from the diaspora in Alexandria. The first chapters a description of the suffering of the ideal righteous man, who is persecuted and even killed by the godless:

> If the righteous man is God's son, he will help him,
> and will deliver him from the hand of his adversaries
> (2.18; cf. 2.13, 16).

There are clear parallels here to the passion narrative in the synoptic gospels. Presumably there is some relationship between the suffering wise man and son of God and the 'servant of God' in Isa. 53. After his death the righteous man is counted among the 'sons of God', i.e. the angels (5.5).[86] In the Hellenistic Jewish romance of *Joseph and Asenath*, Asenath, the daughter of an Egyptian priest, and other non-Jews on a number of occasions call Joseph 'son of God' because of his supernatural beauty and wisdom; however his brother Levi only calls him 'one beloved of God', and according to Batiffol's edition he is 'like a son of God'. This is probably meant to express the thought that he belongs to the sphere of God: one might even talk of his 'angelic' character.[87] A *fragment of text from*

---

heavenly Holy of Holies, who addressed him: 'Ishmael my son, bless me.' According to the legend of the ten martyrs (Jellinek 6, 21), Ishmael is addressed by the Metatron, God's vizir, as 'my son'. Presumably in the original form God himself spoke here, for in III Enoch 1.8 God himself says to the angels: 'My servants, my seraphim, my cherubim and my ophanim: cover your eyes before Ishmael, my son, my friend, my beloved.' The designation 'my Son' by God, or 'son of God', must have played some role in charismatic and mystic circles of Palestinian Judaism. Memar Marqah calls Moses *br byth d'lh*, 'son of the house of God' (IV §1, p. 85, Macdonald), and rabbinic literature knows the *'phamiliā^c of God as a technical term, i.e. the angels as the *'phamiliā^c šel ma^{ca}lā'*, cf. Hag. 13b; Sanh. 99b, etc., see S. Krauss, *Griechische und Lateinische Lehnwörter im Talmud, Midrasch und Targum*, 2, 1899, 463. The term can signify the heavenly hosts and also the heavenly council of the wise (Sanh. 67b). Cf. the prayer 'May it be thy will, O Lord our God, to make peace in the *phamiliā^c* above and the *phamiliā^c* below . . .' (Ber. 16b/17a).

[86] See L. Ruppert, *Der leidende Gerechte*, 1972, 78f., 84, 91; K. Berger, *ZTK* 71, 1974, 18ff.

[87] Joseph and Asenath 6.2–6; 13.10; 21.3; but see 23.10 (= Batiffol 75, 4f.); see M. Philonenko, *Joseph et Aséneth*, 1968, 85ff., who seeks to explain the title from Jewish-Hellenistic wisdom speculation in Egypt. Calling Joseph the son of God does not do away with Jacob's paternity

Cave 4 at Qumran shows that the tradition of the *king* as a 'son of
God' was not completely lost. The text has messianic quotations
from the Old Testament. Nathan's oracle in II Sam. 7.14, 'I will
be his father and he will be my son', is transferred to the 'shoot of
David', i.e. the Davidic Messiah, 'who will appear . . . in Zion at
the end of days' (4QFlor I, 11f.). Psalm 2 is also quoted a little
later, but unfortunately the fragment breaks off in the first few
verses, so that Ps. 2.7 does not appear. It follows from another
fragment that the birth of the Messiah will be God's work:[88]
'. . . when (God) brings it about that the Messiah is born among
them' (1QSa 2, 11f.). The messianic reference of Ps. 2.7 and other
similar passages is not completely lost even among the *rabbis*, for
all their anti-Christian polemic. The term 'son of God' appears
often in another text from Cave 4, in Aramaic, which presumably
comes from a Daniel apocryphon with eschatological contents.
Although it is sixteen years since it was purchased, it has only been
published in a provisional and fragmentary form. J. A. Fitzmyer
supplements it and translates it as follows:

> [. . . But your son] shall be great upon the earth [O King! All (men)
> shall] make [peace], and all shall serve [him. He shall be called the
> son of] the [G]reat [God], and by his name shall he be named.
> He shall be hailed (as) the Son of God, and they shall call him
> the Son of the Most High (*brh dy 'l yt'mr wbr 'lywn yqrwnh*). As
> comets (flash) to the sight, so shall be their kingdom. (For some)

(7.5; 22.4). The nearest parallel to this terminology seems to me to be
T. Abraham 12, where Abel, the son of Adam, functions as judge of souls.
He sits in heaven on a crystal throne that blazes like fire, as a 'wonderful
man, glittering like the sun, like to a son of God' (Recension A: ὅμοιος
υἱῷ θεοῦ). Cf. also the promise to Levi in Test. Levi 4, 2: 'The Most
High has now heard your prayer, to separate you from unrighteousness
and for you to be a son, helper and servant to him.' See J. Becker, *Untersuchungen zur Entstehungsgeschichte der Testament der zwölf Patriarchen*,
AGAJU 8, 1970, 263f. According to Ezekiel the Tragedian's drama, God
addresses Moses from the burning bush: 'Be of good cheer, my son
(ὦ παῖ), and hear my words.' Text in B. Snell, *Tragicorum Graecorum
Fragmenta*, I, 293, line 100. According to Josephus, *Antt.* 2, 232, the new-
born child Moses is a παῖς μορφῇ τε θεῖος.
[88] Cf. E. Lohse, TDNT 8, 361f.; G. Vermes, *Jesus the Jew*, 1973, 197ff.
W. Grundmann, in *Bibel und Qumran*, Festschrift H. Bardtke, 1968, 86–
111.

year[s] they shall rule upon the earth and shall trample everything
(under foot); people shall trample upon people, city upon ci[t]y . . .
until there arises the people of God, and everyone rests from the
sword.

J. T. Milik supplements the passage in a different way and conjectures that the Seleucid usurper Alexander Balas is the son
of God, but Fitzmyer sees him as a Jewish ruler. Nor is it possible to rule out a collective interpretation in terms of the Jewish
people, like the Son of Man in Dan. 7.13. The parallels to
Jesus as the messianic son of God in Luke 1.32, 33, 35, to
which Fitzmyer draws explicit attention, are also interesting. We
shall have to wait for the publication of the whole text before
drawing further conclusions, and it is possible that the riddle
of the text will never be satisfactorily solved. However, it makes
one thing clear, that the title 'Son of God' was not completely
alien to Palestinian Judaism.[89]

It may, however, be objected that all this has to do with the
designation of distinguished men as 'sons of God' and not with the
transference of divine nature to a man, much less with statements
about pre-existence and mediation at creation. However, there is
at least an indication of a connection between a man and the world
of heavenly 'sons of God' in the Wisdom of Solomon and Joseph
and Asenath. In the following section I would like to discuss two
Jewish texts, one from Palestine and one from the diaspora, in
which this barrier is clearly broken.

[89] Billerbeck, III, 19ff. There is also evidence there for polemic against
the Christian conception of 'the Son'. In Pesikta R.37 (Friedmann, 163a),
Jer. 31.20: 'Ephraim is my beloved son', is transferred to the suffering
Messiah b. Joseph. After his exaltation he is appointed judge over the
peoples. See p. 71 below. In the Targum on Ps. 89.27 God promises the
Davidic king, i.e. the Messiah: 'He will call on me: "Thou art my Father,
my God and the power of my redemption!"' *hū' yiqrē li 'abbā 'att . . .*;
cf. the κράζειν of the spirit in Rom. 8.15 and Gal. 4.6. The roots of the
address 'abba' in primitive Christianity – which certainly goes back to
Jesus – could lie here, see below p. 63, n. 116. In Ex. R. 19.7, R. Nathan
(about 160) refers Ps. 89.28, 'And I will make him my firstborn', to the
Messiah, Bill., III, 258. For the new 'Son of God' text from Qumran see
J. A. Fitzmyer, *NTS* 20, 1973/74, 391ff. Milik's interpretation is appearing in *HTR*.

III.(b)   *Jewish mysticism: Metatron*

In the so-called *Third Hebrew Book of Enoch*, which derives from
Jewish mysticism, following Gen. 5.24 the man *Enoch is caught up
into the highest heaven and is transformed into the fiery form of an
angel.* As *'Metatron'* he is set on a throne alongside God, appointed
above all angels and powers, to function as God's vizir and plenipotentiary. He is possibly given the title 'prince of the world',
indeed he is even called the 'little Yahweh'. The parallel to New
Testament statements about the enthronement of the exalted
Christ has long since been recognized,[90] and this passage is also
clearly dependent on the earlier Son of Man tradition which
appears, e.g., in Ethiopian Enoch 70;71. The only difference is that
in the time of the rabbis, titles like Son of Man and Son of God
could no longer be used because of competition with Christianity.
Instead, Enoch is given by God the mysterious designation *'na͑ar'*,
young man.[91] This could be substituted for christological titles
like 'Son' or 'Son of Man' which could no longer be used. Such a
view would be supported by the rabbinic warning against confus-
ing this Metatron with God himself, as 'his name is like that of his
Lord'.[92] When the rabbinic mystic and later apostate Elisha ben

[90] 'Prince of the world': III Enoch 30.2; 38.3; cf. also Ex. R. 17.4;
Hag. 12b; Yeb. 16b; Hull. 60a, etc.; 'little Yahweh': 12.5; 48C, 7; 48D,
1, no. 102. G. Sholem, *Jewish Gnosticism, Merkabah Mysticism and Talmudic Tadition*, 1960, 44ff., has questioned whether the 'prince of
the world' was originally identical with Metatron. The designation *͑ebed*
(YHWH) also appears at 48D, 1, no. 17, see H. Odeberg, II, 28, 174, and
III Enoch 1.4; 10.3; etc. See J. Jeremias, *TDNT* 5, 1968, 688, n. 256.
According to Num. R. 12.12, as heavenly high priest he offers the souls
of the righteous as an expiation for Israel. III Enoch 15 (B), 1, declares
him to be greater than all *'elōhim*. For influence on christology see H. R.
Balz, *Methodische Probleme der neutestamentlichen Christologie*, WMANT
25, 1967, 87–112; O. Michel, *Der Brief an die Hebräer*, KEK [12]1966, 105;
K. Berger, *NTS* 17, 1970/71, 415. Jaoel in the Apocalypse of Abraham is
a related mediator figure. The Metatron speculation is in turn taken up
by the Gnostic *Pistis Sophia* and the Book of Jeu, see Odeberg, I, 188ff.
[91] III Enoch 2.2; 3.2; 4.1, 10; cf. Odeberg, II, 7f.; I, 80; for Mandaean
parallels, 68f., and gnostic parallels, 191; the latter are evidently dependent
on earlier Jewish speculation. According to Yéb. 16b he is not only *na͑ar*,
youth, but also *zāqēn*, old man (Ps. 37.25).
[92] Sanh. 38b; cf. III Enoch 12.5: 'And he called me the little (lesser)
Yahweh in the presence of his whole *phamiliā'* (see above, n. 85), as it is

Abuya saw Metatron enthroned in glory in a vision, he is said to
have cried out, 'Truly, there are two divine powers in heaven!'
This recognition is said to have been the reason for his apostasy
from Judaism.[93] The interpretation given by Akiba of the thrones
in Dan. 7.9 shows that analogous conceptions could also be transferred to the Messiah: one is for God and the other is for David,
i.e. the Messiah. R. Jose the Galilean retorted indignantly: 'Akiba,
how long will you go on profaning the Shekinah . . . ?'[94]

III.(c) *The Prayer of Joseph*

Of course, even here it can be said that this tradition is an analogy
to the exaltation christology and explains the appointment of a
man to a godlike status, granting him absolute power to rule, but
does not explain *pre-existence* before all time, mediation at creation,
sending and incarnation. Further help is given us here by a text
from the Greek-speaking diaspora. In his commentary on John,
Origen quotes a fragment from a Jewish apocryphon, the so-called
Prayer of Joseph. There *Jacob-Israel*, the tribal ancestor of the
people of God, appears as an incarnate 'archangel of the power of
the Lord and supreme commander among the sons of God'. As
such he was 'created before all the works of creation' – together
with the other patriarchs Abraham and Isaac – and received from

---

written: 'For my name is in him' (Exod. 23.21). For the connection of
other angels with the tetragrammaton see 29.1 and 30.1 and Odeberg, II,
104f. Here we have an analogy to the transference of the title Kyrios (in
the LXX originally the Qere for the tetragrammaton) to the exalted
Christ. K. Berger, *ZTK* 71, 1974, 19, n. 36, gives a similar verdict; he
also refers to Jaoel in Apoc. Abr. 10.

[93] III Enoch 16.2, cf. Hag. 15a. For this sacrilege of the arch-apostate
Elisha (= Acher), Metatron is punished with sixty strokes of fire. Here is
an interpretation which is hostile to Metatron and denounces this kind of
mystical speculation about the heavens as dangerous. For rabbinic polemics
against the 'two powers' see H. F. Weiss, *Untersuchungen zur Kosmologie
des hellenistischen und palästinischen Judentums*, TU 97, 1966, 324f.

[94] Sanh. 38b, par. Hag. 14a. The messianic interpretation of the Son of
Man by Akiba also follows from this. Cf. also Billerbeck, I, 486; above
all, the interpretation of Anani in I Chron. 3.24 as 'son of the clouds', i.e.
as Messiah. See also the exaltation messianology in Pesikta Rabbati below,
p. 71, no. 127.

God the name Israel, 'the man who sees God, for I am the first-born of all living beings to whom God gave life'. He descended incognito to earth; the angel Uriel, who stood far below him, burned with envy against him and fought with him at the river Jabbok (Gen. 32.25ff.), but was overcome by Jacob, who referred to his own incomparably higher status. Exodus 4.22, '*Israel is my firstborn son*', which is applied collectively to the people of Israel, is evidently interpreted here in terms of a supreme, pre-existent spiritual being (πνεῦμα ἀρχικόν) which takes human form in Jacob and becomes the tribal ancestor of the people of Israel. Jacob-Israel can therefore also proclaim to his sons the whole future of the people of God because he has read it on the heavenly tablets of destiny.[95]

III.(d)   *Pre-existent Wisdom*

Mediation at creation, which we have so far missed, meets us continually in the Jewish wisdom tradition from the third century BC onwards. Wisdom already appears as God's *beloved child, born*

[95] Origen, *In Joh.* 2.31, §189f. (GCS 10, 88f.), cf. Origen, *In Gen.* 1.14 (3.9), in Eusebius, *PE* 6, 11, 64 (GCS 43, 1, 356). Text also in A.-M. Denis, *Fragmenta Pseudepigraphorum quae supersunt graeca*, 1970, 61f.; id., *Introduction aux pseudépigraphes grecs . . .*, 1970, 125ff., and the more detailed article by Jonathan Z. Smith, 'The Prayer of Joseph', in *Religions in Antiquity. Essays in Memory of E. R. Goodenough*, 1968, 253–94. Smith stresses the connections with Jewish mysticism and wisdom speculation and points to the Jewish origin of the fragment: 'Rather than the Jews imitating Christological titles, it would appear that the Christians borrowed already existing Jewish terminology' (272). Some rabbis also interpret Exod. 4.22 not primarily in terms of the collective Israel, but in terms of the patriarchs, so e.g. R. Nathan in Ex. R. 19. 7: God says to Moses: 'Just as I have made Jacob a firstborn, for it says "Israel is my firstborn son", so I will make the king Messiah a firstborn, as it says: "I will make him my firstborn" ' (Ps. 89.28). Cf. III Enoch 44.10 (Odeberg): 'Abraham my beloved, Isaac my chosen, Jacob my firstborn.' J. Z. Smith reaches the conclusion: 'The PJ may be termed a myth of the mystery of Israel. As such it is a narrative of the descent of the chief angel Israel and his incarnation within the body and of his recollection and ascent to his former heavenly state' (287). H. Windisch, *Neutestamentliche Studien für G. Heinrici*, UNT 6, 1914, 225, n. 1, already saw the significance of this fragment: its 'phrases recall wisdom speculation in the same way as does Col. 1.15'. Cf. also A. D. Nock, *Essays*, 2, 931f.

before all the works of creation and present at the creation of the world, in the fundamental wisdom hymn of Prov. 8.22ff.:

> When he marked out the foundations of the earth,
> then I was beside him as his darling;
> and I was daily his delight,
> rejoicing before him always,
> rejoicing in his inhabited world
> and delighting in the sons of men (8.29f.).

This unique mediator in creation and revelation acquires a function in Judaism in the Hellenistic period which (with a pinch of salt) might be compared with the Platonic world-soul or the Stoic Logos.[96] It gives the world its order and men their rationality: God himself 'poured her out on all his works' (Sir. 1.9). But the Ben Sira who stressed the universality of Wisdom in this statement also proclaimed its extreme exclusiveness in a way which is only understandable against the background of the spiritual struggle of his time. Wisdom went through earth and heaven but found no dwelling place:

> Then the Creator of all things gave me a commandment,
> and the one who created me assigned a place for my tent.
> And he said, 'Make your dwelling in Jacob,
> and in Israel receive your inheritance.'
> From primal times, from the beginning, I was created (Syr and V),
> and for eternity I shall not cease to exist.
> In the holy tabernacle I ministered before him,
> and so I was established in Zion.
> In the city which he loved like me I found my rest (Syr and V),
> and in Jerusalem (arose) my dominion.
> So I took place in an honoured people,
> in the portion of the Lord, in his inheritance (Syr) (24.8–12).

That is, the supreme mediator figure leaves the heavenly sanctuary and settles in *one* point on earth, the temple on Mount Zion in Jerusalem, the place which the God of Israel has chosen and on which according to prophetic promise the throne of the Messiah is also to stand.[97] However, this exclusive restriction goes still further.

---

[96] M. Hengel, *Judaism and Hellenism*, I, 153ff., 162ff.
[97] Ibid., 157ff.; J. Marböck, *Weisheit im Wandel*, BBB 37, 1971, 17ff.,

For Ben Sira the divine wisdom is identical with the law of Moses.

> All this is the book of the covenant of the Most High (God),
> the law which Moses commanded us
> as an inheritance for the congregations of Jacob (24.23).

This means that the divine wisdom, a cosmic entity, is sent by God himself to a particular place on earth and at the same time takes the form of the law entrusted to Israel on Sinai. The Jews also took this identification of wisdom and Torah further, at the same time continually stressing its universal, cosmic aspect. For Philo, the Jewish philosopher of religion, as for the rabbis, Wisdom-Torah is comparable to the architectural plan or instrument with which God created the world. Both can also be called *'daughter of God'*.[98] According to Philo, *Quaest. Gen.* 4.97, it is 'daughter of God and first-born mother of the universe'. Whether this designation is merely metaphorical and pictorial or whether the conception of a personified hypostasis can be glimpsed through it is of secondary importance. The two were fundamentally interchangeable. Wisdom is also given comprehensive cosmic significance in the *Alexandrian Wisdom of Solomon*. It is 'a breath of the power of God', 'a pure emanation of the glory of the Almighty', 'a reflection of (his) eternal light', 'an image of his (perfect)

34ff., 63ff.; cf. H. Gese, 'Natus ex virgine', in *Probleme biblischer Theologie, Festschrift G. von Rad*, 1971, 87 = *V om Sinai zum Zion*, 1974, 144f.: 'Wisdom, which became a hypostasis in later wisdom theology, and had to be represented as a child of God created in primal times (Prov. 8.22f.), has a comparable function to the king on Zion as a representative of Yahweh's order. Its identity with Yahweh's revelation to Israel leads to the conception that as the pre-existent divine Logos (Sir. 24.3ff.), like the ark, it can only find a permanent abode on Zion (vv. 7ff.). Thus wisdom theology is at root connected with the messianism associated with Zion, and this connection is presupposed in the relatively early passages in the New Testament which speak of the υἱὸς θεοῦ and the sending of the Son . . . The interpretation of Zion theology in terms of wisdom leads to the idea of the pre-existence of the υἱὸς θεοῦ, and the tradition which saw the time of David as being the primal time and hence, like Micah 5.1, taught the protological origin of the eschatological Messiah, inevitably appeared in a different light.'

[98] M. Hengel, *Judaism and Hellenism*, I, 169ff. For the Torah as 'daughter of God' see ibid., II, 111, n. 418. For wisdom as 'daughter of God' in Philo see *De fuga* 50ff.; *De virtute* 62; *Quaest. Gen.* 4, 97.

goodness'. Here we come up against images and concepts which reappear in the same words in christological statements.[99] On the other hand, Wisdom is not described as a daughter of God, but in even more mythological fashion as his 'cohabitant' (8.3) and 'companion to his throne' (9.4). On the other hand, the righteous man inspired by Wisdom is a 'son of God' (2.18), and Israel too is a 'son of God' (18.13), while the Israelites brought up by Wisdom are 'God's children' (9.4, 7; 12.19, 21; 16.21, etc.). Wisdom is sent out (9.10) in the form of the divine spirit (7.7, 22f.; 9.17f.) and 'enters into holy souls', fills 'friends of God and prophets', i.e. is at work in the holy history of Israel, the children of God (7.27). At the same time, like the Stoic Logos, Wisdom permeates the whole universe (8.1).[100]

III.(e) *Philo of Alexandria*

Wisdom bears very similar traits in the work of Philo of Alexandria, the Jewish philosopher of religion, who is about a generation earlier than Paul. It should, of course be noted that we cannot presuppose any strictly systematic conceptuality in Philo's work. We must reckon with very free and bold associations. For example, Philo can describe God, the 'demiurge' who created the universe, as 'Father', and the divine reason (ἐπιστήμη), which is identical with Wisdom, as the mother of the world, referring explicitly to the wisdom hymn in Prov. 8.22ff., from which we began. 'Having received the divine seed, when her travail was consummated, she bore the only son who is apprehended by the senses, the world which we see.'[8];[1] Here *Jewish wisdom speculation is connected with*

---

[99] Wisdom 7.25; on this cf. B. L. Mack, *Logos und Sophia*, SUNT 10, 1973, 67–72. However, his one-sided interpretation in terms of Egypt misses the point. We have here the typical terminology of religious Hellenistic *koine*, cf. J. M. Reese, *Hellenistic Influence on the Book of Wisdom and its Consequences*, AnalBibl 41, 1970, 41ff. The author is influenced by popular philosophy and the *Hellenistic* Isis aretalogy, which is substantially different from its earlier Egyptian predecessors. Cf. Heb. 1.3; Col. 1.15; II Cor. 4.6.

[100] Cf. P. C. Larcher, *Études sur le livre de la Sagesse* (ÉtBibl), 1969, 329–414: 'La Sagesse et l'Esprit'.

[101] *De ebr.* 30f.; cf. *De fug.* 109: God as father, and Wisdom, 'through

the Platonic doctrine of creation to be found in the Timaeus. To God as Father of the universe there corresponds *the world as son.* Here, however, Philo distinguishes between the *spiritual world of ideas* and the visible world. The former is the '*eldest and first-born son*' and as such is identical with the *Logos*, the divine reason in the world. As mediator between the eternal Godhead and the created, visible world he is at the same time God's 'image' (εἰκών).[102] Philo can describe him in many different ways: impersonally as the 'spiritual world' or in personified form as the heavenly high priest, the sinless mediator, the spiritual primal man, the spokesman, the archangel, indeed as the second god (δεύτερος θεός), who, neither created nor uncreated, is God's messenger and ambassador, and rules the elements and the stars as his governor.[103] The visible world, on the other hand, is the 'younger son', and time the

---

whom the universe came into existence', as mother of the High Priest, i.e. the Logos; similarly *Quod det. pot.* 54. See B. L. Mack, op. cit., 145. For the whole question see also H. Hegermann, *Die Vorstellung vom Schöpfungsmittler* ... TU 82, 1961, and H. F. Weiss, *Untersuchungen zur Kosmologie des hellenistischen und palästinischen Judentums*, TU 97, 1966, 248–82. A. S. Carman, 'Philo's Doctrine of the Divine Father and the Virgin Mother', *AJT* 9, 1905, 491–518, and A. Maddalena, *Filone Alessandrino*, 1970, 298–317: 'Il figlio e il padre'; 345–58: 'Dal figlio al padre'.

[102] In *Conf. ling.* 62f. the '*semaḥ*' = *anatole* of Zech. 6.12, which is in itself messianic, is interpreted in terms of the eldest and 'first-born son', i.e. the Logos. For his position as mediator see *Quis rer. div.* 205f. Cf. also *Conf. ling.* 146; *De agric.* 51; *De somn.* 1, 215; *Quod det. pot.* 82; *Spec. leg.* 1, 96, etc. For the Logos as *eikon* see F.-W. Eltester, *Eikon im Neuen Testament*, BZNW 23, 1958, 35ff.

[103] E. Schweizer, *TDNT* 8, 355f.; B. L. Mack, op. cit., 167ff. It is improbable that Egyptian Horus mythology underlines the concept of the Logos as 'son' and 'image', as Mack supposes. Mack underestimates the Middle-Platonic tradition in which Philo is situated. The light terminology is too widespread in antiquity for far-reaching historical conclusions to be drawn from it. All attempts to interpret Philo predominantly in terms of a single cause (Egyptian mythology, theology of the mysteries, gnosticism, Old Testament and Judaism) are misleading and do not do justice to the complex synthetic character of Philo's thought. For the Logos as 'second God' see *Quaest. Gen.* II, 62 = Eusebius, *PE* 7, 13, 1: 'Nothing mortal can be made in the likeness of the most High One and Father of the universe, but (only) in that of the second God, who is his Logos'; cf. Rom. 8.32 and H.-F. Weiss, op. cit., 261, n. 8. However, see the remarks about θεός and ὁ θεός in *Somn.* 1, 228ff., see below, 80f.

'grandson of God'. The 'younger son' also functions as mediator;[104] he can 'teach me as a son about the Father and as a work about the master workman'.[105] Philo is *remarkably restrained in transferring the designation 'son of God' to men.* In *Quaest. Gen.* 1, 92 (on Gen. 6.4) his basis for calling the angels 'sons of God' is that they are incorporeal spirits who are not fathered by a man. He adds the observation that Moses also calls 'good and excellent men' sons of God, whereas he calls the wicked only 'bodies'. In *Spec. leg.* 1, 318, on the basis of a combination of Deut. 13.18 and 14.1, he comes to the conclusion 'that men who "do what is pleasing (to nature) and what is good" are sons of God'. Physical descent plays no part here; in principle this does away with any restriction to the nation of Israel. This restraint of Philo's in transferring the term to men is particularly clear in *Conf. ling.* 145ff. First of all, quoting Deut. 14.1 and 32.18, he stresses that all those who have knowledge of the uniqueness of God are called 'sons of the one God'. This is supplemented in traditional Stoic fashion: they 'hold (moral) beauty to be the only good', in order to destroy what is morally bad, that is, pleasure. Philo then adds a qualification: 'But if there is anyone who is as yet unfit to be called a son of God', then he should submit himself 'to the Logos, to God's first-born, who holds the eldership among the angels', the 'archangel' and the 'one with many names', who is at the same time also called 'beginning, name, word of God, man after the image and the one who sees, namely Israel' (. . . κατὰ τὸν πρωτόγονον αὐτοῦ λόγον, τὸν ἀγγέλων πρεσβύτατον. . . · καὶ γὰρ ἀρχὴ καὶ ὄνομα θεοῦ καὶ λόγος καὶ ὁ κατ' εἰκόνα ἄνθρωπος καὶ ὁ ὁρῶν, Ἰσραήλ, προσαγορεύεται).

Referring to Gen. 42.11, 'We are all sons of one man', i.e. Jacob-Israel, he then stresses that those who 'are not fit to be considered sons of God' may be at least sons 'of the most holy Logos', God's 'invisible image'. This is not a matter of physical descent, but of the 'paternity of souls raised to immortality by virtue' (149). Here the saving function of the Logos is particularly clear. Only he, 'the firstborn of God', can make men worthy of being called 'sons of God' through spiritual rebirth. The interpretation of

---

[104] *Quod deus imm.* 31f.; *De ebr.* 30ff. (quot. Prov. 8.22).
[105] *Spec. leg.* 1, 41.

'Israel', of the man who sees God, as '*archē*' and 'oldest archangel'
at the same time sheds light on the Prayer of Joseph, which has
already been mentioned, though Philo's language has a stronger
philosophical stamp. Evidently speculations of this kind were not
unusual in diaspora Judaism.

It is therefore all the more remarkable that Philo hardly ever
applies the term 'son of God' to a particular figure in salvation
history. Of course he is fond of speaking of spiritual procreation,
without a father, and in this context can at one point call Isaac
'son of God', but this predicate is not applied to the historical
patriarch. In an allegorical interpretation of his name it means 'the
best of all the good emotions', 'inner laughter of the heart', which
God 'gives as a means to soothe and cheer truly peaceful souls'
(*Mut. nom.* 130f.). The designation is only applied to Abraham at
one point, in connection with the interpretation of Gen. 18.17:
'Shall I hide (what I plan) from *Abraham*, my friend (LXX on the
other hand only has 'my servant', παῖς μου)?' The wise man who
is thus a friend of God 'has passed beyond the bounds of human
happiness; he alone is nobly born, for he has registered God as his
father and become *by adoption* his only son' (μόνος γὰρ εὐγενὴς
ἅτε θεὸν ἐπιγεγραμμένος πατέρα καὶ γεγονὼς εἰσποιητὸς αὐτῷ μόνος
υἱός). In connection with this, the wise man is praised, in good
Stoic fashion, as the sole true rich man, free man and king
(*Sobr.* 56f.).[106]

---

[106] Cf. *Quaest. Gen.* 4, 29 on 18.33, where the encounter of God with
Abraham is depicted as the ecstasy of the wise man. This encounter cannot be of permanent duration, but the wise man must be prepared to
return, for 'not everything is to be done by the sons in the sight of the
Father . . .' In *Quaest. Gen.* 4, 21, Abraham is called 'my servant', follow-
ing the LXX of Gen. 18.17, similarly *All. leg.* 3, 18. K. Berger (*ZTK* 71,
1974, 7, and *NTS* 20, 1973/74, 34f., n. 132) would see a Hellenistic-
Jewish tradition about an unpolitical kingdom in the interpretation of
Abraham as the wise man, the adopted son of God, the rich man, the
free man and the king. The (ironic) conclusion of Horace's epistle to
Maecenas shows that these themes are based entirely on Stoic tradition
(*Ep.* 1, 106ff.):
> *ad summam*: sapiens *uno minor est Iove* dives,
> liber, *honoratus, pulcher* rex *denique regum*,
> *praecipue sanus* – nisi cum pitvita molesta est
> (unless he is plagued with a cold).

Instead of 'son of God', Philo prefers to use 'man of God' (ἄνθρωπος θεοῦ), which goes back to Old Testament models.[107] This restraint is all the more striking since, probably as the result of Hellenistic influence, the boundaries between the divine world and man are blurred in the case of individual figures like the patriarchs and Moses. Thus in *Quaest. Ex.* 2, 29 he interprets the statement in 24.2 that Moses alone is allowed to approach God as meaning that the soul, inspired by God with prophetic gifts, 'comes near to God in a kind of family relation, for having given up and left behind all mortal kinds, it is changed into the divine, so that such men become kin to God and truly divine.' In *Quaest. Ex.* 2, 46 Philo calls this transformation a 'second birth', incorporeal and without involving a mother, brought about through the 'Father of the universe' alone. [108] In an 'eschatological' tractate *De praem. et poen.* 165ff., finally there is a description of the miraculous return of Israel, in which three 'Paracletes' are involved to achieve 'reconciliation with the Father' (πρὸς τὸν πατέρα τακαλλαγαί): God's goodness, intercession and the reformation of those returning home. They have 'no other goal than to find favour with God, *as* sons may with their father'.

Although Philo accordingly does not use 'son of God' frequently in his great work, the term has a considerable breadth of variation. In the cosmic sphere, where its focal point is to be found, it takes

---

Thus already E. Bréhier, *Les idées philosophiques et religieuses de Philoe d'Alexandrie*, ³1950, 233ff.: 'Le fils de Dieu . . . n'est donc que le sage au sens stoïcien, sans qu'il y ait trace d'une relation personelle.'

[107] The designation 'ma.ı of God' can be used simultaneously both for the Logos, i.e. the heavenly primal man, and for the wise man who lives in accord with the Logos. For the term cf. LXX Deut. 33.1; Josh. 14.6 = Moses; I Kingd. 2.27; 9.7–10 = Samuel; III Kingd. 12.24; 13.4–31; 17.24; IV Kingd. 1.9–13, etc. = Elijah; 4.7ff. = Elisha. For Philo, see Bréhier, op. cit., 121ff. In I Enoch 15.1, the Enoch who is transported to God in heaven is ὁ ἄνθρωπος ὁ ἀληθινός (or τῆς ἀληθείας).

[108] For Philo's teminology see R. A. Baer Jr, *Philo's Use of the Categories Male and Female*, ALGHJ 3, 1970, especially 55ff.: 'The divine impregnation of the soul.' The regular description of God and the powers subordinate to him as spiritual begetters is intended to present him as 'the source of all goodness and virtue' (61). Salvation history with its individual specific figures retreats right into the background in the face of this present, mystical relationship with God.

up the speculations of Jewish wisdom and of Plato's *Timaeus*; its application to men is usually prompted by Old Testament statements, though they are interpreted in Stoic fashion. Despite the strong Hellenistic stamp, this restraint in the use of metaphor might be connected with a concern to preserve God's transcendence over the world. Of course it stands in striking contrast to Philo's favourite speculations about a 'begetting' or a 'birth' from God. Statements from the Old Testament and Judaism and Hellenistic mythology or philosophy flow into one another almost without a break: in this way Philo shows the wide possibilities of a Greek interpretation of Jewish tradition.

6

The Problem of the Rise
of Early Christology

We have sketched out extremely briefly Jewish terminology relating to the Son of God and the thought-patterns involved with it: pre-existence, mediation at creation and sending into the world. It would seem that there is substantial building material here which would be used by the early church in the conception of its christological outlines. The remarkable number of names applied to Wisdom and the various ways of conceiving of it, and even more the similar variety in the case of Philo's Logos, show us that it is misleading to unravel the web of christological titles into a number of independent and indeed conflicting 'christologies', with different communities standing behind each. To adopt this approach brings one as near to historical reality as if one were to suppose that there was an independent 'Logos doctrine' behind each of the names given to Philo's Logos. Such a method only opens up a wide range of historical absurdities. This should also be noted in connection with the rise of christology. Ancient man did not think analytically or make differentiations within the realm of myth in the way that we do, but combined and accumulated his ideas in a 'multiplicity of approximations'. The more titles were applied to the risen Christ, the more possible it was to celebrate the uniqueness of his saving work.[109] We should also remember that in the sources which we possess, as elsewhere in antiquity, we have only a very small, and

[109] Philo says that Logos and Wisdom have 'many names': *Conf. ling.* 146: 'But if anyone is not worthy to be called son of God, let him strive to take his place under the Logos, his (God's) first-born, the eldest among the angels, who is archangel and has many names (πολυώνυμος).' According to *Leg. all.* 1, 43, the 'exalted heavenly wisdom' which is identical with the Logos or described as his mother is said to have many names. Moses

often quite fortuitous, section from a very much larger range of tradition.

The question now is, how far can this mosaic collection of Jewish sources help us to make a hypothetical reconstruction of the development of the Son of God christology in the brief twenty years between the primal event of the death and resurrection of Jesus on which the community was founded and the development of Paul's mission after the apostolic council?

First and foremost, we must remember that what happened cannot just have been a simple reproduction of earlier Jewish speculations about hypostases and mediators. Earliest christology has a quite original stamp, and is ultimately rooted in the contingent event of the activity of Jesus, his death and resurrection appearances. A history-of-religions comparison can only explain the

---

(*Mut. nom.* 125) and the wise man (*Ebr.* 82), and indeed 'divine powers' (*Somn.* 2, 254), have the same epithet applied to them. That in the view of antiquity to have many names was an indication of superior status is evident not only from the way in which seventy names are conferred on Metatron (III Enoch 3.2; 4.1; 48D, 1, 1, 5, 9) but also from the multiplicity of the names of God himself, III Enoch 48B, cf. Philo, *Decal.* 94. The 'pluriform name of God' (τὸ τοῦ θεοῦ πολυώνυμον ὄνομα) should not be wantonly misused. Whereas divine anonymity was seen to be a sign of primitive peoples, multiplicity of names was seen to be a sign of honour: for the Stoa see Diogenes Laert., 7, 135, 147; Ps. Aristot., *De mundo* 7 (401a, 13ff.). Cf. already *Hom. Hymn. Dem.* 18, 32, 'The son of Kronos with the many names' (= Hades), and the appeal to Dionysus 'of the many names' (Sophocles, *Ant.* 1115), Cleanthes, *Hymn to Zeus*, line 1 (SVF 1, 121, lines 34f.): 'Zeus, supreme among the immortals, ruler of the universe, with the many names', and Aristides, *Or.* 49, 29ff. (Keil, 346): 'Zeus has received all the great names which befit him.' 'Isis of the many names' is well-known: Apuleius, *Met.* 11, 5, 2: *cuius numen unicum multiformi specie, ritu vario, nomine multiiugo totus veneratur orbis.* See also the great Isis aretalogy, POx 1380. For the whole matter see E. Bickerman, 'Anonymous Gods', *Journal of the Warburg Institute* 1, 1937/38, 187ff.: H. Bietenhard, *TDNT* 5, 298f. The connection of the many names of Wisdom and the Logos in Philo with the Egyptian Isis aretalogy in B. L. Mack, op. cit., 110, n. 2, is one-sided. This is a very widespread phenomenon. For christology see H. von Campenhausen in connection with the Fourth Gospel, *ZNW* 63, 1972, 220f.: 'This abundance of "names" is no doubt deliberate. Jesus himself in his uniqueness is the sole content of the Gospel. Each possible title is no more than a reference, and none can describe Jesus completely as he is in truth.'

derivation of individual themes, traditions, phrases and functions, and not the phenomenon of the origin of christology as a whole. At the same time, we must also consider the possibility of 'unparalleled' innovation. Even now we have not really progressed very far beyond a judgment which is particularly significant because it was made by such a distinguished scholar of Hellenistic religion as A. Deissmann: 'The origin of the cult of Christ (and that means, of christology) is the secret of the earliest Palestinian community.' Our considerations will have to begin here.

I. *The early confession in Romans 1.3f.*

First of all, I would like to go back to a Pauline text about the Son of God which I have so far kept in the background. The unanimous opinion of scholars is that it contains an early confession. Paul quotes it in the introduction to his letter to the Romans, a community which he did not found. Perhaps he uses this formula to indicate the common creed which they shared. At this point Paul says two things about the 'Son of God' who is the content of his gospel:

> Who was descended from the seed of David according to the flesh and designated Son of God in power according to the Spirit of holiness by his resurrection from the dead (Rom. 1.3f.).

In recent years, more has been written about this than about any other New Testament text.[110] We may spare ourselves the trouble of reporting the many hypotheses about the development of the formula. All attempts at reconstruction are more or less hypothetical. It is clear that two contrasting statements are set side by side here, both of which concern the Son of God (περὶ τοῦ υἱοῦ αὐτοῦ, 1. 3a):

---

[110] See the list in E. Käsemann, *An die Römer*, 1973, 2; K. Wengst, *Christologische Formeln und Lieder des Urchristentums*, SNT 7, 1972, 112ff. G. Eichholz, *Die Theologie des Paulus im Umriss*, 1972, 123ff.; E. Brandenburger, *Frieden im Neuen Testament*, 1973, 19ff. E. Schweizer, *Neotestamentica*, 1963, 180ff.; P. Stuhlmacher, *EvTh* 27, 1967, 374–89, are still important.

1. His human descent is through David. This gives the earthly basis of his messianic status in the context of salvation history.

2. However, the emphasis is on the second expression. By virtue of the resurrection – or chronologically, after the resurrection – he is appointed Son of God in 'divine' power (δύναμις) and in a 'spirit-like', i.e. heavenly, mode of being, which shares in the divine glory.

It would therefore be too one-sided to seek to understand being a Son of God only in 'legal' and 'non-physical' terms.[111] This modern alternative is inadequate. For to talk of Jesus as Son of God is at the same time to make a statement about the 'transcendent' being of the risen Christ with God in his glory, into which he has been 'transformed'. However, in this formula it is striking that Paul does not speak expressly of the pre-existence and sending of the Son, although he may presuppose it in the introduction; indeed from the isolated wording scholars infer that the appointment as Son of God is only brought about through the resurrection from the dead. We may conclude from this that here we really do have a very early confession which is 'pre-Pauline' in the strict sense of the term. It might presumably go back in a simpler form to the first Jewish-Christian community in Jerusalem. H. Schlier suggested as its original form:

> Jesus Christ of the seed of David,
> appointed Son of God
> through the resurrection of the dead.[112]

Paul, on the other hand, certainly understands it in terms of his theology of pre-existence which we find, for example, in the Philippians hymn, where the crucified Christ is given the title 'Kyrios' in the act of exaltation. The nearest Jewish parallel would be the exaltation, transformation and enthronement of the man Enoch, who is also addressed by God with a wealth of titles, including that of 'the little Yahweh'.

---

[111] H. Conzelmann, *An Outline of the Theology of the New Testament*, 1969, 105.

[112] H. Schlier, 'Zu Rö 1, 3f', in *Neues Testament und Geschichte. Festschrift O. Cullmann*, 1972, 207–18, here 213.

II. *The historical background to Romans 1.3f.*

The two-membered confession shows the twofold root of christology extremely well.

The first root is the earthly Jesus from the seed of David. The expression in the first member describes him as Messiah designate. As such he goes to his death. Over his cross, as the political statement of his crime, stood the words 'King of the Jews'. This title runs through the whole passion narrative like a scarlet thread and cannot therefore simply be rejected as a late construction by the community.[113] The early Christian formulations of belief go on to repeat in numerous variations the claim that 'The Messiah (Christ) died for us' or 'for our sins'. The shameful death of the Messiah-designate was an unheard-of scandal which from the beginning compelled the primitive community to interpret this horror in terms of the need for it if the Old Testament promise of salvation were to be fulfilled. This is not, of course, the question here. The death of Jesus is only presupposed implicitly in the statement about the resurrection.

[113] M. Hengel, *Nachfolge und Charisma*, BZNW 34, 1968, 42ff. That the charge of being 'king of the Jews' was tantamount to rebellion in the eyes of the Roman administration is shown by the characterization of the Jewish kings in Tacitus, *Hist.* 5, 8: '*Tum Iudaei Macedonibus invalidis, Parthis nondum adultis (et Romani procul erant), sibi ipsi reges imposuere.*' Only the Romans had the right to appoint and depose kings within their empire, see Josephus, *BJ* 1, 282: Mark Anthony is resolved 'to make Herod king of the Jews'. On the other hand, according to *Antt.* 14, 384, the Hasmonean Antigonus forfeited his kingdom because he had been appointed by the Parthians. According to Dio Cassius 49, 22, 6 he was executed as a rebel by the axe, having been first bound to a stake and flogged, 'which is something that no king of the Romans had suffered' (cf. Strabo, according to Josephus, *Antt.* 15, 9). For the mockery of Jesus as 'king of the Jews' see not only the Carabas episode in Alexandria (Philo, *In Flacc.* 36ff.), but also the order of Lupus, the Prefect in Alexandria, to mock a Jewish king (Andreas Lukuas of the rebellion of AD 116–117?) in a mime in the theatre, see the *Acta Pauli et Antonini*, col. 1, 1, 4f., *Acta Alexandrinorum*, ed. Musurillo, 1961, 37. We cannot overestimate the scandal of a crucified *Jewish* Messiah king who was to be proclaimed 'Lord' and 'Son of God'. Pilate's question (Mark 15.9, 12), and still more the *titulus* on the cross, are expressions of hostility to Judaism. For the interpretation of the title 'king' and Davidic sonship in charismatic terms and in terms of wisdom see K. Berger, *ZTK* 71, 1974, 1–15.

The event of the resurrection makes up the second root of
christology and its immediate offence. God acknowledged the
condemned man on the cross. So the statement 'God has raised
Jesus' could be described as the real primal Christian confession
which keeps recurring in the New Testament – even more often
than the formula of the dying of Christ.[114] The passive participle
ὁρισθείς in Rom. 1.4 is a typical divine passive, which is a peri-
phrasis of God's own action. It should be noted here that the
resurrection by itself is inadequate to explain the origin of Jesus'
messiahship. The exaltation of a martyr to God was by no means
an indication of his eschatological and messianic, i.e. his unique,
status. The resurrection is especially significant because here God
confirms the crucified 'king of the Jews', his anointed.[115] He brings
about this confirmation by appointing Jesus Son of God, by virtue
of the resurrection from the dead. And so we come to the question
which particularly interests us: why does the confession read 'Son
of God' at this decisive point and not 'Son of Man', or 'Messiah',
or even 'Lord'? We would really expect another title in the context
of the exaltation of Jesus: in Ethiopian Enoch 71.14, God addresses
the exalted Enoch: 'You are the Son of Man who is born for
righteousness', and Ps. 110, which is quite decisive for early
christology, begins: 'The Lord said to my Lord, Sit at my right

[114] From the flood of literature on the resurrection, see B. Rigaux,
Dieu l'a ressuscité, 1973, esp. 311ff.; P. Stuhlmacher, 'Das Bekenntnis zur
Auferweckung Jesu von den Toten und die Biblische Theologie', *ZTK*
70, 1973, 365–403, and the third number of *TQ* 153, 1973, on 'the origin
of resurrection faith', with contributions by R. Pesch, W. Kasper, K. H.
Schelkle, P. Stuhlmacher and M. Hengel.

[115] Cf. N. A. Dahl, 'Der gekreuzigte Messias', in H. Ristow – K. Matthiae, *Der historische Jesus und der kerygmatische Christus*, 1960, 161:
'. . . it could be concluded from the appearances of the risen Jesus that he
was alive and had ascended into heaven, but not that he was the Messiah
. . . The resurrection meant that Jesus had been put in the right by God
over against his adversaries. Had he been crucified for messianic claims,
then – and only then – belief in his resurrection would have had to become
belief in the resurrection of the crucified Messiah.' Similarly J. Jeremias,
New Testament Theology, I, 255: 'Faith in the resurrection of a murdered
messenger of God certainly does not amount to belief in his messiahship
(cf. Mark 6.16). Furthermore, the scandal of the crucified Messiah is so
enormous that it is hardly conceivable that the community should have
presented itself with such a stumbling block.'

hand . . .' The keyword 'Lord' appears here as in Philippians. The Old Testament and Jewish statements about the Son of God are, as we saw, both confusingly varied and very obscure: in contemporary Judaism in particular, 'Son of God' is not really used as a title for the Messiah. A first reply to this might be: more than any other title in the New Testament, the title Son of God connects the figure of Jesus with God. He is the beloved (Mark 1.11; 9.7; 12.6 par.), the only (John 1.14, 18; 3.16, 18; I John 4.9) and the first-born Son (Rom. 8.29; Col. 1.15, 18; Heb. 1.6; cf. Rev. 1.5). This is meant to express the fact that in Jesus, God himself comes to men, and that the risen Christ is fully bound up with God. It may now be objected that this apparently dogmatic information does not add up to a historical proof. There are, however, good historical reasons for it, of which I will name four:

1. An important starting point is Jesus' unique relationship with God, expressed in the address 'Abba', 'dear Father', which it was quite unusual for a Jew to use to God. This alien Aramaic word is a form of address which Paul himself hands on to the communities he founded, and is a sign, effected b7 the Spirit, that the Son makes believers sons of God. Even if Jesus probably did not designate himself 'Son of God' in so many words, the real root of this post-Easter title lies in his filial relationship to God as Father.[116]

2. A further root is the messianic argument from scripture. Jesus was denounced by the leaders of the people to Pilate as an alleged messianic pretender and condemned to death by Pilate. In the events of the resurrection, the oldest testimony to which is Paul's formal account in I Cor. 15.3ff., the early community saw

[116] Rom. 8.15; Gal. 4.5f.; Mark 14.36. J. Jeremias, *The Prayers of Jesus*, SBT II 6, 1967, 11–65; id., *New Testament Theology*, I, 1971, 61ff., 178ff. The original form of the revelation saying in Matt. 11.27 = Luke 10.22 is also an expression of this filial relationship, see op. cit., 56ff. The attempt by K. Berger, *NTS* 17, 1971, 422ff., to derive it from the wisdom tradition of teaching and the understanding of 'teacher' and 'pupil' is, on the other hand, too one-sided. Like Gal. 4.4ff., Rom. 8.15ff. shows that the theme here is the eschatological liberation of the children of God. This already has its roots in Jesus' preaching of the 'kingdom of God' and in his actions. The only explanation of the significance of the Aramaic cry 'Abba' in Paul's Gentile-Christian communities is that it goes back to Jesus himself. See also p. 45, n. 89 above, on Ps. 89.27.

the divine confirmation of Jesus' messianic claim. However, this
Messiahship of the crucified, risen and exalted Jesus went completely counter to the popular, traditional expectation of a political
liberator and learned exponent of the Torah, which is the expectation that had been put about especially by Pharisaism. The missionary preaching of the first witnesses of the resurrection to their
own people derived the force of its argument in the first place from
'scriptural proof', which put prophetic promise before the Torah.
Thus it was possible to read the conjunction of resurrection and the
divine sonship of Jesus out of the ancient oracle given by Nathan
to David (II Sam. 7.12-14): 'I will raise up your seed after you
(*wah^{a}qimōti* = καὶ ἀναστήσω) . . ., and I will establish his kingdom.
He shall build a house for my name, and I will establish the throne
of his kingdom for ever. I will be his father, and he shall be my
son.' My friend Otto Betz has clearly shown that the interpretation
of II Sam. 7.12ff. in terms of the risen Christ clearly lies behind the
early confession in Rom. 1.3f.[117] There are further indications of
the strong influence of II Sam. 7.12-16 on the developing christology of the primitive community in Luke 1.32f.; Acts 13.33f.;
Heb. 1.5, for there is the history of an earlier tradition behind all
these passages. In addition, II Sam. 7.14 is very closely associated
with Ps. 2.7 in the last two passages. A connection between Messiah and Son of God also followed clearly from Ps. 2 and Ps. 89.
Moreover, as 'Son of God' could be used both for the suffering
righteous man and for the charismatic and the wise man, why should
this designation not have been transferred quite deliberately to the
exalted Messiah Jesus? Thus a variety of lines of tradition come
together in the title 'Son of God'.

3. Jesus spoke in a mysterious way of the coming 'Son of Man'
(Aramaic *bar '^{e}nās*), and 'identified' himself with this figure of the
judge to come: I also believe that in the end he was able to speak

---

[117] O. Betz, *What do we know about Jesus?*, 1968, 87ff., 96ff. Cf. also
E. Schweizer, 'The Concept of the Davidic "Son of God" in Acts and its
Old Testament Background', in L. E. Keck/J. L. Martyn (eds.), *Studies
in Luke-Acts*, 1966, 186-93. For a fundamental discussion of the messianic
proof from scripture in relation to the death and resurrection of Jesus see
also J. Jeremias, *Abba*, 1966, 205, on the influence of Isa. 53 (which is
hardly to be doubted).

of himself in veiled form as 'the (Son of) Man'. This is the only explanation of how this mysterious title was given such a central significance in all the gospels as an exclusive self-designation of Jesus, although it was not a current messianic title, and for that reason evidently could not be used in early Christian mission preaching either. It has no real kerygmatic significance. True, there is mention in the synoptic gospels of the suffering Son of Man and the Son of Man who is to come, but not of belief in him. The two contemporary Jewish texts which speak of the Son of Man already identify him with the Messiah.[118] Things were no different in primitive Christianity. The resurrection served only to a limited degree as proof for the truth of Jesus' proclamation of the Son of Man: God has shown that the crucified Jesus is himself the Son of Man, and as such he will return in the function of judge and bringer of salvation. Now on linguistic grounds alone it would seem obvious, by the law of analogy, that the *bar '"nās(ā)* (Son of Man) who had been confirmed and exalted by God should also be confessed as *bar '"lāh(ā)* (Son of God). This was all the more likely since the 'Son of Man' had at the same time been exalted over all the heavenly 'sons of God' and had all power given into his hand as God's eschatological 'plenipotentiary'. The development which has been outlined here with the utmost brevity, leading to the statement contained in Rom. 1.3f. about the Son of God who is appointed through the resurrection, may have taken place in Palestine itself in a relatively short time. Its foundation lay in the inner consistency of a combined consideration of the preaching and actions of Jesus, his death and the event of the resurrection. Paul, in describing his call near Damascus, which took place between AD 32 and AD 34, as a revelation of the Son of God by God himself, is in my view already presupposing the central significance of this title for that time.[119] In the vision he sees at his call, he is sure of 'the

[118] Eth. Enoch 48.10; 52.4; IV Ezra 13; cf. U. B. Müller, *Messias und Menschensohn in jüdischen Apokaeypsen und in der Offenbarung des Johannes*, SNT 6, 1972, 52ff., 81ff., 111ff. For the rabbinical exegesis of Dan. 7.13 see Billerbeck, I, 486, and Justin, *Dial c. Tryph.* 32.

[119] Gal. 1.15f.; see n. 19 above. Cf. M. Hengel, in *Neues Testament und Geschichte, Festschrift O. Cullmann*, 1972, 62.

identity of the heavenly Messiah with the crucified Jesus'.[120] Jesus, the son of David, was none other than the risen Son of God. The message of the Christians against which Paul the Pharisee and the scribe fought so bitterly was not a diabolical deception, but God's eschatological truth.

4. This development towards the use of υἱὸς θεοῦ as a central honorific title was strengthened by the fact that it was possible to translate the Hebrew ʿebed with παῖς and then interpret it as 'Son'. This explains why 'servant of God' (παῖς θεοῦ) as a christological title has already faded right into the background in the New Testament texts. But we may assume that its influence in earliest Christianity was never as strong as is sometimes supposed. It is, for instance, questionable in the extreme whether υἱὸς θεοῦ in the baptism pericope in Mark 1.11 has suppressed an original παῖς θεοῦ.[121] Thus the confession 'Son of God' is primarily an explicit expression of Jesus' *exaltation*.

III. *Pre-existence, mediation at creation and sending into the world*

But how are we to explain the move towards ideas of *pre-existence, mediation at creation* and the *sending* of the Son of God into the world, which already have central significance for Paul?

---

[120] J. Weiss, *Earliest Christianity*, I, 1937 reprinted 1959, 191 (italicized by the author), cf. 161. We do not know whether Paul, as a Pharisee of the Diaspora, already believed in the existence of a heavenly messianic figure and if so, in what form. Conjectures were made by the history of religions school (they were particularly crass in e.g. M. Brückner, *Die Entstehung der paulinischen Christologie*, 1903) about a pre-Christian Hellenistic Jewish speculation concerning a pre-existent heavenly *Messiah*, but they have no direct foundation in any sources known to us. We only have access to the wisdom tradition. Of course, the literature of Hellenistic Judaism is almost completely lost, apart from Philo, Josephus and a few small fragments. We do not know, for example, what traditions lie behind the revelation of the eschatological high priest (T. Levi 18). On the other hand, the assumption of a pre-Christian Jewish 'Christ-gnosis', as suggested by W. Schmithals, is quite without foundation.

[121] Cf. J. Jeremias, *Abba*, 1966, 191–216. For the pericope about Jesus' baptism (Mark 1.9–11) see F. Hahn, *Christologische Hoheitstitel*, 1963, 301ff., 340ff.; this is questioned by F. Lentzen-Deis, *Die Taufe Jesu nach den Synoptikern*, 1970, 186ff., 262ff.

It is possible and indeed probable that they were first developed among those Greek-speaking Jewish Christians who were driven out of Jerusalem and began the mission to the Gentiles in the Hellenistic cities of Palestine, Phoenicia and Syria. On the other hand, Paul already uses these expressions as though they had established forms. Direct pagan influence is extremely improbable, if only because of the ethnic composition of these earliest mission communities. The Jewish Christians were always the spiritual driving force which determined the content of the theology. In fact they put their stamp on the whole of the first-century church. Unfortunately the history of religions school paid too little attention to this decisive point. The men who carried on the spiritual controversy with Judaism most sharply during the first century AD come from Judaism: Stephen; the Pharisee Paul; and the authors of the First, Second and Fourth Gospels, Hebrews and Revelation. Another predominant group was that of the so-called God-fearers, who were already closely associated with Judaism before their change to the new faith: the author of the Third Gospel and Acts may well come from their circles.[122]

There is also an *inner consistency* in the further development of christology. The confession of the exaltation of Jesus as Son of Man and Son of God in the resurrection and his appointment as God's eschatological plenipotentiary immediately posed for earliest Christianity the question of the relationship of Jesus to other intermediary figures, whether the supreme angels or Wisdom-Torah, which was at least partially thought of as a personification. It was also necessary to reconsider the relationship between the previous means of salvation in Judaism, temple worship and the Torah, and the exalted Son of God and mediator of salvation. This led to a critical distinction between Christianity and Judaism.[123] Certainty

[122] F. Siegert, 'Gottesfürchtige und Sympathisanten', *JSJ* 4, 1, 1973, 109–64; M. Hengel, 'Zwischen Jesus und Paulus', *ZTK* 72, 1975, 151–206.
[123] Against Klaus Berger, *Die Gesetzesauslegung Jesu*, WMANT 40, 1972, 17ff., we do not find within the pre-Christian Judaism of the diaspora, let alone in Palestine, a real and fundamental criticism of the law, that is, one with a religious motivation, which, say, rejected the whole of the ritual law and concentrated only on the moral commandments. The

that the 'time of the Messiah' had dawned in the works, death and
resurrection of Jesus also provided the impulse for a fundamental
change of attitude towards the law of Moses. The true will of God
was no longer embodied in the Torah of Sinai but in the teaching
of the Messiah Jesus, and his accursed death on the cross (Deut.
21.23) could and indeed must put in question the law of Moses as
an *ultimate* authority. Even in a messianic context, the exodus and
the revelation of the law on Sinai was the real, normative saving
event. Christians now consistently transferred it to the person of
Christ and his work. The statement at the end of the Torah (Deut.

---

radical reformers in Jerusalem after 175 BC strove for complete assimilation
to paganism, and this was also usually the aim of a Jew who broke with
the law of the fathers. The Jewish critics of the law of whom Philo speaks
(*Agr.* 157; *Vit. Mos.* 1, 31; *Conf. ling.* 2ff.), or the radical allegorists (*Migr.
Abr.* 89ff.), were on the fringe of Judaism and hardly had any influence
worth mentioning, see H. A. Wolfson, *Philo*, 1, ³1962, 82ff., and I. Heine-
mann, *Philons griechische und jüdische Bildung*, 1932 reprinted 1962, 454ff.
At the decisive initial stage, the early Christian criticism of the law was
hardly influenced by this lax assimilative Judaism. Paul does not idly call
himself a former 'Zealot' for the tradition of the fathers (Gal. 1.14). On
the other hand, the early Christian criticism of the law which emerges in
Palestine itself is not oriented on secular emancipation but entirely on a
new radical understanding of the will of God. In other words, it must have
had an eschatological basis, and ultimately goes back to an original authority, namely Jesus himself. Of course, a reference to a 'new Torah of
messianic times' is also questionable (against W. D. Davies, *Torah in the
Messianic Age and/or the Age to Come*, JBL Monograph Series 7, 1952,
and H. J. Schoeps, *Paul*, 1961, 171ff.). At best the rabbis knew of reflections on a partial transformation of the law when sin had come to an end,
in connection with the question of the 'grounds of the Torah', see now
P. Schäfer, *ZNW* 65, 1974, 27–42. Paul merely thought through consistently and radically, to the end, the partial criticism of the Torah in a
christological and soteriological perspective which had already been introduced by Jesus and was taken further by the Hellenists of Stephen's
group (Acts 6.11, 13f.). If God's saving revelation in his Christ was really
universal and final, it must also be valid for all men; if God's Christ was
the ground of salvation, then the law of Moses could no longer be regarded as a way to salvation. God's Christ stood above the law which
according to Deut. 21.23 had delivered him over to God's curse. Similarly,
Jesus' sacrificial death made all temple sacrifice meaningless. He alone
was now the propitiatory sacrifice, the sacrifice of the covenant, the atoning sacrifice, the true passover lamb, indeed the high priest and the place
of reconciliation in one. Even the Jewish-Christian Ebionites rejected
sacrifice. See M. Hengel, *ZTK* 72, 1975, 190ff.

34.10): 'And there has not arisen a prophet since in Israel like
Moses, whom the Lord knew face to face, none like him for all the
signs and the wonders which the Lord sent him to do' is corrected
by Jesus in terms of John the Baptist in Luke 16.16 and in terms of
himself in Matt. 11.27 = Luke 10.22. The earliest christology
must already have robbed it of its force.

Following the well-known saying in the Epistle of Barnabas,
'Behold I make the last things as the first things' (6.13), the
eschatological awareness of the earliest community was matched
by a certain interest in protology. Only the one who has control
over the beginning has the whole matter in his grasp. The beginning therefore had to be illuminated by the end, and ultimately the
idea of pre-existence was a favourite means of bringing out the
special significance of particular phenomena for salvation. One
might perhaps say that it expressed the common Near Eastern view
that there was a correspondence between the heavenly original
and earthly reality in typical Jewish fashion, by means of a projec-
tion back into primal time. The pre-existence of the eschatological
redeemer could already be read out of Micah 5.1 or Ps. 110.3:
he was begotten by God, older than the dawn of creation (see n. 49
above). We also find further statements about the pre-existence of
the Son of Man in Enoch 48.6; 62.7: he is said to have been elected
by God before the creation of the world; there is also mention of
the pre-existence of his name (48.3; cf. 69.26). To this corresponds
the pre-existence of the name of the Messiah in rabbinic sources.[124]
As in the case of the relationship between a personified hypostasis
and purely metaphorical language, the transition here from mere
'ideal' pre-existence (that is, to some extent only in the thought of
God) to 'real' pre-existence is fluid. Moreover, the concept of 'pre-
existence' is not yet understood in the sense it later acquires during
the Arian dispute as uncreatedness and timeless, eternal being with
God. In the first place it denotes a 'being before the creation of the

[124] Cf. U. B. Müller, Messias und Menschensohn, 47ff.: 'Like the Messiah
in IV Ezra, the Son of Man in I Enoch is a pre-existent factor in salvation,
a part of the world already created by God, which will only appear at the
end of time' (49). For the rabbis see Billerbeck, II, 334–52, above all,
335: Pes. 54a Bar.; Targ. Zech. 4.7, etc.; 346f.: speculations about the
pre-existent soul of the Messiah from Amoraean times.

world'. Nevertheless, there were also changes here. Thus as early
as Prov. 8.22f., 'being born' also stands alongside verbs about being
created. At least Wisdom or the Logos must always have been
associated with God. Indeed one could not conceive of God without his Wisdom.[125] The more christological reflection progressed,
the more it was inevitably involved in trinitarian questions. According to later rabbinic tradition, reference was made to Gen. 1.2 'and
the spirit of God hovered' to prove the 'pre-existence' of the
Messiah before creation, because this phrase meant the spirit of
the Messiah (Pes. R. 33, 6; cf. Gen. R. 2, 4).[126] A related text

[125] Prov. 8.22: *qānāni* = he created me; 8.23: read *nesakkōti* = 'I was
skilfully made', see H. Gese, in *Probleme biblischer Theologie. Festschrift
G. von Rad*, 1971, 81f. = *Vom Sinai zum Zion*, 138f., who also reads this
form (instead of *nāsakti*, which has the same consonants) in Ps. 2.6: 'But
I was created (in a wonderful way) as his king on Zion . . .'; 8.24: *ḥōlalti*,
'I was born in travail'. Concepts like 'begetting', 'bringing forth', 'reflecting' and 'flowing' are even more predominant in Philo and Wisdom as
over against those of creating and forming. Philo can call the Logos
eternal: 'The head of all things is the eternal Logos of the eternal God'
(*Quaest. Ex.* 2, 117; of course here we could have a Christian interpretation
in the Armenian text, see the continuation. Cf. the *re'šit* in Gen. 1.1;
Prov. 8.22; Col. 1.18; Eph. 1.22; cf. H. F. Weiss, *Kosmologie*, 265ff.).
According to *Quis rer. div. her.* 205f., the 'oldest Logos' and 'archangel',
who was given the task by the Father and Creator of the world 'to divide
the creation from the Creator', was, as mediator, 'neither uncreated like
God . . . nor created (like the creatures), but in the middle between the
two extremes'. As such he is 'spokesman for . . . mortals' and 'the ruler's
envoy to the servants'. 'For like a herald I bring to creatures the message
of peace of the one who has resolved to abolish wars, the God who constantly watches over peace.' The later distinction between the *logos
endiathetikos* and the *logos prophorikos* in Theophilus of Antioch (*Ad
Autolyc.* 2, 10) indeed already goes back to Philo, who developed Stoic
conceptuality in speculative fashion.

[126] According to Gen. R. 2, 4, R. Simeon b. Lakish (middle of the third
century AD) interpreted Gen. 1.2 in terms of the four world kingdoms:
tōhū = Babylon; *bōhū* = the Medes, the kingdom of Haman; darkness =
Javan (Macedonia); the deep (*tᵉhōm*) = the power of wickedness (Rome).
' "And the spirit of God hovered", this is a reference to the spirit of the
king Messiah, as is said in Isa. 11.2: "The spirit of Yahweh rests upon
him" '; cf. Lev. R. 14.1: 'the spirit of the king Messiah'. On the other
hand, according to Yalqut Ps. 139, §5 (265a), Gen. R. 8, 1 and Midr.
Tanchuma Tarzia (Buber, 153a), Simeon b. Lakish interpreted the spirit
in Gen. 1.2 in terms of the soul of Adam. According to Theodor's edition,
manuscript D likewise has 'king Messiah' in Gen. R. 8, 1 (p. 56). Probably

identifies the primal light of creation in Gen. 1.4 with the light of the Messiah which God conceals under his throne. At Satan's request, God shows him the Messiah hidden under the throne, whereupon Satan falls to the ground, for he has seen his own annihilation and that of his followers (Pes. R. 36, 1).[127] *Thus there was an inner necessity about the introduction of the idea of pre-existence into christology.* Eberhard Jüngel is quite right when, from the standpoint of a systematic theologian, he passes the judgment: 'It was more a matter of consistency than of mythology.'[128] With pre-existence, however, statements about the sending of the Son took on their fullest form. Angels or men of God and prophets of the Old Testament had already been said to have been sent by God, and according to Mal. 3.23 the sending of Elijah is promised for the end-time; in a similar way the Jewish Sibyl could talk of the sending of the messianic king.[129] Luke takes up this theme in Acts 3.20: '. . . that times of refreshing may come from the presence of the Lord, and that he may *send* the Christ appointed for you, Jesus . . .' Given pre-existence, however, sending now presupposes

---

Simeon b. Lakish put forward both interpretations, and it is illegitimate simply to push the reference to the Messiah or his soul to one side as an allegory (as happens in Billerbeck, II, 350). Pes. R. 33, 6 (Friedmann, 152b) shows that the idea continued to exercise influence: 'What is the proof that the Messiah has existed since the beginning of the creation of the world? "And the spirit of God hovered." That is the king Messiah! For we read, "And the Spirit of the Lord will rest on him" (Isa. 11.2).'

[127] Pes. R. 36, 1 (Friedmann, 161a/b). Sections 36 and 37 show the Messiah ben Ephraim as a pre-existent figure who obediently takes upon himself the suffering intended by God for the sins of Israel and allows himself to be sent into the world. After his liberation from suffering he is exalted, enthroned and glorified by God in heaven. Billerbeck's conjecture that this homilectic Midrash only came into being about AD 900 is questionable. J. Bamberger, *HUCA* 15, 1940, 425ff., conjectures on the basis of certain political information that sections 34–37 were composed between 632 and 637. The traditions which it contains are for the most part considerably earlier. Obviously Christian influence is possible and indeed probable here. We can, however, see those forms which Jewish messianology was able to accept even after the separation from Christianity and despite the polemical controversy with it. Would things have been so very different in the pre-Christian period?

[128] E. Jüngel, *Paulus und Jesus*, ²1964, 283.

[129] Sib. 3, 286 (Cyrus?); 5, 108, 256, 414f.

a descent from the heavenly sphere, humiliation and incarnation as depicted in the Philippians hymn (the analogy is with Wisdom in Sir. 24). It is typically Jewish that in the exposition of christology, pre-existence, mediation at creation and the idea of sending the Son into the world were all developed chronologically *before the legends of the miraculous birth of Jesus.* The tradition behind the prologue to the Fourth Gospel is 'earlier' than the infancy narratives of Matthew and Luke in their present form. That is the most obvious place to talk of 'Hellenistic' influence, even if the form chosen is that of the Jewish Haggadah. Thus the problem of 'pre-existence' necessarily grew out of the combination of Jewish ideas of history, time and creation with the certainty that God had disclosed himself fully in his Messiah Jesus of Nazareth. The 'simple gospel of Jesus' was not, then, delivered over to pagan mythology; on the contrary, the threat of myth was overcome by the radical trinitarian character of the idea of revelation.

Once the idea of pre-existence had been introduced, it was obvious that the exalted Son of God would also attract to himself the functions of Jewish Wisdom as a mediator of creation and salvation. Even Wisdom, which was associated with God in a unique way from before time, could no longer be regarded as an independent entity over against the risen and exalted Jesus and superior to him. Rather, all the functions of Wisdom were transferred to Jesus, for 'in him are hid all the treasures of wisdom and knowledge' (Col. 2. 3). Only in this way was *the unsurpassibility and finality of God's revelation* in Jesus of Nazareth expressed in a last, conclusive way. The exalted Jesus is not only pre-existent, but also shares in the *opus proprium Dei*, creation. Indeed, he accomplishes the work of creation at the behest and with the authority of God, just as he also determines events at the end of time. No revelation, no speech and no action of God can take place without him or beside him. So it is the pre-existent Christ who must accompany Israel on its journey through the wilderness as the 'spiritual rock' (I Cor. 10.4). According to Wisdom 10.17 it was the divine Wisdom which guided Israel on its miraculous journey, and Philo identified the rock from which Moses drew water, like the manna, with Wisdom or the Logos (*Leg. all.* 2, 86; *Det. pot.* 115ff.). Palestinian exegesis,

on the other hand, had the people led on their journey through the
wilderness by the Shekinah of Yahweh. As the exegesis in I Cor.
10.4 is not typically Pauline, and Paul does not otherwise draw
positive connections with the time of Moses – indeed he interprets
the consequences of this event to the Corinthians in a negative way
– we must assume that this exegesis comes from non-Pauline
Greek-speaking Jewish Christianity. The stream of tradition which
included this christology influenced by pre-existent Wisdom was
surely broader than Paul's letters suggest. The Logos christology
of the Johannine prologue about fifty years after Paul is therefore
only the logical conclusion of the fusion of the pre-existent Son of
God with traditional Wisdom, though of course the concept of
'*sophia*', which was always threatened by mythological speculation,
had to give place to the clear 'Logos', the Word of God. The prologue, too, is therefore certainly not to be derived from gnostic
sources, but stands in an established context of tradition within
Christianity and Judaism.[130] The christological climaxes of the
Fourth Gospel, like 1.1: '. . . and the Word was with God and the
Word was God', or 10.30: 'I and the Father are one', mark the
goal and the consummation of New Testament christology.

Now for the Son of God to take on the all-embracing functions
of Wisdom as mediator was also to shatter to pieces the function
of the law in the ordering of the world and the salvation of men.
For the Jews, the law was identified with Wisdom and its functions
were authoritative and had an ontological basis. Paul, the former
Pharisee and scribe, drew the ultimate radical consequences here.
Other people before him had pondered what changes in the law
were to be made as a result of the exegesis of the true will of God
in the message of Jesus the Messiah, but Paul's pointed expression

[130] See already the considered criticism by W. Eltester, 'Der Logos und
sein Prophet', in *Apophoreta*, BZNW 30, 1964, 109–34: '. . . that I would
like to see stronger stress on the connection between the prologue and
Alexandrian Judaism. This happened in earlier scholarship before Bultmann. I think that gnostic connections were only communicated by means
of Hellenistic Jewish literature, of which no more than a fragment has
been preserved' (122, n. 30). 'Gnostic connections' can be completely
ignored in the prologue; Jewish Hellenistic thought, which we may
picture as having been extremely varied, is a quite adequate explanation.

'Christ is the end of the law, that everyone who has faith may be justified' (Rom. 10.4) is a fundamental expression of the unique soteriological function of the crucified and exalted Jesus as the all-embracing, final, eschatological revelation of God which challenges the claim of the law in principle. It is not just Moses, but God's Christ alone, who brings salvation. Paul's appeal to the Corinthians, 'God made Christ Jesus our wisdom, our righteousness and sanctification and redemption' (I Cor. 1.30), in essentials embraces all the functions of salvation which the pious Jews ascribed to Wisdom-Torah. Behind this break stood an inexorably consistent piece of christological thinking. It must have been a fatal scandal to his Jewish contemporaries for God's Wisdom no longer to be communicated by the venerable body of law which Moses received on Sinai but by a seducer of the people who was broken on the cross.[131] We cannot therefore over-exaggerate the scandal of Pauline christology and soteriology, precisely *because* it was fed from Jewish sources. Of course this scandal was not so much grounded in the teaching of the pre-existent Son of God, as H. J. Schoeps believed, but in the christologically motivated abrogation of the law, its abolition as a way of salvation by the cross and resurrection of Jesus.

The connection between Jesus and Wisdom had thus been prepared for by Jesus' own preaching during his ministry, the form of which was very much in the wisdom tradition. The primitive Palestine community collected the unique wisdom teachings of the Messiah in the nucleus of the logia source, just as earlier the wise sayings of King Solomon, David's son, had also been collected together. Of course, in the case of Jesus, 'more than Solomon is here' (Luke 11.31 = Matt. 12.42). He was seen already as the representative of divine Wisdom, and the features of Wisdom which we also find in the case of the Son of Man in the Jewish

---

[131] For Jesus' opponents, the high-priestly Sadducees and the Pharisees who were faithful to the Torah, Jesus was not only a figure who had met with human failure, but a perverter of the people who had been judged by God: see M. Hengel, *Nachfolge und Charisma*, 43ff. The contrast between his claim and his shameful death had to be interpreted as the divine judgment. That is why Paul, the Pharisee and zealot for the law, became a persecutor of the community.

Similitudes of Ethiopian Enoch were transferred to him.[132] Here is another confirmation that the development of christology was from the beginning concerned with synthesis: otherwise it was impossible to give satisfactory expression to the eschatological uniqueness of God's communication of himself in the man Jesus. Not only mediation at creation but also the designation of Christ as 'God's image' (εἰκών) was taken over from the wisdom tradition of Greek-speaking Judaism. At the same time, this concept created associations between the pre-existent Christ and the figure of the first, heavenly Adam, the 'primal man', who in Philo is identical with the Logos and the 'firstborn son', though it is striking that Paul does not see Christ as the protological primal man of Gen. 1 and 2, but as the heavenly, eschatological Adam, who as a 'life-giving spirit' overcomes death.[133] The 'first Adam', the

[132] F. Christ, *Jesus Sophia. Die Sophia-Christologie bei den Synoptikern,* ATANT 57, 1970; H. Koester/J. M. Robinson, *Trajectories through Early Christianity,* 1971, 71ff., 179ff., 219ff. For the unique words of the Messiah see M. Hengel, *TQ* 153, 1973, 267, n. 42: Ps. Sol. 17.43; T. Levi 18.1; Targ. Isa. 53.5, 11, cf. Luke 4.16ff. Here I follow F. Mussner, *Galaterbrief,* 86, n. 43, in believing that there is no 'existence of a special "Q group" ' among the early Christian communities, with a quite specific, distinctive theology without a kerygma of the cross and resurrection. Still less are these, as S. Schulz asserts, sayings of the exalted Jesus. There is no mention of the exalted Christ in Q, which with few exceptions is concerned throughout with the words of the earthly Jesus. As the spirit was regularly present in Christian prophets in the liturgy, there was no need to record and hand down what he had made known; what was important was the teaching of the earthly Jesus, who had now been removed from the community, and this was seen as the apocalyptic wisdom-teaching of the Messiah. The reason why there is no kerygma of the passion and the resurrection is that this was not part of the proclamation of Jesus. The best solution to the riddle of Q is to take Q seriously as a record of the teaching of Jesus. The basic theory of S. Schulz, *Q. Die Spruchquelle der Evangelisten,* 1972, 5, is that 'Earliest Christianity, long (!) before Paul wrote his letter, ... was from the beginning a complex entity with a variety of traditional material and different outlines of the kerygma, which indicate different independent communities.' In this form it is untenable and misleading.

[133] For Christ as the 'image of God', II Cor. 4.4; Col. 1.15; cf. J. Jervell, *Imago Dei,* FRLANT 76, 1960, 173ff., 197ff., and especially 227ff., on the 'divine status of Christ'; F.-W. Eltester, *Eikon im Neuen Testament,* BZNW 23, 1958, 130ff. For Adam and Christ see I Cor. 15.44–49. Here Paul breaks through the protological speculation of the diaspora synagogue

primal man, does not have any function as eschatological redeemer in Judaism, either. Now if Christ is identical with the heavenly, *pre-temporal* 'image of God', that also means that he was '*of divine nature*', as we hear at the beginning of the Philippians hymn. Thus, although he is clearly subordinate, the Son no longer stood on the side of creation alone, but also on the side of God. Only through the incarnation, which is 'consummated' in his death on the cross, does he receive a share in human destiny and can he be regarded as reconciler and intercessor for men. Jesus was now no longer just the perfect righteous man, chosen by God, who was in complete accord with God's will, a model for discipleship, but in addition the divine mediator who out of the Father's love for lost men obediently gave up his heavenly communion with the Father and took on human form and human destiny, a destiny which led to a shameful death on the cross. Thus incarnation and death become an unsurpassable expression of the divine love. Neither Graeco-Roman nor Jewish tradition knew of such a 'myth'. In the Son, God himself came to men and was involved with their deepest distress, therein to reveal his love to all creatures. Only as the broken figure on the cross was Jesus – paradoxically – the exalted one, the Lord, to whom, as God's eschatological 'plenipotentiary', were subjected even those powers which had apparently triumphed over him at his ignominious death (Phil. 2.6–11; I Cor. 2.8; II Cor. 8.9). It is understandable that bold christological sketches of this kind were not at first presented in the form of speculative prose, but in hymns inspired by the spirit (I Cor. 14.26; cf. Col. 3.16; Eph. 5.19; Rev. 5.9, etc.); the language most appropriate to God's 'inexpressible grace' (II Cor. 9.15) was the hymn of praise inspired by the Spirit. The quotation of such a hymn in teaching or paraenesis shows that it quickly acquired 'the status of a sacred text' in the same way as Old Testament statements.[134]

---

with his very specific eschatology. There is no longer any need to look for a gnostic background. On the other hand, the apocalyptic Son of Man could very well underlie the 'last Adam' of I Cor. 15.45. For Jewish speculation about Adam see J. E. Ménard, *RSR* 42, 1968, 291f.

[134] R. Deichgräber, *Gotteshymnus und Christushymnus in der frühen Christenheit*, SUNT 5, 1967, 188f.

IV. *Kyrios and Son of God*

This development in christology progressed *in a very short time*. Its final result was that the statements in the Old Testament in which the inexpressible divine name, the tetragrammaton YHWH or its Qere in the Greek Bible, Kyrios, 'Lord', was used, were now transferred directly to the *Kyrios Jesus*. Paul can already give Joel 3.5, 'Everyone who calls upon the name of the Lord will be saved' (Rom. 10.13; cf. Acts 2.21), as the basis for the key acclamation 'Κύριος Ἰησοῦς'. In the original text, Kyrios refers to God himself, but for Paul the Kyrios is Jesus, in whom God makes a full disclosure of his salvation. From the time of the history of religions school there has been an inclination to derive this terminology from the mystery cults with their 'Kyria Isis' or 'Kyrios Sarapis', but this is a quite senseless undertaking.[135] Quite apart from the

---

[135] This old theory of W. Bousset and W. Heitmüller has enjoyed great popularity down to quite recent times, see S. Schulz, 'Maranatha und Kyrios Jesus', *ZNW* 53, 1962, 125–44; W. Kramer, *Christ, Lord, Son of God*, SBT 50, 1966, 96ff.; P. Vielhauer, *Aufsätze zum NT*, ThB 31, 1965, 166, in a quite irrelevant, one might almost say 'scholastic', piece of polemic against F. Hahn, *Christologische Hoheitstitel*, FRLANT 83, 1963, 67–125. Whereas Hahn for the most part gives a convincing account of the historical situation, Vielhauer is still completely oriented on the old and unexamined theories of the history of religions school; similarly K. Wengst, *Christologische Formeln und Lieder des Urchristentums*, SNT 7, 1972, 131ff. To assert that the title Kyrios was 'a general predicate of gods in Hellenistic cults . . . above all in the mysteries' (134) is facile and simply misleading. Where and from what point are the gods of Eleusis and Dionysus, the real mystery gods, 'generally' given the title 'Kyrios'? Since when has it been possible to demonstrate that Attis and Mithras were 'mystery gods' (see above, pp. 25ff., n. 54)? From what point and whereabouts in Syria (which is the important question for us) do they appear, along with the title Kyrios? One exception is the 'Kyria Isis' from the first century BC. Possibly in her case – and in the case of Sarapis, as H. Stegermann conjectures in his work on the title Kyrios, which unfortunately has yet to be published – there is a reaction against the usurping of the title Kyrios by the Jews, who used the word 'Lord' as Qere for the tetragrammaton. (In Egypt they were numerous and influential.) To use 'Kyrios' in the absolute as a divine title is essentially un-Greek. We find the designation 'Lord' that much more frequently in a variety of forms in connection with Semitic deities in Syria, Palestine and Mesopotamia, the Jews not excepted. Thus 'Kyrios' appears quite often as a title for local Baalim who were accorded the functions of Zeus, or even for Egyptian

fact that Sarapis only became a mystery god at a late date and then
remained on the fringe of the mysteries,[136] the title 'Kyrios' is not
typical of the mysteries. Moreover, we have no evidence for mysteries in Syria in the first century BC (see pp. 27ff., above). The

---

deities in the later period. The title expresses a personal relationship with
the deity, which was so important for the oriental. Angels, too, could be
addressed as 'Kyrios' and were called 'kyrioi'. For 'Lord' was not only a
divine title or mode of address, but also the title for all kinds of distinguished people, including the Herodian kings and not least the emperor
after the time of Claudius. Finally, it is striking that the Greek title
'Kyrios' is very rarely used of gods even in the Syrian inscriptions before
the second century AD. This whole question calls for a thorough investigation, which I hope to make in due course. The critical observation made
by K. Berger, *NTS* 17, 1970/71, 413, is quite correct: 'The claim, however, persists. It is quite mysterious how it could have been possible in
terms of the history of the tradition for Jesus to be identified with a Hellenistic cult deity. The theory that Gentile Christians alone were responsible for this transference is untenable, because there is early evidence for
the title, and "pure" Gentile Christianity is a fiction.' I can therefore
only agree with Vielhauer's polemical remark, 'Problems are not solved
by ignoring them' (166). The only question is who has so far ignored the
decisive problem, namely what the sources say! For this whole question
see also M. Hengel, in *Neues Testament und Geschichte, Festschrift O.
Cullmann*, 1972, 55ff., and above all W. Foerster, *Herr ist Jesus*, 1924,
with its excellent collections of material. See especially 79ff. on the
mystery cults: 'Popular religion formed the basis for the later mysteries.
Where *kyrios* had not already been used, it did not appear in the mysteries,
either with Attis or with Mithras. The Isis mysteries indicate that even
where *kyrios* was a customary usage, it was used less often in the mysteries.
The corresponding term there is ἄνασσα, queen, which means "ruler" '
(89). Foerster's conclusions are largely confirmed by more recent material,
see the continuation of his work in *TDNT* 3, 1039–58.

[136] A. D. Nock, *Essays*, 2, 799: 'Apart from one possible exception in a
papyrus, there is no other indication of any mysteries of Sarapis himself.'
See the verdict of the best authority, P. M. Fraser, *Ptolemaic Alexandria*,
1972, 1, 265, and 2, 419, n. 20. It is probable that the papyrus mentioned
by Nock (PSI 1162, third century AD) also contains no reference to the
mysteries. See id., *Opuscula Atheniensia* 3, 1969, 4, n. 1. It should also be
noted that the new god created by Ptolemy I in the early empire was
markedly less significant outside Egypt. This significance only increased
as a result of Vespasian's enthronement in Alexandria in 69 BC and then
again through Hadrian. The god reached his greatest period as universal
god in the third century AD. The very isolated references to Sarapis
mysteries are late and their meaning is disputed. Presumably he only became a mystery god occasionally through his identification with Osiris

and in conjunction with the Isis mysteries, for which there is similarly evidence after the first century AD. See L. Vidman, *Isis und Sarapis bei den Griechen und Römern*, RVV 29, 1970, 126ff., and id., *Sylloge inscriptionum religionis Isiacae et Sarapiacae*, RVV 28, 1969, no. 758 = CIL II, 2395c from Portugal, third century AD. No. 326, second century AD Prusa, and no. 295, Tralles, are uncertain. That the Eumolpid Timotheus of Eleusis was involved in the foundation of the cult (Tacitus, *Hist.* 4, 83, and Plutarch, *Is. et Osir.* 28, 362A) is still no proof that it had the character of a mystery. Neither the number of places where the mysteries of Isis (and Osiris) could be performed nor the number of initiates should be over-estimated. These were 'exclusive clubs', 'as the mysteries in all the oriental mystery religions in imperial times were very expensive' (Vidman, *Isis und Sarapis*, 127). The kind of 'solemn initiation' which Apuleius describes, e.g. at Cenchraea and Rome, 'could only take place where there was a well-appointed temple with a number of priests who also acted in these mystic games' (op. cit., 131). Nor is it a coincidence that both Sarapis inscriptions and archaeological evidence for Syria, Phoenicia and Palestine are relatively rare. See Vidman, *Sylloge*, 180ff., and G. J. F. Kater-Sibbes, *Preliminary Catalogue of Sarapis Monuments*, 1973, 76ff. The same holds for the Isis cult, see F. Dunand, *Le culte d'Isis dans le bassin oriental*, 1973, 3, 122ff.: with very few exceptions, the spread of the cults of Isis and Sarapis in Syria can be demonstrated only in the time of the empire: 'En Palestine, que ce soit sur le littoral ou à l'intérieur du pays, les traces du culte isiaque sont très rares' (132). The situation in Rome and Italy is different, see M. Malaise, *Les conditions de pénétration et de diffusion des cultes égyptiens en Italie*, 1972. Here too, however, intensive expansion only begins with the Flavians (407ff.). The few Isis inscriptions from Syria and Palestine, see L. Vidman, *Sylloge inscriptionum religionis Isiacae et Sarapiacae*, 1969, 181–6, contain no references to mysteries: *kyrios/kyria* appears only in an Artemis inscription, three or four times for the emperor and twice for the city goddess of Gerasa (κυρία πατρίς), i.e. *not* for the mystery gods. The reason why Sarapis sometimes attracted the title Kyrios is that, like Asclepius, as a god connected with salvation, dreams and oracles, he had a personal relationship to believers. This was similarly the case with Kyrios in the Christian community right from the beginning. It means, however, that personal relationship with the exalted Christ cannot first have been established in alien pagan cults. That the 'Lord Jesus' *could* be seen as a kind of new cult-deity at a later stage in typically Hellenistic mission communities of an almost exclusively Gentile-Christian stamp is another chapter in the story. It was possible, for example, in Corinth, and then led to corresponding misunderstandings among certain groups, but it was certainly not yet the case for the 'pre-Pauline' and 'early Pauline' mission. These groups hardly exercised any theological influence in the early period. The element coming from the Jewish Christians or the God-fearers was simply too strong for this. For the problem see already J. Weiss, *Earliest Christianity*, 1937 reprinted 1959, 31ff., 161f., 172f., 233f.

development from 'rabbi' or 'mari', used as a respectful form of
address to Jesus, to the fully developed Kyrios can be shown to
have as stringent an intrinsic consistency as the development in the
use of the term Son of God.[137] Here Ps. 110.1, the most important
Old Testament proof passage for the development of christology,
acquired a quite decisive role.[138] Philo, too, can say in *Somn.* 1, 157
that Jacob saw the *Kyrios* on the heavenly ladder in his dream
(Gen. 28.13), meaning by it the 'archangel', i.e. the Logos, in
whose form God reveals himself. Here he distinguishes between a
proper mention of ὁ θεός and an improper mention with the mere
θεός, which means 'his eldest Logos' as mediator of revelation
(1, 228–230).

Finally, I would like to call attention to just one more example
which shows that even in Palestine itself, the Essenes of Qumran
in their eschatological exegesis could transfer Old Testament passages, the original text of which clearly meant God himself, to a
mediator or redeemer figure near to God. This is the well-known
fragment from Cave 11 in which the prince of light and adversary
of darkness, Michael-Melchizedek, appears as eschatological victor
over all the powers of evil and ushers in the eschatological year of
jubilee (according to Lev. 25.8), which is identical with the proclamation of liberation in Isa. 61.1 (cf. Luke 4.17ff.).[139] The first

---

[137] F. Hahn, *Christologische Hoheitstitel*, 74ff.; M. Hengel, *Nachfolge
und Charisma*, 46ff., cf. above, p. 46, n. 92: Metatron's name too 'is like
that of his Lord'. According to Philo, the name Kyrios embodies a special
dynamis of God. Cf. now J. A. Fitzmyer, n. 89 above, 386ff.

[138] See already H. Windisch, against W. Heitmüller and W. Bousset,
in *Neutestamentliche Studien, Festschrift G. Heinrici zum 70. Geburtstag*,
1914, 229, n. 1: 'Furthermore, Ps. 110 should also be taken into account
as the biblical basis for the earliest Christian and Pauline doctrine of the
heavenly Kyrios and for its origin and development.' Windisch conjectures
that Ps. 110.3 prompted Paul to fuse the idea of the Messiah with Wisdom
in Prov. 8.22. Presumably this step was already taken in the Greek-
speaking Jewish-Christian community which existed before, or better
alongside, Paul. The later rabbinic application of Ps. 110 to Abraham was
virtually a last resort.

[139] A. S. v. d. Woude, 'Melchisedek als himmlische Erlösergestalt in den
neugefundenen eschatologischen Midraschim aus Qumran Höhle XI',
OTS 14, 1965, 354–73; M. de Jonge/A. S. v. d. Woude, *NTS* 12, 1965–66,
301–26; J. A. Fitzmyer, *JBL* 86, 1967, 25–41 = *Essays on the Semitic*

thing which is striking here is that this supreme angelic figure in Qumran is evidently identified with the priest-king Melchizedek of Salem according to Gen. 14.18ff., i.e. an originally human form. It is therefore no coincidence that in Hebrews Melchizedek becomes the type of Christ, the heavenly high priest. In this fragment, Ps. 82.1, 'God has taken his place in the divine council; in the midst of the gods he holds judgment', is interpreted in terms of the eschatological judgment of Michael-Melchizedek on the angels who are hostile to God. It is still more remarkable that the confession of the messenger of peace in Isa. 52.7, 'who says to Zion, "Your God is king" ', does not apply to God himself but again to his plenipotentiary Melchizedek-Michael. The kingdom of God is identical with that of his vizir. According to the most recent reconstruction by Milik, the text says, 'and "your God", that means (Melchizedek, who will deliver) them (from) the hand of Belial'.[140] God's plenipotentiary Michael-Melchizedek, the prince or angel of light, is at the same time the victorious eschatological counterpart of Belial, the 'prince of darkness', who in a new text is called *malki-resa*[c] and appears along with the thrice-named prince of light, *malki-zedeq*, in a vision of Amram, the father of Moses.[141] This unique significance of Michael-Melchizedek among the Jewish Hasidim of the Maccabean period and later among the Essenes of Qumran is confirmed by his role as eschatological mediator of salvation in Dan. 12.1f., where Michael, 'the great prince', emerges as Israel's ally and ushers in the last events. He also appears in the Apocalypse of the Symbolic Animals (Eth. Enoch 90.14, 17, 20ff.), which comes from the same time, and above all the War Scroll, where God sends Michael as 'heavenly redeemer':

Background of the New Testament, 1971, 245–67. There is now a fundamental study by J. T. Milik, 'Milkî-ṣedeq et Milkî-reša[c] dans les anciens écrits juifs et chrétiens', *JJS* 23, 1972, 95–144. Cf. also F. du Toit Laubscher, *JSJ* 3, 1972, 46–51.

[140] See the text in Milik, op. cit., 98f., lines 10, 23–25.

[141] J. T. Milik, '4Q Visions de 'Amram et une citation d'Origène', *RB* 79, 1972, 77–79. Both 'Malki-reša[c]' and 'Malki-ṣedeq' 'have power over all the sons of Adam', Fr. 1, line 12 (p. 79). One 'rules over all darkness' and the other 'over all light and over all (that belongs to God)', Fr. 2, lines 5f. Cf. also the already-known text 1QS 3. 18ff.

And he will send eternal succour to the company of his (re)deemed by the might of the angel of the powerful one(?)[142] for the kingdom of Michael in eternal light; to enlighten with joy the covenant of Israel . . .; *to raise up among the gods* ('*elim* = angels) *the kingdom of Michael* and the kingdom of Israel above all flesh (1 QM 17, 6–8).[143]

One could also refer to the Old Slavonic book of Enoch, where Melchizedek – apparently the great-grandson of Enoch and the nephew of Noah – is begotten and born in miraculous fashion, appointed priest and transported by Michael into the garden of Eden, an indication that that idea of the virgin birth was not completely alien at least to Greek-speaking Judaism.[144] Philo, on the other hand, interprets the priest-king from Salem of Gen. 14.18f. as 'the priestly Logos' (*Leg. all.*, 3, 82). The patristic interpretation of Melchizedek as an angel may also go back to Jewish traditions. Even the gnostic Melchizedekians who are described by Hippo-

[141] The *ml'k h'dyr'* can be translated in three different ways: see the commentary by J. v. d. Ploeg, *Le rouleau de la Guerre*, 1959, 177. With A. S. v. d. Woude, I read *hā'addir* in the sense of a construct. The 'mighty one' would then be God. Another possibility is to take *h'dyr* as hiphil with the following *lmšrt myk'l*: 'he glorifies the rule of Michael'. It seems to me less probable that it should be interpreted as an adjective with the preceding noun without an article, as this is first attested in Mishnaic Hebrew.

[143] 1QM 17, 6f. For the part played by Michael in Qumran see Y. Yadin, *The Scroll of the War of the Sons of Light against the Sons of Darkness*, 1962, 134ff.; O. Betz, *Der Paraklet*, AGSU 2, 1963, 64ff., 149ff., who also draws attention to the relationships with christology and especially to the Paraclete in John. The *hārim* corresponds to the New Testament (ὑπερ)-υψοῦν, cf. Phil. 2.9. For the interpretation of the heavenly mediator and redeemer figure Melchizedek-Michael see J. T. Milik, *JJS* 23, 1972, 125: 'Milkî-ṣedeq est par conséquent quelque chose de plus qu'un ange créé, ou même le chef des bons esprits, identifiable à Michaël (comme le soulignent à juste titre les éditeurs hollandais). Il est en réalité une hypostase de Dieu, autrement dit le Dieu transcendant lorsqu'il agit dans le monde, Dieu lui-même sous la forme visible où il apparaît aux hommes, et non pas un ange créé distinct de Dieu (Ex. 23, 20).' There are interesting connections with Philo here. In *De agr.* 51, Philo interprets Ex. 23.20 in terms of God's '*true reason, the firstborn Son*' (τὸν ὀρθὸν αὐτοῦ λόγον καὶ πρωτόγονον υἱόν) who is appointed by God like a 'governor of the Great King' to rule the world; cf. also *Migr. Abr.* 174.

[144] A. Vaillant, *Le livre des secrets d'Hénoch. Texte slave et traduction française*, 1951, 69ff. (chs. 22f.). The narrative displays no Christian features. It is also improbable that the virgin birth would be ascribed by a Christian to an Old Testament figure.

lytus and Epiphanius hardly developed out of the exegesis of the Epistle to the Hebrews, and may also have Jewish roots. Among other things, they asserted that 'Melchizedek is greater than Christ, and Christ is only his image' (Hippolytus, *Phil.* 7, 36). Anti-Christian and anti-gnostic polemic is the reason why the rabbis partially devalued the figure of Melchizedek and no longer interpreted Ps. 110. 1, 4 in terms of the Messiah but in terms of Abraham. Thus there was probably a preparation for the typological relationship between the Son of God and the priest-king in *Hebrews* in the Haggadic exegesis of the various Jewish groups.[145]

[145] Cf. G. Wuttke, *Melchisedech der Priesterkönig von Salem*, BZNW 5, 1927, 18ff., 27ff.; G. Bardy, 'Melchisédech dans la tradition patristique', *RB* 35, 1926, 496ff.; 36, 1927, 25ff.; J. A. Fitzmyer, *Essays on the Semitic Background of the New Testament*, 1971, 221ff. 245ff.; cf. M. de Jonge and A. S. v.d. Woude, '11Q Melchizedek and the New Testament', *NTS* 12, 1965/66, 301ff.; O. Michel, *Der Brief an die Hebräer*, KEK ¹²1966, 257ff.

7

The Son in the Epistle
to the Hebrews:
The Crucified and Exalted Jesus

A not unimportant difference between the New Testament and the
majority of Jewish texts is of course that New Testament christology *a priori* put the exalted Jesus, as Son, *above all angelic beings*
(not least because of his close association with the pre-existent
wisdom of God). A real *angel christology* could only become significant right on the fringe of the Jewish-Christian sphere. Jewish
angelology is, in fact, already substantially transcended in the
Melchizedek text from Qumran. At any rate, in his great work *The
Formation of Christian Dogma*, Martin Werner much exaggerated
the role of 'angel christology' in early Christianity.[146]

[146] M. Werner, *Die Enstehung des christlichen Dogmas*, [1]1941; [2]1953,
302ff. (an abridged translation appeared in English, *The Formation of
Christian Dogma*, [3]1957, 120ff.); this was already questioned by W.
Michaelis, *Zur Engelchristologie im Urchristentum*, ATANT 1, 1942. See
also J. Barbel, *Christos Angelos*, Bonn dissertation 1941; H.-J. Schoeps,
Theologie und Geschichte des Judenchristentums, 1949, 8off.; R. N. Longe-
necker, 'Early Christological Motifs', *NTS* 14, 1967–68, 528ff. The pene-
tration of certain themes of 'angel christology' in the 'post-apostolic'
period, e.g. in the Shepherd of Hermas, is closely connected with the
collapse of theological reflection generally. Cf. e.g. L. Pernveden, *The
Concept of the Church in the Shepherd of Hermas*, Stud. Theol. Lund 27,
1966, 58ff., 'The Son of God and Michael'. In certain areas where there
was a pre-Christian angel cult under Jewish influence, e.g. in Phrygia,
people were particularly open to 'angel syncretism', as Colossians shows.
Cf. L. Robert, *Hellenica* 10, 434, n. 2, and CRAI, 1971 613f. The constant influence of Jewish apocrypha, with speculations about angels and
hypostases, on early Christian popular piety, must also be taken into
account, see e.g. C. Colpe, *JbAC* 15, 1972, 8ff., on the Apocryphon of
Peter from Codex VI of Nag Hammadi, where Jesus appears to the

The Epistle to the Hebrews follows earlier Christian tradition closely in making a fundamental distinction between the pre-existent and exalted Son and the angels, and in putting the Son far above the angels by virtue of his association with the Father:

> He reflects the glory of God (cf. Wisd. 7.25f.)
> and bears the very stamp of his nature,
> upholding the universe by his word of power.
> When he had made purification for sins,
> he sat down at the right hand of the Majesty on high,
> having become as much superior to the angels
> as the name he has obtained is more excellent than theirs.
> For to what angel did (God) say at any time,
> 'Thou art my Son, today I have begotten thee'?
> Or again, 'I will be to him a father, and he shall be to me a son'?
> And again, when he brings the firstborn into the world, he says,
> 'Let all God's angels worship him.'[147]

In this context we should note that Judaism was also familiar with the theme of the jealousy of angels, who were given a lower status

---

disciples in the form of a healing angel, Lithargoel. The 'ancestral angelic folklore' of Jewish-Christian circles could now live on 'as angel christology' (op. cit., 10f.). Traces of this can be followed as far as Origen. However, in contrast to the colourful world of images in Jewish-Christian angelology, theological reflection followed the course to the divinity of Christ in the unity of the revelation of Father and Son with intrinsic consistency.

[147] Heb. 1.3–6. For the dispute over the christology of Hebrews and its soteriological and anthropological interpretation see E. Grässer, in *Neues Testament und christliche Existenz, Festschrift für Herbert Braun*, 1973, 195–206. For the interpretation of the introductory verses of the epistle see id., EKK 3, 1971, 55–91. For the theme of Christ's superiority to the angels see 1 Clem. 36.2, which in my view already presupposes knowledge of Hebrews. The rather later Shepherd of Hermas shows that the question of the relationship of Christ to the angels was acute in Rome at the end of the first century and the beginning of the second. In contrast to G. Theissen, *Untersuchungen zum Hebräerbrief*, SNT 2, 1969, 120ff., 'gnostic themes' should not be presupposed in Hebrews, much less in Philo, unless the term 'gnostic' is clearly differentiated from later Gnosticism. The abundant use, or better misuse, of the term 'gnostic' only serves to confuse matters. See on the other hand the detailed historical investigation by O. Hofius, *Katapausis*, WUNT 11, 1970, and id., *Der Vorhang vor dem Throne Gottes*, WUNT 14, 1972, who has clearly brought out the many strata in the Jewish background to the letter. These was still no division between an 'orthodox' and a 'heretical' Judaism before AD 70.

than a particularly distinctive man, in the context of the creation of
Adam, the bestowing of the law on Israel and the ascension and
exaltation of particular figures of salvation history like Enoch-
Metatron, Moses, or the martyr high priest Ishmael b. Elisha.
According to later rabbinic teaching, the righteous man was
'greater than the angels, for the angels, unlike the righteous man,
cannot hear the voice of God without fear. The angel Gabriel followed Daniel and his companions like a pupil going behind his
master.'[148] Of course, the primitive Christian exaltation christology
left all these intermediary stages behind in a bold move in christological thinking. E. Lohmeyer is quite right in stressing in his
interpretation of Heb. 1.1ff. that the essential point here is that the
christological outline of Phil. 2.6–11 is being made more precise.
Here the 'notion of equality with God is defined (more exactly);
the metaphysical determination "Son" frees it from the indefinite-
ness which the phrase "being in the form of God" still carries with
it.' The subjection of 'everything in heaven' to the name of Jesus
(Phil. 2.10f.) corresponds to his superiority over the angels (Heb.
1.4). But the 'heir of the universe' (Heb. 1.2, cf. 4b) is the exalted
Kyrios. 'Thus the divine nature of the "Son" in Hebrews is so to
speak established from the beginning. The approach here is the
same as in the hymn which Paul quotes; the difference is that it is
made more precise in terms of the metaphysical substantiality of
Christ.'[149] The decisive feature here is that a strict paradox is
maintained: the humiliation of Jesus to the point of his shameful
death on the accursed cross, which was such a scandal for ancient
man, whether Jew or Greek (I Cor. 1.18ff.), is sustained in an un-
broken and indeed remorseless way. The basic theme of the Epistle
to the Hebrews, on which there are many variations, is the representative atoning suffering of the Son. Neither his temptation
(2.18) nor his loud cries and tears in prayer (5.7) are suppressed.
'He endured the cross, despising the shame' (12.2). It is no coinci-

[148] R. Mach, *Der Zaddik in Talmud und Midrasch*, 1957, 110; cf. also
P. Schäfer, *Rivalität zwischen Engeln und Menschen. Untersuchungen zur
rabbinischen Engelvorstellung*, Studia Judaica VIII, 1975.
[149] E. Lohmeyer, *Kyrios Jesus. Eine Untersuchung zu Phil 2,5–11*,
reprinted 1961, 77f.

dence that Cicero, in his second speech against Verres (5, 165), speaks of crucifixion as the '*crudelissimum taeterrimum supplicium*'. 'So Jesus also suffered . . . in order to sanctify the people through his own blood. The reforelet us go forth to him outside the camp, bearing his *shame*' (13.12f.).[150] One might almost regard the whole of Hebrews as a large-scale development of the christological theme which is already present in the Philippians hymn. It is remarkable that at the very point where the divine sonship and pre-existence of the exalted Christ are stressed, the shame of his passion also stands in the centre. This is true for Paul, for the author of Hebrews and – in a somewhat different form – for the Second (Mark 15.39) and Fourth Evangelists (John 19.5). The '*doxa*' of the Son of God cannot be separated from the shame of his cross. The Fourth Evangelist gives classic form to this idea: the crucified Jesus is the exalted Christ (3.14; 8.28). Conversely, it is probably no chance that the Hellenist Luke keeps his distance from both the christology of the pre-existent Son of God and the saving significance of the cross. The tense christological struggle in the ancient church could never completely free itself from this paradoxical dialectic. The Scythian monks in Constantinople were still fighting over the recognition of the disputed 'theopaschite formula': *unus ex trinitate passus est carne*, in the sixth century AD. For traditional Greek ideas of God oriented on Parmenides' way of thinking, the idea of the suffering of the pre-existent Son of God was and remained an intolerable scandal. The 'theologically progressive' intellectuals of the second century AD therefore fled from this intolerable paradox of the christological confession into gnostic docetism. Here was one of the chief reasons for the success of the gnostic type of thinking in the church of the second and third centuries AD.

[150] See my forthcoming study, 'Mors turpissima crucis', in *Rechtfertigung. Festschrift für E. Käsemann zum 70. Geburtstag*, 1976, und 'Die christologischen Hoheitstitel im Urchristentum', in *Der Name Gottes*, ed. H. V. Stietencron, 1975, 90–111.

8
Theological Conclusions

With this glance forward we have gone far beyond the horizon of our investigation, which has been no more than an attempt to understand better the christological development of the first twenty dark years between about AD 30 and AD 50, by means of the title Son of God, at the same time casting light on its historical background. In so doing we came up against a multiplicity of Jewish ideas about a mediator and redeemer, from Enoch-Metatron through Wisdom and the Logos to Melchizedek-Michael. We discovered not only analogies but also fundamental differences. A demonstration of parallels in the history of religions always sharpens one's awareness of the difference and the new elements which came out in primitive Christianity. Precisely in order to express the uniqueness of the revelation of the *one* God in a hostile world and his history with the chosen people Israel, ancient Judaism was able to make use of many different conceptions of intermediaries. These intermediary figures were differentiated from God and yet closely connected with him. They acquired special significance in the final eschatological events. It is understandable that post-Christian Judaism partly retracted these forms of expression: polemical differentiation from Christian and gnostic 'heretics' made rethinking necessary. However, Jewish mysticism shows that even at a later time it was felt undesirable and impossible to give them up altogether. Investigation of the significance of the Jewish Hekalot and Merkabah literature for early Christian christology has still a wide field to explore, as Billerbeck in his great commentary unfortunately paid too little attention to these texts, Odeberg's exegesis of the Gospel of John has remained a torso and Jewish scholars have often underestimated the significance of them, for apologetic reasons.[151]

[151] The two works by O. Hofius cited in n. 147 are an excellent example

These forms of Jewish thought and language concerned with a mediator of revelation and salvation at the beginning and the end of time almost forced earliest Christianity to interpret Jesus' preaching and actions, his claim to be God's eschatological messianic ambassador, his unique connection with the Father, the imminence of whose salvation he announced, his shameful death and his resurrection, which was interpreted as exaltation, in a concentrated form as a *unique, 'eschatological' saving event*. The general apocalyptic framework of earliest Christianity, in which the revelation of the 'saving power' of God through this Jesus was expressed, from the beginning irresistibly forced the development of christological thought in this direction. The goal was to articulate God's communication of himself, his speaking and acting in the Messiah Jesus, in quite unsurpassable, final – 'eschatological' – form. The roots of this development were twofold: first, Jesus' claim to messianic authority, in which he announced the imminence of the rule of God, i.e. the saving love of the Father, to the lost, and secondly the disciples' certainty that God had raised his crucified Messiah Jesus. It was impossible to stop at a simple adoptionist christology or an understanding of Jesus as a new lawgiver, because this would have continued to give God's action in creation and in primal times, as with his people Israel under the old covenant, an independence from his conclusive, eschatological revelation in Jesus, which was open to misinterpretation. With strictly consistent christological thought, the early communities were concerned with the *whole revelation of God*, the *whole of salvation* in his Christ Jesus, which could not remain one 'episode in salvation history' among others. In Jesus, God himself comes to men with the fullness of his love. It was through a christology in terms of the pre-existent Son of God, which was apparently so scandalous and, according to a widespread opinion, 'mythological',

---

of the way in which these texts can be used to illuminate the New Testament. The two texts published by J. Strugnell, 'The Angelic Liturgy at Qumran . . .', *Congress Volume Oxford 1959*, SVT 7, 1960, show that we may already presuppose the heavenly Merkabah speculation in pre-Christian times. Unfortunately the great work by G. Scholem is still used too little for New Testament exegesis.

that the way was shown towards overcoming the danger of a
syncretistic, mythical speculation. It is no coincidence that the
most fully developed christology of the Gospel of John has particularly attracted thinkers like Schleiermacher and Bultmann who
have been so strictly concerned with 'demythologizing'.

In a concern to express the revelation of the love of God in this
Jesus, for which no reasons could be given from the human side, in
such a way that it could be proclaimed as a missionary message, a
'gospel' to 'Jews and Greeks', the earliest Christian community
created with astonishing speed a christology in which he appeared
as the fulfiller of the promises of the old covenant, the sole mediator
of salvation, indeed as the one fulfiller of God's revelation from the
beginning. Far from opening the floodgates to mythologizing, to
raise him to be Son of God and Lord *above* all heavenly powers and
to set him 'at the right hand of the Father' restricted this possibility. This is demonstrated by the course of later gnosticism,
where in an abundance of mythological speculations Christ was
often degraded to becoming *one* divine emanation *among many
others*. Nor was the scandal of the cross removed by this christological development; rather, as far as ancient man was concerned,
it was immeasurably increased. There may have been many crucified righteous men in the ancient world: Plato's paradigm in
Republic 361E was well-known to the educated men of the time.
But for Jews and Greeks the crucified Son of God was an unheard-of
idea.[152] The danger of ditheism was also averted, for the Son was

[152] Hegesippus in Eusebius, *HE* 2, 23, 12: ὁ λαὸς πλανᾶται ὀπίσω Ἰησοῦ
τοῦ σταυρωθέντος, and the objections of the Jew Trypho in Justin,
Dialogue 10.3: 'But we cannot understand ... how you can set your
hopes on a crucified man (cf. 8.3) and expect good of him, although
you do not observe God's commandments.' 90.1: 'However, you must
prove to us whether he had to be crucified and die such a shameful and
dishonourable death, which is accursed by the law, since something like
this is unthinkable to us'; see also 137, 1ff. and the *Altercatio Simonis
Judaei et Theophili Christiani*, 2, 4, ed. Harnack, TU 1, 1883, 28f., and
E. Bratke, CSEL 45, 25f., and E. Bammel, *VigChr* 26, 1972, 259ff., with
a text from the *Toledoth Jesu*. From the Hellenistic world see Lucian's
taunt about the 'crucified sophist' and his worshippers, *Peregr.* 13, and
11; also the charges of Celsus, Origen, *C. Celsum* 2,9, and the well-known
taunt crucifix on the Palatine. W. Bauer, *Das Leben Jesu im Zeitalter der
neutestamentlichen Apokryphen*, 1909 reprinted 1967, 467ff., gives a survey

involved in a complete union of action and love with the Father
(John 3.35; 8.19, 28, 40; 15.15; cf. 1.18; 10.30; 17.11, 21–26) to
whom he ultimately hands all things over in complete obedience
(I Cor. 15.28). For that very reason he could not become the symbol of man's self-redemption. Modern dogmatic theologians are
fond of contrasting christologies 'from above' and 'from below',
but this is a false alternative that goes against the course of New
Testament christology, which develops in an indissoluble dialectic
between God's saving activity and man's answer. God's Yes,
which precedes all human action, stands not only at the end of this
course (John 1.14; 3.16), but already at its beginning (Luke 4.18 =
Isa. 61.1; Mark 2.17; Matt. 11.19; Luke 9.20). Jesus the Son, in
eternal communion with the Father, was *not* understood by the
community in the way that Ernst Bloch would have us believe, as
the 'Son of Man' who, like a second Prometheus, stormed heaven
for himself and thus won divine worth for humanity. The Son who
was sent into the world and obediently took upon himself human
existence 'under the law' (Gal. 4.4), and indeed a slave's death, was
not regarded as a religious hero like Heracles, who put human
achievement on a new level. These objectifications, which are all
too familiar from Christian tradition and all too alien to outsiders
because of the extreme 'mythological' form of their expression,
may now seem odd or even scandalous to us. But we should not
allow ourselves to be discouraged from attempting to understand
them better. The disqualification of expressions of this kind, which
often seems scientific but is really only a matter of primitive
'demythologizing', can sometimes also be a sign of spiritual
naïvety and convenience. In reality, theology will never be able to
dispense with the language of 'myth', with its transcendent meta-
phors, and at this very point we would do well to learn from the
example of the greatest Greek 'theologian', Plato. The 'Son of
God' has become an established, unalienable metaphor[153] of

of Jewish and pagan polemic against the crucified Jesus: 'A God or son
of God dying on the cross! That was enough to put an end to the new
religion' (477). See also above 40ff., n. 83; 61ff., n. 113.
[153] See E. Jüngel, 'Metaphorische Wahrheit', in P. Ricoeur/E. Jüngel,
Metapher. Zur Hermeneutik religiöser Sprache, EvTh-Sonderheft, 1974,
71–122; for 'Son of God' especially 71, 73, 111ff., 118.

Christian theology, expressing both the origin of Jesus in God's being (i.e. his love for all creatures and his unique connection with God) and his true humanity.

I am well aware that the interpretation of expressions of Christian faith is the specific and inevitable task of the systematic theologian, but to end with I would like to make some suggestions for any attempt to consider the significance of the New Testament statements about the 'Son of God'.

This phrase is an expression of the following beliefs:

1. God's love towards all men has taken shape in an unsurpassable way, once and for all, in the one man, Jesus of Nazareth, his beloved Son.

2. The event of this love, i.e. our salvation, is not a this-worldly possibility at human disposal but presupposes the sending by the eternal God of Jesus, who is fully 'in accord with' God's being and will.

3. God's words in the Old Testament, i.e. his revelation in creation and in the history of Israel, the chosen people, lead up to his chosen Messiah Jesus and have their consummation in him, 'the Son'.

4. The death of Jesus on the cross and his resurrection represent the bearing of human guilt and man's mortal destiny by God himself, who 'identifies' himself with the man Jesus and in so doing overcomes guilt and death for us all.

5. Belief in God's disclosure of himself in his Son is the basis for the joyful 'freedom of the children of God', a freedom which participates in God's unlimited 'possibility' in this all too limited world and in a future which – thank God! – is not dependent on a humanity which regards itself as the 'supreme being', but belongs wholly and utterly to God's love.

But let Paul have the last word:

'For all who are led by the Spirit of God are sons of God. For you did not receive the spirit of slavery to fall back into fear, but you have received the spirit of sonship. When we cry, "Abba! Father!" it is the Spirit himself bearing witness with our spirit that we are children of God' (Rom. 8.14f.).

CRUCIFIXION

In the Ancient World and the Folly of
the Message of the Cross

I

The 'Folly' of the Crucified
Son of God

In I Corinthians 1.18 Paul says that in the eyes of 'those who are
perishing', the 'word of the cross' is 'folly'. He goes on to empha-
size the point further in v. 23 by saying that the crucified Christ is a
'stumbling-block' for the Jews and 'folly' for the Gentiles. The
Greek word μωρία which he uses here does not denote either a
purely intellectual defect nor a lack of transcendental wisdom.
Something more is involved. Justin puts us on the right track when
he describes the offence caused by the Christian message to the
ancient world as madness (μανία), and sees the basis for this objec-
tion in Christian belief in the divine status of the crucified Jesus
and his significance for salvation:

> They say that our *madness* consists in the fact that we put a *crucified
> man* in second place after the unchangeable and eternal God, the
> Creator of the world (*Apology* I, 13.4).

Justin later concedes that demons have caused stories to be told
about miraculous powers of the 'sons of Zeus' and of their ascensions to heaven, 'but in no case . . . is there any imitation of the
crucifixion' (55.1).[1] It is the crucifixion that distinguishes the new
message from the mythologies of all other peoples.

---

[1] The remarks in 22.3f. are only apparently a contradiction of this: 'But
if anyone objects (εἰ δὲ αἰτιάσαιτό τις) that he was crucified, this is in common with the sons of Zeus, as you call them, who suffered as we have now
enumerated [in the previous chapter]. For according to the accounts,
their sufferings and death were not all alike, but different. So his unique
passion does not make him out to be inferior – indeed I will, as I have un-
dertaken, show, as the argument proceeds, that he was superior.' These
explicit apologetic remarks also make it clear that the dishonour involved

The 'folly' and 'madness' of the crucifixion can be illustrated from the earliest pagan judgment on Christians. The younger Pliny, who calls the new sect a form of *amentia* (*Epistulae* 10.96.4–8), had heard from apostate Christians that Christians sang hymns to their Lord 'as to a god' (*quasi deo*), and went on to examine two slave girls under torture. Of course the result was disappointing:

> I discovered nothing but a perverse and extravagant superstition.
>
> (*nihil aliud inveni quam superstitionem pravam immodicam.*)

It must have been particularly offensive for a Roman governor that the one who was honoured 'as a god' (*quasi deo carmen dicere*) had been nailed to the cross by the Roman authorities as a state criminal.[2] His friend Tacitus speaks no less harshly of a 'pernicious superstition' (*exitiabilis superstitio*) and knows of the shameful fate of the founder:

> Christus, from whom the name had its origin, suffered the extreme penalty during the reign of Tiberius at the hands of the procurator Pontius Pilate.
>
> (*auctor nominis eius Christus Tiberio imperitante per procuratorem Pontium Pilatum supplicio adfectus erat.*)

The 'evil' (*malum*) which he instigated spread all too quickly to Rome, 'where all things hideous and shameful from every part of the world meet and become popular' (*quo cuncta undique atrocia aut*

---

in the death of Jesus by crucifixion was one of the main objections against his being son of God. Justin attempts to counter this by pointing out that various sons of Zeus are said to have died in different ways and that therefore Jesus is not to be held in less esteem because of the special form of his death. Moreover, the decisive thing is not his death, but what he did: ὁ γὰρ κρείττων ἐκ τῶν πράξεων φαίνεται. Cf. also Justin, *Dialogue with Trypho* 8.3; 10.3; 90.1; 137.1ff. and M. Hengel, *The Son of God*, 1976, 91f.

[2] For Pliny and the Christians see especially R. Freudenberger, *Das Verhalten der römischen Behörden gegen die Christen im 2. Jahrhundert*, MBPF 52, ²1969, 189ff., on the term *superstitio*. Horace, *Satires* 2.3.79f. includes superstition among spiritual ailments:

quisquis luxuria tristive superstitione
aut alio mentis morbo calet ...

(Anyone who is feverish with extravagance or gloomy superstition or some other mental disorder ...)

pudenda confluunt celebranturque, Annals 15. 44.3). Tacitus' precise knowledge of Christians and his contempt for them are probably to be derived from the trials of Christians which he carried out when he was governor in the province of Asia.[3]

In his dialogue *Octavius*, Minucius Felix begins by putting on the lips of his pagan interlocutor Caecilius a pointed piece of anti-Christian polemic, part of which goes back to a work by the famous orator Cornelius Fronto, who lived at the time of Marcus Aurelius. According to Caecilius, Christians put forward 'sick delusions' (*figmenta male sanae opinionis*, 11.9), a 'senseless and crazy superstition' (*vana et demens superstitio*, 9.2) which leads to an 'old-womanly superstition' (*anilis superstitio*) or to the destruction of all true religion (*omnis religio destruatur*, 13.5). Not least among the monstrosities of their faith is the fact that they worship one who has been crucified:

> To say that their ceremonies centre on a man put to death for his crime and on the fatal wood of the cross (*hominem summo supplicio pro facinore punitum et crucis ligna feralia*) is to assign to these abandoned wretches sanctuaries which are appropriate to them (*congruentia perditis sceleratisque tribuit altaria*) and the kind of worship they deserve (9.4).

The Christian Octavius does not find it easy to shake off this last charge. His answer makes it clear that the death of Jesus on the cross was inevitably folly and scandal even for the early Christians. Their pagan opponents quite unjustly assert that Christians worship 'a criminal and his cross' (*hominem noxium et crucem eius*, 29.2). No criminal, indeed no earthly being whatsoever deserves to be regarded as a god. On the other hand, Octavius does not go any

[3] For Tacitus' account of the Christians see H. Fuchs, 'Der Bericht über die Christen in den Annalen des Tacitus', in V. Pöschl (ed.), *Tacitus*, WdF 97, 1969, 558–604; Freudenberger, op. cit., 180ff.; R. Syme, *Tacitus* II, Oxford 1958, 468f., 532f. See also the commentary by E. Koestermann, *Cornelius Tacitus Annalen* IV, 1968, 253ff. His theory that Nero did not persecute the Christians but 'Jewish supporters of the agitator Chrestus, named by Suetonius, *Claudius* 25.4, and wrongly identified by Tacitus with the Christians' (253) is quite untenable. In my view, the *supplicio adfectus* is an echo of the 'slaves' punishment' (*servile supplicium*), cf. Valerius Maximus 8.4.1; *Scriptores Historiae Augustae* 15.12.2 and Hadrian: *ut homicidam servum supplicium eum iure iubete adfici* (quotation according to E. Levy, *Gesammelte Schriften* II, 1969, 476).

further into the person of Jesus and his fate; instead he deals at
some length with the charge of worshipping the cross.

> Moreover, we do not reverence the cross, nor do we worship it. But
> you, who hold your wooden gods (*ligneos deos*) to be holy, also
> worship wooden crosses, as parts of your divine images. For what are
> the military emblems, the banners and standards in your camps, if
> not gilded and decorated crosses? Not only is the form of your signs
> of victory like the structure of the cross; it even recalls a man
> fastened to it (29.6f.).

Indeed, are they not aware that such a 'wooden god' might perhaps
have been part of a funeral pile or a gallows-tree (i.e. a cross: *rogi
. . . vel infelicis stipitis portio*, 24.6)? Octavius cannot deny the
shamefulness of the cross and therefore he is deliberately silent
about the death of Jesus. He seeks to ward off any attack by going
over to the counter-attack – making use of the argument that divine
effigies are contemptible, an argument which was already well tried
in Jewish apologetic: you are the ones who worship crosses and
divine effigies, which in some circumstances have a shameful origin.
He avoids the real problem, namely that the Son of God died a
criminal's death on the tree of shame. This was not appropriate for
a form of argument which was concerned to prove that the one God
of the Christians was identical with the God of the philosophers.
Octavius' evasion of the point indicates the dilemma which all too
easily led educated Christians into docetism.

Augustine has preserved for us an oracle of Apollo recorded by
Porphyry, given in answer to a man's question what he can do to
dissuade his wife from Christian belief. The god holds out little
hope:

> Let her continue as she pleases, persisting in her vain delusions, and
> lamenting in song a god who died in delusions, who was condemned
> by judges whose verdict was just, and executed in the prime of life
> by the worst of deaths, a death bound with iron.
>
> (*Pergat quo modo uult inanibus fallaciis perseuerans et lamentari
> fallaciis mortuum Deum cantans* [compare the wording in Pliny], *quem
> iudicibus recta sentientibus perditum pessima in speciosis ferro uincta mors
> interfecit, Civitas Dei* 19.23; p. 690 CC.)

This oracle, originally in Greek, admirably confirms the verdicts of

Pliny, Tacitus and Caecilius. The one whom Christians claim as
their God is a 'dead God' – a contradiction in itself. And if that
were not enough, he had been condemned justly, as a criminal, by
his judges in the prime of life, i.e. before his time, to the worst form
of death: he had to endure being fastened to the cross with iron
nails.

All this evidence shows us the constantly varying forms of
abhorrence at the new religious teaching. In comparison with the
religious ideals of the ancient world the Christian message had inevitably to be described in Suetonius' words as a 'new and pernicious superstition' (*superstitio nova et malefica, Nero* 16.3). These
accounts, with their marked contemptuous characterizations, are no
coincidence. The heart of the Christian message, which Paul
described as the 'word of the cross' (λόγος τοῦ σταυροῦ), ran
counter not only to Roman political thinking, but to the whole ethos
of religion in ancient times and in particular to the ideas of God held
by educated people.[4]

True, the Hellenistic world was familiar with the death and
apotheosis of some predominantly barbarian demigods and heroes
of primeval times. Attis and Adonis were killed by a wild boar,
Osiris was torn to pieces by Typhon-Seth and Dionysus-Zagreus[5]
by the Titans. Heracles alone of the 'Greeks' voluntarily immolated himself on Mount Oeta.[6] However, not only did all this take

[4] Cf. the polemic of Celsus, Origen, *Contra Celsum* 3.55, against the
'wool-workers, cobblers and laundry workers', and 6.34, against Jesus
himself.

[5] A. Henrichs, *Die Phoinikika des Lollianos*, PTA 14, 1972, 56–79, seeks
traces of a mystery of Dionysus-Zagreus in the human sacrifice depicted
in the fragment of a romance which he has edited for publication. However, the decisive point here seems to me to be that the sacrifice of a child,
eating his heart and drinking his blood, coupled with an oath and other
consequent excesses, are seen by the author and his readers as quite barbarous customs. Naive souls may have imagined that similar things went
on at Christian services.

[6] Cf. M. Hengel, *The Son of God*, 1976, 25f., and on his death, Seneca,
Hercules Oetaeus, 1725f.:

vocat ecce iam me genitor et pandit polos:
venio pater . . .

(See now my father calls me and opens the skies;
Father, I come . . .)

place in the darkest and most distant past, but it was narrated in questionable myths which had to be interpreted either euhemeristically or at least allegorically.[7] By contrast, to believe that the one pre-existent Son of the one true God, the mediator at creation and the redeemer of the world, had appeared in very recent times in out-of-the-way Galilee[8] as a member of the obscure people of the Jews,[9] and even worse, had died the death of a common criminal on

---

He displays his _maiestas_ in dying without any sign of pain (1745f.):

> _stupet omne vulgus, vix habent flammae fidem,_
> _tam placida frons est, tanta maiestas viro._

(The whole crowd stands in speechless wonder, scarcely able to believe the flames, so calm the brow, so majestic the hero.)

The heavenly voice of the exalted Heracles speaks to Alcmene (1966ff.):

> ... _quidquid in nobis tui_
> _mortale fuerat, ignis evictus tulit:_
> _paterna caelo, pars data est flammis tua._

(Whatever in me was mortal and of you has felt the flames and been vanquished: my father's part has been given to heaven, yours to the flames.)

While there may be some parallels between this portrayal of the apotheosis of the son of Zeus and the passion in the gospel of John, it is a far cry from the account in Mark (15.21, 34–36). Heracles' action was imitated by Peregrinus Proteus, who set fire to himself at the Olympic Games of AD 165. See Lucian, _De morte Peregrini_ 20–45, esp. 39: 'I leave the earth and go to Olympus'. My colleague Professor Cancik has pointed out that from its beginnings down to Roman times tragedy has contained the theme of the suffering of heroes (πάθη ἡρώων); cf. Herodotus 5.67, and H. Cancik, 'Seneca und die römische Tragödie', in _Neues Handbuch der Literaturwissenschaft_ III, ed. M. Fuhrmann, Frankfurt-am-Main 1974, 251–60. Of course the heroes of the Greek sagas are not gods who are immortal by nature, but men who by their actions have attained the status and veneration accorded to gods.

[7] See e.g. Plutarch, _De Iside et Osiride_, 22–78; cf. T. Hopfner, _Plutarch, über Isis und Osiris_ II, Prague 1941 (reprinted Darmstadt 1967), 101ff. According to ch. 79 (382f.), Osiris is immaculate and free from any association with transitoriness and death.

[8] For 'Galilean' as a derogatory term used of zealots and Christians to the time of Julian, see M. Hengel, _Die Zeloten_, AGJU 1, Leiden-Köln ²1976, 57ff.; H. Karpp, 'Christennamen', _RAC_ II (1114–1138) 1131.

[9] Celsus in Origen, _Contra Celsum_ 4.36: 'the Jews who cower together in a corner of Palestine', cf. 6.78: 'And you, do you not believe that the son of God sent to the Jews is the most ridiculous makeshift of all?'

the cross, could only be regarded as a sign of madness. The real gods of Greece and Rome could be distinguished from mortal men by the very fact that they were *immortal* – they had absolutely nothing in common with the cross as a sign of shame (αἰσχύνη) (Hebrews 12.2),[10] the 'infamous stake' (*infamis stipes*),[11] the 'barren' (*infelix lignum*) or 'criminal wood' (πανουργικὸν ξύλον),[12] the 'terrible cross' (*maxuma mala crux*) of the slaves in Plautus,[13] and thus of the one who, in the words of Celsus, was 'bound in the most ignominious fashion' and 'executed in a shameful way'.[14] Celsus

[10] I cannot share the view of H.-W. Kuhn (see bibliography), 10f., that Hebrews 12.2 is not influenced by the negative attitude towards crucifixion universal in antiquity, but primarily by the 'biblical Psalter'. The influence of the Psalter and the verdict of antiquity affect one another. For Hebrews 12.2 see now O. Hofius, *Der Christushymnus Philipper 2.6–11*, WUNT 17, 1976, 15ff.

[11] *Anthologia Latina* 415.23f.:

Noxius infami districtus stipite membra
Sperat et a fixa posse redire cruce.

(The criminal, outstretched on the infamous stake, hopes for escape from his place on the cross.)

Cf. also Lactantius, *Institutiones* 4.26.29: the question why God did not devise 'an honourable kind of death' (*honestum . . . mortis genus*) for Jesus, 'why by an infamous kind of punishment which may appear unworthy even of a man, if he is free, although guilty' (*cur infami genere supplicii, quod etiam homine libero quamuis nocente uideatur indignum*). Arnobius, *Adversus nationes* 1.36, makes similar remarks.

[12] Seneca, *Epistulae morales* 101.14; cf. Minucius Felix, *Octavius* 24.6: *deus enim ligneus, rogi fortasse vel infelicis stipitis portio, suspenditur, caeditur. . . .* Behind this is probably to be found the old Roman conception of the *arbor infelix*, consecrated to the gods of the underworld, as a means of execution, see below p. 39. For the 'criminal wood' see the London magical papyrus *PGM* V, 73 (Preisendanz/Henrichs I, p. 184).

[13] See the numerous instances in *ThLL* IV, 1259: *Captivi* 469; *Casina* 611; *Menaechmi* 66, 849 (*abscedat in malam magnam crucem*); *Poenulus* 347 (*i directe in maxumam malam crucem*); *Persa* 352; *Rudens* 518; *Trinummus* 598. The simple *mala crux* is even more frequent. Thus above all in Plautus, but see also Ennius, *Annals* 11, fr. 4 (Argenio, p. 114, lines 349f.): *malo (sic) cruce, fatur, uti des, Iuppiter.* Even more vividly in C. Sempronius Gracchus: *Eo exemplo instituto dignus fuit, qui malo cruce periret* (quoted by Sextus Pompeius Festus, *De Significatu Verborum*, Mueller, p. 150; Lindsay, p. 136).

[14] Origen, *Contra Celsum* 6.10: πίστευσον ὃν εἰσηγοῦμαί σοι τοῦτον εἶναι υἱὸν θεοῦ, κἂν ᾖ δεδεμένος ἀτιμότατα ἢ κεκολασμένος αἴσχιστα, cf. 2.9.68. Achilles Tatius, 2.37.3, calls Ganymede, who was snatched away by an eagle and

puts these phrases in the mouths of Christians as a parody of the
faith which they require: they are very similar to the carefully cal-
culated exuberance in Cicero's documentary 'speech' against Verres
(it was never delivered), in which the orator makes the charge that
the former governor of Sicily inflicted the *crudelissimum taeterri-
mumque supplicium*[15] on a Roman citizen with the utmost haste and
without further investigation, having it carried out immediately.

Some further Greek and Latin evidence may serve to show that
this statement by the great statesman and legal advocate, like other
similar ones, was something more than an isolated 'aesthetic judgment'[16] – as has been suggested recently – remote from the views of
ordinary people and the rest of the ancient world. For example
Josephus, who as Jewish adviser to Titus during the siege of
Jerusalem was witness to quite enough object lessons of this kind,
describes crucifixion tersely and precisely as 'the most wretched of
deaths' ($\theta\alpha\nu\acute{\alpha}\tau\omega\nu\ \tau\grave{o}\nu\ o\emph{i}\kappa\tau\iota\sigma\tau o\nu$). In this context he reports that a
threat by the Roman besiegers to crucify a Jewish prisoner caused
the garrison of Machaerus to surrender in exchange for safe conduct.[17] According to Lucian, the letter T was given its 'evil significance' by the 'evil instrument', shaped in the form of a *tau*, which
tyrants erected to 'hang men on': 'I think we can only punish Tau by
making a T of him.'[18] In the treatise on dreams by Artemidorus, to

---

was like a crucified figure ($\kappa\alpha\grave{i}\ \emph{ε}o\iota\kappa\epsilon\nu\ \emph{ε}\sigma\tau\alpha\nu\rho\omega\mu\acute{ε}\nu\omega$, conj. Jacobs), a $\theta\acute{ε}\alpha\mu\alpha$ ...
$\alpha\emph{ι}\sigma\chi\iota\sigma\tau o\nu,\ \mu\epsilon\iota\rho\acute{\alpha}\kappa\iota o\nu\ \emph{ε}\xi\ \emph{ὀ}\nu\acute{v}\chi\omega\nu\ \kappa\rho\epsilon\mu\acute{\alpha}\mu\epsilon\nu o\nu$. In Origen, *Contra Celsum* 6.34 (cf. 36,
end), Celsus combines in a contemptuous way the nailing of Jesus to the
cross with his lowly trade as a carpenter and mocks Christian talk of the
'tree of life' and the 'resurrection of the flesh through the wood (of the
cross)': 'What drunken old woman, telling stories to lull a small child to
sleep, would not be ashamed of muttering such preposterous things?' Cf.
Minucius Felix, above, p. 3.

[15] 2.5.165: *apud te nomen civitatis ne tantum quidem valuisse ut dubita-
tionem aliquam (crucis), ut crudelissimi taeterrimique supplicii aliquam parvam
moram saltem posset adferre.* (That this mention of his citizenship had not
even so much effect on you as to produce a little hesitation or to delay even
for a little the infliction of that most cruel and disgusting penalty.)

[16] Thus H.-W. Kuhn (see bibliography), 8.

[17] *BJ* 7.202ff. (the quotation comes from 203); cf. Lucian, *Prometheus* 4.
He calls the crucified Prometheus (see pp. 11f. below) an $o\emph{i}\kappa\tau\iota\sigma\tau o\nu\ \theta\acute{ε}\alpha\mu\alpha\ \pi\tilde{\alpha}\sigma\iota$
$\Sigma\kappa\acute{v}\theta\alpha\iota\varsigma$.

[18] *Iudicium vocalium* 12: $\tau\tilde{\omega}\ \gamma\grave{\alpha}\rho\ \tau o\acute{v}\tau o\nu$ (viz. the 'Tau') $\sigma\acute{\omega}\mu\alpha\tau\acute{i}\ \phi\alpha\sigma\iota\ \tau o\grave{v}\varsigma$

dream that one is flying among the birds can only be of ill omen for criminals, 'for it brings the death penalty to criminals, and very often through crucifixion'.[19] Similarly, in his didactic astrological poem, Pseudo-Manetho enumerates the criminals who must justifiably expect crucifixion, and includes among them murderers, robbers, mischief-makers (ἐμπεδολώβας) and deceivers:

> Punished with limbs outstretched, they see the stake as their fate; they are fastened (and) nailed to it in the most bitter torment, evil food for birds of prey and grim pickings for dogs.

> (στρεβλὰ κολαζόμενοι σκολοπηίδα μοῖραν ὁρῶσιν
> πικροτάτοις κέντροισι προσαρτηθέντες ἐν ἥλοις,
> οἰωνῶν κακὰ δεῖπνα, κυνῶν δ' ἑλκύσματα δεινά.)[20]

This evidence from the third century AD shows how widespread was the death penalty and the use of crucifixion even in the later empire; nor had there been any change in the negative attitudes towards crucifixion. From the time of Plautus, that is, from the third century BC onwards, there is evidence of the use of *crux* as a vulgar taunt among the lower classes. It can be found on the lips of slaves and prostitutes,[21] and is comparable with *furcifer, cruciarius*

τυράννους ἀκολουθήσαντας καὶ μιμησαμένους αὐτοῦ τὸ πλάσμα ἔπειτα σχήματι τοιούτῳ ξύλα τεκτήναντας ἀνθρώπους ἀνασκολοπίζειν ἐπ' αὐτά. ἀπὸ δὲ τούτου καὶ τῷ τεχνήματι τῷ πονηρῷ τὴν πονηρὰν ἐπωνυμίαν συνελθεῖν. ('For they say that their tyrants, following his figure and imitating his build, have fashioned timbers in the same shape and crucify men upon them; and that it is from him that the sorry device gets its sorry name.')

[19] *Oneirocriticon* 2.68 (Pack, p. 192): πανούργοις δὲ πονηρόν. τοὺς γὰρ ἀλιτηρίους κολάζει, πολλάκις δὲ καὶ διὰ σταυροῦ; cf. 2.56 (p. 185): κακούργῳ μὲν ἰδόντι σταυρὸν βαστάσαι σημαίνει, similarly 1.76 (p.82); Plutarch, *Moralia* 554 A/B (see p. 77 below): *Anthologia Graeca* 9.378 (Beckby, III, p. 234) and 9.230 (III, p.658).

[20] *Apotelesmatica* 4.198ff. (Koechly, p.69). Prof. Cancik conjectures ἔνηλοι for the difficult ἐν ἥλοις. The adjective ἔνηλος is attested by the old glossaries with the meaning 'nailed', see Liddell and Scott, 9th ed., 1940, s.v. Cf. 1.148f. (p.90): ἄλλον δ'ἀκλειῶς μετέωρον ἀνεσταυρώσας, οὗ τέτατ' ἀνδροφόνοις περὶ δούρασιν ἡλοπαγὴς χείρ, similarly 5.219ff. (p. 108). On this see F. Cumont, *L'Égypte des astrologues*, Brussels 1937, 197 n. 1.

[21] See *ThLL* IV, 1259; Plautus, *Aularia* 522; *Bacchides* 584; *Casina* 416 (conj. Camerarius); *Persa* 795; Terence, *Eunuch* 383; Petronius, *Satyricon* 126.9; cf. 58.2: *crucis offla* (=*offula*), *corvorum cibaria*, 'gallows-bird', 'carrion'.

or even *patibulatus*:[22] an English equivalent might be 'gallows-bird', 'hang-dog'. The abusive *i in malam maximam crucem* thus meant something like 'Be hanged!'[23] Varro, Cicero's contemporary, uses the offensive word *crux* as a vivid illustration for his etymological theory: *lene est auribus cum dicimus 'voluptas', asperum cum dicimus 'crux' . . . ipsius verbi asperitas cum doloris quem crux efficit asperitate concordet* (to say 'pleasure' is gentle on the ears, but to say 'cross' is harsh. The harshness of the latter word matches the pain brought on by the cross).[24] The learned man presupposes that everyone will accept this argument. We may no doubt assume that this horrible word did not sound any better in the ears of a slave or foreigner (*peregrinus*) than it did to a member of the Roman nobility.

Even Paul's Greek audience could hardly have approved of the λόγος τοῦ σταυροῦ, much less the Jews who could see the Roman crosses erected in Palestine, especially when they could hardly forget the saying about the curse laid upon anyone hanged on a tree (Deut. 21.23). A crucified messiah, son of God or God must have seemed a contradiction in terms to anyone, Jew, Greek, Roman or barbarian, asked to believe such a claim, and it will certainly have been thought offensive and foolish.

[22] *Cruciarius*: ThLL IV, 1218: Seneca the Elder, *Controversiae* 7.6.2f., 6; Apuleius, *Metamorphoses* 10.7.5, etc.; cf. Isidore of Seville, *Etymologiae* 10.48f.: 'one worthy of the cross' (*cruciarius eo quod sit cruce dignus*). *Patibulatus*: Plautus, *Mostellaria* 53; cf. Apuleius, *Metamorphoses* 4.10.4.
[23] ThLL IV, 1258f.: Plautus, *Asinaria* 940; *Bacchides* 902; *Casina* 93, 641, 977; *Curculio* 611, 693; *Menaechmi* 915, 1017; *Mostellaria* 1133; *Poenulus* 271, 495, 511, 789, 1309 etc.; cf. p. 7 n. 13 above.
[24] *De lingua latina quae supersunt*, ed. Goetz/Schoell, p. 239. (I am grateful to Prof. Cancik for this comment.)

2

Prometheus and Dionysus: the 'Crucified' and the 'Crucifying' God

The only possibility of something like a 'crucified god' appearing on the periphery of the ancient world of the gods was in the form of a malicious parody, intended to mock the arbitrariness and wickedness of the father of the gods on Olympus, who had now become obsolete. This happens in the dialogue called *Prometheus*, written by Lucian, the Voltaire of antiquity. When describing how his hero is fastened to two rocks in the Caucasus, Lucian uses all the technical terms of a crucifixion: Prometheus is to be nailed to two rocks above a ravine in the sight of all, in such a way as to produce the effect of 'a most serviceable cross' (ἐπικαιρότατος . . . ὁ σταυρός).[1] Hermes and Hephaestus carry out their gruesome work like two slaves, threatened by their strict master with the same punishment if they weaken. The climax comes with the charge

---

[1] *Prometheus* 1: προσηλῶσθαι, . . . καὶ οὗτος ἅπασι περιφανὴς εἴη κρεμάμενος, . . . οὔτε γὰρ ταπεινὸν καὶ πρόσγειον ἐσταυρῶσθαι χρή . . . . ὑπὲρ τῆς φάραγγος ἀνεσταυρώσθω ἐκπετασθεὶς τὼ χεῖρε . . . 2: . . . ἀντὶ σοῦ ἀνασκολοπισθῆναι αὐτίκα (nailed up . . . and he will be in full sight of everyone as he hangs there . . . We must not crucify him low and close to the ground . . . crucify him above the ravine with his hands stretched out . . . be crucified in your stead). For the model see Hesiod, *Theogony* 521f., and Aeschylus, *Prometheus* 52ff. Possibly Hesiod and Aeschylus already depicted the binding of Prometheus after the manner of an *apotympanismos*, see p. 70 below. Hesiod, *Theogony* 521, speaks of a post or pillar to which the god is fastened: δεσμοῖς ἀργαλέοισι μέσον διὰ κίον' ἐλάσσας (bound with inextricable bonds, driving a shaft through the middle). W. Marg, *Hesiod, Sämtliche Gedichte*, Zürich-Stuttgart 1970, 227f., conjectures 'a stake of shame (i.e. a pillory) . . . which was perhaps originally one of the pillars of heaven'. See Κεραμόπουλλος (see bibliography), 60–6; cf. also L. Gernet (see bibliography), 295f., 306 and 316; P. Ducrey (see bibliography), 210 n. 1 and the vases on plates I and II. Apollodorus 1.7.1 speaks of Prometheus being nailed.

made by Prometheus, the Titan, against Zeus: Prometheus is
ashamed that Zeus could be so petty and so vengeful as to 'deliver
so old a god to crucifixion' (ἀνασκολοπισθησόμενον πέμπειν
παλαιὸν οὕτω θεόν, ch. 7). It was necessary to make man in the
image of the gods, 'for I believed that the divinity was incomplete
without a counterpart and that only a comparison would show it to
be the happier being' (ch. 12). Moreover, worship of the gods and
sacrifice had been made possible only by the gift of fire: 'You have
crucified the author of the honour and the sacrifice offered to you!'
(ch. 17). Even Hermes, who is rarely at a loss for a word, cannot find
fault with these arguments of the γενναῖος σοφιστής; he tries to
console Prometheus by speaking of his gifts as a seer. Thus
reconciliation is achieved at the end. As a μάντις Prometheus
prophesies his own liberation by Heracles and his complete
rehabilitation – a crucified god can at best be tormented for a while;
he can never die.[2] It does not seem to me to be a coincidence that
the author of this biting parody in his *De morte Peregrini* mocks
Christians as 'poor devils' (κακοδαίμονες) 'who deny the Greek
gods and instead honour that crucified sophist and live according
to his laws'.[3]

A distinction should be made between the 'crucifixion' of the

---

[2] For the theme of the crucified Prometheus in connection with a parody
of the gods see also Lucian, *Iuppiter confutatus* 8 and *De sacrificiis* 6:
Prometheus was more than usually φιλάνθρωπος, καὶ τοῦτον εἰς τὴν Σκυθίαν
ἀγαγὼν ὁ Ζεὺς ἀνεσταύρωσεν (though well disposed to men, he was brought by
Zeus to Scythia [the barbarian land *par excellence*], where he was crucified);
Dialogi deorum 5 (1).1. There are also allusions to the crucifixion of Prometheus in Martial, *Liber spectaculorum* 7.1ff.; Ausonius, *Technopaegnion*
(*De historia*) 10.9ff. (Peiper, p. 163). One might also compare Andromeda,
who is freed by Perseus, see Manilius, *Astronomica* 5.551ff. (Housman, p.
71, see below, p. 77), and Aristophanes, *Thesmophoriazusae* 1011; also
Euripides, *Andromeda* frs. 122–8 (Nauck, pp. 397ff.); see also p. 70 below.
According to Philostratus, *Heroicus* 19.17 (Kayser II, p. 214). Heracles
crucifies the centaur Asbolus and writes 'this epitaph for him': 'I Asbolus,
who fear the punishment of neither men nor gods, hang on the pointed,
resinous fir, giving a great meal to the long-lived ravens.'

[3] *De morte Peregrini* 13: τὸν δὲ ἀνεσκολοπισμένον ἐκεῖνον σοφιστὴν αὐτὸν
προσκυνῶσιν καὶ κατὰ τοὺς ἐκείνου νόμους βιῶσιν. Cf. 11: ... ὃν ἔτι σέβουσι, τὸν ἄνθρωπον
τὸν ἐν τῇ Παλαιστίνῃ ἀνασκολοπισθέντα, ὅτι καινὴν ταύτην τελετὴν εἰσῆγεν ἐς (*sic*) τὸν
βίον (whom they still worship, the man crucified in Palestine, because he
introduced this new religion into life).

rebellious Titan Prometheus by Zeus, the father of the gods, and
the report in Diodorus Siculus (3.65.5) about the crucifixion of the
wicked *Lycurgus* by *Dionysus*. The two are quite different. Lucian's
account is a bitterly angry mockery of the gods; Diodorus' account,
on the other hand, is unique in ancient literature and derives from
the genre of the historicizing, euhemeristic romance. According to
E. Schwartz it goes back to the Alexandrian writer Dionysius
Scytobrachion.[4] Lycurgus, king of Thrace, is said to have broken
peace treaties with Dionysus, who had come from Asia as conqueror of the world. Thereupon Dionysus crossed the Hellespont
and 'defeated the Thracian forces in battle. Lycurgus, whom he
took prisoner, he blinded, tortured in every conceivable way and
finally crucified' (καὶ τὸν Λυκοῦργον ζωγρήσαντα τυφλῶσαί
τε καὶ πᾶσαν αἰκίαν εἰσενεγκάμενον ἀνασταυρῶσαι). This
account has no religious connections; it is not even critical of
religion, as is the case with Lucian. Rather, it is a realistic political
representation of an idea which was particularly popular in
Hellenistic times, that of Dionysus as conqueror of the world,
which was adorned with the colours of the romance of Alexander.
A cruel practice from the Persian and Macedonian wars underlies
the motif of crucifixion. This was used as a punishment for rebellious vassals and usurpers. Plato was already familiar with it, and
it had also been employed by Alexander and the Diadochi (see
below, pp. 27ff., 73f.). The punishment of Lycurgus appears for
the first time in Homer, who simply records that Zeus blinded the
'enemy of the gods' because of his wickedness towards the Maenads
and the child Dionysus:

> The immortals, who live in blessedness, were angry with him, and
> Zeus the son of Cronos struck him blind. He did not live long after
> this, for he was hateful to all the immortal gods. No, I take no
> delight in fighting against the blessed gods (Diomede, in *Iliad*
> 6.138–41).

---

[4] See Drexler, 'Lykurgos', in: W. H. Roscher, *Ausführliches Lexikon
der griechischen und römischen Mythologie* II, 2 (1897–99), 2194, and E.
Schwartz, *De Dionysio Scytobrachione*, Diss. Bonn 1880, 46. Cf. Heracles
and Asbolus (above, p. 12 n. 2).

The extraordinary paucity of the theme of crucifixion in the mythical tradition, even in the Hellenistic and Roman period, shows the deep aversion from this cruellest of all penalties in the literary world.

3

Docetism as a Way of Removing the 'Folly' of the Cross

With its paradoxical contrast between the divine nature of the pre-existent Son of God and his shameful death on the cross, the first Christian proclamation shattered all analogies and parallels to christology which could be produced in the world of the time, whether from polytheism or from monotheistic philosophy. We have points of comparison for the conceptions of exaltation, ascension and even resurrection. But the suffering of a god soon had to be shown to be mere simulation, rapidly followed by punishment for those humans who had been so wicked as to cause it: good examples of this are some stories about the god Dionysus: the fate of Lycurgus, which has already been mentioned, his fortunes among the pirates[1] or the account of his capture by Pentheus in the *Bacchae*.[2] Prometheus' words in Aeschylus, 'See what I, a god, suffer at the hands of gods' ($\emph{i}\delta\epsilon\sigma\theta\acute{\epsilon}$ μ'$o\hat{\iota}a$ $\pi\rho\grave{o}s$ $\theta\epsilon\hat{\omega}\nu$ $\pi\acute{a}\sigma\chi\omega$ $\theta\epsilon\acute{o}s$, 93), are the exception which proves the rule. Thus the basic theme of christology, the humiliation and ignominious death of the pre-existent redeemer, presented in the first verse of the hymn in Philippians 2.6–11, is obscured, rather than elucidated, by reference

---

[1] *Homeric hymns* 7.12ff.: 'They attempted to bind him with crude bonds, but the bonds would not hold him and the withes fell far away from his hands and feet.' The hymn is a late one, from the Hellenistic period.

[2] Euripides, *Bacchae* 515ff.: the god must not suffer, and Pentheus will have to do penance for his arrogance in wanting to bind the god. Cf. 614ff.:

Dionysus: I delivered myself easily, and with no trouble.
Chorus: Did not Pentheus bind your hands with coils of chains?
Dionysus: It was here I scorned him; thinking that he fettered me he neither touched nor grasped me, but fed on fantasy.

to a pagan pre-Christian redeemer myth.[3] In particular, the
gnostic 'docetism' which did away with the scandal of the death of
Jesus on the cross in the interest of the impassibility of the God of
the philosophers demonstrates that the gnostic systems are secondary attempts at an 'acute Hellenization' of the Christian creed, i.e.
necessary consequences of a popular philosophical influence. On
many occasions in the Graeco-Roman world we come across the
idea that offensive happenings should not be ascribed to revered
divine beings or demi-gods themselves, but only to their 'repre-
sentations'. Thus Ixion, inflamed with love for Hera the spouse of
Zeus, does not embrace the goddess herself but a cloud which has
taken her shape – and as a punishment for his wickedness is bound
to the wheel of the sun.[4] Helen, the daughter of Zeus and Leda, was
really transported by Hermes to Egypt, where she remained safely
until the conquest of Troy, whereas Paris possessed in 'empty
delusion' (δοκεῖ μ'ἔχειν κενὴν δόκησιν, οὐκ ἔχων) her phantom (εἴδωλον), 'made out of heavenly ether' ((ὁμοιώσασ' ἐμοὶ
εἴδωλον ἔμπνουν οὐρανοῦ ξυνθεῖσ' ἄπο) by Hera, who grudged
Helen to Paris. This is what he took away to an adulterous union
in Troy.[5] According to Ovid's *Fasti* (3.701ff.), the goddess Vesta
carried off Caesar, her priest, to the heavenly halls of Jupiter immediately before his murder, and the assassins' weapon stabbed
only his phantom:[6]

> *ipsa virum rapui simulacraque nuda reliqui;*
> *quae cecidit ferro Caesaris umbra fuit.*
> *ille quidem caelo positus Iovis atria vidit*
> *et tenet in magno templa dicata foro.*

[3] M. Hengel, *The Son of God*, 1976, 33ff.; on Phil.2.6ff. see now O.
Hofius, *Der Christushymnus Philipper 2.6–11*, WUNT 17, 1976.
[4] See Weizsäcker, Roscher II, 1, 766ff.; Waser, *PW* X, 2, 1373ff.
[5] Euripides, *Helena* 31ff.; cf. *Electra* 1283f.; also Bethe, *PW* VII,
2.2833ff. We can already find a man being transported by a god and being
replaced by an εἴδωλον in Homer, *Iliad* 5, 311ff., 344ff., 445ff., 449ff., where
Aeneas is rescued by his mother Aphrodite and Apollo. For Heracles see
Odyssey 11.601ff.
[6] See E. Bickerman, 'Consecratio', in *Le culte des souverains dans
l'Empire romain*, Entretiens sur l'antiquité classique 19, Vandoeuvres-
Genève 1973, (1–25) 15f. The model for the transporting of Caesar seems
to be that of his ancestor Aeneas.

(I myself carried the man away, and left nothing but his phantom behind. What fell by the sword was Caesar's shade. Transported to the sky he saw the halls of Jupiter and in the great Forum he has a temple dedicated to him.)

For Celsus or his Jewish authority, Jesus should have demonstrated his divinity by being transported either at the time of his capture or later, from the cross.[7]

The current trend in exegesis concerned with christology away from a one-sided orientation on the abysses of gnosticism towards a special concern with the Pauline theology of the cross is to be welcomed, because here we find ourselves confronted with the indispensable characteristic of Paul's preaching. Indeed, here we have the theological centre of the New Testament itself, which is grounded on the representative death of the messiah Jesus, a fact which cannot be dissolved into any kind of docetism, ancient or modern. It is important not to blur the sharp contours of Paul's remarks about the cross of Christ by including them in a questionable and hypothetical 'theology of the cross' which is supposed to extend to Justin, the gnostics of the second century AD and the apocryphal acts of the apostles.[8] The later interpretation of the

---

[7] Origen, *Contra Celsum* 2.68: εἰ δ'οὖν τό γε τοσοῦτον ὤφειλεν εἰς ἐπίδειξιν θεότητος, ἀπὸ τοῦ σκόλοπος γοῦν εὐθὺς ἀφανὴς γενέσθαι ('But if he was really so great he ought, in order to display his divinity, to have disappeared suddenly from the cross.') Cf. pp. 7f. n. 14 above.

[8] This danger is to be found in the account given by H.-W. Kuhn (see bibliography). After what I feel to be a questionable discussion of crucifixion in antiquity (3–11), he immediately continues with the role of the cross in Christian gnosticism (11ff.) and only comes to Paul at the end (27ff.). The great variety of speculative gnostic interpretations of the cross (see W. Foerster etc. (ed.), *Gnosis* I, ET London 1972; II, 1974; index II, 327 s.v. 'Cross'), contrast abruptly with both Paul and with the synoptic accounts, indeed even with that of John. In connection with the question of the meaning of the cross in earliest Christianity it is best to use these interpretations as a contrast; besides, no one has claimed that there was some kind of unitary 'early Christian theology of the cross' during the first and second centuries AD. Later interpretations had expressly apologetic significance; they are historically conditioned and questionable answers to the reproach of the 'folly' of the cross, see Justin, *Apology* I. 55.8, where διὰ λόγου is to be understood in terms of a rational demonstration. For these manifold apologetic possibilities see H. Rahner, *Greek*

cross which can be seen from Ignatius onwards, in symbolic-allegorical or cosmic terms, has little in common with Paul's λόγος τοῦ σταυροῦ. When Paul began his missionary activity, Christianity was not what it later became at the time of Pliny the Younger or Justin Martyr; it was still a completely unknown Jewish sect in Palestine and the adjoining areas of Syria. It was only a few years since the death of the founder, and personal recollection of events beforehand and afterwards was still alive in the community: I Corinthians 11.23ff.; 15.3ff. (and especially v.6) show that even Paul was not completely unaware of this, despite his 'distance' from the Jesus tradition.[9] Anyone who seeks to deny completely Paul's commitment to the *earthly* figure of the crucified Jesus makes him a docetic theologian.

At the same time, however, this means that for Paul and his contemporaries the cross of Jesus was not a didactic, symbolic or speculative element but a very specific and highly offensive matter which imposed a burden on the earliest Christian missionary preaching. No wonder that the young community in Corinth sought to escape from the *crucified* Christ into the enthusiastic life of the spirit, the enjoyment of heavenly revelations and an assurance of salvation connected with mysteries and sacraments.[10] When in the

---

Myths and Christian Mystery, London 1962, pp.46ff. and Index, p.392, s.v. 'Cross'; also G. Q. Reijners (see bibliography).

[9] This was not so total and so radical as is usually assumed today. Precisely because of the scandal of the cross, it was impossible to be a missionary in the ancient world, proclaiming a crucified messiah and Son of God, without saying something about the activity and the death of this man. Moreover, a need for information is a fundamental human characteristic, especially in connection with a new and revolutionary message. Paul preached to people with a thirst for knowledge, not to stones! P. O. Moe, *Paulus und die evangelische Geschichte*, Leipzig 1912, long ago said what had to be said on the matter. Of course others, like Peter and the missionaries associated with him, had much more to tell about Jesus than Paul had: this could have caused Paul some difficulties on his mission.

[10] It is time to stop talking about 'gnosticism in Corinth'. What happened in the community does not need to be explained in terms of the utterly misleading presupposition of a competing gnostic mission. This never existed, except in the mind of some interpreters. What happened in Corinth can easily be explained in terms of the Hellenistic (and Jewish) milieu of this Greek port and metropolis.

face of this Paul points out to the community which he founded that his preaching of the crucified messiah is a religious 'stumbling block' for the Jews and 'madness' for his Greek hearers, we are hearing in his confession not least the twenty-year experience of the greatest Christian missionary, who had often reaped no more than mockery and bitter rejection with his message of the Lord Jesus, who had died a criminal's death on the tree of shame. This negative reception which was given to the Pauline theology of the cross is continued in the anti-Christian polemic of the ancient world. Walter Bauer was quite right in the remarks with which he concluded his account of the views of the passion of Jesus held by Jewish and pagan opponents of Christianity: 'The enemies of Christianity always referred to the disgracefulness of the death of Jesus with great emphasis and malicious pleasure. A god or son of god dying on the cross! That was enough to put paid to the new religion.'[11] There is an admirable illustration of this in the well-known caricature of a crucified figure with an ass's head from the Palatine with the inscription 'Alexamenos worships god' ($'A\lambda\epsilon\xi\acute{a}$-$\mu\epsilon\nu o\varsigma\ \sigma\acute{\epsilon}\beta\epsilon\tau\epsilon\ [= \sigma\acute{\epsilon}\beta\epsilon\tau\alpha\iota]\ \theta\epsilon\acute{o}\nu$). There should be no doubt that this is an anti-Christian parody of the crucified Jesus. The ass's head is not a pointer to some kind of gnostic Seth-worship, but to the Jewish derivation of Christian faith. One of the regular themes of ancient anti-Jewish polemic was that the Jews worshipped an ass in the temple.[12]

Less well-known is another caricature on a tile which comes

[11] *Das Leben Jesu im Zeitalter der neutestamentlichen Apokryphen*, Tübingen 1909 (reprinted 1967), 477. Cf. 476: 'How could they have avoided his suffering and dying? Here, if anywhere, their opponents would have been able to make the most devastating criticisms. Jesus had been tried and executed, and not as an innocent man, a new Socrates. On the contrary, he was prosecuted as a criminal, found guilty, sentenced and delivered over to death.'

[12] E. Dinkler, *Signum Crucis* (see bibliography), 150ff.; I. Opelt, 'Esel', *RAC* VI, 592ff.; J.-G. Préaux, 'Deus Christianorum Onocoetes', in *Hommages L. Herrmann*, Brussels-Berchem 1960, 639–54; see also E. Bickermann, 'Ritualmord und Eselskult', *MGWJ* 71, 1927, 171–87; 255–64. The charge of worshipping an ass was raised as early as 200 BC by Mnaseas of Patara. See now M. Stern, *Greek and Latin Authors on Jews and Judaism* I, Jerusalem 1974, 97ff.

from the first half of the fourth century AD and depicts someone
carrying a cross. It was discovered in Oroszvár in Hungary, ancient
Gerulata in the province of Pannonia. The figure is dragging a
Latin cross and his tongue is hanging out under its weight. K. Sági
sees this as 'an interesting testimonial to the reaction against
Christianity, which gradually acquired a dominant position in
parallel with the consolidation of the sole rule of Constantine the
Great'.[13] Here too the pagan who drew the picture has focused his
ridicule on the main point of offence which was caused by the new
religion.

   Separated from the particular death of Jesus on the cross, the
Pauline 'word of the cross' would become vague and incomprehensible speculation. At least as far as Paul is concerned, we must
challenge the assertion made in the most recent investigation of the
subject that 'there is no direct route from the historical cross to
theological talk of the "cross"'.[14] The one thing which made Paul's
preaching the offensive 'word of the cross' was the fact that in it the
apostle interpreted the death of Jesus of Nazareth, i.e. of a specific
man, on the cross, as the death of the incarnate Son of God and
Kyrios, proclaiming this event as the eschatological event of salvation for all men. Even the apostle's own suffering is exclusively to
be understood in terms of this historically *unique* event (Rom. 6.10:
ἀπέθανεν ἐφάπαξ). The shame and contempt which the apostle
had to endure is illuminated and explained by the fact of the shameful death of Jesus on the cross. It cannot be detached from this and
be interpreted independently. The enigmatic expression in Colossians 1.24 does not come from the apostle; it is deutero-Pauline. In
my view it already presupposes Paul's martyrdom – perhaps in
Nero's persecutions. Thus for Paul's preaching, the words
σταυρός/σταυροῦν still retained the same original cruelty and abhorrence which was also obvious to the ancient world outside
the Christian tradition, though we find it remote. What Paul says
in I Corinthians 1.17–24 can only be understood against this background. For Paul, therefore, the word has certainly not faded to the

---

[13] K. Sági, 'Darstellung des altchristlichen Kreuzes auf einem
römischen Ziegel', *Acta Antiqua* 16, 1968, (391–400) 400 and pl. 5.
[14] H.-W. Kuhn (see bibliography), 29.

point of becoming a mere 'theological cipher'. Any assertion to this effect merely demonstrates the tenuous link of contemporary exegesis with reality and its insipid and unhistorical character. In other words, the utter offensiveness of the 'instrument for the execution of Jesus' is still to be found in the preaching of Paul.

Thus we can understand all too well how in the pseudo-scientific, popular Platonic arguments used in Gnosticism, this scandal, which deeply offended both religious and philosophical thought in antiquity, was eliminated by the theory that the Son of God had only *seemed* to be crucified. In reality he did not suffer at all. We can see how easily even the orthodox apologist found himself in difficulties here from the laborious argument in Minucius Felix's *Octavius* which has been described on pp. 3f. above. In contrast, worship remained the right place for making public confession of the scandalous paradox of the crucifixion. This is evident not only from the earliest hymns to Christ but also from Melito's *Homily on the Passion*, where it is expressed in polished rhetorical form:[15]

> He who hung the earth [in its place] hangs there, he who fixed the heavens is fixed there, he who made all things fast is made fast upon the tree, the Master has been insulted, God has been murdered, the King of Israel has been slain by an Israelitish hand. O strange murder, strange crime! The Master has been treated in unseemly fashion, his body naked, and not even deemed worthy of a covering, that [his nakedness] might not be seen. Therefore the lights [of heaven] turned away, and the day darkened, that it might hide him who was stripped upon the cross.

[15] 96f.; cf. O. Perler, *Méliton de Sardes, Sur la Pâque*, Source Chrétiennes 123, 1966, 194f.

4

Crucifixion as a 'Barbaric' Form of Execution of the Utmost Cruelty

The instances given so far have been an attempt to show that for the men of the ancient world, Greeks, Romans, barbarians and Jews, the cross was not just a matter of indifference, just any kind of death. It was an utterly offensive affair, 'obscene' in the original sense of the word. In the following pages we shall make a further attempt to illuminate the attitude of the ancient world to crucifixion in more detail.

As a rule, books on the subject say that crucifixion began among the Persians. This is true to the extent that we already find numerous references to crucifixion as a form of execution among the Persians in Herodotus, and these can be supplemented by later evidence from Ctesias.[1] However, according to the ancient sources crucifixion was regarded as a mode of execution used by barbarian peoples[2] generally, including the Indians,[3] the Assyrians,[4] the Scythians[5]

[1] Herodotus 1.128.2; 3.125.3; 3.132.2; 3.159.1: Darius has three thousand inhabitants of Babylon crucified; 4.43.2, 7; 6.30.1; 7.194.1f.; Thucydides 1.110.1; also Ctesias (according to Photius) *FGH* 688 F 14.39: Amastris 'crucifies' the Egyptian usurper Inarus on three crosses (presumably this was a matter of impaling his corpse): καὶ ἀνεσταύρισεν μὲν ἐπὶ τρισὶ σταυροῖς; F 14.45: Amastris has the Caunian Alcides crucified; for the treatment of the corpse of the younger Cyrus see Xenophon, *Anabasis* 3.1.17, and Plutarch, *Artaxerxes* 17.5; because of this Parysatis, the queen mother, has the officer who dishonoured Cyrus' body on the orders of Artaxerxes II flayed and crucified, Ctesias F 16.66. Cf. Ezra 6.11 and Haman's cross, Esther 5.14; 7.9f., see below, pp. 84f.

[2] This was already observed by Justus Lipsius, *De Cruce*, Amsterdam 1670, 47ff.: Book I ch. XI is headed '*Apud plerasque gentium cruces fere usitatas*'.

[3] See the threatening letter sent by the Indian king Stabrobates to Semiramis: Diodorus Siculus, *Bibliotheke* 2.18.1.

[4] The Assyrian king Ninus has the Median king Pharnus crucified:

and the Taurians.[6] It was even used by the Celts, who according to Posidonius offered their criminals in this way as a sacrifice to the gods,[7] and later by the Germani[8] and the Britanni,[9] who may well have taken it over from the Romans and combined it with their own forms of punishment. Finally, it was employed by the Numidians and especially by the Carthaginians, who may be the people from whom the Romans learnt it.[10] Crucifixion was not originally a typically Greek penalty; however, the Greeks did have related forms of execution and partially took over crucifixion (see below, pp. 69ff.). Both Greek and Roman historians were fond of stressing *barbarian* crucifixions, and playing down their own use of this form of execution. Mithridates,[11] the arch-enemy of Rome, and two kings of Thrace, the cruel Diegylis and his son Ziselmius, who

---

Diodorus 2.1.10. Lucian, *Iuppiter confutatus* 16: Sardanapalus becomes king and has the valiant (ἀνὴρ ἐνάρετος) Goches crucified. Of course these reports have no historical value. For an older form of execution see the impalement among the Assyrians: *ANEP* 362, 368, and the bas-relief of the storming of Lachish, 373.

[5] Cyrus is crucified by the Scythians: Diodorus Siculus, 2.44.2; cf. Justin, *Epitome* 2.5.6; Tertullian, *Adversus Marcionem* 1.1.3: 'the crosses of the Caucasus' (*crucibus Caucasorum*).

[6] Euripides, *Iphigenia in Tauris* 1429f.: King Thaos wants to have the strangers hurled down from a rock or fastened to a stake (or impaled). For the Thracians see n. 12 below.

[7] Diodorus Siculus 5.32.6: καὶ περὶ τὰς θυσίας ἐκτόπως ἀσεβοῦσι · τοὺς γὰρ κακούργους ... ἀνασκολοπίζουσι τοῖς θεοῖς ... (And they are monstrously impious in their sacrifices; for they crucify evildoers for their gods.)

[8] Tacitus, *Annals* 1.61.4; 4.72.3, but cf. *Germania* 12.1: *proditores et transfugas arboribus suspendunt* (they hang traitors and deserters on trees). See also Dio Cassius 54.20.4; Florus, *Epitome* 2.30 = 4.12.24.

[9] Tacitus, *Annals* 14.33.2: *sed caedes patibula, ignes cruces, tamquam reddituri supplicium, et praerepta interim ultione, festinabant* (they made haste with slaughter and the gibbet, with fires and crosses, as though the day of reckoning must come, but only after revenge had been snatched in the interval). Cf. Dio Cassius 62. 7.2 and 11.4.

[10] Numidians: Sallust, *Bellum Iugurthinum* 14.15; Caesar, *Bellum Africum* 66. Carthaginians: Polybius 1.11.5; 24.6; 79.4f.; 86.4; Diodorus Siculus 25.5.2; 10.2; 26.23.1; Livy 22.13.9; 28.37.2; 38.48.13; Valerius Maximus 2.7 ext. 1: Justin, *Epitome* 18.7.15; Silius Italicus, *Punica* 1.181; 2.435f.

[11] Appian, *Mithridatic Wars* 97; cf. Valerius Maximus 9.2, ext. 3.

was even worse, were cited as deterrent examples in the Hellenistic period.[12]

A particular problem is posed by the fact that the *form* of crucifixion varied considerably. Above all, there is not always a clear distinction between the crucifixion of the victim while he is still alive and the display of the corpse of someone who has been executed in a different fashion. In both cases it was a matter of subjecting the victim to the utmost indignity. As a rule, Herodotus uses the verb ἀνασκολοπίζειν of living men and ἀνασταυροῦν of corpses. Ctesias, on the other hand, uses only ἀνασταυρίζειν for both. The common factor in all these verbs is that the victim – living or dead – was either nailed or bound to a stake, σκόλοψ or σταυρός. The texts do not always make it clear whether cross-beams were used here. Polycrates of Samos, for instance, the most famous example in antiquity, was not crucified in the strict sense; he was lured by the satrap Oroites into Persian territory, killed 'in an unspeakable (cruel) way' and his body fastened to a stake: ἀποκτείνας δέ μιν οὐκ ἀξίως ἀπηγήσιος Ὀροίτης ἀνεσταύρωσε (Herodotus, *History* 3.125.3). Nevertheless, later tradition saw him as the prototype of the crucified victim whose fate represented a sudden change from supreme good fortune to the uttermost disaster.[13] After Herodotus the words ἀνασκολοπίζειν and ἀνασταυροῦν became synonyms. Josephus, for example, uses only *(ἀνα)*σταυροῦν, while Philo on the other hand uses only ἀνασκολοπίζειν for the same thing. However, neither of the two verbs appears in the only detailed account of a crucifixion given by Herodotus. According to him, the Athenian general Xanthippus had the satrap Artayctes executed for religious offences at the very place where Xerxes had once built a bridge over the Hellespont: 'They

[12] Diodorus Siculus 33.15.1: 34/35.12.1: impalements are recorded of the father and crucifixions of the son.

[13] Cicero, *De finibus* 5.92; Valerius Maximus 6.9 ext.2; Fronto, *Epistula de bello Parthico* (van den Hout I, pp. 208f.); Lucian, *Charon* 14; Dio Chrysostom, *Oratio* 17 (67).15; cf. also the interpretation in Philo, *De providentia* fr. 2.24f., following Eusebius, *Praeparatio Evangelica* 8.14.24f. (Mras, GCS 43.1, pp. 468f.), and the Armenian version 2.25: 'by which he met a gruesome fate'. For Philo his crucifixion is the ultimate punishment for his wicked life.

nailed him to planks and hung him there ([πρὸς] σανίδας προσ-
πασσαλεύσαντες ἀνεκρέμασαν). And they stoned Artayctes' son
before his eyes.'[14] We have very few more detailed descriptions,
and they come only from Roman times: the passion narratives in the
gospels are in fact the most detailed of all. No ancient writer wanted
to dwell too long on this cruel procedure.

Even in the Roman empire, where there might be said to be
some kind of 'norm' for the course of the execution (it included a
flogging beforehand, and the victim often carried the beam to the
place of execution, where he was nailed to it with outstretched
arms, raised up and seated on a small wooden peg),[15] the form of
execution could vary considerably: crucifixion was a punishment
in which the caprice and sadism of the executioners were given full
rein. All attempts to give a perfect description of *the* crucifixion in
archaeological terms are therefore in vain; there were too many
different possibilities for the executioner. Seneca's testimony speaks
for itself:

> I see crosses there, not just of one kind but made in many different
> ways: some have their victims with head down to the ground; some
> impale their private parts; others stretch out their arms on the gibbet.
>
> (*Video istic cruces, non unius quidem generis, sed aliter ab aliis fabricatas:
> capite quidam conuersos in terram suspendere, alii per obscena stipitem
> egerunt, alii brachia patibulo explicuerunt.*)[16]

From Josephus we have an eyewitness account of the fate of Jewish
fugitives who attempted to escape from besieged Jerusalem:

> When they were going to be taken (by the Romans), they were forced
> to defend themselves, and after they had fought they thought it too

[14] Herodotus 9.120, cf. 7.33: ζῶντα πρὸς σανίδα διεπασσάλευσαν. I. Barkan
(see bibliography), 69f., conjectures an instance of *'apotympanismos'* here,
see pp. 69ff. below.

[15] For the *sedile* see H. Fulda (see bibliography), 149ff.; for nailing,
J. Blinzler (see bibliography), 375ff. (ET 264f.). Cf. below p. 31 n. 25.

[16] *Dialogue* 6 (*De consolatione ad Marciam*) 20.3; cf. *Martyria Petri et
Pauli* 60 (Lipsius I, p. 170). Y. Yadin, 'Epigraphy' (see bibliography),
believes that epigraphical and anatomical evidence must lead us to suppose
that the crucified figure discovered at Jerusalem was fastened to the cross
upside down. For 'spitting' the victim as a variation see p. 69 n. 1 below.
Apuleius, *Metamorphoses* 8.22.4f., describes another kind of torture. Cf.
Suidae Lexicon (Adler III, p. 223.10ff.) *s.v.* Κύφωνες: a slow death at the
pillory similar to crucifixion.

late to make any supplications for mercy: so they were first whipped, and then tormented with all sorts of tortures, before they died and were then crucified before the wall of the city (μαστιγούμενοι δὴ καὶ προβασανιζόμενοι τοῦ θανάτου πᾶσαν αἰκίαν ἀνεσταυροῦντο τοῦ τείχους ἀντικρύ). Titus felt pity for them, but as their number – given as up to five hundred a day – was too great for him to risk either letting them go or putting them under guard, he allowed his soldiers to have their way, especially as he hoped that the gruesome sight of the countless crosses might move the besieged to surrender: 'So the soldiers, out of the rage and hatred they bore the prisoners, nailed those they caught, in different postures, to the crosses, by way of jest (προσήλουν . . . ἄλλον ἄλλῳ σχήματι πρὸς χλεύην), and their number was so great that there was not enough room for the crosses and not enough crosses for the bodies.'[17]

The same sort of thing probably happened on the direct instructions of the emperor at the time of the first persecution of Christians by Nero in Rome. This is probably the way in which the famous and disputed passage in Tacitus, *Annals* 15.44.4, is to be interpreted:

> *Et pereuntibus addita ludibria, ut ferarum tergis contecti laniatu canum interirent, aut crucibus adfixi atque flammati, ubi defecisset dies, in usu(m) nocturni luminis urerentur.*

> (And additional derision accompanied their end: they were covered with wild beasts' skins and torn to death by dogs; or they were fastened on crosses and, when daylight faded, were burned to serve as lamps by night.)

In other words, the *aut crucibus adfixi atque flammati* is not to be deleted as a gloss; rather, crucifixion was the basic punishment to

---

[17] Josephus, *BJ* 5.449–51. For mass crucifixions in Judaea see also *BJ* 2.75 (*Antiquitates* 17.295): Varus before Jerusalem 4 BC; cf. also 2.241: crucifixion of all the Jews taken prisoner by Cumanus; according to *Antiquitates* 20.129 the chief offenders among the Samaritans and the Jews were crucified. Cf. *BJ* 2.253: Felix has a large number of 'robbers' crucified; 2.306, 308: crucifixions by Florus in Jerusalem. A Jewish prisoner at Jotapata (3.321) πρὸς πᾶσαν αἰκίαν βασάνων ἀντέσχεν καὶ μηδὲν διὰ πυρὸς ἐξερευνῶσι τοῖς πολεμίοις περὶ τῶν ἔνδον εἰπὼν ἀνεσταυρώθη τοῦ θανάτου καταμειδιῶν (Though tortured in all kinds of ways and passed through the fire, he told the enemy nothing of those within, and as he was crucified, smiled at death). 5.289: Titus has a Jew, captured during a foray, crucified in front of the walls, εἴ τι πρὸς τὴν ὄψιν ἐνδοῖεν οἱ λοιποὶ καταπλαγέντες (to see whether the rest of them would be frightened). Cf. p. 85 n. 5 below.

which the *addita ludibria* were added.[18] Dio Cassius confirms
Nero's cruel habits in crucifixions – though without, of course,
mentioning Christians, about whom he is silent throughout his
work (63.13.2).

We already learn from Plato's Gorgias that the crucifixion of a
criminal was often preceded by various kinds of torture. There
Polus tries to refute Socrates by a particularly horrifying example –
which is nevertheless probably based on the political realities of the
time:

> If a man is caught in a criminal plot to make himself tyrant, and when
> caught is put to the rack and mutilated and has his eyes burnt out and
> after himself suffering and seeing his wife and children suffer many
> other signal outrages of various kinds is finally crucified (τὸ ἔσχατον
> ἀνασταυρωθῇ)[19] or burned in a coat of pitch, will he be happier than if
> he escaped arrest, established himself as a tyrant and lived the rest
> of his life a sovereign in his state, doing what he pleased, an object of
> envy and felicitation among citizens and strangers alike? (473bc)

Socrates rejects the alternative as a false one, 'for of two miserable
creatures one cannot be the happier', though he goes on to say
that the one who becomes a tyrant is more wretched than the
one who dies under torture – a reply which draws scornful laughter
from his opponent (473de).

Plato takes up the theme again in the famous example of the
innocent sufferer (*Republic* 361e–362a), but now applies it in the
opposite way, which gives his argument a prophetic urgency.
Glaucon compares the completely unjust man with the completely just man (360e). Through his cunning and lack of scruple
the unjust man will acquire power and riches and with them the
appearance of the utmost uprightness, whereas the completely just

---

[18] See also Koestermann, op. cit. (p.3 n.3 above), 257, following
Capocci, who conjectures similar happenings to those depicted in Josephus,
BJ 5.451, or Philo, *In Flaccum* 72.85. For the rich arsenal of atrocities of
this kind see also Seneca, *Dialogue* 5 (= *De ira* 3) 3.6.

[19] Philo, *In Flaccum* 72: after all the preceding tortures ἡ τελευταία καὶ
ἔφεδρος τιμωρία σταυρὸς ἦν (the last and supreme punishment was the cross).
Cf. Eusebius, *Historia Ecclesiae* 3.32.6: καὶ ἐπὶ πολλαῖς ἡμέραις αἰκιζόμενος . . .
καὶ ἐκελεύσθη σταυρωθῆναι (He was tortured for many days and orders were
given for him to be crucified).

man will be looked upon and treated as an unjust man and finally –
here Glaucon apologizes for the vividness and realism of his
language – will be tortured to death:

> The just man will have to be scourged, racked, fettered, blinded, and
> finally, after the uttermost suffering, he will be impaled (τελευτῶν
> πάντα κακὰ παθὼν ἀνασχινδυλευθήσεται), and so will learn his lesson
> that not to be but to seem to be just is what we ought to desire.

Plato certainly has Socrates in mind as the example of the completely just man who cares nothing for the views of his fellow-
citizens. It is therefore all the more striking that in contrast to the
'humane' execution of Socrates he envisages the just man being
killed in an extremely barbarous fashion which was quite out of the
ordinary for Athenian citizens. It is significant that Christian
writers – e.g. Clement of Alexandria and the author of the *Acta
Apollonii* – are the first deliberately to take up again the theme of
the crucified just man in Plato. Where other ancient authors
possibly allude to it – with the exception of Lucian (see p. 83
below) – they leave out any account of crucifixion, which was
offensive to them.[20] As at a later date Demosthenes, when defend-
ing himself against a trumped-up charge of murder (*Oratio* 21.105,
against Meidias), describes 'being nailed up' (προσηλοῦσθαι) as the
worst form of execution, we must assume that crucifixion or similar
forms of execution were not completely foreign even to the Greeks
(see pp. 69ff. below).

The combination of crucifixion and torture beforehand was also
customary among the Carthaginians and in the relatively 'normal'

---

[20] Plato is probably thinking of a particularly cruel form of '*apotympanismos*' (see below, pp. 70f.). For Christian interpretation since the *Acta
Apollonii* 39f. and Clement of Alexandria, *Stromateis* 5.108.2f.; 4.52.1f.,
see E. Benz (see bibliography), 31ff. Allusions to just men suffering without crucifixion are found in Maximus of Tyre, *Dialexeis* 12.10 (Hobein,
pp. 156f.); Cicero, *De republica* 3.27, following Carneades; cf. Seneca,
Dialogue 2 (*De constantia sapientis*) 15.1. H. Hommel, 'Die Satorformel
und ihr Ursprung', *ThViat* 1952, (108–180) 124–33, supplements and
corrects Benz, pointing to Macedonian parallels, see p. 72 n. 12 below.
Significantly enough, the rare word ἀνασκινδα(υ)λεύειν only reappears in
the church fathers with express reference to Plato, see Eusebius, *Praeparatio Evangelica* 12.10.4; Theodoret, *Graecarum Affectionum Curatio* 8
(PG 83,1012).

course of execution among the Romans; at the least, a flogging was carried out before the execution.[21] However, the torture which came first probably helped to shorten the actual torments of crucifixion, which were caused above all by the duration of the suffering. A later text explicitly states that hanging on the gallows (*furca*), which gradually took the place of crucifixion after the time of Constantine and the later Christian emperors of the fourth century, was essentially a more humane punishment:

> But hanging is a lesser penalty than the cross. For the gallows kills the victim immediately, whereas the cross tortures for a long time those who are fixed to it.
>
> (*sed patibuli* (= *furca*) *minor poena quam crucis. Nam patibulum adpoenos statim exanimat, crux autem subfixos diu cruciat.*)[22]

Following Livy (30.43.13), Valerius Maximus (2.7.12) says that the older Scipio punished Roman deserters at the end of the Second

---

[21] See J. Blinzler (see bibliography), 321ff. (ET 222ff.), who refers to *Digest* 48.19.8.3, according to which many people even died during the torture. Cf. Dionysius of Halicarnassus, *Antiquitates Romanae* 5.51.3: μάστιξι καὶ βασάνοις αἰκισθέντες ἀνεσκολοπίσθησαν ἅπαντες (after being tormented with whips and tortures, all were crucified), and 7.69.1f.: Diodorus Siculus 18.16.3, see p. 74 n. 15 below. Nero was threatened with flogging as a death penalty *more maiorum* (Suetonius, *Nero* 49.2): *nudi hominis cervicem inseri furcae, corpus virgis ad necem caedi* (the criminal was stripped, fastened by the neck in a fork, and then beaten to death with rods). According to the saga it was carried out publicly as early as by King Tarquinius Superbus: Dio Cassius 2, fr. 11.6; the victims were bound naked to the stake before the eyes of their fellow-citizens and flogged to death: ἐν τοῖς τοῦ δήμου ὄμμασι σταυροῖς τε γυμνοὺς προσέδησεν καὶ ῥάβδοις αἰκισάμενος ἀπέκτεινεν (Boissevain I, p. 27). Scipio Africanus maior acted in this way in Spain to preserve military discipline (Dio Cassius 16 after Zonaras 9.10.8 [I, p. 251]), and C. F. Fimbrias used the punishment in Macedonia in the Mithridatic war (Dio Cassius 30–35, fr. 104.6 [I, p. 348]); the last Hasmonean king Antigonus was humiliated in this way in 38 BC and then executed with the axe, 'which no other king had endured from the Romans' (Dio Cassius 49.22.6). Cf. M. Fuhrmann, 'Verbera', *PW* Suppl. IX (1589–97) 1590ff. For the combination of flogging and crucifixion see Livy 22.13.9; 28.37.3: *laceratosque verberibus cruci adfigi iussit* (when they had been beaten with lashes he ordered them to be fastened to the cross).

[22] Isidore of Seville, *Etymologia* 5.27.34 (Lindsay). Apuleius, *Metamorphoses* 8.22.5, comes near to a crucifixion: a slave is tied to a tree and slowly tortured to death (*per longi temporis cruciatum*). See Fulda (see bibliography), 115f.

Punic War more harshly (*grauius*) than the Latin allies: he crucified
the former as renegades and traitors, but beheaded the latter as
treacherous allies.

> *hos enim tamquam patriae fugitiuos crucibus adfixit, illos tamquam*
> *perfidos socios securi percussit.*

In Epistle 101 to Lucilius, Seneca makes a spirited defence
against Maecenas of the possibility of suicide as the last way to freedom in unbearable suffering. In the form of a verse, Maecenas
compares the illnesses and griefs of his old age with the torments
of the crucified man; nevertheless, he is determined to hold on to
life at any price:

> Fashion me with a palsied hand,
> weak of foot and a cripple.
> Build upon me a crook-backed hump,
> Shake my teeth till they rattle.
> All is well if my life remains.
> Save, oh, save it, I pray you,
> Though I sit on the piercing cross.
>
> (*Debilem facito manu, debilem pede coxo,*
> *Tuber adstrue gibberum, lubricos quate dentes;*
> *Vita dum superest, benest; hanc mihi, vel acuta*
> *Si sedeam cruce, sustine.*)

For Seneca, on the other hand, a life which can be compared with
the torments of hanging on the cross, with only a peg to support
the body, and in which the only comfort is the outcome of the
execution, death, is no longer worth living:

> Is it worth while to weigh down on one's own wound and hang
> impaled on a gibbet in order to postpone something which is the
> balm of troubles, the end of punishment?
>
> (*Est tanti vulnus suum premere et patibulo pendere districtum, dum*
> *differat id, quod est in malis optimum, supplicii finem?*)

A lengthy process of dying is no longer worthy of the name of 'life'.
There follows a description of the gradual expiry of the victim of
crucifixion which is unique in ancient literature:

> Can anyone be found who would prefer wasting away in pain dying
> limb by limb, or letting out his life drop by drop, rather than expiring

once for all? Can any man be found willing to be fastened to the
accursed tree, long sickly, already deformed, swelling with ugly weals
on shoulders and chest, and drawing the breath of life amid long-
drawn-out agony? He would have many excuses for dying even
before mounting the cross.

*(Invenitur aliquis, qui velit inter supplicia tabescere et perire membratim
et totiens per stilicidia emittere animam quam semel exhalare? Invenitur,
qui velit adactus ad illud infelix lignum, iam debilis, iam pravus et in
foedum scapularum ac pectoris tuber elisus, cui multae moriendi causae
etiam citra crucem fuerant, trahere animam tot tormenta tracturam?)*[23]

In view of the evidence from antiquity, it is incomprehensible that
some scholars could have stated recently that crucifixion was 'by
nature a bloodless form of execution'.[24] Statements of this kind,
which go against all the historical evidence, are prompted by the
questionable tendency to draw a dividing line between New
Testament remarks about the bloody sacrificial death of Jesus and
the Pauline *theologia crucis*, which is still held in high esteem. It
should be noted that in Roman times not only was it the rule to
nail the victim by both hands and feet,[25] but that the flogging

[23] Cf. *Dialogue* 3 (*De ira* 1) 2.2: *alium in cruce membra diffindere* ('another to have his limbs stretched upon the cross'), as a climax at the end
of an enumeration of gruesome forms of death; *Dialogue* 5 (*De ira* 3), 3.6:
*eculei et fidiculae et ergastula et cruces et circumdati defossis corporibus ignes
. . . uaria poenarum, lacerationes membrorum* (the torture horse, the cord,
the gaol, the cross and fires encircling living bodies implanted in the
ground and the different kinds of punishments . . . the rending of limbs);
see also Valerius Maximus 6.9 ext. 5, the macabre account of the crucified
Polycrates; Cicero, *in Pisonem* 42: *An ego, si te et Gabinium cruci suffixos
viderem, maiore adficerer laetitia ex corporis vestri laceratione quam adficior ex
famae?* (Or if I were to see you and Gabinius fixed to a cross, should I feel
a greater joy at the laceration of your bodies than I do at that of your
reputations?); Apuleius, *Metamorphoses* 6.32.1: *et patibuli cruciatum, cum
canes et vultures intima protrahent viscera* (the torment of the gibbet, where
dogs and vultures shall drag out her innermost entrails).
[24] E. Brandenburger (see bibliography), 18; cf. id., 'Kreuz', *TBLNT*
II, 1, 1969, 826f.: 'Indeed crucifixion is . . . by its very nature (!) a bloodless affair'. For an answer I can only refer to Josephus, *Antiquitates* 19.94.
Cf. also J. Jeremias, *The Eucharistic Words of Jesus*, London and New
York 1966, 223, who puts forward the same view as Brandenburger, but
from a very different perspective.
[25] J. Blinzler (see bibliography), 361f., 377ff. (ET 250, 264f.); J. W.
Hewitt, 'The Use of Nails in Crucifixion', *HTR* 25, 1932, 29–45; cf. *inter
alia* Philo, *De posteritate Caini* 61; *De somniis* 2.213; Achilles Tatius,

which was a stereotyped part of the punishment would make the blood flow in streams. Binding the victim to the cross only with bonds remained the exception.[26] Presumably Jesus was so weakened by loss of blood that he was unable to carry the beam of the cross to the place of execution; this is also the best explanation of his relatively speedy death. The 'ugly weals on shoulders and chest' in Seneca's macabre description are probably a reference to the consequences of the flogging.

The evidence from Seneca and elsewhere also shows that even where crucifixion is only used as a simile or metaphor, its gruesome reality could very well be before the eyes of the writer. In essentials, this will also be the case with Christian talk of the cross up to the time of the edict of toleration in AD 311. Not only were crosses set up all over the empire, but Christians themselves will either have been executed on the cross or at least will have to have reckoned with crucifixion or similar punishment.[27]

2.37.3; Plutarch, *Moralia* 499D; Pliny the Elder, *Historia Naturalis* 28.41, 46; Ps. Manetho, *Apotelesmatica* 4.199; 1.149; Seneca, *Dialogue* 7 (*De vita beata*) 19.3; Lucan, *De Bello Civili* 6.543–7; Apuleius, *Metamorphoses* 3.17.4; Galen, *De usu partium* 12.11 (Kühn IV, p.45); Artemidorus, *Oneirocriticon* 2.56; Lucian, *Prometheus* 1.2; *Dialogus deorum* 5(1).1 (see above p.11 n.1). In Xenophon of Ephesus, *Ephesiaca* 4.23, binding to the cross is mentioned as an Egyptian custom for reasons connected with the narrative, and therefore as an exception; but cf. Chariton 4.3.6: the hero is not to be wounded at his crucifixion. See now also the discovery of a skeleton of a crucified man in Jerusalem in which the nail is still in the heel bones: N. Haas, 'Anthropological Observations on the Skeletal Remains from Giv'at ha-Mivtar', *IEJ* 20, 1970, (38–59) 49ff. and P. Ducrey, 'Note' (see bibliography).

[26] Fulda (see bibliography) 161ff. saw this as an intensification. Pliny the Elder, *Historia Naturalis* 28.46, and the witch in Lucan, *De Bello Civili* 6.543f., 547, know of the magical use of nails and bonds employed at a crucifixion.

[27] Cf. Justin, *Dialogue with Trypho* 110.4; Tertullian, *Apologeticus* 12.3: *crucibus et stipitibus imponitis Christianos* (You put Christians on crosses and stakes); 50.12; *Ad nationes* 1.3.8; 1.6.6; 1.18.1; *De anima* 1.6; 56.8, etc. Eusebius, *Historia Ecclesiae* 2.25.5; 3.32.6: Simeon son of Clopas of Jerusalem under Trajan according to Hegesippus; 8.8.10. Further instances in P. Garnsey (see bibliography), 127f. n.10.

5

Crucifixion as the Supreme
Roman Penalty

All this also helps us to understand how in his speech against Verres
Cicero could already describe crucifixion as the *summum supplicium*.[1] The continuing legal tradition which can be seen here is
brought to an end by the jurist Julius Paulus about AD 200. In the
Sententiae compiled from his works towards AD 300, the *crux*
is put at the head of the three *summa supplicia*. It is followed, in
descending order, by *crematio* (burning) and *decollatio* (decapitation). In the lists of penalties given in the sources, *damnatio ad
bestias* often takes the place of decapitation as an aggravated penalty.
This shows that *decollatio* was not always included among the
summa supplicia. Similarly, in the Greek East we find during the
early imperial period in a Lycian inscription, in Philo and in an
edict of the Egyptian prefect the threat of the ἀνωτάτω τιμωρία or
κόλασις but without a further mention of crucifixion.[2] At the same

---

[1] *In Verrem* 2.5.168: *Adservasses hominem* (P. Gavius) *custodiis Mamer-
tinorum tuorum, vinctum clausum habuisses, dum Panhormo Raecius veniret*
('You would have kept him with your Messinian friends, chained and
locked up, till Raecius arrived from Panhormus', in order to prove that
the accused was a Roman citizen); *cognosceret hominem, aliquid de summo
supplicio remitteres* ('should he identify the man you would no doubt lessen
the extreme penalty'). 169: Verres' crime is less against Gavius than against
Rome and Italy: *Italia autem alumnum suum servitutis extremo summoque
supplicio adfixum videret* (Italy might see her son as he hung there suffer
the worst extremes of tortures inflicted upon slaves). Cf. Philo, *In Flaccum*
72 (see p.27 n.19); Florus, *Epitome* 1.18=2.2.25: *nec ultimo sive carceris
seu crucis supplicio* (nor by the final punishment of prison or cross), and
Cicero's rhetorical questions, *In Pisonem* 44.
[2] Paulus, *Sententiae* 5.17.2 (Krüger, *Collectio librorum iuris anteiustiniani*
II, p.126); Minucius Felix, *Octavius* 9.4 (above, p.3). For an enumeration
of these supreme penalties see also Sallust, *Bellum Iugurthinum* 14.15;

time the *Sententiae* give catalogues of crimes which are punished by
crucifixion, including desertion to the enemy, the betraying of
secrets, incitement to rebellion, murder, prophecy about the welfare
of rulers (*de salute dominorum*), nocturnal impiety (*sacra impia
nocturna*), magic (*ars magica*), serious cases of the falsification of
wills, etc.[3] Here we can see the further development of capital
punishment during the later empire. Of course because of its harshness, crucifixion was almost always inflicted only on the lower class
(*humiliores*); the upper class (*honestiores*) could reckon with more
'humane' punishment. Here we have a real case of 'class justice'.
The class distinction became particularly significant after the
introduction of universal Roman citizenship by Caracalla; however, it had already been in effect previously, especially among the

---

Seneca the Elder, *Controversiae* exc. 8.4; Lucan, *De Bello Civili* 10.365;
Apuleius, *Metamorphoses* 6.31.1; 32.1; Xenophon, *Ephesiaca* 4.62f.;
Justin, *Dialogue with Trypho* 110.4; cf. pp. 77f. n.26. For the *summa
supplicia* as 'aggravated forms of the death penalty' see P. Garnsey (see
bibliography), 124. Professor Louis Robert has called my attention to an
inscription, a better reading of which has recently been published, which
comes from Myra in Lycia and from the time of Claudius. According to
this the imperial legate, of senatorial rank, who was entrusted with the
administration of the new province, scourged a slave who had accepted
some doubtful documents for the city archives, although he had been
warned against this, and threatened that if he offended again he would be
punished most severely: 'and with a demonstration of this kind (i.e. the
flogging), I made it clear to him that if he offended against the administration again . . . I would compel the rest of the city slaves to forget their
earlier negligence not only with blows but with the supreme penalty
against him (οὐ πληγαῖς μόνον, ἀλλὰ καὶ τῆι ἀ[νω]τάτωι κολάσει αὐτοῦ); M. Wörrle,
'Zwei neue griechische Inschriften aus Myra zur Verwaltung Lykiens in
der Kaiserzeit', in: *Myra*, Istanbuler Forschungen 30, 1975, (254–300)
256 lines 14–19. For the ἀνωτάτω τιμωρία see op. cit., 281 n.681: Philo, *In
Flaccum* 126; L. Mitteis/U. Wilcken, *Grundzüge und Chrestomathie der
Papyruskunde*, Berlin 1912, I, 2, no.439 = E. M. Smallwood, *Documents
Illustrating the Principates of Gaius, Claudius and Nero*, Cambridge 1967,
no.381: edict of the prefect of Egypt of 29.4.42 AD against soldiers who
oppressed the populace: κατὰ τούτου τῇ ἀνωτάτω χρήσομαι τειμωρίᾳ. In the
Myra inscription the reading quoted above is to be preferred to an earlier
one which presupposes a reference to crucifixion here.

[3] Paulus, *Sententiae* 5.19.2; 21.4; 23.2, 16; 25.1; 30b.1. See also U.
Brasiello, *La repressione penale in diritto romano*, Naples 1937, 248ff.; P.
Garnsey, op. cit., 122–31; A. Zestermann (see bibliography), 25f.

foreigners (*peregrini*).[4] The important thing here is that *crux, bestiae, ignis* were regarded as aggravated punishments and not as mere variables.[5] In terms of severity, crucifixion can only be compared with the 'popular entertainment' of throwing victims to the wild beasts (*bestiis obici*); however, this was not listed among the *summa supplicia* as 'the regular forms of execution . . ., because whether or not it was carried out depended on the chance circumstance that such a popular festival had been arranged . . .'.[6] By comparison crucifixion was a much more common punishment; it could be carried out almost anywhere, whereas *bestiis obici* required a city arena and the necessary facilities. Of course, crucifixion too could serve as a 'popular entertainment'; according to Philo (*In Flaccum* 72.84f.) this was the case with the torture and subsequent crucifixion of Jews in Alexandria by the prefect Flaccus. It could also happen in mime as in the representation of the execution of the robber chief Laureolus, at which a great deal of artificial blood flowed; both these instances date from the time of Caligula (AD 37–41).[7] Juvenal wished that the actor Lentulus were on a real cross in this fearsome piece; it was an abomination to the satirist that the actor, as a member of the upper class, should debase himself by such a performance (8.187f.). Under Domitian a real criminal seems to have played the part of the robber chief: we read how he was hung on a cross and torn to pieces by a Scottish bear (Martial, *Liber Spectaculorum* 7):

Laureolus, hanging on no unreal cross, gave up his vitals defenceless

[4] For the aggravation of capital punishment see E. Levy, 'Die römische Kapitalstrafe', in *Gesammelte Schriften* II, 1963, 325–78, esp. 353ff.; cf. id., 'Gesetz und Richter im kaiserlichen Strafrecht, Erster Teil', ibid., (433–508) 487f. Cf. also G. Cardascia, 'L'apparition dans le droit des classes d'"honestiores" et d'"humiliores"', *RHDF* 58, 1950, 305–36, 461–85; for penal law see 319ff.

[5] Thus U. Brasiello, op. cit., 246ff., 26off.; endorsed by G. Cardascia, op. cit., 321 n.7. Brasiello (257) defines the *summum supplicium* as 'massima tortura' or 'pene con cui si tormenta nel modo più doloroso il condannato', but see P. Garnsey (see bibliography), 122f.

[6] T. Mommsen (see bibliography), 927.

[7] Josephus, *Antiquitates* 19.94; cf. Suetonius, *Caligula* 57.4; Tertullian, *Adversus Valentinianos* 14.4, cf. J. G. Griffith, *Mnemosyne* 15, 1962, 256ff. For torture, crucifixion and burning in the arena see also Seneca, *Epistulae morales* 14.5; cf. p. 27 n. 18 above.

to a Caledonian bear. His mangled limbs lived, though the parts
dripped blood and in all his body was nowhere a body's shape.

(nuda Caledonio sic viscera praebuit urso
non falsa pendens in cruce Laureolus
vivebant laceri membris stillantibus artus
inque omni nusquam corpore corpus erat.)

A similarly cruel form of execution was devised for the slave girl
Blandina during the persecution of Christians in Lyons.[8] Nero is
said to have covered himself with the hide of a wild animal and to
have tormented the victims hanging on crosses (Dio Cassius
63.13.2). While Martial depicts with satisfaction (or even with an
attack of bad conscience) the crimes which may have been committed by those hanging on the cross, Varro had long since denounced
the barbarism of such a form of punishment:[9]

Are we barbarians because we fasten the innocent to the cross, and
are you not barbarians because you throw the guilty to the wild
beasts?

(nos barbari quod innocentes in gabalum suffigimus homines; uos non
barbari quod noxios obicitis bestiis?)

People were only too well aware of the particular cruelty of this
form of punishment[10] – at one point (*In Verrem* II.5.162) Cicero

[8] Eusebius, *Historia Ecclesiae* 5.1.41: ἐπὶ ξύλου κρεμασθεῖσα προύκειτο βορὰ
τῶν . . . θηρίων · ἢ καὶ διὰ τοῦ βλέπεσθαι σταυροῦ σχήματι κρεμαμένη . . . (suspended on a stake, she was exposed as food to wild beasts. To look at her, as
she hung cross-wise . . .).

[9] Menippus, fr. 24 (p.96, J.-P. Cèbe, *Varron, Satires Ménippées*, Rome
1972). Like *crux* (above, p.9 n.21), *gabalus* is also a taunt: *Anthologia
Latina* 801.2M = *Scriptores Historiae Augustae* 15 (Iulius Capitolinus,
Macrinus) 11.6.

[10] Apuleius, *Metamorphoses* 1.15.4: *sed saevitia cruci me reservasse*
(cruelly kept me for the cross); cf. Seneca, *Epistulae morales* 14.5: *et quic-
quid aliud praeter haec commenta saeuitia est* (and all the other contrivances
devised by cruelty). *Scriptores Historiae Augustae* 6 (Vulcacius Gallicanus,
Avidius Cassius) 4.1f.: *multa extant crudelitatis potius quam severitatis eius
indicia, nam primum milites . . . in illis ipsis locis, in quibus peccaverant, in
crucem sustulit* (there are many indications of savagery rather than strict-
ness, for in the first place . . . he crucified the soldiers in the spot where they
had committed their crimes). Cf. *Scriptores Historiae Augustae* 12 (Iulius
Capitolinus, *Clodius Albinus*) 11.6; 19 (Iulius Capitolinus, *Maximini*)
8.5ff.: *tam crudelis fuit . . . alios in crucem sublatos* (so cruel that he hung
men on the cross); Cicero, *Philippicae* 13.21: *hostis taeterrimus omnibus*

succinctly calls it 'that plague' (*istam pestem*); however, it is almost impossible to find a protest against its use in principle. Cicero twice protested against the crucifixion of Roman citizens, once acting for the prosecution and once for the defence, but he was concerned with quite specific individual instances. He may have accused Verres of having crucified a Roman citizen, P. Gavius, but at the same time he objected that Verres had handed back to their masters a large number of slaves who were suspected of conspiracy to rebellion *instead of* crucifying them.[11] And while the Stoic Seneca ascribes the abomination of crucifixion and other tortures to the worst of all passions, anger, he takes it for granted that criminals have to be executed in this way.[12] We can see here, in the educated world of antiquity, a schizophrenia similar to that which we encounter in connection with the use of the death penalty in large areas of modern society.

It is certainly the case that the Roman world was largely unanimous that crucifixion was a horrific, disgusting business. There is therefore hardly any mention of it in inscriptions; the only evidence from Latin epigraphy which I can find is the pious wish, 'May you be nailed to the cross' (*in cruce figarus = figaris*).[13] As far

---

bonis cruces ac tormenta minitatur (a most hideous enemy is threatening all good men with crucifixion and torture). Justin, *Epitome* 22.7.8: the crucifixion of Bomilcar demonstrates the *crudelitas* of the Carthaginians; Diodorus Siculus 26.23.1: the crucifixion of the members of a Numidian tribe by the Carthaginians is described as ὠμότης.

[11] *In Verrem* II.5.9–13: *hos ad supplicium iam more maiorum traditos ex media morte eripere ac liberare ausus es, ut, quam damnatis crucem servis fixeras, hanc indemnatis videlicet civibus Romanis reservares?* (the quotation is from 12). (When they were already delivered over, in the manner prescribed by tradition, to suffer execution, did you dare to save them, to pluck them from the very jaws of death, intending no doubt that the gallows you set up for the slaves who had been convicted should be kept for Roman citizens who had not?)

[12] Seneca, *Dialogue* 5 (*De ira 3*) 3.6; but cf. *De clementia* 1.23: piety (here the love of parents) was at its lowest ebb after the sack (the ancient punishment for parricide or matricide) became a more frequent sight than the cross (*pessimo loco pietas fuit postquam saepius culleos quam cruces*). Even when the state is to be praised, in which men are rarely punished (*in qua . . . raro homines puniuntur*), one cannot completely avoid cruel punishments. See also below, p. 60.

[13] *CIL IV*, 2082, from Pompeii (strada di Olconio).

as I can tell, the words *crux* or *patibulum* do not appear in Caesar at all, not because he did not use crucifixion as a punishment (for example, in Spain he had three slaves who had been sent out as spies crucified without further ado, *De Bello Hispaniensi* 20.5; cf. *De Bello Gallico* 7.4), but because he did not want to write about that kind of thing. The same may be true of Lucretius, Virgil,[14] Statius, the younger Pliny (who as governor in Bithynia must certainly have condemned offenders to the cross) or Aulus Gellius. Horace talks of crucifixion only in his *Satires* and *Epistles*; Tacitus, too, is restrained in talking about crucifixions, at least in the *Annals*, on the whole mentioning them only as atrocities inflicted by the Germani or the Britanni on Romans. Others, like Valerius Maximus, the older and younger Senecas, and still more, romance writers like Petronius and Apuleius, had fewer hesitations here. The situation is very similar with Greek writers (see pp. 77ff. below). That means, however, that the relative scarcity of references to crucifixions in antiquity, and their fortuitousness, are less a historical problem than an aesthetic one, connected with the sociology of literature. Crucifixion was widespread and frequent, above all in Roman times, but the cultured literary world wanted to have nothing to do with it, and as a rule kept quiet about it.

[14] The only evidence I have been able to find in Virgil is the uncertain Priapean poem *Catalepton* 2a.18, where *crux* and cudgel are menacing thieves (see pp. 66f. n. 2 below).

6

Crucifixion and Roman Citizens

It is usually assumed that there was no question of Roman citizens being executed on the cross, and that the punishment was limited to slaves and *peregrini*. This is only partly correct. There was an archaic, ancient Roman punishment, hanging on the 'barren tree' (*arbor infelix*), which could be imposed even on Romans in cases of serious crime and high treason (*perduellio*). Originally this was probably a way of sacrificing the criminal to the gods of the underworld. According to an old Roman law 'of Romulus' the traitor died 'as a sacrifice for the Zeus of the underworld' (ὡς θῦμα τοῦ κατα-χθονίου Διός, Dionysius of Halicarnassus, *Antiquitates Romanae* 2.10.3). From the third or second century BC this punishment was evidently interpreted as crucifixion.[1] However, with very few exceptions it was hardly ever imposed. When Scipio the Elder crucified deserters who were Roman citizens and had been handed over by the Carthaginians at the end of the Second Punic War, he did so because by their act of high treason they had forfeited the protection

[1] Cf. already T. Mommsen (see bibliography), 919, though in fact he makes too little distinction between the various forms of execution. K. Latte (see bibliography), 1614, does not explain the interpretation of the *arbor infelix* procedure by Cicero as crucifixion. Ovid, *Amores* 1.12, Seneca, *Epistulae morales* 10.1 (*infelix lignum = crux*) and Minucius Felix, *Octavius* 24.7 (*infelix stipes = crux*) are also allusions to the *arbor infelix*. See also C. D. Peddinghaus (see bibliography), 21 and n.139, and C. Brecht, *perduellio*, PW XIX 1, 624f. Servius, *Scholion in Georgica* 1. 501 (Thilo/Hagen III, p.215), says that betrayal of the secret name of the divinity of Rome was punished by crucifixion. The 'hanging up for Ceres' (*suspensumque Cereri necari iubebant*, Pliny the Elder, *Historia Naturalis* 18.3.12) threatened in the Twelve Tables is probably connected with the *arbori infelici suspendere*; T. Mommsen, op. cit., 631f. n.8, sees it as crucifixion, as do P. Garnsey (see bibliography), 128 n.10, and L. Gernet (see bibliography), 292; K. Latte, op. cit., 1614, differs.

of citizenship.[2] Verres had P. Gavius, who has already been mentioned, crucified in Messina with his gaze towards the mother
country because of the nature of the charge made against him, that
he was a spy of the rebellious slaves of Spartacus who were fighting in
Italy.[3] This legal practice was maintained until the time of the late
empire. The jurist Julius Paulus gives crucifixion (*furca* = gallows,
the word which replaced the 'holy' word cross in legal literature after
Constantine) or burning as the punishment for deserters (*transfugae
ad hostes*) and those who betray secrets (*Digest* 48.19.38.1), and
Modestinus, who is a little later (49.16.3.10) gives torture and
bestiae, or the cross.[4] In having Jews who were Roman knights
(ἄνδρας ἱππικοῦ τάγματος) flogged and crucified in Jerusalem in the critical weeks immediately before the outbreak of the
Jewish War in AD 66, the Roman procurator Gessius Florus, like
Verres, will have been punishing acts of high treason (Josephus,
BJ 2.308). Galba, who had studied the law, when governor in
Spain condemned to crucifixion a guardian who had poisoned his
ward for the sake of the legacy; when the condemned man protested that he was a Roman citizen, Galba had him fastened to a
particularly high cross which was painted white (Suetonius, *Galba*
9.2).[5] Of course, Suetonius concludes from this that Galba was

[2] Livy 30.43.13; cf. Valerius Maximus 2.7.12 (see pp.29f. above). The
war had immeasurably intensified the cruelty employed to maintain
military discipline. One example is the action of Pleminius against two
mutinous officers (204 BC), Diodorus Siculus 27.4.4 and Livy 29.9.10;
29.18.14: *uerberatos seruilibus omnibus suppliciis cruciando occidit, mortuos
deinde prohibuit sepeliri* (having flogged them, he executed them by
torturing them with all the torments applied to slaves (p.51 n.1 below)
and then forbade that their bodies should be buried).

[3] Cicero, *In Verrem* 2.5.158ff., 161: *eum speculandi causa in Siciliam a
ducibus fugitivorum esse missum* (sent to Sicily by the leaders of the fugitive
army for spying).

[4] Cf. A. Müller, *Neue Jahrbücher für das klassische Altertum* 17, 1906,
554f.

[5] For the height of the cross as an expression of contempt see Esther
5.14; Artemidorus, *Oneirocriticon*, see below p.77 n.24. Pseudo-Manetho,
Apotelesmatica 1.148; 5.219; *Anthologia Graeca* 11.192 (Beckby III, p.
640), of Lucillius; Justin, *Epitome* 18.7.15: Malchus ordered that his son
Cathalus in Carthage *cum ornatu suo in altissimam crucem in conspectu urbis
suffigi* (with his accoutrements should be fastened to a very high cross in the
sight of the city); 22.7.9: Bomilcar *de summa cruce*; Sallust, *Historiae* fr.

excessive in his punishment of criminals (*in coercendis delictis . . . immodicus*). According to the *Historia Augusta*, which is, however, very unreliable historically, various emperors used crucifixion to maintain military discipline in the army, but the use of the *servile supplicium* (see pp. 51ff. below) was denounced as being especially cruel. Celsus, said to be a usurper under Gallienus, who only ruled for seven days, was crucified after his death *in imagine*, to the delight of the people, while his body was devoured by dogs. By the public display of his corpse on a gibbet the dead usurper was exposed to general abuse and mockery.[6]

There is one classic case in which the death penalty was even asked for over a member of the Roman nobility and a senator, with a reference to the old custom of hanging those guilty of high treason on the *arbor infelix*: this was the trial of C. Rabirius in 63 BC, which was instituted by Caesar. The prosecution was made by the tribune T. Labienus, a committed supporter of Caesar, and the defence was led in a masterly way by Cicero. The accused was charged with the murder of a tribune of the people which had taken place thirty-seven years earlier. When Cicero made his plea to the assembly of the people, the danger of crucifixion had already been averted, and

---

3.9 (Maurenbrecher II, p. 113): (in the case of the pirates) *In quis notissimus quisque aut malo dependens verberabatur aut immutilato corpore improbe patibulo eminens affigebatur* (the most notorious were either hung from the mast and flogged or fastened high up on a gibbet without being tortured first). The usual mutilation was not inflicted, since the victim was to suffer a long time. The manuscripts have *improbi*; Kritzius (Sallust, *Opera* III, 1853, 344f.) reads *improbo* with Corte and refers to Plutarch, *Pompey* 24.

[6] *Scriptores Historiae Augustae* 24 (Trebellius Pollio, *Tyranni triginta* 29.4): *imago in crucem sublata persultante vulgo, quasi patibulo ipse Celsus videretur adfixus* (his image was set up on a cross, while the mob pranced around as though they were looking at Celsus himself nailed to a gibbet). The horror story is probably invented, but it does go back to historical examples, see Hohl, *PW* 2.R.VII, 1, 130. In *Scriptores Historiae Augustae* 19 (Iulius Capitolinus, *Maximini* 16.6), the senate acclaims: *inimicus senatus in crucem tollatur . . . inimici senatus vivi exurantur* (let the foe of the senate be crucified . . . let the foes of the senate be burnt alive). According to Herodian 3.8.1 and Dio Cassius (Xiphilin, *Epitome*) 75.7.3, Septimius Severus had the head of his adversary Albinus publicly impaled in Rome (τὴν δὲ κεφαλὴν ἐς τὴν ˊΡώμην πέμψας ἀνεσταύρωσεν), cf. below p. 60.

the only risk was exile and the confiscation of property. Nevertheless, in the first section of his speech (*Pro Rabirio* 9–17) Cicero once
again described in detail, in a rhetorical *tour de force*, the penalty
with which Rabirius had been threatened. By referring to it he
sought to show that the prosecutor, far from being a friend of the
people (*popularis*), would be quite the opposite, if he wanted to
restore the barbarous customs and the tyranny of the period of the
monarchy. Since H.-W. Kuhn has given a wrong interpretation of
the decisive sentence in this speech, which is often quoted, and in
his recent investigation has drawn misleading consequences from it,
I must go into the matter in more detail.[7] I shall therefore quote the
whole paragraph which includes the sentence in question:

*Misera est ignominia iudiciorum publicorum, misera multatio bonorum,
miserum exsilium; sed tamen in omni calamitate retinetur aliquod
vestigium libertatis. Mors denique si proponitur, in libertate moriamur,*
carnifex vero et obductio capitis et nomen ipsum crucis absit non
modo a corpore civium Romanorum sed etiam a cogitatione, oculis,
auribus. *Harum enim omnium rerum non solum eventus atque perpessio
sed etiam condicio, exspectatio, mentio ipsa denique indigna cive Romano
atque homine libero est* (ch. 16).

(How grievous a thing it is to be disgraced by a public court; how
grievous to suffer a fine, how grievous to suffer banishment; and yet
in the midst of any such disaster we retain some degree of liberty.
Even if we are threatened with death, we may die free men. *But the
executioner, the veiling of the head and the very word 'cross' should be
far removed not only from the person of a Roman citizen but from his
thoughts, his eyes and his ears.* For it is not only the actual occurrence
of these things or the endurance of them, but liability to them, the
expectation, indeed the very mention of them, that is unworthy of a
Roman citizen and a free man.)

As in the second oration against Verres, where the crucifixion of
a Roman citizen is put at the end as a rhetorical climax, with
these sentences the first main part of the speech for the defence

[7] H.-W. Kuhn (see bibliography), 8: 'This saying of Cicero which is so
favoured by theologians (albeit in an abbreviated form) is hardly suitable
for giving a characteristic contemporary example of the understanding of
crucifixion common at the time.' Kuhn himself has 'abbreviated' the
Cicero text very considerably, not to say falsified it, and he has not
verified his conclusions by the ancient sources.

reaches its peak.⁸ The mere fact that C. Rabirius is being tried publicly is an evil, not to mention that he is threatened with the confiscation of his property and banishment. But even in the case of the death penalty against a Roman citizen, the victim is left some freedom if he is allowed to choose for himself the way in which he is to die. This was certainly not the case in the inflicting of the archaic, barbarous punishment of the *arbori infelici suspendere*, which was worthy of a Tarquinius Superbus (*Tarquini, superbissimi atque crudelissimi regis*).⁹ He devised those songs of the torture chamber (*ista . . . cruciatus carmina*), which Labienus, 'the people's friend', had dug up again (ch. 13). Here Cicero is referring to the ancient formula of execution, the most important part of which he quotes himself:

*I, lictor, conliga manus, caput obnubito, arbori infelici suspendito.*¹⁰

⁸ For Cicero's speech and the trial see the introduction to the German translation by M. Fuhrmann, *Marcus Tullius Cicero, Sämtliche Reden* II, 1970, 197ff.; J. van Ooteghem, 'Pour une lecture candide du *Pro C. Rabirio*', *Études classiques* 32, 1964, 234–46; C. Brecht, op. cit. (p. 39 n. 1), 634f.; K. Büchner, 'M. Tullius Cicero', *PW* 2. R. VII 1, 870ff. The trial took place shortly before Cicero's struggle with Catiline over the consulate and the Catiline conspiracy. The situation in Rome was very tense.

⁹ Pliny the Elder, *Historia Naturalis* 36.107: Tarquinius Superbus (not Priscus) had all suicides hung on the cross: *omnium ita defunctorum corpora figeret cruci spectanda civibus simul et feris volucribusque laceranda* (fastened the bodies of all who had died in this way to the cross to be seen by the citizens and to be torn by wild beasts and birds). The shamefulness of crucifixion – even if only of a corpse – becomes particularly clear in this quotation. Cf. also Livy 1.49; Lydus, *De mensibus* 29 (Wünsch, p. 87).

¹⁰ At more length in the account of the trial of the Horatii in Livy 1.26.6f.; cf. 11. According to him the old formula ran: *duumviri perduellionem iudicent; si a duumviris provocarit, provocatione certato; si vincent, caput obnubito; infelici arbori reste suspendito; verberato vel intra pomerium vel extra pomerium* (let the duumvirs pronounce him guilty of treason; if he shall appeal from the duumvirs, let the appeal be heard; if they win, let the lictor veil his head, let him bind him with rope to a barren tree, let him scourge him either inside or outside the *pomerium*). The proceedings were introduced by the command of one of the *duumviri*: *Publi Horati, tibi perduellionem iudico . . . i, lictor, colliga manus*. Livy does not speak of the *crux*: (10) *eum sub furca vinctum inter verbera et cruciatus videre potestis?* but knows of the horrific nature of the punishment: (11) *a tanta foeditate supplicii*; i.e. here the victim is flogged to death; see M. Fuhrmann, 'Verbera', *PW* Suppl. IX, (1589–97) 1591.

(Lictor, go bind his hands, veil his head, hang him on the tree of shame!)

The three terms quoted at the climax of the speech are not, as Kuhn thinks, any three despised forms of execution, including '*inter alia*' the cross, 'but also the worthless covering of the head'.[11] What we have here is a description of the terrible process of the *arbori infelici suspendere*, i.e. crucifixion, following the legal practice of the time: the executioner ties the criminal's hands, covers his head and hangs him on the cross. In any case, Cicero makes a clear distinction between *carnifex, obductio capitis* and the real punishment, the *crux*; only the very name (*nomen ipsum*) of the latter is intolerable for a Roman citizen. The translation chosen by Kuhn, 'the very word cross',[12] illustrates this accentuation clearly. Kuhn's view that what we have here is merely 'the aesthetic judgment of a man with the rank of an *eques*, who stood well apart from the greater mass of the people, even from Roman citizens', represents a complete disregard of historical reality. Cicero was not speaking before the senate, but before the *consilium plebis*,[13] and the whole of his speech for the defence was formulated with a view to its effect on the people. And he was successful. C. Rabirius was acquitted. The passage which immediately follows this one shows that Cicero was skilfully playing on the fears of the common man. On being freed (*manumissio*), even Roman slaves are liberated by the touch of the praetor's staff 'from the fear of all these torments'. There follows an argument *a minori ad maius*: 'Are neither acts (of history), age nor your honours (of citizenship) to protect a man from flogging, from the executioner's hook and finally from the terror of the cross (*a crucis denique terrore*)?'[14] Thus, like the documentation from the second oration against Verres, Cicero's speech *Pro Rabirio* must be seen as important ancient evidence for the horror and disgust felt at crucifixion. In no way can I Corinthians 1.26, 'not many

[11] H.-W. Kuhn, loc. cit.

[12] Ibid., cf. the very similar translation by M. Fuhrmann, op. cit. (n. 91), 209: 'and the mere designation "cross"'.

[13] K. Büchner, op. cit. (p. 43 n. 8 above), 871; this already follows from the address *Quirites*.

[14] *Pro Rabirio* 16; cf. Livy 22.13.9: *et ad reliquorum terrorem in cruce sublato*.

were powerful, not many were of noble birth . . .', a passage which has been so misused, be applied in the opposite sense. Even if the Christians in Corinth, a Roman colony founded by freedmen, were predominantly simple citizens (but cf. Rom. 16.23: Erastus, the city treasurer), they must have found crucifixion quite as horrific a punishment as did the simple citizens of Roman cities, freedmen and slaves at the time of the Civil War.

7

Crucifixion as a Penalty for Rebellious Foreigners, Violent Criminals and Robbers

Crucifixion was already, as in Rome, the punishment for serious crimes against the state and for high treason among the Persians, to some degree in Greece and above all among the Carthaginians. That is, it was a religious-political punishment, with the emphasis falling on the political side; however, the two aspects cannot yet be separated in the ancient world. It was a source of wonder to the Romans that the Carthaginians (unlike the Romans themselves) tended to crucify especially generals and admirals who had either been defeated or who proved too wilful.[1] Crucifixion was also a means of waging war and securing peace, of wearing down rebellious cities under siege, of breaking the will of conquered peoples[2] and of bringing mutinous troops or unruly provinces under control. In contrast to the Carthaginians, the Romans as a rule spared their own nobility and Roman citizens, but otherwise their practice was the same. And we must ask whether at the main crises of the Civil War the threat of crucifixion did not sometimes become a reality.[3]

[1] Polybius 1.11.5; 1.24.6; 1.74.9 etc.; Livy 38.48.12: *ubi in crucem tolli imperatores dicuntur* (where generals are said to be crucified); cf. Valerius Maximus 2.7 ext. 1; Justin, *Epitome* 18.7.15; Livy 28.37.2.

[2] Crucifixions at the sacking or siege of cities: see p. 22 n.1: Babylon; pp. 69f.: Barca in Cyrenaica; p. 73: Tyre (by Alexander); pp. 25f. n. 17: Jerusalem (by Titus and Varus). The fortress of Machaerus was forced into surrender in exchange for safe conduct by the threat of crucifying a prisoner, p. 8.

[3] See Cicero, *Philippicae* 13.21 against Marcus Antonius: *hostis taeterrimus omnibus bonis cruces ac tormenta minitatur* (a most hideous enemy is threatening all good men with crucifixion and torture); Lucan, *De Bello Civili* 7.303f.: Caesar's speech before Pharsalus:

Josephus gives us numerous instances from Judaea (see above, p. 26 n. 17) that it was used excessively to 'pacify' rebellious provincials; the same thing may also have happened in other unruly provinces, though ancient historians tended to pass over such 'trifling matters' in silence.[4] Strabo (3.4.18 = C 165) reports that the wild, freedom-loving Cantabrians in northern Spain continued to sing their songs of victory even when they were nailed to the cross.[5] According to Roman law, rebellious subjects were not 'enemies' (*hostes*), but common 'bandits' (*latrones*, or, as Josephus tends to call the Jewish rebels after the capture of Jerusalem,

---

Aut merces hodie bellorum aut poena parata.
Caesareas spectate cruces, spectate catenas
Et caput hoc positum rostris effusaque membra.

(Today either the reward or the penalty of war is before us. Picture to yourself the crosses and the chains in store for Caesar, my head stuck upon the rostrum and my bones unburied.)

See also Dio Cassius 30–35, fr. 109.4; Valerius Maximus 9.2.3 and Appian, *Bella Civilia* 4.20, for the impalement of the corpses of opponents in the Civil War. Cf. A. W. Lintott (see bibliography), 35ff.

[4] Seneca, *Dialogue* 4 (*De ira* 2) 5.5, gives as an example the fact that in the province of Asia (AD 11/12) the proconsul Volesus had three hundred men executed by the axe in one day, and in full awareness of his *imperium* exclaimed (in Greek): *O rem regiam*. The only other thing that we know about him is that he was later put on trial by the senate for atrocities; we only hear of what he did from Seneca, quite by chance. What would we know about the crucifixions in Palestine without Josephus? Tacitus, *Histories* 5.8–13, does not say a word about them. People tended to be as silent in those days about their own atrocities as dictators and their willing journalists are now.

[5] Cf. Josephus, *BJ* 3.321, about a Jew who was crucified before Jotapata and laughed at the death on the cross devised by his torturers, and 2.153 (the Essenes) and 7.418 (the Sicarii in Egypt); Seneca, *Dialogue* 7 (*De vita beata*) 19.3: . . . *nisi quidam ex patibulo suos spectatores conspuerent* (did not some of them spit upon spectators from their own crosses); Silius Italicus, *Punica* 1. 179ff., the description of a Spanish slave who wanted to be crucified with his master:

> *superat ridetque dolores,*
> *spectanti similis, fessosque labore ministros*
> *increpitat dominique crucem clamore reposcit.*

(He was the master still and despised the suffering; like a mere onlooker he blamed the torturer's assistants for flagging in their task and loudly demanded to be crucified like his master.)

ληστaί). For them the characteristic death penalty was either
crucifixion or being thrown to the wild beasts (*bestiis obici*).[6] We
find evidence for this not so much among historians and orators as
in the romance (then, as now, people lived on a diet of crime, sex
and religion), the popular fable and in astrological and late Roman
legal sources. An essential part of the action of the *Novelle* about
the matron of Ephesus inserted into Petronius' *Satyricon* is the
crucifixion of a group of robbers who are watched over by a soldier
so that relatives do not come and steal the bodies:

> When the governor of the province ordered the robbers to be
> fastened to crosses ...
>
> (*cum interim imperator provinciae latrones iussit crucibus affigi*, 111.5).[7]

The *Metamorphoses* of Apuleius and in the same way the Greek
romances treat the profitable theme of 'robbers and crucifixion'
in great detail.[8] In the view of various Roman jurists, notorious
robbers (*famosi latrones*) should be crucified if possible at the scene
of their misdeeds (*Digest* 48.19.28.15).[9] In the astrological literature

---

[6] M. Hengel, *Die Zeloten*, 31ff.; cf. also R. MacMullen, *Enemies of the
Roman Order*, Cambridge, Mass. 1966, 192ff., 255ff., 350ff. According to
Dio Cassius 62.11.3f., Paulinus said before the battle against the British
leader Boudicca that the Romans were not fighting against enemies of
equal status, but against their slaves. The Romans also looked upon Syrians
and Jews in a similar way, see M. Hengel, *Juden, Griechen und Barbaren*,
SBS 76, 1976, 78f.

[7] Cf. Phaedrus, *Fabulae Aesopi, Appendix Perottina* 15 (Guaglianone,
pp. 101ff.).

[8] The robber theme runs right through Apuleius' romance. The crucifixion theme appears in 1.14.2; 1.15.4; 3.17.4; 4.10.4; 'fatally fettering
him to the tree of torment' (see the translation by R. Helm); 6.31.2;
6.32.1; 10.12.3; cf. also 8.22.4f. 3.9.1f. is typical: *Nec mora, cum ritu
Graeciensi ignis et rota, cum omne flagrorum genus inferuntur. Augetur
oppido, immo duplicatur mihi maestitia, quod integro saltim mori non licuerit.
Sed anus illa ... : 'Prius,' inquit, 'optimi cives, quam latronem istum, misero-
rum pignorum meorum peremptorem cruci adfigatis ...'* (And there was no
long delay, for according to the custom of Greece, the fire, the wheel and
many other torments were brought in; then straightway my sadness increased, or rather was duplicated, because I would not be allowed to die
with whole members. But the old woman said, 'Before you fasten this
thief who has destroyed my wretched children to the cross ...').

[9] Cf. also *Collectio legum Mosaicarum et Romanarum* 1.6 (T. Mommsen,
Collectio librorum iuris anteiustiniani III, p. 138), and M. Hengel, *Die
Zeloten*, 33f.

and the ancient treatises on dreams it almost goes without saying that the just fate of the robber is to die on the cross.[10] The imposition of the penalty of crucifixion upon robbers and rebels in the provinces was under the free jurisdiction of the local governor, based on his *imperium* and the right of *coercitio* to maintain peace and order.[11] Roman provincial administration had no separation between the authority of the army and the police and legal power. In the imperial provinces the governors were also in command of troops; carrying out sentences on rebels and men of violence had a marked military character. The 'robbers' or 'pirates' also, of course, took revenge by sometimes inflicting crucifixion on their victims.[12] As a rule the rural population were grateful when a governor took a hard line against the plague of robbers, which was widespread and from which they suffered severely. And since, under the *Pax Romana* of the first century, times were peaceful, law was relatively secure and the administration functioned well,[13] crucifixion was an

[10] Firmicus Maternus, *Mathesis* 8.22.3, on those born in the seventh segment of Cancer: *quodsi Lunam et horoscopum Mars radiatione aliqua aspexerit, latrocinantes crudeli feritate grassantur. Sed hi aut in crucem tolluntur, aut publica animadversione peribunt* (But if the moon and Mars are both in aspect to the ascendant, robbers act with cruel ferocity. But these will either be crucified or will perish by some public punishment.) Cf. *Catalogus Codicum Astrologorum Graecorum* VIII, 1, 1929, p. 176 lines 13–17. For Pseudo-Manetho see above, p. 9; for Artemidorus' treatise on dreams see pp. 8f. above and 77 below.

[11] For the crucifixion of 'highwaymen' and 'robbers' see e.g. also Chariton 3.4.18; Aesop, *Fabulae* 157, lines 6f. (Hausrath I, p. 184); Phaedrus, *Fabulae Aesopi* 3.5.10; pirates (see pp. 79f.): Hyginus, *Fabulae* 194. Most instances are provided by Josephus, see above pp. 25f., and *Antiquitates* 20.102. According to a version of the romance of Alexander, which was written at the end of the third century AD, Darius threatened Alexander in a letter that he would have him crucified like a common robber chief or as a 'renegade': *Vita Alexandri* cod. L 1.36.5 (van Thiel, p. 54).

[12] Sallust, *Historiae* fr. 3.9 (see p. 40 n. 5 above); Ps. Quintilian, *Declamationes* 5.16 (Lehnert, p. 103); Seneca the Elder, *Controversiae* 7.4.5; Apuleius, *Metamorphoses* 6.31f.; Xenophon, *Ephesiaca* 4.6.2.

[13] There is a background in reality to the well-known homage paid by the sailors of Alexandria to Augustus, Suetonius, *Augustus* 98.2: *per illum se vivere, per illum navigare, libertate atque fortunis per illum frui* ('by him they lived, by him they sailed and by him they enjoyed liberty and good fortune'). The Mediterranean was now free of pirates. In a similar way Augustus purged Italy of highwaymen: Appian, *Bella Civilia* 5.132.

instrument to protect the populace against dangerous criminals and violent men, and accordingly brought contempt on those who suffered it. Because the robbers often drew their recruits from runaway slaves, abhorrence of the criminal was often combined here with disgust at the punishment meted out to slaves. Semi-barbarian and more disturbed areas were an exception here, and refractory and unsettled Judaea was a special case. In the eyes of the average Roman citizen and even of the diaspora Jews the 'dangers from robbers' (κίνδυνοι λῃστῶν II Corinthians 11.26) had a positive connection with the need for a magistrate to wield the sword, who is mentioned in Romans 13.4. The sight of crucified robbers served as a deterrent and at the same time exacted some satisfaction for the victim:

> *ut et conspectu deterreantur alii ab isdem facinoribus et solacio sit cognatis et adfinibus interemptorum eodem loco poena reddita, in quo latrones homicidia fecissent (Digest* 48.19.28.15).

> (That the sight may deter others from such crimes and be a comfort to the relatives and neighbours of those whom they have killed, the penalty is to be exacted in the place where the robbers did their murders.)

Quintilian could therefore praise the crucifixion of criminals as a good work: in his view the crosses ought to be set up on the busiest roads.[14]

---

[14] *Declamationes* 274 (Ritter, p. 124): *quotiens noxios crucifigimus celeberrimae eliguntur viae, ubi plurimi intueri, plurimi commoveri hoc metu possint. omnis enim poena non tam ad (vin)dictam pertinet, quam ad exemplum.* (Whenever we crucify the guilty, the most crowded roads are chosen, where the most people can see and be moved by this fear. For penalties relate not so much to retribution as to their exemplary effect.) For crucifixion at the scene of the crime see also Chariton 3.4.18; Justin, *Epitome* 22.7.8; cf. Alexander Severus, below p. 60.

8

The 'Slaves' Punishment'

In most Roman writers crucifixion appears as the typical punishment for slaves. One might almost say that this was a Roman peculiarity, in contrast to what we know about crucifixion among the Persians, Carthaginians and other peoples. In his second speech against Verres Cicero speaks with rhetorical exuberance of the supreme and ultimate penalty for slaves (*servitutis extremum summumque supplicium*, 5.169, cf. p. 33 n. 1 above). The term 'slaves' punishment' (*servile supplicium*) appears in Valerius Maximus, a contemporary of Tiberius, in Tacitus, in two authors of the *Historia Augusta* and for cruel torturing to death in Livy.[1] How-

---

[1] Valerius Maximus 2.7.12 on the crucifixion of Roman deserters by Scipio Africanus maior in Africa: *non prosequar hoc factum ulterius, et quia Scipionis est et quia Romano sanguini quamuis merito perpesso seruile supplicium insultare non adtinet* (I will not pursue this matter further, both because it concerns Scipio and because Roman blood should not be insulted by paying the slaves' penalty, however deservedly); Tacitus, *Histories* 4.11 (see pp. 59ff. below); cf. 2.72: *sumptum de eo supplicium in servilem modum* (suffered the punishment usually inflicted on slaves); *Scriptores Historiae Augustae* 15 (Iulius Capitolinus, *Macrinus*) 12.2: *nam et in crucem milites tulit et seruilibus suppliciis semper adfecit* (for he even crucified soldiers and always imposed the punishments meted out to slaves); *Scriptores Historiae Augustae* 6 (Vulcacius Gallicanus, *Avidius Cassius*) 4.6: ... *rapi eos iussit et in crucem tolli servilique supplicio adfici, quod exemplum non extabat* (he had them arrested and crucified and punished them with the punishment of slaves, for which there was no precedent). Cf. also Horace, *Satires* I.8.32: *servilibus ... peritura modis.* Livy 29.18.14 uses the formula in connection with executions by Pleminius during the Second Punic War in 204 BC: *dein uerberatos seruilibus suppliciis cruciando occidit, mortuos deinde prohibuit sepeliri* (having flogged them, he executed them by torturing them with all the torments applied to slaves and then forbade that their bodies should be buried); cf. 29.9.10: *laceratosque omnibus quae pati corpus ullum potest suppliciis interfecit nec satiatus vivorum poena insepultos proiecit* (when they had been mangled by every

ever, the matter is to be found portrayed in the crudest terms in
Plautus (*c.* 250 to 184 BC). He is also the first writer, so far as we
know, to give evidence of Roman crucifixions. At the same time,
this poet who presents the world of Roman slaves in an inimitable
way, describes crucifixion more vividly and in greater detail than
any other Latin writer.[2] The antiquity and frequency of the
institution is evident from the much-quoted confession of Sceledrus
in the *Miles Gloriosus*, which was probably written about 205 BC:

> I know the cross will be my grave: that is where my ancestors are, my
> father, grandfathers, great-grandfathers, great-great-grandfathers.
>
> (*scio crucem futuram mihi sepulcrum;*
> *ibi mei maiores sunt siti, pater, auos, proauos, abauos,* 372f.)

For Plautus, slaves have been executed on the cross 'from time im-
memorial'. The deceitful slave Chrysalus is afraid that when his
master returns and finds out about his frauds he will certainly
change his name: '*facietque extemplo Crucisalum me ex Chrysalo*
(he will immediately change me from Chrysalus to Crucisalus,
Bacchides 362), i.e. instead of a 'gold-bearer' he will be a 'cross-
bearer'; that is, he will have to drag his cross to the place of
execution. The slave must always reckon with this cruel death, and
he counters this threat in part with grim 'gallows-humour'.[3]

---

torment which a human body can endure, he put them to death and, not
satisfied with the penalty paid by the living, he cast them out unburied).
The extreme cruelty and shamefulness of the penalty is stressed here.

[2] See G. E. Duckworth, *The Nature of Roman Comedy*, Princeton 1952,
288ff.: 'Master and Slave'. For the dating of Plautus' writings see Sonnen-
burg, 'T. Maccius Plautus', *PW* XIV, 95ff.

[3] Deceit practised by slaves and their punishment in Plautus really requires a monograph to itself. I can only give a few references here: see also
p. 7 n. 13. Cf. *Asinaria* 548ff. (the victory of deceit over all punishment);
Miles gloriosus 539f.; *Mostellaria* 1133; *Persa* 855f.; *Mostellaria* 359ff.: the
slave Tranio,

> *Ego dabo ei talentum primus qui in crucem excucurrerit;*
> *sed ea lege, ut offigantur bis pedes, bis bracchia.*
> *Ubi id erit factum, a me argentum petito praesentarium.*

(I'll give a talent to the first man to charge my cross and take it on con-
dition that his legs and arms are double-nailed. When this is attended
to he can claim the money from me cash down.)

Terence uses the topic of the cross in a much more restrained way, but that may be because he himself had been a slave and did not find it a laughing matter. Since Plautus already takes it for granted that crucifixion is a punishment which has been carried out for ages, both publicly and privately, it cannot first have come to Rome following the First Punic War (264–241 BC). Cicero remarks (*In Verrem* II.5.12) that slaves suspected of rebellion were handed over for crucifixion *more maiorum*. How far the reports of Dionysius of Halicarnassus about the crucifixion of rebellious slaves, which point back towards an earlier period, are historical, remains doubtful; at all events, the historian has depicted the execution of slaves entirely in terms of his own time.[4] According to Livy (22.33.2), in the year 217 BC, the year of the defeat at Lake Trasimene, twenty-five slaves made a conspiracy on the Campus Martius; they were crucified, and the informer received his freedom and 20,000 sesterces. In 196 BC the *praetor peregrinus* M. Acilius Glabrio put down a slave revolt in Etruria with the help of a legion; the *principes*

Stichus 625ff.: Epignomus on the parasite Gelasimus:

... *di inmortales! hicquidem pol summam in crucem
cena aut prandio perduci potest!*
The latter replies: *ita ingenium meumst:
quicumuis depugno multo facilius quam cum fame.*

('Ye immortal gods – what a man! I do believe a dinner or a lunch would induce him to take the highest place at a crucifixion.' 'This is how I'm constituted: there is nothing I find so hard to fight as hunger.')

Cf. Terence, *Andria* 621: Pamphilus: *quid meritu's?* Davos: *crucem* ('What do you deserve?' 'The cross').

[4] *Antiquitates Romanae* 5.51.3; 7.69.1, cf. C. D. Peddinghaus (see bibliography), 24f. See also p. 43 n. 9 on Tarquinius Superbus. Peddinghaus is quite right in stressing that 'there is no definite proof' that crucifixion was introduced via Carthage (25). As Plautus was living and writing as early as the time of the Second Punic War, its significance as a punishment for slaves must be earlier than the Punic Wars, which Peddinghaus gives as a *terminus a quo*. Of course, legendary connections between Rome and Carthage go right back to the sixth century BC. The first trade treaty is said to have been concluded between the two city-states in the year 509 (Polybius 3.23). On the other hand, among the Carthaginians crucifixion was not so markedly a punishment almost exclusively meted out on slaves; it was often inflicted on citizens in cases of high treason.

coniurationis were crucified, and the rest handed back to their owners for punishment (Livy 33.36.3). These accounts suggest that from the state side, crucifixion was practised above all as a deterrent against trouble among slaves and was to be found principally in contexts where the powers of punishment of an individual house-holder, the *dominica potestas*, were no longer sufficient.[5] According to Tacitus there was a special place in Rome for the punishment of slaves (*locus servilibus poenis sepositus, Annals* 15.60.1), where no doubt numerous crosses were set up. We learn from *Annals* 2.32.2 that this horrific place was on the Campus Esquilinus, the counter-part of the hill of Golgotha in Jerusalem.[6] As a result, Horace calls the vulture the Esquiline bird (*Esquilinae alites*), and Juvenal describes the grisly way in which it disposes of corpses even in Rome (*Satires* 14.77f.):

> The vulture hurries from dead cattle and dogs and crosses
> (*vultur iumento et canibus crucibusque relictis*)
> to bring some of the carrion to her offspring.

There may have been similar places of execution, with crosses and other instruments of torture, in every large city in the Roman empire, as a deterrent to slaves and all law-breakers, and as a sign of a strict and merciless régime.

The great slave rebellions in Italy during the second century BC were the occasion for the excessive use of crucifixion as the *supplicium servile*; fear of the threat of danger from slaves aroused hate and cruelty.[7] Of course our information about crucifixions is

[5] In Rome the *tresviri capitales*, as assistants to the praetor, were responsible for law and order. In this capacity they also supervised executions. They already appear in Plautus, *Amphitruo* 155ff.; *Aulularia* 415ff. and *Asinaria* 131; they were feared by slaves. For them and for the decline of private justice practised by the *paterfamilias* see W. Kunkel, *Untersuchungen zur Entwicklung des römischen Kriminalverfahrens in vorsullanischer Zeit*, AAMz NF 56, 1962, 71ff., 115ff., and A. W. Lintott (see bibliography), 102ff.

[6] See also Varro, *De lingua latina* 5.25; Horace, *Satires* 1.8.14ff.; Tacitus, *Annals* 15.40; Suetonius, *Claudius* 25; cf. Catullus, *Carmina* 108.

[7] See W. L. Westermann, 'Sklaverei', PW Suppl. VI, (894–1068) 980f., who refers to Seneca, *Epistulae morales* 47.5: *totidem hostes esse quot servos* ('as many enemies as slaves'), and 976f., with reference to Livy 21.41.10: *non eo solum animo quo adversus alios hostes soletis pugnare velim, sed cum indignatione quadam atque ira, velut si servos videatis vestros arma repente*

completely fortuitous, since it was easier to write about the atrocities of rebellious slaves than about the suffering of those who were defeated. There was also unrest in Italy during the first slave war in Sicily (139–132 BC); according to a later note by Orosius, 450 slaves were *in crucem acti (Historiae* 5.9.4). Florus reports that after the Sicilian revolt had been put down, the remainder of the bandits were punished by fetters, chains and crosses (*reliquias latronum compedibus, catenis, crucibusque, Epitome* 2.7 = 3.19.8). A spotlight is cast on the exceptional cruelty with which larger and smaller slave rebellions were suppressed by the report of Appian that after the final defeat of Spartacus the victor Crassus had six thousand prisoners nailed to the cross on the Via Appia between Capua and Rome (*Bella Civilia* 1.120). Before the battle the slave leader had a Roman prisoner crucified between the armies to warn his followers of their fate if they should be defeated (1.119).[8] When Octavian, later to become Augustus, deposed the former triumvir Lepidus in Sicily in 36 BC, he disbanded the troops of Sextus Pompeius. Contrary to the agreement concluded with Sextus he returned

---

contra vos ferentes (to fight not only with that courage with which you are accustomed to fight against the enemy, but with a kind of resentful rage, as if you saw your slaves suddenly take up arms against you). Cf. also E. M. Štaerman, *Die Blütezeit der Sklavenwirtschaft in der römischen Republik*, Wiesbaden 1969, 238ff., 257ff.

[8] Crucifixions in connection with slave troubles in the second and first centuries BC are also mentioned by Cicero, *In Verrem* II.5.3; similarly Valerius Maximus 6.3.5 and Quintilian, *Institutio oratoria* 4.2.17: the praetor L. Domitius had a shepherd crucified in Sicily after he had killed a boar with a spear, since slaves were prohibited from carrying weapons. Valerius Maximus 2.7.9: L. Calpurnius Piso punished in Sicily a *praefectus equitum* who handed out weapons to slaves: *ut qui cupiditate uitae adducti cruce dignissimis fugitiuis tropaea de se statuere concesserant* . . . (led on by a desire for life they allowed fugitives most worthy of the cross to set up their own trophies). Cf. also C. Clodius Licinus, *Rerum Romanorum Reliquiae* 21 (Peter II, p.78). Dionysius of Halicarnassus, *Antiquitates Romanae* 5.51.3 and 7.69.2, similarly presupposes conditions during the slave wars and transfers them to the early period of Rome. Even Cicero, *Pro rege Deiotaro* 26, does not despise this terminology: *quae crux huic fugitiuo potest satis supplici adferre* (what cross can bring adequate punishment to this fugitive)? Cf. J. Vogt, *Sklaverei* (see bibliography), 49f., 60.

the slaves who had been enlisted to their masters for punishment, and had those without masters crucified (Dio Cassius 49.12.4; cf. Appian, *Bella Civilia* 5.131).[9] In the account which he gives in the *Monumentum Ancyranum* (ch.25), however, he says only that he gave back 30,000 slaves to their masters *ad supplicium sumendum*. The rigorous application of the *servile supplicium* was a consequence of the panic fear of slave rebellions, particularly in Italy, which was constantly fostered by the accumulation of large masses of slaves in the *latifundia* of Italy during the period of Roman 'imperialism' after the Second Punic War. It is all too understandable that this fear sometimes turned into hate.

The Civil War and its proscriptions involved the slaves in a conflict between loyalty to their masters and loyalty to the political authorities, which promised them 10,000 drachmae, freedom and Roman citizenship for the killing of a proscribed master (Appian, *Bella Civilia* 4.11). In at least one instance, however, the indignation of the people compelled the triumviri to crucify a slave who had handed over his master to the killers (Appian, *Bella Civilia* 4.29).[10] Augustus permitted the slave who had betrayed the conspiracy of Fannius Caepio to be nailed to the cross publicly by the father of the conspirator, after the slave had first carried a notice giving the cause of his death around the Forum (Dio Cassius 54.3.7). We also have similar accounts from the second and third centuries AD. Pertinax, himself the son of a freedman, son-in-law of Marcus Aurelius and the capable successor of Commodus (AD 192), who was murdered all too soon, freed all those who had been

[9] Dio Cassius 49.12.4; cf. Appian, *Bella Civilia* 5.131 and Orosius, *Historiae* 6.18.33: *sex milia, quorum domini non extabant, in crucem egit* (he crucified six thousand, who had no masters).

[10] A similar occurrence is said already to have taken place under Tarquinus Superbus (see p. 43 n. 9 above), Scholion in Juvenal, *Satires* 8.266f. (Wessner, pp. 152f.): *Vindicius servus, qui indicaverit filios Bruti Tarquinio portas velle reserare. quos pater securi feriit, servum autem ut conservatorem patriae manu misit et ut delatorem dominorum cruci adfigit* (Vindicius is the slave who gave evidence that the sons of Brutus wanted to open the gates to Tarquinius. The former their father killed with the axe: he freed the slave as a saviour of his country and crucified him as an informer.) For the role of slaves in proscriptions see J. Vogt, *Sklaverei* (see bibliography), 86ff.

condemned on the basis of denunciations by slaves and had those informers who were slaves crucified (*Scriptores Historiae Augustae* 8: Iulius Capitolinus, *Pertinax* 9.10). The same thing happened again when Macrinus became emperor in AD 217 after the murder of Caracalla. He, too, had all the slaves who had denounced their masters under his cruel predecessor crucified (Herodian 5.2.2). The conflict between the orders of a master and the commands of the state, both of which threatened the slave with crucifixion, or between the goodness of a master and the limitations of class, of which crucifixion was a symbol, became a favourite theme of rhetorical declamation.[11]

Slaves thus had relatively little protection against the whim of their masters and therefore against unjust imposition of the *servile supplicium*. The dialogue between a Roman matron and her husband, given by Juvenal (6.219ff.), says more here than many examples:

'"Crucify that slave", says the wife. "But what crime worthy of death has he committed?", asks the husband. "Where are the witnesses? Who informed against him? Give him a hearing at least. No delay can be too long when a man's life is at stake." "What a fool you are!

[11] Cf. e.g. Seneca the Elder, *Controversiae*, exc. 3.9: *crux servi venenum domino negantis* (the crucifixion of a slave who refuses to give his master poison); Ps. Quintilian, *Declamationes* 380: *crux scripta servo non danti venenum*. Both deal with the popular rhetorical theme of the slave who refuses to give his seriously ill master poison to put him out of his misery in order not to be guilty of poisoning under the *lex Cornelia de sicariis et veneficis*, and thus not to be freed in his testament, but handed over to be crucified. The slave apeals to the tribune, i.e. to the imperial court. Seneca the Elder, *Controversiae* 7.6, records another horror story which deals with mixed marriage between freed slaves and freeborn members of the upper class, which was taboo: a master sets his slave free as a reward for his faithfulness and marries him to his daughter, whereas the other slaves in the city are crucified. He is accused of degrading his daughter to the level of being related to *cruciarii*: *Si voles invenire generi tui propinquos, ad crucem eundum est* ('If you want to find your son-in-law's relatives, go to the cross', cf. Plautus, *Miles Gloriosus* 372f., see p. 52 above). Servius, *Commentary on Virgil, Aeneid* 3.551 (Thilo/Hagen I, p.436), reports that after their war against Messene the Spartans put an abrupt end to the illegal relationships between Spartan women and slaves and their offspring: *servos patibulis suffixerunt, filios strangulavere* ('they crucified the slaves and strangled the children'). Here the Roman abhorrence against such liaisons was introduced into Greek history.

Do you call a slave a man? Do you say he has done no wrong? This
is my will and my command: take it as authority for the deed."'

('*Pone crucem servo!*' – '*Meruit quo crimine servus*
supplicium? quis testis adest? quis detulit? audi;
nulla umquam de morte hominis cunctatio longa est.'
'*O demens, ita servus homo est? nil fecerit esto;*
Hoc volo, sic iubeo, sit pro ratione voluntas!')[12]

In his defence of A. Cluentius, Cicero accuses the mother of the
accused of having had a slave crucified and at the same time of having had his tongue cut out, so that he could not give evidence (*Pro
Cluentio* 187). In his speech *Pro Milone* he castigates the extraction
of false testimony from slaves in the time of violent faction-fighting
between the *populares* and the *optimates* (ch. 60). If the slave in-
criminated Clodius, the corrupt faction leader of the *populares*,
against his enemy Milo, he faced the cross (*certa crux*); if he
exonerated him, the liberty he hoped for (*sperata libertas*). The men
of old (*maiores*) had rejected testimony by slaves against their
masters in principle.

Of course there was also criticism of excesses of this kind. For
Horace, a master who has his slave crucified because he sur-
reptitiously tasted some fish soup while bringing it in, 'is quite
mad by any reasonable standard'.[13] This attitude was matched by
Augustus' tendency to curb the whims of slave-owners in favour

---

[12] Seneca the Elder, *Controversiae* 10.5, deals with the case of an Athenian painter who bought an old prisoner of war from Olynthus as a slave
and tortured him to death as the model for a portrait of Prometheus (see
above, pp. 11f.). While the Greek orators utterly condemned the painter, he
was to some extent defended by the Latin ones. Fulda (see bibliography),
56, gives a mediaeval instance of a crucifixion as a model for a painting.

[13] *Satires* 1.3.80ff.: Lucian, *Prometheus* 10 (directed against Zeus): no
one crucifies his cook if he tastes the food. In Horace, *Satires* 2.7.47, a slave
remonstrating with his master says, *peccat uter nostrum cruce dignius*
(which of us commits a sin more worthy of the cross?)? In *Epistles* 1.16.46–
48 Horace reports a conversation with his slave:

'*nec furtum feci nec fugi*' *si mihi dicit*
servus, '*habes pretium, loris non ureris,*' *aio.*
'*non hominem occidi.*' '*non pasces in cruce corvos.*'

(If a slave were to say to me, 'I never stole nor ran away', my reply
would be, 'You have your reward, you are not flogged.' 'I never killed
anyone.' 'You will not feed the crows on the cross.')

of the authority of the state. Seneca even went so far as to remark
with some degree of satisfaction 'that the cruelty of private slave
owners was avenged even by the hands of slaves, who stood under
the certain threat of crucifixion' (*sub certo crucis periculo*, *De
Clementia* 1.26.1).

On the other hand, state justice against slaves continued to be
harsh, and indeed in the time of the empire freedmen and *peregrini*
were increasingly punished with crucifixion in the same way as
slaves. Valerius Maximus reports that – still during the Republic –
a slave denied having murdered an *equus* although he was tortured
six times; finally, however, he confessed and was crucified; another
is said to have been condemned although he kept silent while being
tortured eight times (8.4.2f.). The 'old custom' of executing (often
by crucifixion) all the slaves in a household if the master was
murdered was revived in the time of Nero by a decree of the senate
(Tacitus, *Annals* 13.32.1), and a few years later it was in fact put
into force after the murder of a city prefect, despite the threat of
rebellion among the people (14.42–45). The main argument was
that the great mass of slaves in Rome could not be kept in check
without fear (*non sine metu*, 14.44.3). In the *acta urbis* which
Trimalchio suddenly has read out by his *actuarius* during the
famous feast, a notice appears between information about property
and the selling of cattle and corn: 'The slave Mithridates was
crucified for having damned the soul of our Gaius (= Caligula)'
(Petronius, *Satyricon* 53.3).[14] It is still the case in the *Sententiae* of
the jurist Paulus (5.21.3f.) that the death penalty is threatened not
only on all those who ask questions of astrologers about the
emperor's future and that of the state, but also on the slave who
asks the same question about his master's fate: *Summo supplicio, id
est cruce, adficiuntur* (they will meet the most severe punishment,
the cross). Imperial slaves and freedmen, who could even rise to the

[14] C. D. Peddinghaus (see bibliography), 30, interprets the passage
quite nonsensically in terms of an impalement by king Mithridates. For
the soul of Gaius see Suetonius, *Caligula* 27.3, and Minucius Felix,
Octavius 29.5: *et est eis tutius per Iovis genium peierare quam regis* (safer for
them to swear falsely by the soul of Jupiter than by the soul of the king).
For the whole question cf. Petronius, *Satyricon* 137.2: *si magistratus hoc
scierint, ibis in crucem* ('if the magistrates knew this, you would be crucified').

status of an *eques*, were further threatened by the cruelty of individual rulers. Caligula (Suetonius, *Caligula* 12.2) and Domitian (*Domitian* 11.1) are said to have crucified imperial slaves or freedmen at their whim. Vitellius had a treacherous freedman executed *in servilem modum* (Tacitus, *Histories* 2.72.2), and his opponent Vespasian did the same thing with two former slaves whom Vitellius had freed because of their military 'services', honouring them with the status of *eques*. Tacitus reports with satisfaction the execution of the one who had betrayed Tarracina: the fact that the crucified man was fixed to the cross in the insignia of the equestrian order was a general comfort (*solacium* 4.3.2). Of the other, Asiaticus, he records laconically: 'He paid for his hateful power by a slave's punishment' (*malam potentiam servili supplicio expiavit*, 4.11.3). It is said that after the murder of Heliogabalus in AD 222 Alexander Severus not only reduced the imperial slaves and freedmen whom he had promoted to their former state, but if they had been convicted of calumny and bribery, as a deterrent to others he had them crucified 'on the street which his slaves used most frequently on the way to the imperial palace' (*Scriptores Historiae Augustae* 18: Aelius Lampridius, *Alexander Severus* 23.8). The freedmen and women of private individuals were also endangered in the time of the Empire: the freedwoman of a Roman *eques* who, in league with the priests of a temple of Isis in Rome, had helped him to deceive the woman he longed for, was crucified under Tiberius along with the priests of the Egyptian goddess, who were not Roman citizens but only *peregrini*; the temple was pulled down and the effigy of Isis cast into the Tiber. The seducer himself, however, as an *eques*, escaped with banishment because he had acted in the folly of love (Josephus, *Antiquitates* 18.79f.). In other words, even here the class barriers were strictly maintained.[15]

[15] Cf. Apuleius, *Metamorphoses* 10.12.3: because of an attempt to murder her stepson, a matron is condemned along with her accomplice, a slave: *novercae quidem perpetuum indicitur exilium, servus vero patibulo suffigitur* (the woman was perpetually exiled and the slave fastened to the gibbet). For the distinction between *honestiores* and *humiliores* cf. also *Anthologia Latina* 794.35:

Crimen opes redimunt, reus est crucis omnis egenus.

(Riches buy off judgment, and the poor are condemned to the cross.)

There was evidently a particularly strong suspicion of religious deception and the illegal practice of 'superstitious foreign cults' (*superstitiones externae*: Tacitus, *Annals* 11.15; cf. 13.32.2) among slaves, freedmen and *peregrini*. This is also a partial explanation of the harsh proceedings in the trials of Christians. We have parallels to this in the persecution of the astrologers (Tacitus, *Annals* 2.32), the Celtic druids (Suetonius, *Claudius* 25; Aurelius Victor, *Caesares* 4.2; cf. Pliny the Elder, *Historia Naturalis* 29.54) and in the punishment of those guilty of the ancient Punic practice of child sacrifice. Christians were also accused of such crimes (Minucius Felix, *Octavius* 9.5). A proconsul of Africa, otherwise unknown, punished with utmost severity the priests of 'Saturn', i.e. the Carthaginian god Baal-Hammon, who kept up this ancient practice of child sacrifice. He had them hanged 'on the very trees of their temple, in the shadow of which they had committed their crimes, as though on consecrated crosses (*votivis crucibus exposuit*).' Tertullian, who hands down this information, refers for it to the eyewitness accounts of the soldiers who performed the execution in the name of the proconsul.[16]

It could, of course, be asked whether for slaves and *peregrini*, who had to reckon with the possibility of crucifixion as a punishment, the cross could be such a deterrent horror as to be a hindrance to the message of the crucified redeemer. The answer is that for these people the horror was even more real and related to personal existence than it was for members of the upper classes. Thus the more capable slaves hoped for freedom, which improved their social and legal situation at least to some extent and gave them the possibility of further social improvement; among the ancient bourgeoisie of the self-made men who had made their way up from the mass of the people, the *libertini* played an important role, as is shown by the example of Trimalchio and the numerous imperial freedmen with some degree of power. An alleged son of god who could not help himself at the time of his deepest need (Mark 15.31),

[16] Tertullian, *Apologeticus* 9.2. For child sacrifice see O. Kaiser, 'Den Erstgeborenen deiner Söhne sollst du mir geben. Erwägungen zum Kinderopfer im Alten Testament', in *Denkender Glaube. Festschrift Carl Heinz Ratschow*, Berlin 1976, 24–48 (for the Carthaginians see 42f. n. 65a), and A. Henrichs, *Die Phoinikika des Lollianos*, 1972, 12ff. (15f.) 32ff.

and who rather required his followers to take up the cross, was hardly an attraction to the lower classes of Roman and Greek society. People were all too aware of what it meant to bear the cross through the city and then to be nailed to it (*patibulum ferat per urbem, deinde offigitur cruci*, Plautus, *Carbonaria*, fr. 2) and feared it; they wanted to get away from it. Moreover, early Christianity was not particularly a religion of slaves; at the time of Paul, and much more so with Pliny and Tertullian, it embraced men of every rank, *omnis ordinis*.[17]

This basic theme of the *supplicium servile* also illuminates the hymn in Philippians 2.6–11. Anyone who was present at the worship of the churches founded by Paul in the course of his mission, in which this hymn was sung, and indeed any reader of Philippians in ancient times, would inevitably have seen a direct connection between the 'emptied himself, taking the form of a slave' (ἑαυτὸν ἐκένωσεν μορφὴν δούλου λαβών) and the disputed end of the first strophe: 'he humbled himself and was obedient unto death, even the death of the cross'. Death on the cross was the penalty for slaves, as everyone knew; as such it symbolized extreme humiliation, shame and torture. Thus the θανάτου δε σταυροῦ is the last bitter consequence of the μορφὴν δούλου λαβών and stands in the most abrupt contrast possible with the beginning of the hymn with its description of the divine essence of the pre-existence of the crucified figure, as with the exaltation surpassing anything that might be conceived (ὁ θεὸς αὐτὸν ὑπερύψωσεν). The one who had died the death of a slave was exalted to be Lord of the whole creation and bearer of the divine name Kyrios. If it did not have θανάτου δὲ σταυροῦ at the end of the first strophe, the hymn would lack its most decisive statement. The careful defence of its unity from both poetical and theological criteria by Otfried Hofius can therefore be supported also from its content, the *supplicium servile*: 'If the climax of the first strophe lies – in terms of both language and content – in the mention of the death of the cross, the assertion that in the pre-Pauline hymn the incarnation was understood as the real saving

[17] Pliny the Younger, *Epistulae* 10.96; Tertullian, *Apologeticus* 1.7; *Adversus Nationes* 1.1.2; cf. M. Hengel, *Property and Riches in the Early Church*, ET London and Philadelphia 1975, 36ff. and 64ff.

event and the death merely as its unavoidable consequence can no longer be held to be credible. On the contrary, we are forced to suppose that the hymn already presupposes a firm view of the saving significance of the death of Jesus.'[18]

[18] O. Hofius, *Der Christushymnus Philipper 2,6–11*, WUNT 17, 1976, 17. Cf. 9–17, 56–64. See also M. Hengel, *The Son of God*, 1976, 87f., 91f.

9

The Crucified National
Martyr and Metaphorical
and Philosophical Terminology

There remains the question whether there is any evidence in the
ancient Roman world for a non-Christian, positive interpretation of
death by crucifixion, say as the manner of death of a philosopher or
a national martyr. After all, the death of such figures was a familiar
feature of the ancient world. I have not been able to discover a real
historical instance – leaving aside the ambiguous figure of Polycrates
(see above, p. 24); however, during the course of tradition the figure
of the national hero M. Atilius Regulus was associated with the
cross. As an unsuccessful general, Regulus was captured during an
expedition to North Africa in the First Punic War. The Carthaginians then sent him back to Rome to arrange the exchange of
prisoners or to negotiate a peace treaty with Rome. Once there,
however, he counselled the senate to remain firm. Faithful to his
promise, given under oath, he is then said to have returned to
Carthage, where he was tortured to death by the Carthaginians in
revenge. Traditions about the manner of his death vary widely;
among those mentioned are slow-working poison, being deprived
of sleep, being shut up in a dark room, having his eyelids cut off,
being exposed to blinding light and finally also crucifixion, the last-
mentioned presumably because it was the form of execution
practised in Carthage and was regarded as the *summum supplicium*
which embraced all conceivable tortures.

The historical value of this legend, elaborated by Cicero in
particular, which would 'do full justice to the imagination of a
torturer', is extremely small. 'These unpleasant and historically
spurious heroes are a creation of the rhetoric which exercised such

an unhealthy influence on Roman historiography after the time of
Sulla and of the insipid popular moral philosophy with which we
are familiar from Cicero's writings and which was unconscious of
its own immorality. They were then celebrated for centuries in
declamations composed in prose or poetry.'[1] Above all, Silius
Italicus in the second half of the second century AD cannot go far
enough in his exaggerated and indeed tasteless reverence for the
national martyr:

> I was looking on when Regulus, the hope and pride of Hector's race,
> was dragged along amid the shouts of the populace to his dark
> dungeon, with both hands bound fast behind his back; I was looking
> on when he hung high upon the tree and saw Italy from his lofty cross.
>
> (. . . *vidi, cum robore pendens*
> *Hesperiam cruce sublimis spectaret ab alta, Punica* 2.340–4, cf. 435f.).

Of course, the cross is only one theme among many, and is indeed
a latecomer to the scene. In Book 6 a messenger tells Regulus' son
Serranus of the bestial cruelty of the Carthaginians (*ritus imitantem
irasque ferarum*) and the example given to the whole world by the
veneranda virtus of his father, who suffered torture joyfully (*placido
ore ferentem*). He was deprived of sleep by an instrument of torture.

> That endurance (*patientia*) is greater than all triumphs. His laurels
> will green throughout the ages, as long as unstained loyalty (*fides*)
> keeps her seat in heaven and on earth, and will last as long as virtue's
> name is worshipped (529–50).

It cannot be coincidence that in this last hymn of praise there is no
longer any mention of crucifixion.

Seneca sees Regulus in a similar way as a man who proves
victorious over all the *terribilia* feared by men: 'Many men have
overcome separate trials: Mucius the fire, Regulus the cross,
Socrates poison' (*singula vicere iam multi: ignem Mucius, crucem
Regulus, venenum Socrates* . . ., *Epistulae morales* 98.12). He compares him as a proof of faith and patience (*documentum fidei [et]
patientiae*) with the effeminate Maecenas (see above, p.30), 'who

[1] See P. v. Rohden, 'Atilius 51', *PW* II, 2086–92 (quotation from
2092). Horace gives the simplest evaluation – without the theme of the
cross – in his *Odes* (3.6). Here we simply have *quae sibi barbarus/tortor
pararet* (lines 49f.: he knew what the barbarian torturer was preparing for
him).

spent as many vigils on a feather bed as he did on the cross' (*tam vigilabis in pluma quam ille in cruce*, Dialogue 1, *De providentia* 3.9f.). Florus stresses that Regulus did not sully his honour either by his voluntary return to Carthage or through extreme suffering, whether in prison or on the cross (*nec ultimo sive carceris seu crucis supplicio deformata maiestas*); rather, and this was much more remarkable, he had become a victor over those who had overcome him, indeed he had even conquered fate (*fortuna*) itself (*Epitome* 1.18 = 2.2.25). Even on the cross, the national martyr is accorded the highest honour which the ancient enlightened world could bestow: he was master of his own destiny. For Tertullian, Regulus was the prototype of the pagan martyr, since – in contrast to the others – 'your Regulus readily initiated the novelty of the cross with its manifold and exquisite cruelty' (*crucis vero novitatem numerosae, abstrusae, Regulus vester libenter dedicauit*, Ad Nationes 1.18.3).

The reason why Regulus was said to have been executed on the cross, contrary to all historical reality, may be found in formulations like that in Cicero, *De Natura Deorum* 3.80: *Cur Poenorum crudelitati Reguli corpus est praebitum* (why the body of Regulus was given over to the cruelty of the Carthaginians). The cross was obviously *par excellence* the expression of this *crudelitas*.

We must also make a brief examination of the *metaphorical* terminology which may also be present, in part, in the Regulus legend. *Crux* could be used as an expression for the utmost torment, even including the pains of love, and sometimes it is difficult to decide whether there is a real reference to the instrument of execution or the death penalty, or whether the language is merely metaphorical. The understanding of crucifixion as the *summum supplicium* surely underlies Columella's remarkable statement, 'the ancients regarded the extreme of the law as the extreme of the cross' (*summum ius antiqui summam putabant crucem*, De re rustica 1.7.2). Cicero describes the mere wish to involve oneself in the tyranny of Caesar as *miserius . . . quam in crucem tolli* (*Ad Atticum* 7.11.2), though this did not prevent him at a later stage from doing just that.[2]

---

[2] Cf. also the comment (*Ad Quintum Fratrem* 1.29) on the *eques* Catienus: *illum crucem sibi ipsum constituere, ex qua tu eum ante detraxisses* (set up for himself a cross from which you had earlier taken him down).

More interest is provided by the few instances where the *summum et servile supplicium* appears in philosophical discussion – in connection with the vivid Cynic and Stoic diatribe. Epictetus thinks that it is wrong to provoke an opponent in a legal dispute, since 'if you want to be crucified, wait, and the cross will come' (if it is to come); the decisive thing is to hearken to the Logos in everything (*Diatribes* 2.2.20).[3] Seneca compares desires (*cupiditates*) with 'crosses into which each one of you drives his own nails' (*cruces, in quos unusquisque uestrum clauos suos ipse adigit*); all hang on their own crosses (*stipitibus singulis pendent*) as though brought to punishment (*ad supplicium acti*). There is an echo of the whole thing in the following sentence, which could fit into a Cynic sermon: they are torn apart by as many desires as crosses (*quot cupiditatibus tot crucibus distrahuntur*, Dialogue 7, *De vita beata* 19.3). Cicero attacks the basic Stoic thesis that pain is not really an evil and that the wise man must be *semper beatus*. His terse counter-argument runs: anyone who is put on a cross cannot be happy (*in crucem qui agitur, beatus esse non potest*, *De Finibus* 5.84); he cites Polycrates as an example of his thesis (5.92). Like Seneca, Philo uses the image of crucifixion on several occasions to describe the enslavement of man to his body and the desires which dominate it: souls 'hang on unsouled matter in the same way as those who are crucified are nailed to transitory wood until their death'.[4] The common starting point for these passages is Plato's remark in the *Phaedo* (83cd) that every soul is fastened to the body by desire as though by a nail.[5] The imagery of crucifixion left no room for a

---

Virgil (?), *Catalepton* 2a, 18: *parata namque crux, cave, stat mentula* (beware, for the cross is ready and the penis erect). The threat is of the peasant's Priapic, phallic cudgel. For the pains of grief, Catullus, *Carmina* 99.4: *suffixum in summa me memini esse cruce* (I remember how I hung impaled on the top of the cross).

[3] In the negative sense, 3.26.22, against those who are stretched out 'like crucified figures' in the baths under the hands of the masseur.

[4] Philo, *De posteritate Caini* 61: ἄψυχων ἐκκρέμανται καὶ καθάπερ οἱ ἀνασκολοπισθέντες ἄχρι θανάτου φθαρταῖς ὕλαις προσήλωνται, cf. *De somniis* 2.213 as interpretation of Gen. 40.19; Prov. 25 with reference to Polycrates (see p. 24 n. 13 above).

[5] Cf. Plutarch, *Moralia* 718D; Iamblichus, quoted in Stobaeus, *Anthologia* 3.5.45 (Wachsmuth/Hense III, p. 270).

positive interpretation, apart from the admonition which was widespread in antiquity, that each man had to bear his own fate; here too the metaphor was one of horror and abomination. It is striking that the metaphorical terminology is limited to the Latin sphere, whereas in the Greek world the cross is never, so far as I can see, used in a metaphorical sense. Presumably the word was too offensive for it to be used as a metaphor by the Greeks.

10

Crucifixion in the
Greek-Speaking World

So far the Greek-speaking world, Greece, Asia Minor, Egypt and
Syria, has been deliberately kept at the periphery of our discussion.
The sources for crucifixion, which in the period of the empire
markedly appears as a Roman punishment, are much fuller in Latin
literature than in Greek. However, it would be a mistake to make a
distinction in principle between the Latin 'West' and the Greek
'East', or even between the Persian 'East' and the Greek 'West'.[1]
Pheretime, the mother of the murdered Arcesilaus, the tyrant of
Barca in Cyrenaica, who had those principally involved in the
death of her son crucified round the city wall (Herodotus 4.202.1),
was as Greek as her victims. Herodotus further shows that even the
Athenians could crucify a hated enemy (see pp. 24ff. above); the
phrase 'nail to planks', which appears only here, suggests that a real

[1] C. D. Peddinghaus (see bibliography), 9.11f., draws a somewhat unreliable distinction between 'East' and 'West'; he is followed by E.
Brandenburger (see bibliography), 21. It is also wrong to say that 'putting
a corpse on show on a stake is evidently a practice found only in the East',
as is stated by H.-W. Kuhn (see bibliography), 10 n. 33, also following
Peddinghaus (see p. 46 n. 3 and Diodorus Siculus 16.61.2; Euripides,
Electra 896ff.). As well as crucifixion, there is in the East evidence for
impalement, with the verbs πηγνύναι, ἀναπείρειν, etc.; Euripides, *Iphigenia in
Tauris* 1430; *Rhesus* 513ff.; Diodorus Siculus 33.15.1f.; Dio Cassius
62.7.2; 62.11.4; see also Seneca, *Epistulae morales* 14.5; *Dialogue* 6 (*De
consolatione, Ad Marciam*) 20.3; Fulda (see bibliography), 113–16.
Plutarch, *Moralia* 499D, the passage cited by Kuhn, ἀλλ'εἰς σταυρὸν καθηλώσεις
ἢ σκόλοπι πήξεις, mentions crucifixion and impalement as being presumably
the most gruesome forms of execution known to Plutarch, see below
p. 77. He cites them in order to illustrate the subsequent anecdote of the
fearlessness of the Cyrenaican Theodorus Atheus. The 'East' was no more
cruel than the 'West'. For the impalement of the corpse or head of an
enemy see p. 24, p. 41 n. 6 and p. 47 n. 3 above.

cross was not used in this case, but the '*tympanum*', which was familiar from their own penal law. This was a flat board made up of
planks (σανίδες) on which criminals were fastened for public display, torture or execution. The seventeen victims discovered in the
well-known find of the tomb at Phaleron from the seventh century
BC were fastened with a ring round their necks and hooks round
their hands and feet. This could be seen as an aggravated form of
ἀποτυμπανισμός, which would come very near to crucifixion if the
victim were nailed down instead of being bound or fastened with
curved nails. Mythological analogies are Ixion, Prometheus (see
above, pp. 11ff.) and Andromeda (see below p. 77).[2] In Aristophanes'
Thesmophoriazusai, Mnesilochus, dressed as a woman, is 'tied to the
plank' for impiety (930, 940); he himself believes that he is doomed
to die and will be a sport and food for the ravens (938, 942, 1029).
He is fastened with nails (1003: ἧλος) which can either be loosened
or driven further in; in this way he 'hangs' on the plank (1027,
1053, 1110) like Andromeda, 'distracted and dying, with throat-
cutting agonies riving him' (1054f.), watched over and taunted by a
Scythian bowman who finally threatens to kill him. The whole
scene may only depict a pillory, but it is not far short of a crucifixion.[3] The report of Duris, the historian and ruler of Samos, that
after the capture of the city Pericles had the ten leaders of the
Samians 'bound to planks' (σανίσι προσδήσας) in the market place
of Miletus, and after they had suffered for ten days gave the order to
beat in their skulls with cudgels, is not as improbable as Plutarch,
who is favourably inclined to the Athenians, suggests (*Pericles*
28.3). This is merely an aggravated form of *apotympanismos*, and

    [2] See 'Α. Δ. Κεραμόπουλλος (see bibliography), *passim*. K. Latte (see
bibliography), 1606f., is critical, but he does not do justice to all the arguments put forward by Κεραμόπουλλος. The judgment given by I. Barkan
(see bibliography), 63–72, is very balanced, and probably comes closest to
reality. Cf. also J. Vergote (see bibliography), 143, and C. E. Owen, *JTS*
30, 1929, 259–66. τύμπανον could be used to designate the rack, II Macc.
6.19, 28, and the place of scourging (see Vergote, op. cit., 153f.), which indeed could also be carried out on a stake or cross. The inventiveness of the
torturers was greater than words can describe. The connection with
crucifixion is also stressed by L. Gernet (see bibliography), 290ff. and 302ff.
    [3] See Κεραμόπουλλος op. cit., 27ff.; Barkan, op. cit., 66ff.; Gernet, op.
cit., 304f. Cf. *Suidae Lexicon* s.v. Κύφωνες, above p. 25 n. 16.

the most improbable thing is the duration of ten days for the punishment.[4] In Sophocles' Antigone, Creon threatens not merely to kill those who are in the know about the burial of Polyneices but to hang them alive (ζῶντες κρεμαστοί, 308) unless they speak up. According to a fragment of the comedian Cratinus, slaves were often 'tied to planks'.[5] On the other hand, Menander,[6] Alciphron,[7] Antiphanes[8] and Longus[9] speak of 'hanging'. This, however, is probably not in the sense of killing but of scourging. The word probably also has the same significance in a decree of Antiochus XIII Asiaticus (?), who expelled all philosophers from his sphere of rule. The young men who were found in their company were to be 'hanged' (κρεμήσονται, Athenaeus 12, p. 547b). In the *Tarantinoi* of Alexis the hero would like most of all to 'fasten to the wood' or 'impale' the parasite Theodotus (ἀναπήξαιμ' ἐπὶ τοῦ ξύλου, Athenaeus 4, p. 134a). The Ptolemaic papyri know of both 'hanging'[10] and ἀποτυ(μ)πανίζειν; it must remain open whether the latter was done merely for scourging, or in fact for execution.[11] According to

---

[4] See Κεραμόπουλλος, op. cit., 26f., 31; Barkan, op. cit., 64f.; P. Ducrey (see bibliography), 212. J. Vergote, *RAC* VIII, 116f., conjectures a pillory.
[5] Scholion in Aristophanes, *Thesmophoriazusai* 940 = fr. 341 (Kock, *Comicorum Atticorum Fragmenta* I, pp. 112f.).
[6] *Perikeiromene* 79 (Koerte I, p. 49) = 149 (Allinson, LCL, p. 214). This hanging of slaves as a punishment is to be distinguished from binding them to the block, see Aristophanes, *Equites* 1048; Eupolis, *Demoi*, see C. Austin, *Comicorum Graecorum fragmenta in papyris reperta*, p. 86 (fr. 1.32); Marikas, see p. 100 (fr. 1.153).
[7] *Epistles* 2.13.3 (Schepers, pp. 39f.).
[8] Athenaeus 10, p. 459a.
[9] 4.8.4; 4.9.1 (Hercher, *Erotici Scriptores Graeci* I, p. 309).
[10] *SB* 6739 = *PCZ* 59202 (Edgar II, pp. 61f.), lines 7ff., letter of the *dioikētēs* Apollonius to Zeno, 254 BC: ὁ Ἀμμενεὺς εἰρηκὼς ἃ ἔγραψας πρὸς ἡμᾶς περιαχθεὶς κρεμήσεται ('If Ammeneus said what you have written, he should be brought to us and hung'). κρεμαννύναι appears several times in the sense of 'crucify', e.g. in Appian; cf. also Josephus, *BJ* 7.202; Achilles Tatius 2.37.3.
[11] U. Wilcken, *Urkunden der Ptolemäerzeit* I, Berlin 1927, no. 119, line 37. Wilcken translated the word 'crucify', see the commentary, 562, in connection with Κεραμόπουλλος; there is a reference to PCZ 59202 (see n. 10 above). However, it can simply mean 'kill' here: 'a heightening of the previous ἀποκτενεῖν or only an illustration'. The same is true of O. Guéraud, *ΕΝΤΕΥΞΙΣ*, 1931, no. 86, lines 6,8: here it is most likely to mean 'beat to death'. The difficulties of the term are reflected in Liddell and

the epitomator Justin, Pausanias, the murderer of Philip of Macedon, was arrested soon after the act and crucified; Olympias, who
instigated the murder, went by night and adorned his head with a
golden garland while he was hanging on the cross (*Epitome* 9.7.10).
The anonymous history of Alexander, *POxy* 1798 (fr. 1), reports
that he was handed over to the Macedonian army for *apotympanismos*: τοῖς Μ[ακεδόσι π]αρέδωκε[ν (?). οὗτοι δ']ἀπετυπάν-
[ισαν αὐτό]ν. It is clear from this that Roman historians understood
ἀποτυ(μ)πανίζειν in terms of crucifixion.[12] In the imperial edict
against the imprisoned Christians in Lyons, AD 177 (Eusebius,
Historia Ecclesiastica 5.1.47), ἀποτυμπανίζειν has only the meaning 'to bring to death': the Roman governor then had the Roman
citizens decapitated, 'the others he sent to the beasts' (τοὺς δὲ
λοιποὺς ἔπεμπεν εἰς θηρία).

We need not dwell further on the disputed question of the
correct interpretation of *apotympanismos*, which is used in a number
of different senses, as there are sufficiently clear instances elsewhere of crucifixion being practised by and on Greeks. It has already been said that Plato and probably also Demosthenes were
familiar with this form of execution (see above, pp. 27f.). It is less

Scott's *A Greek-English Lexicon*. The ninth edition, ed. H. Stuart Jones
and R. McKenzie, Oxford 1940, 225, has 'crucify on a plank', which is
surely too one-sided. The supplement, ed. E. A. Barber, Oxford 1968, 21,
corrects this to 'cudgel to death'. Further meanings are 'behead' and 'kill
unmercifully, destroy'. The word can be interpreted in very different
ways, as those bound to the *tympanon* were killed in different ways. III
Maccabees 3.27 is interesting, from Ptolemy's decree against the Jews:
anyone who conceals a Jew αἰσχίσταις βασάνοις (with the most horrible
tortures) ἀποτυμπανισθήσεται πανοικίᾳ (with all his house). This could be the
threat of a form of execution similar to crucifixion. For the many different
uses of (ἀπο)τυμπανίζειν cf. J. Vergote (see bibliography), 153f. and *RAC*
VIII, 119f. At a later date it is mentioned alongside crucifixion and is
distinguished from it. Cf. also Gernet, op. cit., 291ff., 302ff.; P. Ducrey,
op. cit., 210ff.

[12] See U. Wilcken, *Alexander der Grosse und die indischen Gymno-
sophisten*, SAB, phil.-hist.-Klasse 1923 (150–83), 151ff. Wilcken reassesses
Justin's account of the crucifixion of the murderer over against the note in
Diodorus Siculus 16.94.4, who has him killed when trying to escape. He
takes up the interpretation given by Κεραμόπουλλος, 'Thus it is clear that
'ΑΠΕΤΥΠΑΝΙΣΑΝ means the punishment which Justin IX 7,10 describes
as *in cruce pendentis Pausaniae*' (152).

well known that the Athenian admiral Conon, in the service of the
satrap Pharnabazus in 397 BC, crucified the Greek leader of the
mutineers from Cyprus. In the same period, Dionysius I of Syra-
cuse crucified the Greek mercenaries of the Carthaginians whom he
took prisoner. Philip II of Macedon had hung on a gibbet the corpse
of Onomarchus, the despoiler of Delphi, who had fallen in battle.[13]
Alexander the Great carried out crucifixions on many occasions.
The fate of the able-bodied survivors of the siege of Tyre may be a
sufficient example here:[14]

> Then the wrath of the king presented a sad spectacle to the victors,
> for two thousand, for whose killing the general madness had spent
> itself, hung fixed to crosses over a huge stretch of the shore.
>
> (*Triste deinde spectaculum victoribus ira praebuit regis: II milia, in
> quibus occidendis defecerat rabies, crucibus affixi per ingens litoris
> spatium pependerunt*, Curtius Rufus, *Historia Alexandri* 4.4.17).

In the romance of Alexander it is of course the Tyrians who have
Alexander's ambassadors crucified (*Vita Alexandri* 1.35.6). Arrian's
report that Alexander hanged the rebellious Indian prince Musi-
canus 'in his own territory along with those of the Brahmans who
were the instigators of the rebellion' (*Anabasis Alexandri* 6.17.2) is
also very probably a reference to crucifixion.

The Diadochi took further the cruel practice. Perdiccas, the
administrator of the kingdom after Alexander's death, had the
Cappadocian king Ariarathes and all his relatives tortured and
crucified in 322 BC (τοῦτον . . . καὶ τοὺς συγγενεῖς αὐτοῦ
πάντας αἰκισάμενος ἀνεσταύρωσε, Diodorus Siculus 18.16.3);

[13] Conon: *POxy* 842 = FGH 66. XV.5. Dionysius I: Diodorus
Siculus 14.53.4. Onomarchus: Diodorus Siculus 16.61.2: κατακοπεὶς
ἐσταυρώθη; 16.35: ἐκρέμασε. This is not the case in Pausanias 10.2.5 and
Philo, *De providentia* 2.33 = Eusebius, *Praeparatio Evangelica* 8.14.33.
[14] See Justin, *Epitome* 18.3.18; Diodorus Siculus 17.16.4. See M. Hengel,
Juden, Griechen und Barbaren, SBS 76, 1976, 13. Further crucifixions
attributed to Alexander are: Curtius Rufus, *Historia Alexandri* 6.3.14; cf.
7.5.40; 7.11.28; 9.8.16 = Arrian, *Anabasis* 6.17.2; Plutarch, *Alexander*
72.3 = Arrian, *Anabasis* 7.14.4. From the Alexander romance see also the
crucifixion of the murderers of Darius by Alexander, 2.23.4 (van Thiel,
p. 104) and the threat to the ambassadors from Darius, 1.37.3 (p. 54); the
portrait of Alexander here is clearly idealized, and his cruelty is toned
down. Cf. Ducrey, op. cit., 213 and index, 242 s.v.

according to another account, however, he is said to have fallen in
battle (ibid. 31.19.4). During the wars of the Diadochi mass
crucifixions also came to Greece. In 314 BC the daughter-in-law of
Polyperchon, the last 'administrator of Alexander's kingdom, a
warlike woman', who had been given the eloquent nickname
'conqueress of cities' (κρατησίπολις), put down a rebellion in the
city of Sicyon, near Corinth, and had about thirty of its inhabitants
crucified (Diodorus Siculus 19.67.2). Eleven years later Demetrius
Poliorcetes stormed Orchomenus in Arcadia and had its commander Strombichus killed in the same cruel way, along with
about eighty of the defenders who were 'inimically disposed' towards him; however, he enlisted two thousand of the other
mercenaries in his army (Diodorus Siculus 20.103.6). It may be
concluded from the use of crucifixion among the Macedonians and
at the time of Alexander and the Diadochi that it was also to be
found in the Hellenistic monarchies, even if reports of it are sparse.
We know that Antiochus III had the corpse of the usurper Molon,
who had killed himself in battle, 'impaled in the most prominent
place in Media' (ἀνασταυρῶσαι, Polybius 5.54.7); a similar fate
was suffered by the uncle and brother-in-law of the king, Achaeus,
who had set up a monarchy of his own in Asia Minor. After being
betrayed into the hands of Antiochus, he was tortured to death by
mutilation and his body was sewn into an ass's skin and hung
(Polybius 18.21.3). At the command of Ptolemy IV, Cleomenes
king of the Spartans, who had fled to Egypt and committed suicide
after the failure of an attempted coup against the Ptolemies, was
dishonoured in the same way (Plutarch, *Cleomenes* 38f.). There is
some doubt over Justin's report that during the popular rebellion
after the death of the incompetent Ptolemy IV some female members of the current court favourites were crucified (*Epitome*
30.2.7); Polybius 15.33.7ff. knows nothing of this.[15] More trust
may be placed in the report in Josephus that there were also
crucifixions in Judaea during the persecution of those faithful to
the law at the time of the reform under Antiochus IV in 167 BC.

[15] K. Latte (see bibliography), 1606, speaks wrongly of a 'Syrian
revolution'. For the death of Achaeus, Polybius 5.54.7, cf. B. A. van
Proosdij, *Hermes* 69, 1934, 347–50; P. Ducrey, op. cit., 213.

His account could be based on a Hellenistic source (*Antiquitates* 12.256).[16] According to a favourite ancient anecdote, Lysimachus, one of the royal Diadochi, threatened Theodorus Atheus with crucifixion. According to Cicero's account, the latter replied:

> Make, I beg you, your abominable taunts to those purple-robed courtiers of yours; it makes no difference to Theodotus whether he rots on the ground or in the air.

> (*Istis, quaeso, ista horribilia minitare purpuratis tuis. Theodori quidem nihil interest, humine an sublime putescat, Tusculans* 1.102).[17]

A story reported by Strabo points in a similar direction. The grammarian Daphitas is said to have been crucified in Magnesia because of a derogatory epigram against the Attalid(?) kings; however, a parallel tradition in Cicero and elsewhere suggests that he was thrown down from a rock.[18]

[16] On this see E. Stauffer, *Jerusalem und Rom*, Munich 1957, 123ff. He gives an account of crucifixion in Palestine from the Persian period on (which of course needs a critical examination); also the well-considered remarks by C. D. Peddinghaus (see bibliography), 38f. Cf. also *Assumption of Moses* 8.1: *qui confitentes circumcisionem in cruce suspendit* (he crucified those who professed circumcision).

[17] The different versions of the anecdote are given in E. Mannebach, *Aristippi et Cyrenaicorum Fragmenta*, Leiden-Cologne 1961, 59f. The manner of death is not always the same. Plutarch, *Moralia* 499D, quotes the abbreviated anecdote immediately after the mention of crucifixion and impalement (see above, p. 69 n. 1); in *Moralia* 606B Theodorus is threatened with death in an iron cage. Cicero, the earliest witness, could have formulated the threat in terms of crucifixion *ad hoc*. Alexander threatens the martyr philosopher Anaxarchus the same way in *Gnomologium Vaticanum* 64. The background of the anecdote is the Cynic contempt for any form of piety towards the dead or towards funeral rites, which were so important in antiquity: see already Teles (Hense, p. 31), and the evidence given here. Seneca the Elder, *Controversiae* exc. 8.4, is typical: *Omnibus natura sepulturam dedit; naufragos fluctus, qui expulit, sepelit; suffixorum corpora a crucibus in sepulturam defluunt; eos qui vivi uruntur, poena funerat.* (Nature has given forms of burial for all: the wave which flings shipwrecked mariners into the sea also buries them; the bodies of those fastened to crosses decompose; the penalty itself incinerates those who are burnt alive.) Cf. M. Hengel, *Nachfolge und Charisma*, BZNW 34, 1968, 6 n. 16.

[18] Strabo, *Geography* 14.1.39. There is a parallel Latin tradition in Cicero, *De fato* 5; Valerius Maximus 1.8, ext. 8, cf. also *Suidae Lexicon* s.v. 'Daphitas'. The division in the tradition could derive from a confusion between κρημνέναι, 'hang', 'crucify' (Appian, *Mithridatic Wars*, 97), and κρημνίζειν, 'cast down'. For the whole question see Crusius, *PW* IV, 2134f.

Further evidence that insubordinate intellectuals had to reckon
with the possibility of crucifixion under the Diadochi kings is probably to be found in an epigram which Philip V of Macedon composed as a reply to an impudent epigram composed by Alcaeus of
Messene over Philip's defeat at Cynoscephalae:

> Leafless and without bark, O traveller, on this hill-top
> Stands for Alcaeus a cross, towering aloft in the sun.

> Ἄφλοιος καὶ ἄφυλλος, ὁδοιπόρε, τῷδ' ἐπὶ νώτῳ
> Ἀλκαίῳ σταυρὸς πήγνυται ἠλίβατος
>
> (Plutarch, Titus Flaminius 9.4).

Here the king threatens the poet with a gruesome fate should he
fall into his hands. These examples show that even in the pre-
Roman, Hellenistic period, crucifixion was not unknown as a
punishment for state criminals in the Greek-speaking East as well.
On the other hand, clear instances of the crucifixion of slaves only
occur more frequently under Roman rule.

The epitaph of a master murdered by his slave, from Amysos in
Caria, finally records that the citizens of the town – and not the
Roman authorities – 'hung the murderer alive for the wild beasts
and birds of prey'.[19] It dates from the second or first century BC.
Roman influence may already be evident here, since in 133 BC
Attalus III had made over his kingdom to the Romans.

Whereas it seems clear so far that crucifixion and impalement –
the two are closely connected – appear in connection with crimes of
lèse-majesté and high treason, or in the context of acts of war, in the
Roman period this form of execution appears more frequently as a
punishment for slaves and violent criminals from among the
population of the provinces. H.-W. Kuhn's conclusion, drawn
from the relatively few reports of crucifixion in Greece and Asia

[19] The Collection of Ancient Greek Inscriptions in the British Museum IV,
2, ed. F. H. Marshall, 1916, no. 1036: ἀλλὰ πολῖται ἐμοὶ τὸν ἐμὲ ῥέξαντα τοιαῦτα
θηρσὶ καὶ οἰωνοῖς ζωὸν ἀνεκρέμασαν. Cf. K. Latte (see bibliography), 1606; for
the 'hanging' of slaves see above, p. 71. The text of the inscription also
appears in L. Robert, Études Anatoliennes 3, Paris 1937, 389 n. o. M.
Rostovtzeff, The Social and Economic History of the Hellenistic World III,
London 1941, 1521 n.76, asks whether this execution may not have taken
place in connection with the slave revolt of Aristonicus. However, what we
have here is an individual action: the slave had killed his master Demetrius, who had got drunk at a banquet, and set fire to the house.

Minor during the first 150 years of the common era, is misleading; it is not the case 'that crucifixion was not perhaps as frequent as is usually supposed in this important missionary area of early Christianity'.[20] First, we have relatively few sources from this period. For orators like Dio Chrysostom,[21] Aristides or Maximus of Tyre, or learned writers like Plutarch, the crucifixion of slaves and robbers was an unappetizing theme; still, Plutarch knew well enough that 'every criminal condemned to death bears his cross on his back' (καὶ τῷ μὲν σώματι τῶν κολαζομένων ἕκαστος κακούργων ἐκφέρει τὸν αὑτοῦ σταυρόν).[22] Honorific inscriptions and epitaphs also had other things to record than cruel executions. However, the 'completely certain evidence'[23] that we lack is abundantly supplied by the Greek romances, the satires of Lucian the Syrian, the treatise on dreams by Artemidorus of Ephesus,[24] the medical[25] and not least the astrological literature, where the constellation of Andromeda brought an especial threat of the cross. Bad nativities in connection with Mars and Saturn also threatened crucifixion and other *summa supplicia*.[26] Here there were fewer

---

[20] H.-W. Kuhn (see bibliography), 10.

[21] He mentions only the classic case of Polycrates (17.15, see above p. 24): 'he met with no easy death, but was crucified by that barbarian and thus perished' (μηδὲ ῥᾳδίου γε θανάτου τυχεῖν, ἀλλ᾽ ἀνασκολοπισθέντα ὑπὸ τοῦ βαρβάρου διαφθαρῆναι).

[22] Plutarch, *Moralia* 554A/B; cf. 554D: στρεβλοῦν ἢ κρεμαννύναι τὸν πονηρόν. See also p. 69 n. 1 above on 499D.

[23] H.-W. Kuhn, op. cit. The term 'completely certain evidence' as applied to ancient history needs to be defined here. There are only various degrees of probability.

[24] Artemidorus, *Oneirocriticon* 1.76; 2.53; 2.68; 4.33; 4.49. Even in the late dream book by Achmes, *Oneirocriticon* 90 (Drexel, pp. 54f.), the theme of crucifixion as a form of execution appears in various modes.

[25] Galen, *De Usu Partium* 12.11 (Helmreich II, p.214): ἢ σταυρῷ προσηλωμένον; cf. also the unburied bodies of robbers put on display on a hillside, on which Galen was able to pursue anatomical studies: *De Anatomicis Administrationibus* 3 (Kühn II, p.385).

[26] Andromeda: Manilius, *Astronomica* 5.553: *et cruce uirginea moritura puella pependit* (and the virgin maiden hung dying on the cross). Cf. *Liber Hermetis Trismegisti* XXV, ed. Gundel, AAM phil.-hist. Abteilung, NF 12, 1936, p. 51, 25f.: *crucifixos facit propter Andromedam; Catalogus Codicum Astrologorum Graecorum* VIII.1, ed. F. Cumont, 1929, p. 248.16ff. Mars and Saturn: *Liber Hermetis* ... XXVI, p. 79, 26–32: *Saturnus et Mars in ascendente* ...; *et natus malum coniugium habebit et ipse erit prauus mali*

aesthetic constraints about calling a spade a spade: the atmosphere here was closest to the reality of everyday life and thus to the thoughts and feelings of ordinary people. One might go on to ask

---

consilii . . . et plures eorum moriuntur a daemonibus . . . quoniam et cruc(i) plures affixi mortui sunt et decollati sunt vel mutilati sunt membra vel vivi combusti fuerunt (the one born when Saturn and Mars are in the ascendant will have a bad marriage and he himself will be wicked and of evil counsel . . . and many of them will die from demons . . . since many have died fastened to crosses or have been decapitated or their limbs have been mutilated or they have been burnt alive); they are very dangerous for the fugitive slave: *Catalogus Codicum Graecorum* V.3, ed. I. Heeg, 1910, p. 84. 29f.: ἐὰν δὲ ὁ μὲν Ἄρης ἐκ τῶν εὐωνύμων, ὁ δὲ Κρόνος ἐκ τῶν δεξιῶν αὐτὴν περιέχωσιν, ὁ φυγὼν ἀνασταυρωθήσεται (If [the moon] is between Ares on the left and Cronos on the right, the fugitive will be crucified). Firmicus Maternus, *Mathesis* 6.31.58 (Kroll/Skutsch II, 164): '*Si vero cum his Saturnus fuerit inventus, ipse nobis exitium mortis ostendit. Nam (in) istis facinoribus deprehensus severa animadvertentis sententia patibulo subfixus in crucem tollitur*' (But if Saturn is found in conjunction with these, it shows us a deadly fate. For those who are detected in such crimes are punished with a severe sentence, fastened to the stake and crucified). See also *Catalogus* VIII.1, ed. F. Cumont, 1929, p. 176, 15f., for the case of a very bad constellation: καὶ ἀνασταυρούμενον δηλοῦσι, τὸν τοιοῦτον *(i.e. ληστήν . . . καὶ ἀνδροφόνον)* (and they show that such a man [i.e. a robber . . . and murderer] will be crucified); op. cit. VIII.4, ed. P. Boudreaux-F. Cumont, 1922, p. 200, 12f.: μαρτυρηθεὶς δὲ ὁ Ἄρης ὑπὸ Ἡλίου, ἀπὸ δήμου ἢ πλήθους ἢ βασιλέων ἀναιρεῖ σταυρουμένους ἢ ἀποκεφαλιζομένους ἢ θηριομαχοῦντας (shown by Ares under the sun that they will be crucified or beheaded or put to the beasts by the people or by the rabble or by kings); p. 201.22f.: ὁ Κρόνος ὑπογείῳ, Ἄρης μεσουρανῶν νυκτὸς ποιοῦσιν ἐσταυρωμένους καὶ ὑπὸ ὀρνέων βεβρωμένους (Cronos at its nadir and Ares in mid-heaven by night indicate those who are crucified and eaten by birds); cf. op. cit. IX.1, ed. S. Weinstock, 1951, p. 150.23f.: μετὰ σπονδύλου ἀνθρώπου ἐσταυρωμένου (with the vertebra of a crucified man). Firmicus Maternus, *Mathesis* 6.31.73 (II.169); 8.6.11 (II.298: *aut tolluntur in crucem, aut crura illis publica animadversione franguntur* (they are either crucified or their legs are broken by public sentence); 8.22.3 (II, 237), see above p. 49; 8.25.6 (II, 333f.): *In XVIII parte Librae quicumque habuerit horoscopum, in crucem iussu imperatoris tolletur, aut praesente imperatore torquebitur, aut iussu principali suspendetur* (anyone who has the ascendant in the eighteenth degree of Libra will be crucified at the order of the emperor or will be tortured in the presence of the emperor or will be hung on his orders). But there was not only the possibility that the emperor might have citizens crucified. Under the constellation of Mars and the moon a tyrant could meet with the same fate: *Catalogus* XI.1, ed. C. O. Zuretti, 1932, p. 259.8: τὸν τύραννον ἑαυτὸν ἀπαρτᾶν λέγε ἢ σταυρούμενον. Cf. also F. Cumont, op. cit. (above p. 9 n. 20), 296ff., and Pseudo-Manetho, *Apotelesmatica* 1.148f.; 4.197ff.; 5.219ff., see n. 20 above.

what 'completely certain evidence' – which Kuhn misses for the
East – we have for crucifixion in this period from Roman Gaul,
from Spain – apart from the one account about Galba (see above,
p. 40), North Africa and the Danube provinces. There, too, was it
only a very rare form of execution? Lastly, the very places which
were the centres of Paul's activity were also centres of Roman
power. Corinth, Philippi, Troas, Pisidian Antioch, Lystra and
Iconium (this last at least from the time of Hadrian) were Roman
colonies, and in Syrian Antioch, Ephesus, Thessalonica and
Corinth there were Roman provincial governors who followed
Roman legal practice, especially in capital cases. As a Roman
citizen, Paul himself will have been well informed about the execution of Roman justice and his own rights as a citizen (Acts 25.11f.).
Moreover, from the evidence that we have for crucifixion in the
Greek-speaking provinces, we may conclude that the cross was
very well known to every slave and peasant in this part of the
empire also. Attitudes to it may have been different. The Palestinian
peasant, his sympathies with the freedom movement, saw in it the
feared and hated instrument of repression employed by his Roman
overlords, whereas the majority of the inhabitants of the Greek
cities will have regarded it as a horrible but nevertheless necessary
instrument for the preservation of law and order against robbers,
violent men and rebellious slaves. In the East, in particular, the
end of the Civil War and the beginning of the Principate brought
great relief, increased security and economic revival, which was
highly esteemed by the urban population.

Moreover, on the whole the evidence for crucifixion in this area
is not as sparse as all that. In 97 BC, Q. Mucius Scaevola, as proconsul of Asia, had a slave and chief agent of the tax farmers
executed on the cross immediately before he was due to be freed
(Diodorus Siculus 37.5.3).[27] During the First Mithridatic War, in
88 BC, after the capture of the island of Sciathos, Q. Bruttius Sura
had crucified slaves who were in the service of Mithridates (Appian,
Mithridatic Wars 29). The execution of pirates by the young Caesar

---

[27] Freeing him would have made the *servile supplicium* impossible, see
above pp. 44f. For the crucifixions of Mithridates VI of Pontus, see above,
p. 23 n. 11.

in Pergamon about 75 BC is well known.[28] Suetonius (*Iulius* 74.1)
has the interesting but probably secondary version that with his
proverbial clemency Caesar had the pirates' throats cut before
crucifixion in order to spare them suffering (*iugulari prius iussit,
deinde suffigi*). In AD 44 Claudius restricted the freedom of the island
state of Rhodes because the Rhodians 'had crucified some Romans'
(ὅτι 'Ρωμαίους τινὰς ἀνεσκολόπισαν, Dio Cassius 60.24.4). As a
civitas foederata atque libera, which had been a faithful ally of Rome
for almost 250 years, Rhodes had independent capital justice. The
background to this event is, however, obscure.[29] According to
Suetonius, Domitian had Hermogenes, a writer from Tarsus,
executed because of some objectionable allusions in one of his
books, while the unfortunate slaves who had written it out were
crucified out of hand (*Domitian* 10.1).[30] As evidence from Egypt
I have found the report of a trial from the first century AD; unfortunately the text is very fragmentary. It contains a hearing of
four defendants before a high Roman official, presumably in Alexandria. One of the accused is to be flogged, and there is a mention
of crucifixion towards the end (σταυροποίαν [π]είσεται).[31] The

---

[28] Plutarch, *Caesar* 2.2–4; Valerius Maximus 6.9.15.

[29] Dio Cassius 60.24.2. M. P. Charlesworth, *CAH* X, ²1952, 682,
conjectures 'a riot in which some Roman citizens were crucified'; similarly
D. Magie, *Roman Rule in Asia Minor* I, Princeton 1950, 548. In II, 1406,
Magie conjectures an identification with the *seditio* which Tacitus, *Annals*
12.58.2, reports for AD 53: *redditur Rhodiis libertas, adempta saepe aut
firmata, prout bellis externis meruerant aut domi seditione deliquerant* (The
Rhodians recovered their liberties, so often forfeited or confirmed as the
balance varied between their military service abroad and their serious
offences at home). Possibly this *seditio* merely consisted in the fact that the
people of Rhodes wanted to show their power of jurisdiction as a *civitas
libera*.

[30] It remains obscure whether this happened in Rome or somewhere
in the East.

[31] *POxy* 2339; this is evidently a genuine account of the proceedings.
That no crucifixion appears in the literary *Acta Alexandrinorum* can be
explained, in my view, by the fact that this despised form of execution
was below the status of the respected citizens of Alexandria who are
celebrated here. From the time of the Ptolemies onwards there were two
forms of flogging as a punishment practised in Alexandria. The worse
kind, scourging, was only carried out on criminals from the lower classes.
Flaccus punished the thirty-eight members of the Jewish Gerousia in this

editor connects the text with unrest among the Greeks and Jews during which, according to Josephus, there were numerous executions. This, of course, only made matters worse (*BJ* 2.489). For the time of Caligula Philo reports torture and crucifixions of Jews in the amphitheatre of the Egyptian capital (*In Flaccum* 72, 84f.). In the romance of Xenophon of Ephesus, which probably comes from the second century AD, the prefect of Egypt has the unfortunate hero crucified on a false charge; however, in a miraculous way the crucified man is rescued by the divine Nile, and the woman who has denounced him (and has murdered her husband) suffers the due penalty.[32]

A brief word should also be said about the Greek romances generally. Crucifixion of the hero or heroine is part of their stock in trade, and only a higher form of this 'recreational literature', as represented say by Heliodorus' *Aethiopica*, scorns such cruelty. In the *Babyloniaca* written by the Syrian Iamblichus, the hero is twice overtaken by this fearful punishment, but on both occasions he is taken down from the cross and freed.[33] Habrocomes, the chief figure in the romance by Xenophon of Ephesus which has already been mentioned, is first tortured almost to death and later crucified. Even his beloved, Anthea, is in danger of being crucified after she has killed a robber in self-defence.[34] However, heroes cannot on any account be allowed to suffer such a painful and shameful death – this can only befall evil-doers.[35] Chariton of Aphrodisias,

---

way (Philo, *In Flaccum* 75). In the account of the trial one of the accused with an Egyptian name protests against the flogging: he claims that it is against the law and threatens success in war. The alleged crucifixion mentioned by R. Taubenschlag, *The Law of Greco-Roman Egypt in the Light of the Papyri*, Warsaw [2]1955, 434 n.25 (BGU 1024.8–11) is in fact an execution by the sword. Of course we have only a very few accounts of capital cases from Egypt.

[32] *Ephesiaca* 4.2.1ff.; 4.4.2 (Hercher, *Erotici Scriptores Graeci* I, pp.374f.).
[33] Iamblichus, *Babyloniaca* 2 and 21 (Hercher I, pp.221, 229), according to Photius, *Bibliotheca*.
[34] Xenophon, *Ephesiaca* 2.6; 4.2.1ff.; 4.6.2 (Hercher I, pp.351f., 374f., 378).
[35] Ibid., 4.4.2 (Hercher I, p.277): Cyno, who murdered her husband; Chariton 3.4.18 (Hercher II, p.57): the robber Theron at the tomb of

who was perhaps still writing in the first century AD, gives a vivid
description of crucifixion as a punishment for slaves: sixteen slaves
from the domains of the satrap Mithridates escaped from their
lodgings, but were recaptured and, chained together by necks and
feet, were led to the place of execution, each carrying his own cross.
'The executioners supplemented the necessary death penalty by
other wretched practices such as were effective as an example to the
rest(of the slaves)', i.e. the whole proceedings were designed above
all as a deterrent. The hero of the romance is saved at the last
moment, just before he is to be nailed to the cross.[36]

There are further indications of the relatively frequent use of
crucifixion. Lucian, for example in his portrayal of the arrival of the
dead in the underworld,[37] or a pseudonymous letter of Diogenes,[38]

Callirhoe, whom he has sold to slave-dealers; cf. the crucifixion of the
murderers of Darius on the tomb of the dead ruler in the Alexander
romance, see above, p. 73 n. 14.

[36] Chariton 4.2.6ff.; 4.3.3ff.; cf. 5.10.6 (II, pp.72f., 75, 103). K.
Kerényi, *Die griechisch-orientalische Romanliteratur in religionsgeschichtlicher Beleuchtung*, Darmstadt ²1962, investigates the theme of crucifixion
and suffering in the Greek romances in detail (109ff.; 123ff.; delivery from
the cross and transfiguration). However, his idea that the ancient Egyptian
Ded-column of Osiris underlies the theme of the cross (110ff.) and his
introduction of gnostic writings are misleading. The ancient romance
writers wanted to introduce tension into their stories with 'crime, sex and
religion', but they were not concealing any mysteries. The verdict of R.
Merkelbach, *Roman und Mysterium in der Antike*, Munich and Berlin
1962, 180, is more restrained: he seeks to see crucifixion as an 'initiation
test' (cf. 191). However, this too is improbable. Crucifixion simply
represents the supreme threat to the hero, and screws up tension to the
highest pitch. See the criticism of Kerényi in A. D. Nock, *Essays on
Religion and the Ancient World* I, ed. Z. Stewart, Oxford 1972, 170, who
rightly points out that crucifixion plays no part in the mysteries: Osiris
was not crucified.

[37] *Cataplous* 6: τοὺς ἐκ δικαστηρίου . . . παράγαγε, λέγω δὲ τοὺς ἐκ τυμπάνου καὶ
τοὺς ἀνεσκολοπισμένους (Bring in the output of the courts, I mean those who
died by the *tympanon* and by the cross), cf. also *De morte Peregrini* 45 and
Sextus Empiricus, *Adversus Mathematicos* 2.30, where crucifixion is miss-
ing and there is mention only of prison and the *tympanon*.

[38] Diogenes, *Epistle* 28.3 (Hercher, p.242): οὔκουν πολλοὶ μὲν ἐπὶ τῶν
σταυρῶν κρέμανται, πολλοὶ δὲ ὑπὸ τοῦ δημίου ἀπεσφαγμένοι (many are hung on the
cross and many have their throats cut by the executioner). Cf. the anecdote
ascribed to him, Diogenes Laertius, *Vita Philosophorum* 6.45.

indicate that its significance in the Greek-speaking world was by no means inconsiderable. In Lucian's dialogue *Piscator* (ch. 2), the philosophers are summoned by Socrates to consider how they are to kill the free-thinking Parrhesiades. The first proposal from the assembled company is, 'I think he should be crucified'; the next speaker agrees: 'Yes, by Zeus, but before that he must be flogged'; there then follows putting out his eyes and cutting off his tongue. There could be a distant allusion here to Plato's just man crucified (see above, p. 28). At all events, death by crucifixion seems to be taken for granted as the *summum supplicium*. On the basis of the examples given here, which could certainly be multiplied further, we may conclude that in the Greek-speaking East crucifixion was no less well-known, feared and abhorred than in the Latin West – particularly among the lower classes.[39]

All this leads to a final conclusion which it is difficult to resist. When Paul spoke in his mission preaching about the 'crucified Christ' (I Corinthians 1.23; 2.2; Galatians 3.1), every hearer in the Greek-speaking East between Jerusalem and Illyria (Romans 15.19) knew that this 'Christ' – for Paul the title was already a proper name – had suffered a particularly cruel and shameful death, which as a rule was reserved for hardened criminals, rebellious slaves and rebels against the Roman state. That this crucified Jew, Jesus Christ, could truly be a divine being sent on earth, God's Son, the Lord of all and the coming judge of the world, must inevitably have been thought by any educated man to be utter 'madness' and presumptuousness.

[39] I have deliberately left aside instances where crucifixion seems to have been introduced secondarily into the earlier Greek traditions, e.g. in the two fables of Hyginus, no. 194 on the zither player Arion and the pirates, and no. 257 on Phalaris of Selinunte and the two Pythagorean friends, which Schiller turned into his famous ballad 'Die Bürgschaft'.

I I

Crucifixion among the Jews

The history of crucifixion in Judaea and in the Jewish tradition really needs a separate investigation; I have therefore deliberately kept the μωρία of the cross among the 'Gentiles' (I Corinthians 1.23) in the foreground. H.-W. Kuhn is quite right in stressing that the σκάνδαλον τοῦ σταυροῦ for the Jews according to I Corinthians 1.23; Galatians 5.11 has a religious character going back to Deuteronomy 21.23.[1] Y. Yadin has demonstrated by means of the Qumran temple scroll that in the Hellenistic-Hasmonean period crucifixion was practised as the form of death penalty applied in cases of high treason – probably for this very reason; it was taken over from the non-Jewish world. The *arbori infelici suspendere* in severe cases of *perduellio* in Rome is something of an analogy here.[2] Anyone who had betrayed his own people to a foreign enemy had to be subjected to the utmost dishonour. This explains the crucifixion of 800 Pharisees by Alexander Jannaeus[3] and the remarkable report, already handed down in the Mishnah, that Simeon b. Shetah had seventy or eighty 'sorceresses' 'hung' in Ashkelon; in my view what we have here is a polemical encipherment of the

[1] H.-W. Kuhn (see bibliography), 36f.
[2] Y. Yadin, *Pesher Nahum* (see bibliography). The objections made by J. M. Baumgarten (see bibliography) are not at all convincing.
[3] Josephus, *BJ* 1.97f.; *Antiquitates* 13.380–3, cf. *BJ* 1.113; *Antiquitates* 13.410f.; see J. M. Allegro, *Qumran Cave 4*, I, DJDJ V, 1968, 37–42, no. 169; 4QpNah 3–4 col. I.4–9; see also J. Strugnell, 'Notes en marge du volume V des "Discoveries in the Judaean Desert of Jordan"', *RdQ* 7, 1969–71, (163–276) 207. For Jannaeus' banquet before those who were crucified see Iamblichus, *Babyloniaca* 21 (Hercher I, p.229): King Garmos, garlanded and dancing, holds a banquet with flute-players in front of the hero's cross. For the killing of women and children before the eyes of those who were crucified see Herodotus 4.202.1 and 9.120.4.

Pharisaic counter-reaction against the Sanhedrin after the death of Alexander Jannaeus, under queen Salome, when the Pharisees who had reached positions of power in the state took vengeance on the Sadducean advisers of the dead king and repaid them with like for like. The proud Sadducean priests and officers were transformed into pagan witches in a radical polemical transformation. The striking thing about this anecdote is that Ashkelon was the only city in Palestine which the Hasmoneans had not sacked.[4]

It is all the more significant that Herod broke with this tradition of execution and it can hardly be a coincidence that not a single crucifixion is reported by Josephus from his time. Did the king want to dissociate himself from Hasmonean custom? This mass murderer would surely not have had humane considerations in mind. The excessive use made of crucifixion by the Romans in the pacification of Judaea meant that from the beginning of direct Roman rule crucifixion was taboo as a form of the Jewish death penalty. This change can also be inferred from rabbinic interpretation of Deuteronomy 21.23. Varus had already had two thousand prisoners crucified around Jerusalem,[5] and AD 70, the year of terror, brought a sorry climax in this respect too. Nevertheless, the cross never became the symbol of Jewish suffering; the influence of Deuteronomy 21.23 made this impossible. So a crucified messiah could not be accepted either. It was here that the preaching of the earliest Christians caused particular offence in the mother country itself. It also explains why the theme of the crucified faithful plays no part in Jewish legends about martyrs. The cross had become too much a sign of the passion of Jesus and his followers – though in the Talmudic literature we have a whole series of references to the crucifixion of Jews during the later empire.

[4] Mishnah, *Sanhedrin* 6.5, cf. *j.Sanh.* 23c. This tradition, which completely contradicts the whole of the later rabbinic legal tradition, cannot be pure invention. I regard it as a tradition which has been encoded in the interests of polemic. Those in the know would be fully aware of its meaning. Josephus, *BJ* 1.113, and above all *Antiquitates* 13.410f., shows that the Pharisees took bloody revenge. For 'hanging' as a punishment for high treason see also Targum Jonathan II on Num.25.4; M. Hengel, *Nachfolge und Charisma*, BZNW 34, 1968, 64 n.77.

[5] See p. 26 n. 17 above. Cf. *Assumption of Moses* 6.9: *aliquos crucifigit circa coloniam eorum.*

12

Summary

I have attempted to give a survey of the use of crucifixion as a penalty in the Graeco-Roman world, as a contribution towards a better understanding of Paul's remark about the μωρία of the λόγος τοῦ σταυροῦ. The following points may be made in conclusion. I am well aware that this study remains essentially incomplete, for now at the end I should really begin all over again with a detailed exegesis of the evidence about the cross in the writings of Paul. As it is, I am breaking off where theological work proper ought to begin. The preceding chapters are no more than 'historical preliminaries' for a presentation of the *theologia crucis* in Paul. The reader must therefore excuse me if I now do no more than hint at some of the theological lines which mark out the further possibilities of progress, along with a summary of the historical results.

1. Crucifixion as a penalty was remarkably widespread in antiquity. It appears in various forms among numerous peoples of the ancient world, even among the Greeks. There was evidently neither the desire nor the power to abolish it, even where people were fully aware of its extreme cruelty. It thus formed a harsh contradiction to the idealistic picture of antiquity which was inaugurated by Winckelmann in terms of 'noble simplicity and quiet greatness' (*edle Einfalt und stille Grösse*). Our own age, which is proud of its humanity and its progress, but which sees the use of the death penalty, torture and terror increasing in the world rather than decreasing, can hardly pride itself on having overcome this ancient contradiction.

2. Crucifixion was and remained a political and military punishment. While among the Persians and the Carthaginians it was

imposed primarily on high officials and commanders, as on rebels, among the Romans it was inflicted above all on the lower classes, i.e. slaves, violent criminals and the unruly elements in rebellious provinces, not least in Judaea.

3. The chief reason for its use was its allegedly supreme efficacy as a deterrent; it was, of course, carried out publicly. As a rule the crucified man was regarded as a criminal who was receiving just and necessary punishment. There was doubtless a fear that to give up this form of execution might undermine the authority of the state and existing law and order.

4. At the same time, crucifixion satisfied the primitive lust for revenge and the sadistic cruelty of individual rulers and of the masses. It was usually associated with other forms of torture, including at least flogging. At relatively small expense and to great public effect the criminal could be tortured to death for days in an unspeakable way. Crucifixion is thus a specific expression of the inhumanity dormant within men which these days is expressed, for example, in the call for the death penalty, for popular justice and for harsher treatment of criminals, as an expression of retribution. It is a manifestation of trans-subjective evil, a form of execution which manifests the demonic character of human cruelty and bestiality.

5. By the public display of a naked victim at a prominent place – at a crossroads, in the theatre, on high ground, at the place of his crime – crucifixion also represented his uttermost humiliation, which had a numinous dimension to it. With Deuteronomy 21.23 in the background, the Jew in particular was very aware of this. This form of execution, more than any other, had associations with the idea of human sacrifice, which was never completely suppressed in antiquity. The sacrifice of countless hordes of people in our century to national idols or to the 'correct' political view shows that this irrational demand for human sacrifice can be found even today.

6. Crucifixion was aggravated further by the fact that quite often its victims were never buried. It was a stereotyped picture that the crucified victim served as food for wild beasts and birds of prey. In this way his humiliation was made complete. What it meant for a man in antiquity to be refused burial, and the dishonour which

went with it, can hardly be appreciated by modern man.

7. In Roman times, crucifixion was practised above all on dangerous criminals and members of the lowest classes. These were primarily people who had been outlawed from society or slaves who on the whole had no rights, in other words, groups whose development had to be suppressed by all possible means to safeguard law and order in the state. Because large strata of the population welcomed the security and the world-wide peace which the empire brought with it, the crucified victim was defamed both socially and ethically in popular awareness, and this impression was heightened still further by the religious elements involved.

8. Relatively few attempts at criticism or even at a philosophical development of the theme of the boundless suffering of countless victims of crucifixion can be found. At best, we can see it in the Stoic preaching of the $\dot{a}\pi\dot{a}\theta\epsilon\iota a$ and $\dot{a}\rho\epsilon\tau\dot{\eta}$, the calmness and virtue of the wise man, where in some circumstances the torment of the man dying on the cross could be used as a metaphor. Here crucifixion became a simile for the suffering from which the wise man can free himself only by death, which delivers the soul from the body to which it is tied. In the romances, on the other hand, crucifixion made for exciting entertainment and sensationalism. Here the suffering was not really taken seriously. The accounts of the crucifixion of the hero served to give the reader a thrill: the tension was then resolved by the freeing of the crucified victim and the obligatory happy ending.

9. In this context, the earliest Christian message of the crucified messiah demonstrated the 'solidarity' of the love of God with the unspeakable suffering of those who were tortured and put to death by human cruelty, as this can be seen from the ancient sources. This suffering has continued down to the present century in a 'passion story' which we cannot even begin to assess, a 'passion story' which is based on human sin, in which we all without exception participate, as beings who live under the power of death. In the person and the fate of the one man Jesus of Nazareth this saving 'solidarity' of God with us is given its historical and physical form. In him, the 'Son of God', God himself took up the 'existence of a slave' and died the 'slaves' death' on the tree of martyrdom (Philippians 2.8), given up

to public shame (Hebrews 12.2) and the 'curse of the law' (Galatians 3.13), so that in the 'death of God' life might win victory over death. In other words, in the death of Jesus of Nazareth God identified himself with the extreme of human wretchedness, which Jesus endured as a representative of us all, in order to bring us to the freedom of the children of God:

> He who did not spare his own Son,
> but gave him up for us all,
> will he not also give us all things with him? (Romans 8.32)

This radical kenosis of God was the revolutionary new element in the preaching of the gospel. It caused offence, but in this very offence it revealed itself as the centre of the gospel. For the death of Jesus on the cross is very much more than a religious symbol, say of the uttermost readiness of a man for suffering and sacrifice; it is more than just an ethical model which calls for discipleship, though it is all this *as well*. What we have here is God's communication of himself, the free action through which he establishes the effective basis of our salvation. In ancient thought, e.g. among the Stoics, an ethical and symbolic interpretation of the crucifixion was still possible, but to assert that God himself accepted death in the form of a crucified Jewish manual worker from Galilee in order to break the power of death and bring salvation to all men could only seem folly and madness to men of ancient times. Even now, any genuine theology will have to be measured against the test of this scandal.

10. When Paul talks of the 'folly' of the message of the crucified Jesus, he is therefore not speaking in riddles or using an abstract cipher. He is expressing the harsh experience of his missionary preaching and the offence that it caused, in particular the experience of his preaching among non-Jews, with whom his apostolate was particularly concerned. The reason why in his letters he talks about the cross above all in a polemical context is that he deliberately wants to provoke his opponents, who are attempting to water down the offence caused by the cross. Thus in a way the 'word of the cross' is the spearhead of his message. And because Paul still understands the cross as the real, cruel instrument of execution, as the instrument of the bloody execution of Jesus, it is impossible to

dissociate talk of the atoning death of Jesus or the blood of Jesus from this 'word of the cross'. The spearhead cannot be broken off the spear. Rather, the complex of the death of Jesus is a single entity for the apostle, in which he never forgets the fact that Jesus did not die a gentle death like Socrates, with his cup of hemlock, much less passing on 'old and full of years' like the patriarchs of the Old Testament. Rather, he died like a slave or a common criminal, in torment, on the tree of shame. Paul's Jesus did not die just any death; he was 'given up for us all' on the cross, in a cruel and a contemptible way.

The theological reasoning of our time shows very clearly that the particular form of the death of Jesus, the man and the messiah, represents a scandal which people would like to blunt, remove or domesticate in any way possible. We shall have to guarantee the truth of our theological thinking at this point. Reflection on the harsh reality of crucifixion in antiquity may help us to overcome the acute loss of reality which is to be found so often in present theology and preaching.

BIBLIOGRAPHY

I. Barkan, *Capital Punishment in Ancient Athens*, Chicago 1936
J. M. Baumgarten, 'Does *tlh* in the Temple Scroll refer to Crucifixion?',
JBL 91, 1972, 472–81
E. Benz, *Der gekreuzigte Gerechte bei Plato, im Neuen Testament und in
der alten Kirche*, AAMz 1950, no. 12
J. Blinzler, *Der Prozess Jesu*, Regensburg ⁴1969; ET of 2nd ed., *The
Trial of Jesus*, Westminster, Md, 1959
E. Brandenburger, 'Σταυρός, Kreuzigung Jesu und Kreuzestheologie',
WuD NF 10, 1969, 17–43
E. Dinkler, 'Jesu Wort vom Kreuztragen', *Signum Crucis. Aufsätze zum
Neuen Testament und zur Christlichen Archäologie*, Tübingen 1967,
77–98
id., 'Das Kreuz als Siegeszeichen', ibid., 55–76
id., 'Kreuzzeichen und Kreuz. Tav, Chi und Stauros', ibid., 26–54
id., 'Zur Geschichte des Kreuzsymbols', ibid., 1–25
P. Ducrey, *Le traitement des prisonniers de guerre dans la Grèce antique, des
origines à la conquête romaine*, Paris 1968
id., 'Note sur la crucifixion', *MusHelv* 28, 1971, 183–5
H. Fulda, *Das Kreuz und die Kreuzigung. Eine antiquarische Untersuchung . . .*, Breslau 1878
P. Garnsey, *Social Status and Legal Privilege in the Roman Empire*,
Oxford 1970
L. Gernet, *Anthropologie de la Grèce antique*, Paris 1968, 288–329
E. Grässer, '"Der politisch gekreuzigte Christus". Kritische Anmer-
kungen zu einer politischen Hermeneutik des Evangeliums', in *Text
und Situation. Gesammelte Aufsätze zum Neuen Testament*, Gütersloh
1973, 302–30
M. Hengel, *The Son of God. The Origin of Christology and the History of
Jewish-Hellenistic Religion*, ET London and Philadelphia 1976
H. F. Hitzig, 'Crux', *PW* IV, 1901, 1728–31
M. Kähler, 'Das Kreuz. Grund und Mass der Christologie', *Schriften
zur Christologie und Mission. Gesamtausgabe der Schriften zur Mission*,
ed. H. Frohnes, ThB 42, 1971, 292–350
E. Käsemann, 'Die Gegenwart des Gekreuzigten', in *Deutscher Evan-
gelischer Kirchentag Hannover 1967. Dokumente*, Hanover 1967,
424–37, cf. 438–62

id., 'The Saving Significance of the Death of Jesus in Paul', *Perspectives on Paul*, ET London and Philadelphia 1971, 32–59

'Α. Δ. Κεραμόπουλλος, Ὁ ἀποτυμπανισμός. Συμβολὴ ἀρχαιολογικὴ εἰς τὴν ἱστορίαν τοῦ ποινικοῦ δικαίου καὶ τὴν λαογραφίαν, Βιβλιοθήκη τῆς ἐν 'Αθήναις 'Αρχαιολογικῆς 'Εταιρείας 22, Athens 1923

G. Klein, 'Das Ärgernis des Kreuzes', in *Ärgernisse. Konfrontationen mit dem Neuen Testament*, Munich 1970, 115–31

H.-W. Kuhn, 'Jesus als Gekreuzigter in der frühchristlicher Verkündigung bis zur Mitte des 2. Jahrhunderts', *ZTK* 72, 1975, 1–46

K. Latte, 'Todesstrafe', *PW* Suppl VII, 1940, 1599–1619

H.-G. Link, 'Gegenwärtige Probleme einer Kreuzestheologie. Ein Bericht', *EvTh* 33, 1973, 337–45

A. W. Lintott, *Violence in Ancient Rome*, Oxford 1968

J. Lipsius, *De Cruce libri tres*, Amsterdam 1670

W. Marxsen, 'Erwägungen zum Problem des verkündigten Kreuzes', *NTS* 8, 1961/62, 204–14

J. Moltmann, *The Crucified God*, ET London and New York 1974

T. Mommsen, *Römisches Strafrecht*, 1899 reprinted Berlin 1955

F.-J. Ortkemper, *Das Kreuz in der Verkündigung des Apostels Paulus. Dargestellt an den Texten der paulinischen Hauptbriefe*, SBS 24, [2]1968

C. D. Peddinghaus, *Die Entstehung der Leidensgeschichte. Eine traditions-geschichtliche und historische Untersuchung des Werdens und Wachsens der erzählenden Passionstradition bis zum Entwurf des Markus*, Diss. Heidelberg 1965 (typescript)

G. Q. Reijners, *The Terminology of the Holy Cross in Early Christian Literature as based upon Old Testament Typology*, Diss. Nijmegen 1965

L. Ruppert, *Jesus als der leidende Gerechte? Der Weg Jesu im Lichte eines alt- und zwischentestamentlichen Motivs*, SBS 59, 1972

J. Schneider, σταυρός κτλ., *TDNT* VII, 1971, 572–84

W. Schrage, 'Leid, Kreuz und Eschaton. Die Peristasenkataloge als Merkmale paulinischer *theologia crucis* und Eschatologie', *EvTh* 34, 1974, 141–75

J. Stockbauer, *Kunstgeschichte des Kreuzes. Die bildliche Darstellung des Erlösungstodes Christi im Monogramm, Kreuz und Crucifix*, Schaffhausen 1870

A. Strobel, *Kerygma und Apokalyptik. Ein religionsgeschichtlicher und theologischer Beitrag zur Christusfrage*, Göttingen 1967

V. Tzaferis, 'Jewish Tombs at and near Giv'at ha-Mivtar, Jerusalem', *IEJ* 20, 1970, 18–32

J. Vergote, 'Les principaux modes de supplice chez les anciens et dans les textes chrétiens', *Bulletin de l'Institut Historique Belge de Rome* 20, 1939, 141–63

id., 'Folkswerkzeuge', *RAC* VIII, 1972, 112–41

J. Vogt, 'Crucifixus etiam pro nobis', *Internationale katholische Zeitschrift* 2, 1973, 186–91

id., *Sklaverei und Humanität*, Historia Einzelschriften 8, Wiesbaden ²1972

P. Winter, *On the Trial of Jesus*, SJ 1, ²1974 (rev. and ed. by T. A. Burkill and G. Vermes)

Y. Yadin, 'Epigraphy and Crucifixion', *IEJ* 23, 1973, 18–22

id., 'Pesher Nahum (4Q pNahum) Reconsidered', *IEJ* 21, 1971, 1–12

A. Zestermann, *Die Kreuzigung bei den Alten*, Brussels 1868

THE ATONEMENT

I

Preliminary Questions

No human death has influenced and shaped the world of late antiquity, and indeed the history of mankind as a whole down to the present day, more than that of the Galilean craftsman and itinerant preacher who was crucified before the gates of Jerusalem in AD 30 as a rebel and messianic pretender. Thousands of men had been executed by crucifixion there by the Roman prefects and later procurators, in the sixty-five years, or thereabouts, between the transformation of Judaea into a Roman province and the end of the Jewish War. The internal Jewish tradition in the Talmudim and Midrashim has completely suppressed these countless victims of the Roman governing power down to the time of the destruction of the Second Temple. Josephus' work, preserved thanks to the Christian tradition, mentions a very few names, but apart from that, they have all been forgotten.[1] The fact that this one Galilean was not forgotten, but had a unique effect on world history, especially by means of his death, is connected with the way in which this death was interpreted: it became the foundation of Christian faith. In what follows, the most important question that we shall have to answer is: how did it come about that the disciples of Jesus could proclaim that cruel, disastrous execution of their master as the saving event *par excellence*? In other words, how did the crucifixion of Jesus come to take its place at the centre of early Christian preaching?[2] How was it that this infamous death could so quickly be interpreted as a representative, atoning, sacrificial death, and in what interpretative framework was such an understanding possible at all?

New Testament scholars usually attempt to come close to the
basic event on which the Christian community was founded by
means of form-critical and traditio-critical analyses of the earliest
pieces of tradition that we have. We shall also have to adopt this
approach in the following pages, but by itself it is not enough to
provide an answer to our question. We shall have to understand
that in a broader historical context.

As a result, I have to begin with a quite different, rather unusual
question. How did the *Gentile audience* in the Graeco-Roman
world understand this strange new message of the crucified and
risen Son of God and Redeemer? Were its categories, for example
that of the representative atoning death of Jesus, completely alien
to people who did not know either the Old Testament or the Jewish
Haggadah? Or, barbarous and offensive as the new doctrine of
salvation must have seemed to the educated, did it not also contain
basic concepts which were quite familiar to people in Ephesus,
Corinth or Rome?

Another preliminary point should be made here. One of the
most important historical distinctions with which New Testament
scholarship has worked since the emergence of the history-of-
religions school is the sharpest possible division between the 'Old
Testament and Jewish' and the 'Hellenistic' tradition. This distinction became almost a tenet of faith for German scholarship,
which divided 'conservative' from 'critical' theologians. Of course,
over the last few years – slowly enough – the view has spread that
this abrupt distinction is far too blurred, and indeed is sometimes
positively misleading. The Jews of the time of Jesus and the
apostles had been living for about four hundred years under the
influence of Greek civilization, with its scientific and technical
superiority, even in the mother country of Palestine, and in any
case the world of late antiquity forms a relative cultural and spiritual unity, which moreover spoke a common, elementary religious
koinē, spreading even beyond the linguistic barriers of the Semitic
and Greek worlds. Only if we take this fact into account can we
provide a historical explanation for phenomena like the origin of the
Septuagint and the literature of Greek-speaking Judaism, which
extended as far as Palestine itself, or the astonishing missionary

success of the Jewish-messianic sect of the Christians which from its base in Judaea penetrated so rapidly into the Graeco-Roman world. The Jewish upper classes in Palestine were also largely bilingual, and the allegedly 'anti-Hellenistic' Pharisees and the rabbinate which developed from them after AD 70 were deeply influenced by their cultural environment. It would not be much of an exaggeration to describe the whole of Judaism in the Hellenistic Roman period as 'Hellenistic Judaism'. New Testament scholarship can no longer escape this recognition.[3]

Now of course it is strange that despite this growing insight, when it comes to the question of the origin of the soteriological interpretation of the death of Jesus the old dispute between 'Hellenists' and 'Judaizers' has flared up again in a new and acute way. Particularly in Germany during the last ten years, over against the more traditional view that the interpretation of the death of Jesus as a representative atoning death comes from Old Testament and Jewish sources, it has been argued with some emphasis that in the last resort the 'death of Jesus for us' is to be derived from Greek sources and was first developed in the Hellenistic (Jewish-Christian) community.[4] In contrast to that, there were supposed to be quite different earlier, typically Jewish, categories of interpretation, which could be traced back to the earliest Palestinian community, and perhaps even to the proclamation of Jesus himself: first, that prophets are killed by their own people, and secondly, that the righteous man is exalted to God only through suffering and death.[5] This conflict points to a real problem. If the tradition of the earliest, Aramaic-speaking, Jewish community in Palestine were thought to be solely responsible for the interpretation of the death of Jesus on the cross as an event bringing about salvation and atonement for the whole world, it would be hard to understand how this particular interpretation emerges so strongly in the 'missionary literature' of the New Testament which is addressed to Gentile Christians, for example the Pauline corpus, Hebrews and I Peter, whereas in the Palestinian tradition about Jesus to be found in the synoptic gospels it appears only in a very few places. In comparison with it, the tradition of the murder of the prophets is predominant in the Logia source (Q) and the theme of the 'suffering righteous' in the passion narrative. Of course we would immediately have to ask whether they are in fact so typically 'Jewish' or 'un-Hellenistic', and whether distinctions of this kind do not prove relatively unhelpful in understanding the New Testament texts.

(ii) *The apotheosis of the dying hero*

It is surely right that among the Greeks and Romans – to put it cautiously – a whole series of closer and more distant analogies can be found to the interpretation of the death of Jesus as a *presupposition for his exaltation* and also as a representative atoning death for others. This is also true not least of terminology, but it is not just limited to that. I shall begin with a number of well-known instances. We find a voluntary acceptance of death, as the way to divine honour indicated by the gods, in a number of places in Greek myth, and in particular in connection with its most prominent figures, above all the two most popular heroes of antiquity, Heracles and Achilles. 'While the pyre was burning, it is said that a cloud passed under Heracles and with a peal of thunder wafted him up to heaven',[6] whereas the son of Peleus decided to rush off into battle against Hector, despite the warning of his divine mother, in order to meet the murderer of his beloved friend: '. . . and then I myself will accept my fate, when Zeus and the other immortal gods resolve to bring it about'. A short but glorious life seemed more desirable than a long but inglorious one.[7] In the post-Homeric saga, Thetis carries aloft the corpse of her son; in Pindar he appears as the judge of the dead (*Olympian Odes* 2,77), while other poets transport him to Elysium or to the island of Leuke in the Black Sea, where he is venerated as a god and leads an immortal life. However, one could also point to historical figures, e.g. Empedocles. To some degree depending on the audience, the saga describes how he leapt into Etna to achieve his own apotheosis, or experienced a miraculous transportation by night (Diogenes Laertius 8.67f.). There is also Plato's account of the death of Socrates, which has quite a different form. Faithful to the inner command of the god, Socrates fulfilled his task in Athens and, mindful of the laws of the city, did not try to escape the unjust death penalty imposed on him, but fearlessly drank the cup of hemlock. In this way he becomes the prototype of the martyr who looks death fearlessly in the eye for the sake of the truth – in the last resort a divine truth – which he represents.[8] We might well ask whether the theme of the 'innocent sufferer', suffering for the truth of the law, which makes such an evocative appearance in the Hellenistic period, is as Jewish as all that. It may also be influenced decisively by the ideal of the martyred philosopher, which is substantially older than the specifically Jewish transfiguration of the death of the pious and the righteous. Any historical investigation which is to do justice to the New Testament cannot be content with stressing the tradition of the Old Testament and Judaism, important though that may be; it must also pay very close attention to the Graeco-Roman world, where the problems become particularly interesting at the point where Jewish and Greek conceptions have already become fused in the pre-Christian period. By the providence of God, the New Testament is written in Greek, and not Hebrew or Aramaic.

The ancient ideal of the *voluntary heroic apotheosis achieved through death* also appears in the person of the Cynic – and erstwhile Christian – Peregrinus Proteus, who immolated himself in Olympia in AD 165. The satirist Lucian described his life and death in a malicious account. He is said to have hurled himself on to the burning pyre with the cry 'May the gods of my mother and father be gracious to me', and as in the Romulus saga and the apotheosis of the Roman emperors, his transportation to heaven is confirmed by eyewitnesses (Lucian, *Peregrinus* 36.39f.). Parium, his home town, erected a statue of him which, according to the testimony of the Christian apologist Athenagoras (26), is said to have brought about miracles. Here Peregrinus followed the example of Heracles, the Indian Brahmans and the strict Cynic doctrine that death is on no account to be feared because it brings the liberation of the soul. In contrast to Lucian's caricature, many contemporaries seem to have thought highly of the philosopher for his strict standards: he did not hesitate to attack the emperor, the government and the mightiest men in the Empire, and as a result was banished from Rome.[9] The fact that according to Lucian, Peregrinus taught that

he was dying 'for men's welfare' (ὑπὲρ τῶν ἀνθρώπων), to teach
them to despise death and to overcome their fears (ἐγκαρτερεῖν
τοῖς δεινοῖς, 23, cf. 33), might well suggest that he was parodying
the attitudes of Christian martyrs.

These instances of voluntary death as the way towards deifica-
tion could be supplemented by numerous legends about the transportation or ascension of the living and the dead to the gods: from
Romulus and Alcmene through the legendary poet Aristeas, mentioned by Herodotus, to the transportation of Caesar and the later
emperors and their apotheoses.[10]

(iii) *Dying for the city and for friends*

On the other hand, it is striking that while we have the transportation of two living men, Enoch and Elijah, in the Old Testament,
there is no instance of the transportation of anyone who has died,
much less of a numinous transfiguration of death or even of a
divine glorification of the dead. In a radical way, which is unique
in the ancient world, death is robbed of its religious autonomy in a
way which makes the cult of the dead, widespread among mankind
and particularly in the ancient world, quite impossible. One might
almost say that the fact that the deceased ancestors in Israel ceased
to be *autonomous* numinous beings was a revolutionary development. The exclusive revelation of God to his people does not allow
any special cult of 'heroes'. True, there are rites of mourning regu-
lated by law and custom, and on death a man joined the 'community
of his fathers', but belief in Yahweh did not allow any kind of worship of the dead or any cultic or magical dealings with them. Where-
ever anything of this kind appears on the periphery – as with the
witch of Endor (I Sam. 28) – it is condemned out of hand as a
religious evil.[11]

It is all the more significant that in the Hellenistic period, probably under the influence of the spirit of the age, a degree of autonomy was restored to the realm of the dead, even in Palestine and
Babylonia – albeit strictly governed by belief in Yahweh's omnipo-
tence.

For this reason, the glorification or even the superhuman transfiguration of the martyr is completely alien to the Old Testament. It simply does not occur in ancient Israel. The martyrdom of the faithful becomes an independent problem only in the latest book of the Old Testament canon, the apocalypse Daniel (11.33ff.), which was written in 165 BC, about the time of the climax of the Maccabean revolt. This is only possible because at the end, to some degree as God's answer, there is a statement of the resurrection hope (12.2f.). For this reason, the literary form of the account of a martyrdom is unknown to the Old Testament texts, because it presupposes not only the resurrection hope, which overcomes death, but also a particular interest in the person of the martyr as a heroic witness, and also in his suffering. Our first examples, II Macc. 6; 7, were written by a Jew with Greek education, who was, however, familiar with Palestinian piety.[12] By contrast, in ancient Israel there are hardly any examples of dying for Israel, the Law or the sanctuary, which are stressed as heroic actions.[13] There was no room here for praise of 'the acts of the dead': the sole concern was for the glory of God: 'Not unto us, O Lord, not to us, but to thy name give glory' (Ps. 115.1). Whenever there is any mention of dying for God's sake, as in Ps. 44.22: 'Nay, for thy sake we are slain all the day long, and accounted as sheep for the slaughter', this is not done to celebrate those who are killed in this way, or to praise human bravery, but to accuse God, who refuses to help the innocent people:

> Rouse thyself! Why sleepest thou, O Lord?
> Awake! Do not cast us off for ever!
> Why dost thou hide thy face?
> Why dost thou forget our affliction and oppression?
> (Ps. 44.24f.)

Death, which for Greeks and Romans is so glorious on the battle-field, is without reservation God's judgment and mystery; even in the case of a Jonathan, the friend of David who is portrayed in such sympathetic terms, or so God-fearing a king as Josiah. The lament about the mysterious person who is 'pierced' (Zech. 12.10ff.), which is probably connected with the tradition of Josiah's death, conceals more than it reveals.[14] His death remains an insoluble riddle. Even the heroic end of Samson, the Hebrew Heracles, who takes vengeance on his enemies by his own death (Judg. 16.26–30), seems like an alien body in ancient Israel. True, there are some references to individual prophets who are killed (Jer. 26.20ff.; II Chron. 24.20ff.) or persecuted, along with the Deuteronomistic accusations of the murder of prophets in Israel (cf. Neh. 9.26) but there is no real report of a prophetic martyrdom, far less any hints of a 'theology of martyrdom'.[15] The theme of the murder of the prophets serves as a basis for God's judgment on his people; there is still no interest in the dying prophets themselves and in the circumstances of their death. The death or the suffering of the pious at the hand of the wicked is not yet an independent theme. Commemoration of the martyr prophets and the legends associated with them (even including the veneration of their tombs) only begins to become more prominent in Palestine in the Hellenistic period. This was prompted, as far as I can see, by veneration of the tombs of Greek heroes.

A representative death to atone for the guilt of others can therefore be found at best on the periphery of the Old Testament – for example in Isa. 53, which K. Koch rightly describes as an 'erratic block'.[16] There is a good deal of argument about the interpretation and influence of this text even now, which we shall have to consider later (see pp. 57ff. below). As a rule, the possibility of such representation is rejected out of hand, since 'a person may die only for his own sins'.[17] Moses' request to God to forgive the sins of his people or to be able to die for them is expressly rejected by God himself: 'I blot out from my book only those who have sinned against me.'[18]

Again, we find examples of heroic 'dying for the people or for the Law' only in the Hellenistic period, above all after the time of the Maccabean rebellion. In I Maccabees, which was originally written in Hebrew, Mattathias admonishes his sons: 'Show zeal for the Law, and give your lives for (ὑπέρ) the covenant of our fathers.' The theme of glory appears a little later: 'And receive great honour and an everlasting name.'[19] Josephus presents this invitation in an even more Graecized version: 'So prepare your souls, so that, if necessary, you can die for the Law'; here he is clearly making use of a Greek formula known since Aristotle.[20] Subsequently, similar assertions can often be found in the mouth of Jewish martyrs and freedom fighters within Jewish Hellenistic writing.[21] The description of the heroic act of Eleazar, one of the Maccabee brothers, who killed a Seleucid elephant and was crushed by the beast's fall, is typical of the new, thoroughly Greek-sounding understanding of heroic death: 'He supposed that the king was upon it. So he gave his life to save his people and to win for himself an everlasting name.' [22] We shall have to return to this and other Jewish texts on a number of further occasions. At this point, however, it should already be noted that the Old Testament background is not enough to explain it.

The situation among the *Greeks* is quite different. For them, from the classical period onwards, ἀποθνῄσκειν ὑπέρ and more rarely also (ἐπι)διδόναι ἑαυτὸν ὑπέρ, or similar formulae with περί or πρό, so familiar from New Testament christological formulae, were a stereotyped expression for the voluntary sacrifice of a man's life in the interests of his *native city, his friends, his family* or – quite peripherally – also philosophical truth. Since this terminology, so far as I can see, has hardly been investigated at all in existing litera-ture, I must dwell on it somewhat longer. The following study makes no claim to completeness. Rather, it has the character of a compilation of the fruits of relatively chance reading.

To deal with the phenomenon, a composite verb ὑπεραπο-θνῄσκειν was even formed. We find its content presented in an overwhelming way in Euripides' *Alcestis*, where Alcestis is pre-pared to die for her husband Admetus, whereas his old parents refuse to perform this service,[23] or in the *Phoenissae*, where Creon's son Menoeceus is ready to sacrifice himself for his country against his father's will. Creon wants 'to die as an atoning sacrifice for the city',[24] but his son sets off secretly: 'I am going, and will deliver the city, and I will give up my life to die for this land' (εἶμι καὶ σώσω πόλιν ψυχήν τε δώσω τῆσδ' ὑπερθανεῖν χθονός).[25] The re-solve of Heracles' daughter Macaria in the *Heraclides* is very much the same: she is prepared to sacrifice herself to save her kinsfolk: 'I voluntarily give my life for them, not under compulsion.'[26] In Plato's *Symposium*, dying for the beloved is stressed as a special

expression of the unique power of Eros (179B ff. : καὶ μὴν ὑπεραποθνῄσκειν γε μόνοι ἐθέλουσιν οἱ ἐρῶντες).[27]

From the classical period onwards there are virtually innumer-
able statements which praise vicarious death in battle for the city.
In essentials, the idea itself goes back to Homer. Hector himself
urges on the Trojans:

> Go, fight at the ships in close groups,
> and if any of you, wounded by arrow or sword, should meet
>   death and fate,
> let him lie in death; it is no disgrace to die fighting for one's
>   country.
>
> (οὐ οἱ ἀεικὲς ἀμυνομένῳ περὶ πάτρης/τεθνάμεν)

We hear a very similar note from the Spartan poet Tyrtaeus:

> For it is honourable to be killed, to fall in battle among the
> foremost fighters as a brave man, for one's country.
>
> (τεθνάμεναι γὰρ καλὸν ἐνὶ προμάχοισι πεσόντα
> ἄδρ' ἀγαθὸν περὶ ᾗ πατρίδι μαρνάμενον)

Round about the same time the Ephesian Callinus wrote:

> For it is a glorious and honourable thing when a man fights
> for his country, his children and his wife.[28]
>
> (. . . ἀνδρὶ μάχεσθαι γῆς περί)

After the time of the Persian wars, the fame of dead heroes was
written on numerous honorific inscriptions and epitaphs for all to
see. From the many examples let me mention just one of the
earliest pieces of evidence, the memorial in Locrian Opus to those
who fell at Thermopylae:

> τούσδε ποτὲ φθιμένους ὑπὲρ Ἑλλάδος ἀντία Μήδων
> μητρόπολις Λοκρῶν εὐθυνόμων Ὀπόεις.
>
> Opus, metropolis of the Locrians of righteous laws,
> mourns for these who perished in defence of Greece against
>   the Medes.[29]

In the *Menexenus*, Plato's Socrates calls this praise of those who
have fallen for the city, 'who have accepted death in exchange for
the salvation of the living', both an appropriate praise of the fathers

and also a legitimate piece of self-esteem.[30] Pindar could celebrate dying for the city unequivocally as a religious sacrifice:

Hearken, O war-shoot, daughter of war! Prelude of spears!
To whom soldiers are sacrificed for their city's sake,
In the holy sacrifice of death.
(... ᾷ θύεται ἄνδρες ὑπὲρ πόλιος τὸν ἱερόθυτον θάνατον).[31]

Most recently, J. Gnilka has wanted to brush aside this wide-ranging evidence with its religious implications by observing that here 'the death which is died for others saves them exclusively from physical and material distress', or that 'the fame and reputation of the cause or institution under attack will be increased in an earthly and public context', and then goes on to conclude that 'these texts do not have any kind of theological significance'.[32] However, here he completely misunderstands the nature of ancient religion. It is taken for granted that dying for one's native city, its gods, holy laws and temples, for the tombs of dead ancestors and families, always also has an essentially religious character, and those who have fallen in battle for these supreme goods are worshipped as heroes, i.e. as divine beings. Even in Plutarch's time (about AD 100), those who fell at Plataea (478 BC) had sacrifices offered to them year by year as those 'who had died for the freedom of Greece', and the souls of the dead were summoned to taste the sacrificial blood.[33] The encomium of Simonides of Ceos at the celebration for all those who died at Thermopylae similarly expresses a deep religious sensibility:

... glorious is their destiny, fair their fate; *for an altar they have a tomb*, for libations remembrance, for wine mourning. No decay, no all-vanquishing time will deface this shrine of brave men, and the glory of Greece has made its abode in this hallowed precinct.[34]

Making heroes of those who had died in the Greek fight for freedom against the Persians introduced a new development. This is also connected with the fact that the unexpected victory over the Great King and the repulse of the Persian yoke was celebrated as a historical saving event, which more than any other historical event formed the basis for a general sense of being Greek which transcended all internal political differences.[35] In retrospect, it was explained more and more in religious terms; from now on other warriors, benefactors and saviours of cities were elevated and became demigods.[36] In this context there was a predilection for stressing that the dead had died not just for an individual *polis* but 'for Greece'. This is the case in the legendary answer of Leonidas, in which he rejected Xerxes' offer of shared rule over Greece: 'Death for Greece (ὁ ὑπὲρ τῆς Ἑλλάδος θάνατος) seems to me better than sole rule over my fellow countrymen.' His death was seen as a heroic sacrificial death for all Greece, in a deliberate parallel to the death of king Codrus (see below, pp. 13f.), and other figures from the mythical primal period. This model may even have influenced the motif of sacrifice in the plays of Euripides; at the same time it comes close to the Roman *devotio*.[37]

Of course the theme of 'dying for the fatherland' took on its greatest significance in political rhetoric. It appears for the first time in Thucydides in the famous speech of Pericles in honour of those who fell in the first year of the war, 431: 'who made the finest sacrifice for the city. For together they yielded up their bodies, and in return each received praise which does not grow old . . .'[38] We have a similar-sounding formula in the story of the three men in the burning fiery furnace, Dan. 3.28: 'They yielded up their bodies rather than serve and worship any god except their own God,' which is probably an indication that even in the early Hellenistic periods this 'surrender formula' had also found its way into Aramaic-speaking Judaism.[39]

Isocrates' *Panegyric*, which is fond of this formula, says that the fallen 'counted it worse to incur shame with their (fellow) citizens than to die in the right way for the city' (ἢ καλῶς ὑπὲρ τῆς πόλεως ἀποθνῄσκειν).[40] We also find similar statements somewhat less frequently in other Attic orators,[41] and not infrequently with later authors.[42] According to Cicero, the question '*Honestumne sit pro patria mori?*' is a rhetorical exercise.[43] Even in the *Acta Appiani*, which come from the sphere of the Alexandrian Acts of Martyrs, belonging to the time of Commodus, Heliodorus encourages the gymnasiarch Appian, whom the emperor has condemned to death, as he is led out to execution: 'Go, my son, die! It will bring you fame to die for a fatherland which is so sweet. Do not be afraid!' (τρέχε, τέκνον, τελεύτα. κλέος σοί ἐστιν ὑπὲρ τῆς γλυκυτάτης σου πατρίδος τελευτῆσαι. μὴ ἀγωνία).[44]

Obviously, dying for the *polis* was also included in the philosophers' catalogues of duties. Plato's *Menexenus* is dominated by this theme (see above, p. 10); in his *Nicomachean Ethics*, Aristotle associated the obligation to die for one's native city with giving up one's life, if necessary, 'for one's friends'. This extension of the *patris* to friends also indicates a loosening of the ties of the city which were supplemented – or even replaced – by the philosophical bond of friendship. E. Schwartz comments: 'Where the state can no longer be the foundation for a common ethic, voluntary φιλία insinuates itself'. This tendency is continued in the Hellenistic period. The Stoics after Chrysippus said that to sacrifice one's life for one's country or for one's friends was foremost among the reasons which justified one's voluntary death. On the other hand, for Epicurus and his followers, who were averse to all political activities, it was the mark of the wise man only 'in some circumstances to die for a friend'. Epictetus, too, limits himself to dying for friends.[45] This requirement is close to John 15.13 and Paul's remark in Rom. 5.6. However, for Paul, that the Son accepted death for God's *enemies* (Rom. 5.5–10) was a quite incomparable event.

By contrast the Cynics, who saw themselves as citizens of the world, rejected dying for institutions, along with dying for the state, war and the family, though – as the example of Peregrinus Proteus shows – they called for utter contempt of death.[46]

Romans and Greeks were familiar from childhood onwards with this ideal of representative dying for the community, as expressed in Horace's well-known and much misused verse *'dulce et decorum est pro patria mori'*.[47] This was one of the basic lessons of the ancient school. An exceptional instance of this 'dying for one's country' was the *voluntary self-sacrifice of a select individual* in the sense of 'one for all', e.g. the king or the general. Ancient texts relatively often mention the heroic example of Codrus, the legendary last king of Athens, who on the basis of an oracle went out to meet the enemy alone in slave's clothing; unrecognized, he was killed by them and in so doing saved Athens.[48] It was a favourite practice to cite the names of such heroes in rhetorical lists of examples. Cicero begins such a list with the comment: 'A noble death sought willingly for one's country is thought by orators not only to be praiseworthy but also to be happy' (*Clarae vero mortes pro patria oppetitae non solum gloriosae rhetoribus sed etiam beatae videri solent*). Even Vercingetorix delivered himself up to the Romans in order to spare his people,[49] and the emperor Otho, who had come to power in a somewhat disreputable way, displayed the ancient Roman attitude after receiving news of his defeat against Vitellius: 'Go to the victor and pay homage to him. I myself will free me from myself, that through this action, too, all men may learn that you have chosen the kind of emperor who not only sacrifices you for himself, but also sacrifices himself for you' (ὅστις οὐχ ὑμᾶς ὑπὲρ ἑαυτοῦ ἀλλ' ἑαυτὸν ὑπὲρ ὑμῶν δέδωκε). Despite the refusal of the soldiers, 'but we will all die *for you*', he killed himself. Dio Cassius cannot avoid praising him for this: 'after he had lived the most wicked of all men, he died in the most noble way'.[50]

The relatively well-educated conservative Christian Clement of Rome uses this theme of the sacrifice of an individual hero for the whole people in order to move the refractory Corinthians, as far as possible, to depart in the interest of peace in the community: 'Many kings and rulers, when a time of pestilence has set in, have followed the counsel of oracles, and given themselves up to death, that they might rescue their subjects through their own blood.' He probably has in mind here the ancient Roman custom of the *devotio* of the general, or is thinking of the kind of lists that we have in Cicero and other orators. As a biblical Jewish counterpart, Clement mentions Judith, who 'gave herself up to danger . . . for love of her country and her people in their siege',[51] i.e. a Jewish *Novelle* of the Maccabean period, which has typically Hellenistic features.

This theme is given a christological turn in the 'prophecy' of the high priest Caiaphas (John 11.50) that it is better 'that one man should die for the people, and that the whole nation should not perish'. In the archaic *devotio* already mentioned, the general dedicated himself or others to the gods of the underworld with the aim of also delivering his opponents over to the underworld by means of his own sacrificial death. If he then escaped with his life, for the rest of his life he was regarded as *impius*. The underlying idea of the *unum pro multis dabitur caput*[52] could also be formulated as a rabbinic rule: 'It is better that this man should be killed than that the community should be punished for his sake.'[53] Among the Christian church fathers after Clement of Alexandria, the classical Greek concept of ὑπεραποθνῄσκειν was then transferred to the atoning death of Jesus, whereas Celsus reproaches the disciples of Jesus for 'neither dying with him nor for him', but denying him.[54]

(iv) Dying for the law and for truth

Voluntary death for the common good of one's city or one's friends *could also be transferred to spiritual ends.* Only through this transference did there come into being the real 'idea of the martyr', which then at a later stage became very significant in Judaism and even more so in Christianity. After all that has already been said, I need not stress further that it, too, is clearly Greek in origin. We already find a beginning of the transference of readiness to fight (and to die) for one's homeland into the spiritual sphere in the fine saying of Heraclitus: 'The people must fight for the law as for the wall' (μάχεσθαι χρὴ τὸν δῆμον ὑπὲρ τοῦ νόμου ὅκωσπερ τείχεος). εὐνομία to some degree formed the spiritual and social wall of a city, which in many circumstances protected it even against its own citizens. In the last resort, it is not human, but divine in origin: 'All human laws draw their sustenance from the one divine law.' For that very reason the νόμος calls for the sacrifice of all one's life.[55] Demosthenes finds it terrifying that the ancestors of the Athenians 'dared to die, so that the laws would not be destroyed' (προγόνους ὑπὲρ τοῦ μὴ καταλυθῆναι τοὺς νόμους ἀποθνῄσκειν τολμᾶν), but they themselves no longer dared even to punish transgressors.[56] Plato's Socrates goes one stage further in the *Apology* (32a): to have any effect at all, anyone who really wants to fight for the right (τὸν τῷ ὄντι μαχούμενον ὑπὲρ τοῦ δικαίου), must renounce all ambition for political office. So in his own defence he will 'not yield to anyone through fear of death', just as earlier in a court of judgment he had been the only one to vote against an unjust judgment, despite the threats of the majority, because he believed that he 'must run the risk to the end with law and justice on my side', rather than follow the majority 'in an unjust judgment through fear of imprisonment or death' (32b/c). His refusal to escape from prison, despite the threat of execution, because of his respect for the laws of the city, sets the final seal on his attitude. For the ancient world, including Hellenistic Jews and Christians, he thus became the first example of the steadfast martyr for truth and justice.[57]

One further example worth mentioning is Hermias, the friend of Aristotle, who was crucified by the Great King. At the last, he sent from the cross a message to his friends that he had not done anything 'unworthy of philosophy or shameful'. Aristotle dedicated a paean to him, glorifying him along with Heracles, the Dioscuroi, Achilles and Ajax:

> O virtue, hard for the mortal race to attain,
> noblest prize that life can win,
> for the sake of your beauty, O virgin,
> death would be an enviable fate in Greece
> (σᾶς πέρι, παρθένε, μορφᾶς
> καὶ θανεῖν ζαλωτὸς ἐν ῾Ελλάδι πότμος)
> and to endure fierce untiring labours
> . . . for the sake of your fair form
> the nursling of Atarneus
> left the sunlit world.
> The Muses will make you immortal . . .

He too was a philosophical witness for truth against the cruelty of the tyrant.[58]

The Jewish freedom fighters in the time of the Maccabees could take up this philosophical tradition of fighting and dying for law, righteousness and divine truth, and use it to create a new type of martyr. However, a hitherto little noted verse in Ben Sira, who connects the new spirit of the age with the Old Testament tradi-

tion, shows that this idea had already entered Palestinian Judaism
before the trial of fortitude under Antiochus IV Epiphanes: 'Fight
to the death for righteousness and Yahweh will fight for you' ('*ad
ham-māwet hē'āṣeh 'al haṣ-ṣedeq weyhwh nilḥām lākh*). His grandson
translates: ἕως θανάτου ἀγώνισαι περὶ τῆς ἀληθείας, καὶ κύριος
ὁ θεὸς πολεμήσει ὑπὲρ σοῦ.[59] Here we can already see something of the spirit which inspired, say, Mattathias and his sons a
generation later. In II Macc. 13.14 Judas admonishes his followers
before the battle 'to fight boldly to the death for (περί) law,
sanctuary, city, fatherland and constitution', with the battle cry
'To God the victory' (θεοῦ νίκην, see p. 9 above). At this point
the distinction between Palestinian and Hellenistic Judaism proves
to be very relative and virtually meaningless. True, 'dying for the
truth' appears much more rarely in ancient witnesses than dying
'for the *polis*' or for '*friends*', but – leaving aside Socrates – the fact
that it is not completely absent even there is evident from the
discussions which the hero of Philostratus' *Vita Apollonii* has with
his two pupils Demetrius and Danis about the meaning of philosophical martyrdom before Apollonius voluntarily submits to
Domitian's judgment in Rome. Demetrius advises him to escape,
since a 'slave's death' is unworthy of philosophy. It befits the
philosopher 'to die in the attempt either to liberate his city or to
protect his parents, children, brothers or kinsfolk, or to die
struggling for his friends, who to the wise man are more precious
than mere kinsfolk.' Damis, the real successor of the teacher, is so
impressed that he begins to question the readiness of the teacher
to die. The execution would certainly be a triumph for the enemies
of philosophy. So on the one hand Damis maintains the theory that
'one ought to die for philosophy' (ἀποθνήσκειν . . . ὑπὲρ
φιλοσοφίας . . . δεῖν) in the sense of dying for one's temples and
city walls, and the tombs of one's ancestors. For many famous men
have gladly died to save such interests as these (ὑπὲρ σωτηρίας γὰρ
τῶν τοιῶνδε). On the other hand, he does not regard such a death
as meaningful now because of its disastrous consequences. Both
are sharply contradicted by the hero: as a child of the East,
dominated by fear, Damis does not know the nature of either true
freedom or philosophy.

The wise man should indeed die for the things that have been mentioned, and of course any man would equally die for them without being wise, for it is an obligation of the law that we should die for freedom and an injunction of nature that we should die for kinsfolk or friends or loved ones. Now all men are the slaves of nature and law, the willing slaves of nature as the unwilling slaves of law. But it is the duty of the wise in a still higher degree to lay down their lives for tenets they have embraced (τελευτᾶν ὑπὲρ ὧν ἐπετήδευσαν). Here are interests which neither law has laid upon us nor nature planted in us from birth, but to which we have devoted ourselves out of mere strength of character and courage. On behalf of these, therefore, should anyone try to violate them, let the wise man pass through fire, let him bare his neck to the axe, for he will not be overcome by any such threats not driven to any sort of subterfuge, but he will maintain his conviction, as firmly as if it were a religion in which he had been initiated.

Since philosophical truth thus represents the ultimate religious obligation for Apollonius, he goes his way unhesitatingly at the risk of his life. In so doing, he does not betray his friends, 'but at the same time I will not betray myself either; but I will boldly wrestle with the tyrant, hailing him with the words of noble Homer, "Mars is as much my friend as yours".'[60]

According to Philostratus, Apollonius' attitude is essentially an illustration of the Cynics' criticism of all institutions: the conclusion shows how the heroic attitude of an Achilles or Hector is the model even for the philosophical ideal of the martyr. It seems to me that there is a knowledge of the gospel passion narratives and the attitude of the Jewish-Christian martyrs and a critical detachment from them. As a 'divine man', Apollonius knows in advance that the tyrant will not get the better of him, that he does not have to die. And indeed he is spirited away in a miraculous manner in the middle of the trial.

(v) *Atoning sacrifice*

In the early Greek period, the sacrifice of the individual for the good of the community was also often understood as an *expiatory sacrifice* to assuage the anger of the gods. Klaus Wengst,[61] who emphatically stressed the Greek origin of ἀποθνῄσκειν ὑπέρ as a vicarious dying for others, wanted to ascribe the conception of cultic atonement only to the Old Testament and Jewish tradition, but he pays too little attention to the rich Greek material. Thus one could well claim that he seems to be inconsistent with his own views. Of course at the same time – as I have already stressed several times – here again we see the relativity of such traditio-historical 'attempts at derivation'. The theme of expiation in the sense of 'purifying the land' from evil and disaster or of 'assuaging' the wrath of the gods was part of the *lingua franca* of the religions of late antiquity. In this context it is particularly striking how many contacts can be demonstrated between ancient Greek ideas and those of the Old Testament. In the Graeco-Roman world in particular, the theme of expiation was often connected with a human sacrifice 'in the sense of an extraordinary atonement'.[62] Because there is a whole series of excellent studies on human sacrifice in the ancient world, representative atoning death and the conceptions and rites associated with it, e.g. the phenomenon of the '*pharmakos*',[63] I do not need to go into as much detail as in my discussion of 'dying for', and in what follows can keep to essentials. Of course at an early stage human sacrifice was already rejected as a barbaric custom, but despite this, in desperate circumstances it was used as a religious and political means in the time of Themistocles, and even under Caesar and Augustus.[64] Furthermore, certain forms of death penalty also had sacrificial features to them.[65] The same figures keep on being mentioned in ancient literature for their sacrifices: by his voluntary sacrifice, Menoeceus[66] atones for the ancient blood-guilt of Oedipus; the sacrifice of Iphigenia recon-ciles angry Artemis and opens up the way for the sack of Troy;[67] the sacrifice of Polyxena appeases the spirit of Achilles and thus guarantees the safety of the victors' return;[68] King Erechtheus is to still the wrath of Poseidon by the sacrifice of a daughter, but instead of one daughter, all three of his daughters go to their deaths.[69]

Greek tragedy above all saw that the theme of the atoning death of individual prominent figures of mythical antiquity remained alive among all strata of the population. For Aeschylus, the sacrifice of Iphigenia takes on decisive significance as the reason for the disaster which comes upon Agamemnon and his family. Sophocles wrote dramas about both Polyxena and Iphigenia.

Above all, however, it was the plays of Euripides at the beginning of the Greek enlightenment[70] which in a striking way took up the theme of an atoning or sacrificial death and explained it in terms of 'voluntary sacrifice of one's life for a higher end'. In six of the extant tragedies (*Alcestis*, *Heraclides*, *Hecuba*, *Supplices*, *Phoenissae*), and in at least three of the lost ones (*Protesilaus*, *Erechtheus* and *Phrixos*), this plays a prominent role.[71]

With the exception of the *Alcestis*, where the 'vicarious death' (ὑπεραποθνῄσκειν), like the 'imitative death' (ἐπαποθνῄσκειν) of Evadne in the *Supplices* and of Laodameia in the *Protesilaus*, is in each case for love, an atoning death always has explicit cultic features. It is striking here that 'in his accounts of sacrificial deaths, even those which are his own invention, the poet has closely followed the Greek sacrificial ritual in every detail'. This is a σφάγιον, i.e. a blood sacrifice, of the kind which is offered to the powers of the underworld before great undertakings, battle, taking an oath or sacrificing to the dead. 'As human sacrifices, of course they have far greater value and greater effectiveness . . . and are in and for themselves guarantees of victory.'[72] An essential feature of this rite was the shedding of blood by cutting the throat in ritual fashion; this provided an association with the underworld which in Euripides is embodied especially by Persephone. It is remarkable how this 'enlightened' tragedian combines an ethical rejection of human sacrifice with a realistic account of this cruel archaic rite. The decisive reason for his doing this was to portray the hero or heroine's voluntary sacrifice of life, by which he gave a last degree of intensification to the conflict of tragedy. Another factor may be that at the same time there was some contribution from the glorification of the sacrificial death for all Greece or for a threatened native city, which was so popular in the political crises of the fifth century.[73] Nevertheless, an element remains which is difficult to elucidate, the knowledge that the primal dark and oppressive experience of the connection between guilt and fate and the need for expiation cannot simply be removed by the reasoning of an enlightenment. Roussel comments:[74]

> nous apercevons le sentiment antique de l'efficacité du sacrifice pour la conservation de la vie sociale. Euripide est pénétré de ce sentiment, et l'a traduit magnifiquement dans son oeuvre . . . Dans tous les périodes de grandes crises, l'utilité pratique du dévouement total de l'individu à la communauté ne se traduit-il pas par le sentiment mystique de la valeur expiatoire et pro-pitiatoire du sang librement répandu?

Indeed, we also owe to Euripides the most irrational, ecstatic and cruel of all the ancient dramas, the *Bacchae*, in which the fearful end of Pentheus essentially also represents a sacrifice. Above all through his plays, which were so frequently performed, the idea of the heroic, voluntary and vicarious sacrificial death for the good of the homeland became familiar to the whole Graeco-Roman world.

Of course the subject appears in ancient sagas very much more frequently than in the mythical material used by Euripides. In the seventh century, i.e. already in the historical period, the 'crime of Cylon', a political murder in a holy place, as a result of which plague broke out in Athens, is said to have been expiated by the voluntary sacrifice of two young men.[75] This theme was especially popular in connection with the self-sacrifice of sisters, who in deep need save their threatened homeland through their common sacrificial death.[76] W. Burkert would describe this sacrifice of virgins, which is particularly prominent in Euripides also, from primal hunting and fighting societies, who used this rite to prepare themselves for going out to battle.[77] At all events, the archaic character of this motive is obvious.

Some examples are impressive to the New Testament scholar simply because of the cultic language they use. Thus the two daughters of Orion in Aeonia in Boeotia declare themselves ready in time of plague to propitiate the two gods of the underworld (ἱλάσσασθαι τοὺς δύο ἐριουνίους θεούς) by 'accepting death for their fellow citizens' (ὑπὲρ ἀστῶν θάνατον ἐδέξαντο). Of their own free will they offered themselves to the gods as sacrifices (αὐτοῖς ἑκοῦσαι θύματα γίνονται). However, Hades and Persephone had mercy on them and transported them as stars to the heavens. Their fellow citizens built a temple to them, 'with annual celebrations and sacrifices for the propitiation of the dead'.[78] The tourist Pausanias was able to visit the pyre and ashes of two other Boeotian sisters who are said to have sacrificed themselves willingly in place of their father in order to save their native city of Thebes.[79] In Athens, the daughters of the primal king Erechtheus (see n. 69 above) were not the only ones to kill themselves to assuage the wrath of Poseidon. According to a kindred saga, the three daughters of Leo, the Leokorai, were sacrificed during a plague or a famine. People also built a sanctuary in their honour, the Leokorion.[80] There is a similar account of the four daughters of Hyacinthus, an immigrant from Lacedaimonia to Athens.[81] Aglauros, one of the daughters of Cecrops and a priestess of Athens, is said to have hurled herself from the walls to save the city as a result of an oracle of Apollo when war threatened. She also had a sanctuary, in which the ephebes of Attica swore their oath.[82] The theme of the purity of those consecrated always played a decisive role in these virgin sacrifices. The theme itself remains almost the same, though names and individual features from these sagas could easily be exchanged, confused and varied. This shows the importance of the actual theme.

Men, too, offered themselves as sacrifices in a similar way. Reference has already been made to king Codrus of Athens. When the Dioscuroi invaded Attica, a foreigner by the name of Marathon is said to have sacrificed himself willingly before the battle;[83] the city received its name from him. The saga is possibly an invention from the Persian period, in the same way as Euripides 'invented' the sacrifice of Macaria, the daughter of Heracles.[84]

Finally, one could also refer to the representative death of one individual for another. Quite apart from the death of Alcestis for her husband Admetus (see p. 9 above), the theme appears in the case of the wise centaur Cheiron, who, wounded by Heracles'

poisoned arrow, made over his immortality to Prometheus in order
to avoid eternal putrefaction. We find the same thing in the imperial
period in the form of a promise to make over one's own life for the
emperor, as in the case of Augustus, Caligula, Otho or Hadrian.[85]

This list of examples could be continued, but I must break it off
at this point. One fixed ingredient of almost all these traditions is
that the voluntary sacrifice did not rest on a man's own decision,
but followed the divine demand of an atoning sacrifice to deliver the
people, the land or a family, which was given by a seer or an
oracle, often that of Delphi.[86]

Conceptions universal in antiquity, widespread and going back
to the earliest period, underlie these sagas of atoning sacrifices
which seem to us to be so cruel.[87] Historical and psychological
explanations of them can no longer bring us complete satisfaction.
The depth of the crisis brought about by guilt and destiny is
matched by the magnitude of the demand for unconditional
sacrifice. At the deepest level, doom and sin were related. The
voluntary nature of such sacrifice, stressed from the time of
Euripides on, gave it ultimate moral stature and made it a model
for citizens.

The Roman *devotio* of a general in desperate situations in war,
already mentioned above, can also be fitted into the framework of
such sacrifice. It is often described directly as an expiatory
sacrifice (*piaculum*). According to Livy, the general P. Decius
hurled himself on his foes 'like a messenger from heaven to
expiate all anger of the gods and to turn aside destruction from his
people and bring it on their adversaries'. All this after he had
dedicated himself as a *devotus* on the basis of a dream.[88] His son
also dedicated himself as a *devotus*, appealing to the example of his
father: 'It is the privilege of our family that we should be sacrificed
to avert the nation's perils. Now I will offer up the legions of the
enemy, to be slain with myself as victims to Earth and the gods of
the underworld.'[89] In his *Pharsalia*, Lucan depicts the death of the
younger Cato as *devotio*, which atones for the blood-guilt of the
civil war. The climax of the remarks addressed to Brutus, a
remarkable mixture of Stoic philosophy, Roman religion and
visions of apocalyptic horror, consists in the following praise: 'So

may it be: may the strict gods of the Romans receive complete expiation, and may we not cheat war of any of its victims. If only the gods of heaven and the underworld would allow this head to expose itself to all punishment as one condemned! The hordes of the enemy cast down Decius, the consecrated one: may the two armies (involved in the civil war) pierce me through. May the barbarians from the Rhine make me the target of their shots, and exposed to every spear, may I receive all the wounds of the whole war. This my blood will ransom all the people; this my death will achieve atonement for all that the Romans have deserved through their moral decline.'[90] The writer of these words, M. Annaeus Lucan, was a contemporary of Paul's, and nephew of Seneca. He died on 30 April, AD 65, at the age of twenty-five, on Nero's orders. These words help us to understand why the earliest Christian message made sense in Rome.

If we look for a summary characterization of these expiatory rites and those involved in them, we come up against the term *pharmakos*, the specifically Greek form of the 'scapegoat'. We find it in archaic times in a number of cities, especially in Ionia, and including Athens. There year by year a particular man was driven out of the city or even killed in accordance with a fixed rite of humiliation to secure the purification of the country.[91] The best-known example of this custom is the driving out or stoning of two people during the feast of Thargelia in Athens, which was dedicated to Apollo: 'one for the men and one for the women' (ἕνα μὲν ὑπὲρ τῶν ἀνδρῶν, ἕνα δὲ ὑπὲρ τῶν γυναικῶν). Istrus, a pupil of Callimachus, who lived in the third century BC, derived it from a certain Pharmakos who had stolen the sacred vessels belonging to Apollo: he had been caught by the people of Achilles and stoned. This is a preposterous and artificial aetiology, which goes back to one of the Ionian cities, possibly Miletus.[92] We need not trouble ourselves further with the question of the original form and derivation of these ancient rites, over which scholars have been so much in dispute; the important thing to note is its elaboration and interpretation in the late Hellenistic and Roman period.

The most striking thing about the accounts is that as a rule they are concerned with men who are poor, incapable of work, crippled and maimed, who of necessity have 'sold' themselves for the common good; elsewhere, we have condemned criminals. This is in complete contrast to the heroic sagas according to which kings – like Codrus in the garments of a slave – princes or beautiful maidens offered themselves voluntarily for the common good. The scholia on Aristophanes and Aeschylus state in different ways that 'quite worthless and useless people' were 'sacrificed' as *pharmakoi*.[93] They were killed after being taken round the city, outside the gates, either through stoning or through being hurled from a rock. Their being led round the city was usually coupled with a curse.[94] At a later stage people were usually content with driving them beyond the bounds of the city by throwing stones at them. Thus their killing could be described as θύειν or as θυσία. A similar 'sacrifice' was offered on Rhodes to Kronos (ἐθύετο ἄνθρωπος τῷ Κρόνῳ), or they kept a criminal condemned to death until the festival of Kronos and then led him outside the gates (ἔξω πυλῶν) and killed him 'in front of the temple of Artemis Aristobule' (Porphyry, *De abstinentia* 2,54, Nauck p. 279). Heb. 13.12f. might remind its ancient audience of similar analogies.

On the island of Leucas, every year in a sacrifice for Apollo (ἐν τῇ θυσίᾳ τοῦ Ἀπόλλωνος) a criminal was thrown into the sea from a rock to 'ward off evil' (ἀποτροπῆς χάριν). Later, people attempted to fish the unfortunate man out of the sea and bring him to dry land. In this way the original human sacrifice was commuted.[95] Ovid (*Ibis*, 467f.) reports that the citizens of Abdera killed the one 'devoted to death' with a hail of stones. For him the ancient Ionian rite is simply a special form of *devotio*:

Aut te devoveat certis Abdera diebus
Saxaque devotum grandine plura petant.
(Or the city of Abdera could devote you to death on particular days, and catch the one devoted under a hail of stones.)[96]

The scholia interpreted these obscure sentences in rather different ways. According to an earlier tradition, going back to Callimachus (third century BC), year by year the whole city was purified (*uno quoque anno totam civatatem publice lustrabant*) when the people of Abdera stoned one of its citizens whom they had 'devoted' for this day, 'for the salvation of each individual citizen' (*pro capitibus omnium*). Another scholiast says that in Abdera 'a man was *sacrificed for the sins of the citizens*, but people proscribed him seven days earlier, so that in this way he alone would take upon himself the sins of all' (*hominem inmolari pro peccatis civium ut sic omnium peccata solus haberet*). There is clear evidence of the influence of Christian terminology on this last text (cf. I Cor. 15.3; Gal. 1.4: *pro peccatis nostris*; Isa. 53.12: *et ipse peccatum multorum tulit*). In the Diegesis on fragment 90 of the *Aitiae* of Callimachus, which has been preserved on papyrus, of course we only hear that the Abderites bought a man, whom they then fed for a period, and then took him round the city outside the walls as a 'means of purification for the city' (καθάρσιον τῆς πόλεως), finally driving him outside the territory of the city by throwing stones at him.[97] Here the tradition has evidently accentuated the real custom. There also seems to me evidence of the influence of Christian tradition in the poem of the Byzantine writer Tzetzes (twelfth century AD) about the *pharmakos*, which could go back to verses of the poet Hipponax (sixth century BC), who reports of the customs of Ionian cities: 'they took the most hateful of all as to a sacrifice' (cf. Isa. 53.3), τῶν πάντων ἀμορφότερον ἦγον ὡς προς θυσίαν, 'they made the sacrifice at the appropriate place', εἰς τόπον δὲ τὸν πρόσφορον στήσαντες τὴν θυσίαν. The corpse of the *pharmakos* was burnt with the wood of wild trees and his ashes were scattered on the sea.[98]

This theme appears even in a Christian martyr legend in the fifth or sixth century AD, the Martyrdom of Caesarius,[99] which is quite unhistorical and has novellistic features, set in Terracina, between Rome and Naples. There frivolous young men are said to have been convinced that they should live a riotous life for a period at the expense of the community and then on an appointed day be hurled from a rock in full war attire 'for the salvation of the state, the emperor, and the wellbeing of the citizens' (*pro salute rei publicae et principum et civium salubritate*), not to mention their own glory (*et ut nomen habeat gloriae*). The corpses of the victims were brought to the temple of Apollo with great veneration and there burnt; the ashes were kept *pro salute rei publicae et civium*. The saint protested against this barbaric custom and thus caused his imprisonment. The narrative shows how in a later period the ancient rite was elaborated by the inclusion of traditional elements, while at the same time the pagan custom was transformed into an antitype of the Christian veneration of martyrs. It is significant that the traditional killing (or expulsion) of a poor or sick man to purify the city was transformed into an honourable event for the salvation of all.

A very ancient form of purifying a city from plague by stoning a *pharmakos* probably underlies the saga, related by Philostratus, of the overcoming of the plague in Ephesus by Apollonius of Tyana. He had the whole population of the city assembled in the theatre before the statue of Heracles Apotropaeus; in the crowd he saw a poor and apparently blind beggar whom he made the crowd bury under a mountain of stones (in fact he embodied the plague demon). When the stones were taken away, the people found under the corpse of a giant dog (*Vita Apollonii* 4.10). In order to liberate or purify the city, the *pharmakos*, as the incarnation of the disaster which brought the corruption, had to vanish – i.e. either be covered with stones or be plagued in the sea or – as a humane mitigation – be driven out. The Byzantine *Lexica* still report from unknown sources that the *pharmakos* was cast into the sea as a sacrifice for Poseidon with the cry, 'Be our means of atonement, that is, salvation and redemption' (περίψημα ἡμῶν γενοῦ, ἤτοι σωτηρία καὶ ἀπολύτρωσις).)'[100]

When Paul describes himself and other apostles of Jesus Christ as περίψημα and περικαθάρματα τοῦ κόσμου he is taking up this old conception. Both terms had become vicious taunts (I Cor. 4.13). The most impressive description of the '*pharmakos*' in Greek drama is to be found in the figure of Sophocles' Oedipus,[101] who, to atone for the evil which he has unwittingly committed and to rid the land of a murderous curse, blinds himself and allows himself to be driven from home. As a criminal doomed to destruction (ἀσεβής, 1441), he wanders from place to place, homeless and in poverty, until he finds reconciliation, a home and a solution at the sacred shrine of the Eumenides in Colonus in Attica. For in the end death has lost all terrors for him; it is a mysterious transformation:

For no mortal could say what death he died,
but only Theseus.
No gleaming flash of divine fire took him away,
nor a whirlwind from the sea – but he was taken.
It was a messenger from heaven,
or else some gentle, painless opening of the earth.
For without a sigh, or disease, or pain,
he passed away – an end most marvellous,
like no other man.[102]

Thus his end is divine grace

For where as a grace (χάρις)
the night is preserved below,
there is no mourning.[103]

Oedipus, whose peaceful passage over the threshold of death is in
the end veiled in divine mystery, at the same time achieves atonement through his measureless suffering. Thus his figure as portrayed in Sophocles' two plays may now show the most kindred
features in all Greek drama – for all the fundamental differences –
to the story of the passion and resurrection of Jesus in the gospels.
Oedipus, too, knows that one who is well-meaning can intercede
for many and expiate the Eumenides. At the request of the elders to
propitiate the goddesses of the holy place, he sends Antigone:

For I believe that one soul can intercede
for thousands, to expiate this – it approaches in good pleasure
ἀρκεῖν γὰρ οἶμαι κἀντὶ μυρίων μίαν
ψυχὴν τάδ' ἐκτίνουσαν, ἢν εὔνους παρῇ (498f.)

(vi) *The atoning death of Christ and the Graeco-Roman world*

Thus we have answered more than adequately the question with
which we began, whether the pagan audiences in Antioch, Ephesus,
Corinth and Rome could have understood the new message of the
atoning death of Jesus and the conceptions of vicariousness, atonement and reconciliation associated with it. The Gentile who heard
the gospel was quite familiar in his own way not only with the hero's

self-chosen death as a way to apotheosis *per aspera ad astra* and the theme of vicarious dying for others out of love, but also with the notion of a voluntary death as an atoning sacrifice, and he could also understand it in his own way. True, customs of this kind might seem archaic or barbaric to him, but he knew them through myth, patriotic sagas and dramas, and they were at the same time transfigured by the heroic and mythical framework.

The ambivalence of the ancient audience towards narratives of this kind is evident from an account by Plutarch, who was similarly a contemporary of the New Testament writers (*c*. AD 45–120). He tells how the Leuctrides Korai, once violated by the Spartans, appeared to Pelopidas in a dream before the battle of Leuctra. The daughters of Skedasos, they had committed suicide out of shame at their disgrace, and their father had followed suit. Their tombs were in the plain of Leuctra. 'Ever after, prophecies and oracles kept warning the Spartans to be on watchful guard against the Leuctrian wrath' (μηνίμα, cf. Pausanias 9.13.5). The maidens commanded the general to sacrifice a virgin with auburn hair if he wished to win the victory over his enemies. 'The injunction seemed a dreadful and lawless (παράνομος) one to him', but he took the advice of seers and other officers:

Some of these would not hear of the injunction being neglected or disobeyed, adducing as examples of such sacrifice among the ancients, Menoeceus, son of Creon, Macaria, daughter of Heracles; and in later times, Pherecydes the wise man, who was put to death by the Lacedaemonians, and whose skin was preserved by their kings, in accordance with some oracle; and Leonidas, who, in obedience to the oracle, sacrificed himself, as it were, to save Greece; and still further, the youths who were sacrificed by Themistocles to Dionysus Carnivorous before the sea fight at Salamis; for the successes which followed these sacrifices proved them acceptable to the gods. Moreover, when Agesilaus, who was setting out on an expedition from the same place as Agamemnon did, and against the same enemies, was asked by the goddess for his daughter in sacrifice, and had this vision as he lay asleep at Aulis, he was too tender-hearted to give

her, and thereby brought his expedition to an unsuccessful and
inglorious ending. Others, on the contrary, argued against it,
declaring that such a barbarous and lawless (παράνομος)
sacrifice was not acceptable to any one of the superior beings
above us, for it was not the fabled typhons and giants who
governed the world, but the father of all gods and men; even to
believe in the existence of divine beings who take delight in the
slaughter and blood of men was perhaps a folly (ἀβέλτερον),
but if such beings existed, they must be disregarded, as having
no power; for only weakness and depravity of soul could produce
or harbour such unnatural and cruel desires.

(22) While, then, the chief men were thus disputing, and while
Pelopidas in particular was in perplexity, a filly broke away from
the herd of horses and sped through the camp, and when she
came to the very place of their conference, stood still. The rest
only admired the colour of her glossy mane, which was fiery red,
her high mettle, and the vehemence and boldness of her
neighing; but Theocritus the seer, after taking thought, cried out
to Pelopidas: 'Your sacrificial victim is come, good man; so let
us not wait for any other virgin; accept and use the one which
heaven offers you.' So they took the mare and led her to the
tombs of the maidens upon which, after decking her with
garlands and consecrating her with prayers, they sacrificed her.[104]

Only Plutarch tells the story in this form. Earlier historians like
Xenophon, and also Diodore, merely report that the sacrifice took
place near the tombs; according to Xenophon the Thebans had
decorated them, since they had been encouraged by an oracle that
they would win there. The romance-like elaboration in Plutarch
shows his own theory of religion. On the one hand there is still a
belief in the efficacy of archaic rites, especially as people revered
the heroes of ancient times who had sacrificed themselves. However, such primal religious sense could not be reconciled with the
purified understanding of religion to be found in the enlightenment.
Human sacrifices were regarded as 'barbaric' and 'criminal', and
the Romans had therefore rightly prohibited them among the

Druids and the Carthaginians. They were not required by any
divine being, least of all by the supreme god, Zeus. If any kind of
demons, i.e. probably the souls of criminals, '*biothanati*', wanted
human blood, they had to be refused it categorically. The division
between ancient religious experience and enlightened ethical
thought is resolved, *providentia dei*, in the happiest of ways. The
seer recognizes that the dream is fulfilled in the filly which comes
trotting along. The battle thus leads to the defeat of the Spartans
and the end of their predominance in Greece.

The message of the death of Jesus of Nazareth, the Son of God,
on the cross for all men was not incomprehensible even to the
educated audience of the Gentile world. Its linguistic and religious
categories were largely familiar to this audience. Nevertheless, the
primitive Christian preaching of the crucified Messiah must have
seemed aesthetically and ethically repulsive to them and to be in
conflict with the philosophically purified nature of the gods. The
new doctrine of salvation had not only barbarian, but also
irrational and excessive features. It appeared to contemporaries as
a dark or even mad superstition.[105] For this was not the death of a
hero from ancient times, suffused in the glow of religion, but that
of a Jewish craftsman of the most recent past, executed as a
criminal, with whom the whole present and future salvation of all
men was linked. Because of this, the earliest Christian mission
always spoke also of the teaching, the actions and the passion of the
Messiah from Galilee. The narrative about his messianic person
was part of the preaching of the cross.

On the other hand, the Christian message fundamentally broke
apart the customary conceptions of atonement in the ancient
world and did so at many points. For example, it spoke not of
atonement for a particular crime, but of universal atonement for
all human guilt. Furthermore, it was decisive that God's grace was
given, not as the result of the heroic action of a particular man, but
by God himself, through Jesus, the Son, who was delivered over to
death (II Cor. 5.18ff.). In other words, men no longer need to
assuage the wrath of God through their actions. God, as subject of
the saving event, reconciled to himself his unfaithful creatures,
who had become his enemies. Finally, the Christian message took

on its ultimate acuteness and urgency as a result of its *eschatological* character. The atoning death of the Son of God and reconciliation came about in the face of the imminent judgment of the world. All this was said in language and conceptuality which was not essentially strange to the men of the Greek and Roman world.

When fundamental difficulties in understanding arise, they are felt not by the audience of ancient times, Jewish or Gentile, but by us, the men of today. However, precisely because of this difficulty in understanding today, we must guard against limiting, for apologetic reasons, the fundamental significance of the soteriological interpretation of the death of Jesus as vicarious atonement in the context of the earliest Christian preaching. Today we find not only a 'fundamentalist' but also a radical critical biblicism, which seeks to strip Jesus and the earliest Christian message, as far as possible, of all that it regards as 'mythological' and therefore as theologically obsolete. Over against this, as scientific exegetes, we must attempt to illustrate, first of all, the origin of this central expression of the faith of the earliest church with all the philological and historical means at our disposal, so that we can understand it in terms of its earliest presuppositions.

2

The Origin of the Soteriological Interpretation of the Death of Jesus

An attempt to answer the questions raised at the end of the previous chapter should also help us to answer three further basic questions which arise out of what has been said so far:

(*a*) What was the specific feature of the primitive Christian expression of the vicarious atoning death of Jesus which distinguished it from analogous Greek and Jewish conceptions? Why was this message evidently offensive and at the same time victorious, and what made it new?

(*b*) To what degree is there a connection between the soteriological interpretation of the death of Jesus and the Old Testament and Jewish tradition, especially as right at the very start primitive Christianity was a Jewish Palestinian movement of an apocalyptic and messianic character?

(*c*) At the same time this raises the question of the age and the origins of this tradition. Does it enter the early primitive Christian kerygma at a relatively late stage as a secondary 'interpretative element', perhaps only in the so-called Hellenistic Jewish-Christian community, or from the beginning was it a constitutive element of the Christian message?

One might also ask: did it only so to speak come in by means of later theological reflection by the 'Hellenistic community' or is it inseparably bound up with the Easter event itself? Indeed, in essence does it perhaps go back to the words and actions of Jesus himself?

An answer to the third question will also provide answers to the first and second.

(i) *Pauline formulae and pre-Pauline tradition*

The best and most sensible method is to turn to the earliest texts, the authentic letters of Paul, which were written only twenty to twenty-five years after the event which founded the earliest community. They bring us closest in time and content to the earliest preaching of the primitive community to which we have access.

By contrast, the account of the earliest period of the community in Acts is about thirty years later, and despite the use of 'archaic' material in the speeches of Peter, which are significant for our questions, the hand of the redactor is very evident. In contrast to the account given by Luke of what is supposed to be the earliest primitive Christian kerygma in the speeches in Acts, with the best will in the world one cannot claim that statements about the vicarious death of Jesus 'for us' play only a minor role in the letters of Paul. Formulae and statements which express the saving significance of the death of Jesus are too frequent and too varied in the writing of the greatest missionary and theologian of primitive Christianity to be ignored, and the stereotyped form of some of them already points back to earlier traditions.

The fact that soteriological formulae of this kind retreat right into the background in the synoptic tradition is quite another matter. Nevertheless, even there we find explicit formulae at two highly significant points: Mark 10.45 (= Matt. 20.28) and then in the tradition of the Last Supper (Mark 14.24 = Matt. 26.28). The fact that they are otherwise lacking is no indication that they were unknown to the authors of the synoptic gospels. The reason for their lack of prominence is rather that understandably they do not play a central role in the proclamation of Jesus. In the first place he sought to announce the dawn of the kingdom of God, and in the face of this task his own fate retreated into the background. It is even possible that Luke's unique restraint over against a soteriological interpretation of the death of Jesus may be explained by the fact that this first historian of early Christianity is oriented on the Jesus tradition, which is exemplary as far as he is concerned.

By contrast the allegedly independent, decidedly post-Easter 'theologies' of the so-called Q or Marcan 'communities', detached completely from the person of Jesus, are artificial products of modern exegesis. We may not refer to them in any way to claim that in earliest Christianity there was also a kerygma in which the death and resurrection of Jesus played no part, or only a small part. Q and Mark did not set out to present 'community theology', but primarily the message and the work of Jesus. Where in Mark the influence of the theology of the evangelist becomes visible, the death of Jesus becomes important too (below pp. 42ff.).

In Paul we find stereotyped expressions about the atoning death of Jesus chiefly in two forms: first, in statements which express the *'giving up'* of Jesus for our salvation, connected with the composite verb παραδιδόναι or the simple διδόναι. This so-called 'surrender formula' is, of course, very variable, so it is taking a liberty to describe it as a fixed formula.[1] In two cases God himself is the one who 'gives up'. One is in Rom. 8.32, where he appears as subject: 'He who did not spare his own Son but gave him up for us all.' Here the first line has a reference to Gen. 22.12, the sacrifice of Isaac (καὶ οὐκ ἐφείσω τοῦ υἱοῦ σου τοῦ ἀγαπητοῦ δι'ἐμέ).

On the other hand, in the two-membered formula of Rom. 4.25 we find a divine passive:

Who was given up (ὃς παρεδόθη) for (διά) our trespasses and raised for (διά) our justification.

It is very probable that this statement depends on Isa. 53.12. In Gal. 1.4; 2.20 and the Deutero-Pauline texts Eph. 5.2, 25; Titus 2.14 and I Tim. 2.6, Christ is the subject who gave up his life himself 'for us'. In the last instance this surrender of his life is described as a 'ransom' (ἀντίλυτρον); thus the verse proves to be a variant of the earlier Semitic-type expression, Mark 10.45, in the Greek tradition.

In all the Pauline and Deutero-Pauline texts the preposition is *hyper*, with the exception of Rom. 4.25, where the *dia* goes back to the influence of Isa. 53.12 LXX, and Gal. 1.14, where the textual variant *peri* is possibly original. Of course there is much dispute as to the origin of this 'surrender formula'. If we look for an Old Testament model, we quickly come upon Isa. 53, where in the LXX the verb *paradidonai* appears three times for the surrendering of the servant of God and is twice related to 'our sins' (53.6, 12).

This is in accordance with the traditional interpretation,[2] which, however, is now under considerable attack. As Werner Grimm has shown very recently,[3] we should also add Isa. 43.3f., as this text has relatively close· connections with the earliest form of our tradition, Mark 10.45.[4] Of course, this does not yet have any decisive bearing on the 'antiquity' of this tradition. We shall therefore begin by leaving aside this whole complex and turn to other more important and more fixed groups of formulae in Paul, as they help us more to make a proper historical move back to the obscure 'pre-Pauline' period of the formation of early Christian formulae.

The second, so-called 'dying formula',[5] is primarily limited to Paul himself. Its best known expression is to be found in the summary of Paul's gospel with a catechetical form to be found in I Cor. 15.3b: Χριστὸς ἀπέθανεν ὑπὲρ τῶν ἁμαρτιῶν ἡμῶν. Otherwise, however, Paul usually uses this formula in an abbreviated form: Χριστὸς ἀπέθανεν ὑπὲρ ἡμῶν (or something similar). Here the shorter form only becomes fully comprehensible in the light of the longer form: ὑπὲρ ἡμῶν means 'for the forgiveness of our sins', by which we have separated ourselves from God. This is the case even in the pre-Pauline and extra-Pauline tradition, as Paul uses the plural 'sins' and the conception of forgiveness only very rarely. Isaiah 53 may have some influence on the longer form. This could be indicated not only by the striking ὑπὲρ τῶν ἁμαρτιῶν (cf. Gal. 1.4) but also by the κατὰ τὰς γραφάς, which is unique for Paul. The constitutive elements of both the longer and shorter formulae are the subject Χριστός; the aorist ἀπέθανεν, which refers to a unique, unrepeatable event of the past (cf. Rom. 6.9f.); and the preposition ὑπέρ with the genitive, which contains the soteriological interpretation. Of course this formula too is variable, and its particular form depends on the context. The subject Χριστός in the formula appears seven times (I Cor. 15.3; Rom. 5.6, 8; 14.9; I Cor. 8.11; Gal. 2.21; I Peter 3.18; cf. also I Thess. 5.10); the verb ἀποθνῄσκειν in the aorist on the other hand appears ten times (I Cor. 15.3b; Rom. 5.6, 8; Rom. 14.9; I Cor. 8.11; II Cor. 5.14, 15 twice; Gal. 2.21; I Thess. 5.10 aorist participle; I Peter 3.18 as a *varia lectio* of ἔπαθεν).[6] Paul uses the preposition ὑπέρ even more often in the soteriological sense, and in addition it also dominates the surrender formulae. I Cor. 1.13; II Cor. 5.21; Gal. 3.13; indeed even Rom. 6.2, 8–10 seem to me to be dependent on the dying formula.

For Paul, the long form of I Cor. 15.3b is part of a 'paradosis' which he handed on to the Corinthians, on the founding of the community in AD 49/50, as a 'key element' (ἐν πρώτοις) and summary of his gospel. For him this is a matter of objective events taking place in time and space which at the same time possess ultimate, unsurpassable, in short, 'eschatological' saving significance.

In I Cor. 15.3–5 (or –8), in essentials we have a highly compressed historical account presented in credal form, which of course is inseparably fused with theological interpretative elements. These include above all the ὑπὲρ τῶν ἁμαρτιῶν ἡμῶν but also the subject Χριστός, which in this confessional text has its original significance as a title and points to the death of the Messiah. For Greeks, Χριστός was completely unusual as a name, this is still evident from the way in which in Suetonius (and probably also in Tacitus)[7] it is confused with the slaves' name Χριστός; however, Christians in Antioch and in the Pauline communities were of course very well aware of the derivation of this unique name from the biblical eschatological expectation.

Along with the resurrection formula θεὸς ἤγειρεν τὸν Ἰησοῦν ἐκ νεκρῶν, the short formula Χριστὸς ἀπέθανεν ὑπὲρ ἡμῶν is the most frequent and most important confessional statement in the Pauline epistles and at the same time in the primitive Christian tradition in the Greek language which underlies them. The significance of I Cor. 15.3f. lies in the fact that here two formulae were linked together in an expanded form, whereas the other relatively infrequent two-membered formulae in Paul which link statements about dying and rising again are mostly abbreviated. I Corinthians 15.3 is therefore nearest in content to the two-membered formula Rom. 4.25, which has an independent tradition

from it. Thus if we are concerned with the age of the paradosis I Cor.
15.3f., the starting point is clear.[8] Paul passed it on in fixed form
to the young Christians in Corinth on the founding of their
community, and he retains it unaltered five or six years later when
he writes I Corinthians. The christological basis of the Pauline
kerygma has a firm shape and did not undergo any essential
metamorphoses. Evidently the tradition of I Cor. 15.3 had been
subjected to many tests in the long missionary activity of the apostle.
In content it points back through the people it lists (leaving aside
Paul himself) to Palestine and above all to Jerusalem. Thus this
piece of tradition explains why, despite all difficulties, the apostle
tries to hang on so persistently, to some degree almost at any price,
to the link he has with the centre of Judaism. One might assume
that it had already had fundamental significance in Paul's fourteen-
year-long missionary work in Syria and Cilicia, indeed that it had
even provided the common starting-point for the meeting between
Paul and Barnabas and the pillars in Jerusalem (Gal. 2.1–10),
from which agreement might be sought.[9] In terms of content it was
the foundation of that 'gospel' which Paul proclaimed to the
Gentiles and which he 'put before' the Jerusalem authorities
(Gal. 2.2). The closing sentence in I Cor. 15.11 gives a specific
indication of this: 'Whether then it was I or they, so we preach and
so you believed.' The ἐκεῖνοι who preach the same thing as Paul
are the preachers of the gospel from Peter on who are listed here.
At the same time, we should not forget that when he founded the
community in Corinth, Paul was accompanied by a missionary
partner from Jerusalem, Silas-Silvanus (I Thess. 1.1; Acts 15.40).
Thus one could say that the form of the paradosis goes back to the
early period of Paul's activity in Antioch and Syria, and indeed
even back as far as Damascus, but that its content in nearly all its
statements refers back to Jerusalem. The much disputed question
whether there was an original Aramaic form loses its significance in
the light of this. For the Greek-speaking Jewish-Christian community had its roots in Jerusalem itself. Jerusalem was a multi-
lingual city with a large Greek-speaking minority. In essentials,
we may assume that from the time of the formation of the community of Jerusalem by the event of Pentecost there was also a

Greek-speaking group there, which then soon became independent and translated the new message and the still living Jesus tradition into Greek.[10]

The long and hotly disputed contrast between 'Hellenistic' and 'Palestinian-Jewish' origins thus becomes a matter of only relative importance – at least as far as 'Hellenistic' origins are concerned. Of course we can hardly assume that Jewish, Aramaic or Hebrew texts came into being in the Diaspora of the Roman Empire outside Palestine – even in Phoenicia and Syria people spoke Greek in the synagogues, and Mesopotamia was part of the Parthian empire – but Greek texts could very well have been written also in Jewish Palestine, in Jerusalem as well as in Tiberias or Sepphoris. 'Hellenistic' and 'Palestinian-Jewish' need therefore no longer be in direct opposition. In any case, we can only talk about the Aramaic-speaking community in Palestine in a very limited and indirect way, because its own tradition has largely been lost. This cannot in any way be identified simply with Q and other parts of the synoptic tradition. In effect we know much more about Jesus than about the community around James; in addition, it is striking that James, the brother of Jesus, who later became leader of the Christian community, plays no part whatsoever in the synoptic tradition. The only mention of him, Mark 6.3 (= Matt. 13.55), has no positive significance whatsoever. This must really tell in favour of its originality.

(ii) The crucified Messiah

Of course, general considerations of this kind only help us to determine very roughly the age of the paradosis; it *may* come from the circle of the Hellenists in Jerusalem, but that is not necessarily the case. In order to fix it more precisely, we need to make a more thorough analysis of its individual elements. Here the subject and predicate Χριστὸς ἀπέθανεν, i.e. 'the Messiah died', are of prime interest.

We know that as a result of the Gentile mission in Antioch round about the middle of the thirties, the messianic title *Christos* gradually became a proper name, and Christians finally came to be called

Χριστιανοί, as a sect bound up with a person. Accordingly, the acclamation Χριστός 'Ιησοῦς became a double name. Of course this process must have taken years, and the messianic, titular meaning of Christ continued to be present in the church at a later stage as well. Like the formula 'God has raised (the man) Jesus from the dead', the phrase 'the Messiah died' had a special, unique significance. That the *man* Jesus *died* meant little, for many men were crucified in Jewish Palestine at that time; incomparably more astonishing was the confession that this *man* Jesus, executed as a criminal, was raised by God. To say that the Messiah had died was a complete reversal of this. It was taken for granted that God would grant victory to the Messiah; the message of his death on the cross, however, was a scandal. For in the light of all our present knowledge, the suffering and dying Messiah was not yet a familiar traditional figure in the Judaism of the first century AD. The figure of the suffering Messiah from the tribe of Ephraim only appears in the rabbinic Haggadah from about the middle of the second century AD, as a result of the catastrophes of AD 70, 115–116 and 132–135. For a Jewish audience, the confession 'the Messiah died . . .' must have been an unprecedented novelty, indeed a scandal which – at least in the light of our present knowledge of extant sources – contradicted the prevailing popular messianic expectation.

It is easy to find the fixed historical starting point for this statement about the death of the Messiah, which sounded so aggressive to a Jewish audience. In Mark's passion narrative[11] Jesus is handed over by the supreme Jewish authorities to the Roman prefect as a messianic pretender; he is condemned by Pilate on the basis of his own confession; he is mocked by the soldiers as king of the Jews, and finally crucified as such. The charge on which he is crucified, as stated on the *titulus*, together with the mockery of the leaders of the people at the crucified Messiah, is an expression of Jesus' complete human failure, which then culminates in the desperate cry from Ps. 22.2.

In recent times, attempts have been made to see the death of Jesus not so much in traditional terms, as that of the suffering messianic servant of God; instead, the widespread theme of the 'righteous sufferer' has been used to interpret the passion of Jesus, and reference has been made in this connection to the use of the psalms of suffering in the Marcan passion narrative. Here we are supposed to have a version of the pattern of the humiliation and exaltation of the innocent, of a similar kind to the one which also appears in Wisdom 2–5. A one-sided introduction of this theme, however, misinterprets the intention of the passion in Mark. The pattern of the humiliation and exaltation of the righteous is far too general and imprecise to interpret the event which Mark narrates so skilfully and with such deep theological reflection. He is concerned with the utterly unique event of the passion and crucifixion of the Messiah of Israel which is without any parallel in the history of religion. For Mark, the few psalms of suffering which illuminate individual features of the suffering and death of Jesus, like Psalms 22 and 69, are exclusively *messianic* psalms, such as Psalms 110 and 118. The 'righteous' does not appear in connection with Jesus either in the two psalms or in Mark; it is only Matthew with his rabbinic training who makes the Messiah Jesus into an exemplary ṣaddiq. Where features from the suffering of the righteous man appear, for example in the mocking of Jesus, they are also in a messianic key. The suffering 'of the righteous' is to be integrated completely and utterly into the suffering of the Messiah. *The Messiah alone is the righteous and sinless one par excellence.* His suffering therefore has irreplaceable and unique significance.

The category of the 'martyr prophet' is another one which is inadequate for understanding the passion of Jesus: in Mark 12.1–11 a very clear distinction is made between the unique, 'beloved' son and heir and the different servants who are sent first. The *unmessianic* interpretation of the person and work of Jesus which has become customary in Germany from the time of Wrede not only obstructs a historical and theological understanding of the emergence of the early christology of the first community, but hinders a real understanding of the passion of Jesus. At this point I can only point emphatically to N. A. Dahl, who rightly stressed that resurrection and exaltation could not by themselves serve as a justification for holding Jesus to be Messiah.[12] There was no Jewish doctrine of the appointment of a Messiah and Son of Man through the resurrection and exaltation of a dead man. The appear-

ance of the risen Jesus is therefore in no way an adequate foundation for his messiahship and for the later development of christology,
nor does it give a satisfactory explanation of them.

However, this raises in an even more basic way the question
which dominates the whole of the second half of the Gospel of
Mark and which cannot be answered simply by reference to the
'suffering righteous' and the 'martyr prophet'. Why does the
Messiah–Son of Man have to suffer, according to God's will but
in contradiction to the prevailing contemporary Jewish messianic
tradition as we know it? Mark gives an adequate answer to this
question in Mark 10.45, which he deliberately puts at the end of
the public ministry of Jesus outside Jerusalem, and through the
account of the Last Supper (14.22–25), which at the same time is
the last instruction of the disciples before the passion. Here the
imminent death of Jesus is interpreted in an inclusive, universal
way as being 'for all men', in connection with Isa. 53 and the
covenant sacrifice of Ex. 24.8 (cf. also Zech. 9.11), as a representative atoning death 'for the many'.

No one can say that this theme is completely absent from the
subsequent passion account. How else could we interpret the rending of the veil of the Temple, which set apart the holy of holies, in
Mark 15.38, than by saying that Jesus' death opens the way into
the holy of holies, the place of atonement for the sins of Israel and
of the presence of God, and robs the old cult of its force?[13] The
quotation from Isa. 56.7, that the Temple is 'a house of prayer for
all nations, prepares for this event, and the remark of the Gentile
centurion, who is the first to utter the saving confession of faith as
a representative of 'all nations' or 'the many', shows that the atonement has already become effective. Furthermore, the darkness
which symbolically follows the mocking of the crucified Messiah
about the sixth hour and ends with his cry of forsakenness about
the ninth hour is a sign that the death of Jesus itself was understood
as a saving event (Mark 15.33f., 37). It is clear from all this why
the pattern of the suffering of the righteous man, which has proved
so popular, is also so inadequate for contemporary theological reflection. According to Wisdom 2–5, the righteous sufferer first
achieves salvation only for himself; for others he acts as a model,

or is an accuser of his enemies; in essentials, this is the familiar formula of the *per aspera ad astra*, which we also find in connection with the heroes of the Greek world, and Heracles in particular.

Of course, here to a great extent we are still moving in the sphere of the theological interpretation made by Mark, who presumably wrote his gospel shortly before AD 70. The masterly arrangement of the material at least is his work, even if, as I believe, he took over a much earlier account in his passion narrative. We need to look back further to find the beginnings of the interpretation of the death of Jesus as vicarious atonement. Here a comparison between Mark and the earlier Paul can help us: Mark describes the death of Jesus as the death of the crucified Messiah. He does this with almost penetrating persistence. Between Mark 15.13 and 16.6 he uses the verb σταυροῦν, which was so offensive to ancient ears, eight times, and three times he talks of the σταυρός of the Messiah. Only those who understand how extremely offensive this word will have been to both Jewish and Gentile ears will be able to grasp what that means. Here there is no hagiographical transformation of the scandal: it is expressed openly. The twofold invitation made by the leaders of the people in Mark 15.30 and 32 to Jesus to come down from the cross contains an appeal to transform the scandalous and accursed death into triumph. This offence can still be clearly traced in the later polemic of writers like Celsus (Origen, *Contra Celsum* 2.33–37). Here we come up against the weightiest argument in anti-Christian polemic of both Jewish and Gentile origin. Through his death on the 'cursed tree' Jesus has proved to be a pitiful deceiver and his followers have proved to be dupes. In addition, Jews would inevitably understand talk of a crucified Messiah as blasphemy, because of Deut. 21.23. The Messiah of Israel could never ever at the same time be the one who according to the words of the Torah was accursed by God. It was perhaps for this very reason that the leaders of the people and their clientèle had pressed for the execution of Jesus by crucifixion.[14] This was the most obvious way to refute his messianic claim.

Although countless Jews were crucified under the Seleucids, the Hasmoneans and above all under the Romans, and although there

were so many crucified pious men and teachers, as far as I can see
we find only one reference to a crucified martyr in rabbinic sources:
Jose ben Joezer, the legendary teacher from the time of the
Maccabees.[15] Deuteronomy 21.23 evidently made it difficult to
turn a crucified man into a religious figure or a hero. For that very
reason, Paul describes his message in I Cor. 1.17, with polemical
accentuation, as λόγος τοῦ σταυροῦ; in it he means to proclaim
none other than the Χριστὸς ἐσταυρομένος, i.e. the crucified
Messiah (1.23; cf. 2.2; Gal. 3.1), who was a religious scandal to the
Jews and a delusion to the Greeks.

At this point we come back to the first question about the uniqueness of the proclamation of the universal atoning sacrifice of the
crucified Jesus (see p. 31 above). One feature of it is its unavoidable
offensiveness to ancient ears. Although they have been toned down
to suit Luke's apologetic concern, the allusions in Acts 5.30 and
10.39 show that the interpretation of the death of Jesus on the
cross as a 'curse for us' (Gal. 3.13, following Deut. 21.23) was not
just an exegetical 'discovery' of Paul's.

If we go back from the Paul of the letters to the apostle's conversion, which is to be dated only a few years after Easter, say between
AD 32 and AD 34, the decisive problem is why the young Pharisee
Sha'ul – Paul, with his scribal training, was so intensively occupied
in the persecution and destruction of the community of Christian
'Hellenists' in Jerusalem. Did they not cause offence precisely
through their blasphemous message of the crucified Messiah and
its theological consequences? In Acts 6.13, Stephen, the leader of
this group, is accused of having made attacks 'against this holy
place', i.e. the Temple, 'and the Law' (cf. 6.20; 7.48). The 'zeal'
of the persecutor (Phil. 3.6) must have been directed against these
attempts to shake the foundations of Israel's existence, indeed the
foundation of the whole of creation (Aboth 1.1). But what was the
basis of these attacks on the sanctuary and the Torah? Presumably
the certainty that the death of the crucified Messiah, who had
vicariously taken upon himself the curse of the Law, had made the
Temple obsolete as a place of everlasting atonement for the sins of
Israel, and therefore the ritual Law had lost its significance as a
necessary institution for salvation. There is a definite intrinsic

christological connection between the intentions of such different-sounding sayings as I Cor. 1.23; Mark 15.38; Acts 6.13 and Gal. 3.13.

In Phil. 3.8 the apostle says that the purpose of his radical change of life is 'to win Christ' and thus to receive the new 'righteousness from God' which is given 'through faith in Christ'. This ἵνα Χριστὸν κερδήσω primarily means the appropriation of the death of Christ in which God's righteousness is manifest as saving power. In Rom. 3.21–26 Paul describes the revelation of this righteousness and connects it very closely with the death of Jesus as a vicarious atoning sacrifice. Here we come upon linguistic allusions to the rite performed in the Holy of Holies on Yom Kippur. In his article '*hilastērion*', written more than thirty years ago, Professor Manson already said all that needed to be said about this verse, which is so hotly disputed: 'Christ crucified . . . like the mercy-seat in the Holy of Holies, . . . was the place where God's mercy was supremely manifested'.[16] Here we have one of the few instances in which Paul speaks of the death of Jesus in the categories of the Temple cult. For this he uses an earlier, stereotyped piece of tradition, perhaps because he knew that this language was understood well in Rome. He himself was no longer much concerned with this cultic vocabulary; now that his gaze was turned West, towards Rome and Spain, the cult of the Temple in Jerusalem had faded into the background, even if he had been forced to maintain a link with the church in Jerusalem for the sake of the unity of the church.

Nevertheless, elsewhere in his writings, the cultic language which interprets the death of Jesus as an atoning sacrifice still appears often, usually in relatively stereotyped formulations. This is evidently an earlier – one might say 'pre-Pauline' – linguistic tradition. The reference to the blood of Jesus shed on the cross appears not only in Rom. 3.25, in the context of the atoning sacrifice of Yom Kippur, but also in the paradosis of the Last Supper in I Cor. 11.25, as the sign of the new covenant. Underlying this is probably an interpretation of the self-sacrifice of Jesus as the sacrifice which seals the new covenant. In Romans 5.9 the blood of Jesus is the means by which justification takes place. This statement is closely connected with the preceding v. 8, in which the atoning death of Jesus 'for us, while we were still sinners', is interpreted as a sign of the love of God. The incarnate Son appears in the context of the mission statement in Rom. 8.3 as the atoning sacrifice (περὶ ἁμαρτίας = ḥaṭṭa't), through which God 'judges sin in the flesh'. In II Cor. 5.21, also, the statement that as the sinless one Christ was 'made sin for us' by God (τὸν μὴ γνόντα ἁμαρτίαν ὑπὲρ ἡμῶν ἁμαρτίαν ἐποίησεν) is to be understood to mean that Christ is offered on our behalf as the perfect sin offering. One might also recall I Cor. 5.7: 'Christ our passover is sacrificed', or the intercession of the heavenly high priest at the right hand of God in Rom. 8.34 and the προσαγωγή in Rom. 5.2, the essential basis of which is access to the presence of God in the heavenly sanctuary. Granted, all this does not amount to much, but the multiplicity of themes is all the more striking. Paul contents himself with the relatively frequent and brief formulae concerned with dying and 'surrendering', and remarkably enough, even the theme of the death of Jesus 'for our sins' takes a back place in comparison with the mere 'for us', on the basis of his anthropology. In addition he knows of other concept slike redemption or καταλλάσεσεσθαι or καταλλαγή, deriving from the sphere of interpersonal relationships, a group of words which could also of course be interpreted in a cultic sense (cf. e.g. Sophocles, *Ajax* 744: θεοῖσιν ὡς καταλλαχθῇ χόλου).

As there is a similar multiplicity of cultic terminology in individual deutero-Pauline letters, in I Peter, the Johannine corpus, Revelation, and above all Hebrews, and it is even more prominent here than it is in Paul, it seems likely that this language is not fortuitous and did not arise on the periphery of christological development, but – along with the formulae about dying and 'surrendering' – has a common root. Another indication of this is the use of the metaphor of the sacrificial lamb without blemish for the crucified and exalted Jesus, which we find attested independently in I Peter 1.19; John 1.29, 35f. and Revelation, and which is also to be presupposed in I Cor. 5.7. Underlying this is probably the interpretation of Jesus as the passover lamb, a reference which goes back to the last meal of Jesus with his disciples.

However, the one common root of all this multiple tradition is probably to be discovered where there had been a fundamental break with the atoning and saving significance of sacrifice in the worship of the Temple in Jerusalem and where the theological significance of this break – which did not come about without harsh resistance – had to be worked out. This break was explained in terms of the revolutionary insight that the death of the Messiah Jesus on Golgotha had brought about once and for all – note the significance of the ἅπαξ or ἐφάπαξ in such different texts as Rom. 6.10; I Peter 3.18 and Heb. 7.27; 9.12, etc. – universal atonement for all guilt.

(iii) *The atoning death of Jesus in the earliest community*

Of course this gives rise to further questions:

1. Does the universal soteriological interpretation of the death of Jesus, which necessarily led to a break with the sacrificial cult in the Temple, represent a step which was forced on the Hellenists by what was fundamentally secondary, artificial and scribal reflection compared with the elemental experience of encounter with the risen Lord, and which therefore necessarily presupposes a certain passage of time in the narrow interval which still remained? Or is the recognition of the atoning effect of the death of Jesus just as elemental for all concerned as the certainty that God raised Jesus from the dead?

2. Can we also presuppose an analogous theological insight in the Aramaic-speaking community around Peter and the Twelve? In other words, what is the status of the ultimate unity of the earliest Christian preaching which is attested to by Paul in I Cor. 15.11 and Gal. 2.7–9? Has Paul taken too much on himself here, and do we have to mistrust him?

3. Can the soteriological interpretation of the death of Jesus be derived with some degree of historical probability from the initiative of Jesus himself? Were this the case, we would essentially have answered the first two questions.

First of all a preliminary remark. Here we find a controversy in which a variety of conflicting arguments appear. It is hardly possible

to arrive at real historical *certainty* in this obscure sphere of the
event which gave rise to the earliest Christian community. We
come across this phenomenon often in the earliest history of
Christianity. A fundamental distinction must be made from the
foundation of our faith. My certainty that Christ died for my guilt
is neither strengthened nor attacked by the final results of this
discussion over historical probabilities. There is no historical proof
for the truth of faith. The certainty of faith has a different quality
from historical knowledge. Here we are concerned only with the
simple question: What is more probable after a careful examination
of the sources? Of course, the result of this quest for what is
historically most probable is not without a significance for a better
theological *understanding* of the origin of earliest Christianity, its
preaching and its christology.

Answering the questions raised above is also indissolubly connected with the question of the messianic claim of Jesus. If, as
radical German critics maintain, Jesus never spoke of Messiah or
Son of Man; if – incomprehensibly enough – he was crucified only
as 'rabbi and prophet',[17] as *ḥasid* and *ṣaddiq*, in short as a pious
martyr, the appearances of the risen Jesus could be understood
only as confirmation of his blameless piety, his exaltation to paradise, to the fathers resting there, and as a demonstration of the
proof of his preaching about the kingdom of God, of course with the
qualification that the kingdom of God which he had announced
was still further delayed. True, this would have confirmed in
essentials for the disciples the quite personal 'cause of Jesus' and
put things straight; but they would hardly have gone on in the
extremely vigorous way that they did. The case of Jesus – now
exalted to God – could have been concluded satisfactorily, and the
dawn of the kingdom of God could have been awaited in tran-
quillity. Easter, i.e. the appearances of the risen Jesus mentioned
in I Cor. 15.4ff., in no way explains how the alleged 'rabbi and
prophet' became the Messiah and Son of Man – which also means
the exalted Lord, *maran*, of the community –, in short, how 'the
proclaimer became the proclaimed'. If Jesus had no messianic
features at all, the origin of the Christian kerygma would remain
completely inexplicable and mysterious. In order to bridge this

gap we would be reduced to yet more new and incredible hypotheses. As long as scholarship which calls itself 'critical' does not raise this historical problem properly, it does not deserve the title it bears. In the Judaism of the time there were some authoritative teachers and pious martyrs who were said to have been transported to heaven or taken into the Garden of Eden after their deaths. Not one of them was made Son of Man or Messiah. Nor do we have any indication whatsoever that a martyr prophet could be exalted to be Son of Man through resurrection from the dead. The only 'exaltation' of a man and his identification with the 'Son of Man – Messiah' which is known to us is that of Enoch (Ethiopian Enoch 71). However, he is a hero from primal times with superhuman wisdom and authority. Equally improbable is a lengthy process of tradition, i.e. spread out over a number of years, after the Easter appearances, in which the fundamental features of the primitive Christian kerygma as we find it, say, in I Cor. 15.3, gradually developed, and in which the various christological titles were slowly and successively transferred to Jesus. Here we should no longer reckon in years, but in months or even weeks, and given such short periods of time we are hardly in any position to make subtle distinctions.[18]

The decisive statements must in fact already have been formulated in Greek some time before the calling of Paul. Otherwise there would have been no uproar against Stephen and his friends in the Greek-speaking synagogues of Jerusalem. The usual chronological patterns which are used – without reference to real chronology, – 'early or late traditions', are too indefinite and really do not say anything. We have already seen that the kerygma of the Hellenists, whom Paul fought against and persecuted in Jerusalem, was based on the offensive statement: 'The Messiah died for us (our sins).' Now this formula of 'dying for' (ἀποθνῄσκειν ὑπέρ) is striking because it has no parallel in the Old Testament and the Semitic sphere, though it is frequent in Greek texts, not least those of Hellenistic Jewish provenance from the time of the Maccabees. In contrast to this, the surrender formula clearly goes back to a Semitic basis, as is clear above all from its earliest formulation in the tradition, in Mark 10.45.[19] The formula *nātan* or *māsar napšō 'al* (δοῦναι τὴν ψυχὴν αὐτοῦ ὑπέρ) is variously attested in later Hebrew texts. There is also a Hebraism – presumably from Isa. 53 – in the inclusive, universal significance of πολλοί = *rabbīm* in the sense of πάντες, and the λύτρον ἀντί corresponds with the Hebrew *kōfer taḥat*, which probably goes back to Isa. 43.3f.[20] Thus both formulae, that of the dying of the Messiah and the surrender formula, have different derivations in the history of the tradition.

The Hellenists in Jerusalem, who for the first time recast the primitive Christian message (and the tradition of Jesus) in the Greek language, were linguistically creative in many respects. It is to them that we are presumably indebted for the new and specifically Christian meaning of εὐαγγέλιον, εὐαγγελίζεσθαι; ἀπόστολος, ἐκκλησία, κοινωνία, παρουσία, χάρις, πίστις, ἀποκάλυψις, ἀπολυτρώσις, πρὸ (ἀπὸ) καταβολῆς κόσμου, and so on, and even the phrase ὁ υἱὸς τοῦ ἀνθρώπου (instead of the υἱὸς ἀνθρώπου of the LXX), so mysterious because it has the definite article. We may regard this hermeneutically significant and effective work of translation as a fruit of the enthusiastic experience of the Spirit which came about in the earliest community. The new message was also to be proclaimed to the Jews and godfearers in Jerusalem, the coastal regions of Palestine and the cities of Phoenicia and Syria, indeed to the Diaspora generally, many of whom only spoke Greek. What is more likely than to suppose that the formula Χριστὸς ἀπέθανεν ὑπὲρ (τῶν ἁμαρτιῶν) ἡμῶν, which is pre-Pauline in the full sense of the word, was formed in connection with this creative translation of the new kerygma into Greek? Possibly it was meant to counter statements in the LXX which reject a 'dying for others' (cf. Deut. 24.16; Jer. 38 (31).30; Ezek. 3.18f.; 18.4ff.): the death of the Messiah creates the possibility of representativeness.

Of course this would rule out another obvious possibility. The LXX very often uses the phrase ἐξιλάσκεσθαι περί to translate the Hebrew *kipper 'al*, referring either to people (or pronouns) or to their sins. So here too we find shorter and longer forms (e.g. περὶ ὑμῶν or περὶ τῶν ἁμαρτιῶν ὑμῶν) side by side, with very little difference between them. That this terminology, which makes use of the root ἱλασκ-, also had a certain, albeit limited influence on the soteriological interpretation of the death of Jesus, is shown not only by Rom. 3.25 and Heb. 2.7, but above all by I John, where Christ is twice described as ἱλασμὸς περὶ τῶν ἁμαρτιῶν ἡμῶν (cf. 2.2; 4.10).

This terminology was more directly related to the atoning sacrificial cult of the Temple than the very Greek-sounding formulae of Paul and – as I would suggest – the Hellenists. It is easy to explain why this not directly cultic, Graecized formula was preferred to that of the LXX, which was more connected with the Jerusalem cult: the formula Χριστὸς ἀπέθανεν ὑπέρ . . . expressed the uniqueness of the death of Jesus and its soteriological significance over against the constant atoning sacrifices in the Temple; in contrast to the universal atoning effect of the death of Jesus these latter only had a very limited force and therefore had to be repeated constantly. Presumably the verb *kipper* = ἐξιλάσκεσθαι was too closely associated with the idea of the ever new sacrificial acts of atonement in the cult. By contrast, 'the Messiah died for us' expressed clearly the ἐφάπαξ of reconciliation (Rom. 6.10). The rabbinic tradition, which deliberately restricts the effect of Yom Kippur in a number of ways, rests on an earlier tradition which goes back to the Second Temple. Whereas there, for example, atonement is divided into the three components of conversion, Yom Kippur and man's own death (M. Yoma 8.8 etc.), in the death of Jesus the effective atonement which guaranteed salvation was concentrated on one point: the death of the Messiah on the cross. All purely human action had to fade into the background in the face of that. Paul's idea, which he also assumes the Roman Christians to have heard of, that in the death of Jesus all have died, has its ultimate foundation here (II Cor. 5.14f.; cf. Rom. 6.3f.).

By means of the new kerygmatic formula of the saving significance of the death of the Messiah, the Hellenists stressed the radical newness of the once-and-for-all, eschatological atonement which had taken place on Golgotha, which had been made manifest by the resurrection of Jesus, and now had to be proclaimed to all men. Thus the formula represented a demarcation from the worship of the Temple, which expressed the fundamental, qualitative difference between the dying of Jesus on the cross on Golgotha and the ongoing sin-offerings on Mount Zion. If one so desired, one might say that the atonement achieved through Christ developed its saving power directly, in the heavenly sanctuary, and not just on the altar and in the earthly Holy of Holies. In this way access to the direct presence of God himself had been opened up for the believer.

There are several independent references which tend in this direction: 'For through him we . . . have access (τὴν προσαγωγήν) to the Father' (Eph. 2.18; cf. 3.12; Rom. 5.2). Through the self-sacrifice of the true high priest Jesus we are enabled to 'draw near with confidence to the throne of grace, that we may receive mercy . . .' (Heb. 4.16). We find similar formulae in a christological hymn (I Peter 3.18):

> For Christ also suffered for sins once for all,
> the righteous for the unrighteous,
> that he might bring you to God
> (ἵνα ὑμᾶς προσαγάγῃ τῷ θεῷ).

Behind all these different statements lies an older common tradition.

Nevertheless, the Temple on Mount Zion had not yet lost all its functions; instead of being a place of sacrifice it was a 'house of prayer for all nations'; as one might say, it had become the universal centre of all synagogues. Taking over the familiar formula ἐξιλάσκεσθαι περί from the LXX had furthered the misunderstanding that in fact the death of Jesus was only as important as Temple worship, and stood alongside it; it could not represent the eschatological superseding and abolition of it. In the last resort this is the reason for the astonishing predominance of the preposition ὑπέρ as an expression of the saving efficacy of the death of Jesus in the New Testament texts, as opposed to περί made more familiar through the LXX as a translation of the Hebrew *'al*.

Nevertheless, alongside this, Old Testament references to sacrifice – and indeed an astonishing number and variety of them – were applied to the death of Jesus. This is connected on the one hand with the obvious analogy which it provided, but even more with *the consistent eschatological and christological proof from scripture*. As the Old Testament writings were written as τύποι for the eschatological present (I Cor. 10.11; Rom. 15.4), what they say about sacrifice – understood in the right way – must point beyond them to their eschatological fulfilment in Christ. Atonement through the Temple cult finds its *end and* at the same time also its *fulfilment* in the eschatological saving event on Golgotha. This multiple reference, which expresses both the actual difference between Temple worship and the death of Jesus, together with the analogy between them and an eschatological typology, explains the remarkable fact that in the New Testament texts from Paul to the Johannine corpus the death of Jesus is interpreted, not all that often, but unmistakably and in constantly changing ways, in analogy to the Temple cult. The basis for the multiplicity of these descriptions – very like that of the christological titles – lies in the deliberately chosen 'multiplicity of approaches'.

However, our investigation into origins goes further. Can the soteriological interpretation of the death of Jesus be traced back with some degree of probability only as far as the 'Hellenists', so that we have to suppose that they were the first to express this central idea of the primitive Christian kerygma – under the creative impulse of the *Spirit* – or are there indications which might lead us to look for the origin of this expression of faith in the primal event which brought the church into being?

I have already referred to one of them. As we find it in Mark 10.45, the surrender formula indicates an original Semitic form which must come either from the Aramaic-speaking community or from Jesus himself. A further starting point is the *Lord's Supper*. Both the paradosis in I Cor. 11.23–25, where Paul refers to a historical event with a specific date, and the account in Mark 14. 22–25, contain the interpretation of the death of Jesus as an atoning saving event. In its oldest demonstrable form it is specially bound up with the cup of wine at the Last Supper, and similarly goes back to the Jerusalem community. For in all probability the interpretation of the death of Jesus as a covenant sacrifice along the lines of Ex. 24.8, which is presupposed in the word over the cup in Mark 14.24, and which the (pre-)Pauline tradition expands with a reference to the new covenant of Jer. 31.31, is already to be presupposed in Palestine, since the Targumim (Onkelos and Yerushalmi I)

expressly speak of the atoning effect of the blood rite in the covenant sacrifice of Ex. 24.8, and Mark's version with its Semitic-type
formula τοῦτό ἐστιν τὸ αἷμά μου τῆς διαθήκης τὸ ἐκχυννόμενον
ὑπὲρ πολλῶν also presupposes such an atoning understanding of
the death of Jesus as an eschatological covenant sacrifice.[21] By contrast, the earliest accounts of the Supper in Paul and Mark have no
connection whatsoever with ancient memorial meals for the dead
or mystery celebrations. This is even truer of the pre-Pauline
celebration of the Lord's Supper in the earliest community.

Finally and in conclusion one can also hardly imagine how the
unity of the earliest church – so dear to Paul's heart – could have
been preserved had the community in Jerusalem not shared this
belief in the soteriological efficacy of the death of Jesus. In view of
the daily sacrifice in the Temple, the question whether atonement
took place there or whether God himself had 'finally' brought it
about through the crucifixion of the Messiah must have become
even more urgent.

How can Paul – with relatively few exceptions – content himself
with formulae and not explain in detail the atoning death of the
Messiah 'for us'? The reason is probably that the 'that' in this
formula was in no way controversial, even in Galatia and in the
Roman church which was unknown to him; the problems lay in
the soteriological consequences, say in connection with the ongoing importance of the Torah and the works which it required.
Paul had thought through radically to the end the consequences of
the saving significance of the death of Jesus which the Hellenists
had already sketched out; however, the substance does not derive
first from him nor from the Hellenists – its roots lie deeper.

For example, it is striking that two writings which according to
the tradition of the early church – in my view completely reliable –
must be assigned to the Petrine sphere of tradition, Mark and I
Peter, stress the soteriological interpretation of the death of Jesus
as an atoning death in a marked way, I Peter by an explicit citation
of Isa. 53 (2.17ff.; 3.18f.; cf. 1.18), and Mark in two places in an
archaic Semitic linguistic form. We know very little indeed about
the work of Peter as leader of the Jerusalem community and later
as a missionary. If we assume – and this is still the most likely

thing – that he was executed in Rome during Nero's persecution in AD 64, his activity extended over a period of thirty-four years; it is longer than that of Paul. That it was not without effect is clear from the letters to the Corinthians – despite Paul's vigorous remark in I Cor. 15.10: ἀλλὰ περισσότερον αὐτῶν πάντων ἐκοπίασα, where Paul had to fight against what for him was the threat posed by the Petrine mission – and also from Gal. 1 and 2. We can hardly doubt that Peter had a special theological authority within the first generation of earliest Christian history, and also in the Pauline missionary communities, even if today people sometimes talk about earliest Christianity as though Peter had never existed. The conclusion follows almost of necessity: the Petrine kerygma, too, must have known and shared as its central content the atoning death of Jesus. Otherwise in Antioch Paul would not have been able to argue polemically against it at all, since there would not have been the basic presuppositions for any argument. At first, Peter too 'lived like a Gentile' in Antioch (Gal. 2.14): for him also Christ and not the Torah must have been the foundation of revelation. Conversely, it is hardly credible that the greatest authority of the earliest Christian period could have taken over this central confession at some later stage from the Hellenists – expelled from Jerusalem because of their polemic against the Temple – or invented it on his own authority. If anywhere, its roots must be inseparably bound up with the foundation of his experience of faith.

(iv) Historical and traditio-historical objections

Of course, various objections could be made to this:

1. First, the Temple cult and the legal regulations associated with it still seem to have had some significance for the *Jewish Christians in Judaea*. That can be inferred from James' invitation to Paul to undertake the discharge of Nazirite vows, the tradition of texts from Jesus like Matt. 5.23f., and Luke's notes about the acceptance of priests and zealous Pharisees. On the other hand, we hear from Paul (I Thess. 2.14; cf. Gal. 1.22) that it was the communities in Judaea in particular which were persecuted by the

Jewish authorities, evidently even after the expulsion of the Hellenists. According to Luke, the Sadducean priestly nobility were
the main driving force here; a later wave of persecution was caused
by king Agrippa I (AD 40–44; Acts 12). In AD 62, the chief Sadducee
and then high priest, Annas, son of the Annas of the passion narrative, had James the brother of the Lord and other Jewish Christians
stoned for breaking the Law.[22] According to the apocryphal
anabathmoi Iakobou, James is said to have attacked 'the Temple,
sacrifice and the altar fire';[23] the Pseudo-Clementines, which are
influenced by Jewish Christianity, also rejected the sacrificial cult.[24]
The conjecture made by H. J. Schoeps that the rejection of sacrifice by the Ebionites also makes a soteriological interpretation of
the death of Jesus in the earliest Palestinian community improbable, is untenable; the opposite is the case. The death of Jesus was
presumably one of the causes of the Ebionite criticism of sacrifice,
even if this is no longer clear from the late traditions of the third
and fourth centuries.[25] The constant opposition of the Sadducean
priestly nobility to the Jewish Christians could best be explained
by a permanently critical attitude towards the sacrificial cult on
their part. In my view, it is therefore probable that from the beginning the Jewish Christians adopted a fundamentally detached
attitude to the cult, but were prepared for certain compromises on
account of the world in which they lived. Even the Essenes, who
rejected the real cult in Jerusalem, were ready to honour the
Temple with dedicated gifts (ἀναθήματα).[26] We have no indication
whatsoever that the Jewish Christians in Judaea felt an unconditional obligation to worship on Mount Zion; on the contrary, there
is some evidence that they had a somewhat broken relationship
with it, but had to show a certain compliance if they were to remain
in existence. In my view this is also clear from the tradition about
the Temple tax underlying Matt. 17.24–27, which probably came
into being some time before AD 70, since after the destruction of the
Temple the half-shekel tax had to be paid as a *fiscus Judaicus* in
Rome to the temple of Juppiter Capitolinus. There Jesus stresses
to Simon Peter that as sons of God they are free from the Temple
tax, but that they should nevertheless pay it in order to avoid any
offence. This rejection of the traditional cult must have had very

early roots, as it tended to be weakened under external pressure in the later decades down to AD 70. The best explanation of it is that Jewish Christians in their Palestinian homeland also maintained the fundamental saving significance of the death of Jesus as the sinless Messiah, and no longer ascribed atoning effect to sacrifice in the sanctuary. The special stress on Hos. 6.6 in Matt. 9.13; 12.7 probably derives from Jewish-Christian theology. Hosea 6.6 is cited again in the pseudo-Clementine *Recognitions*, 1.37.2. The legendary account of Hegesippus in Eusebius, about the constant prayer of the Lord's brother in the Temple, does not tell against this. Precisely because the Temple no longer served as a place of sacrifice and atonement, but had become 'a house of prayer' (Mark 11.17–Isa. 56.7), the tradition could develop that James went alone to the Temple and there 'constantly went down on his knees to pray to God and ask him for forgiveness for his people'.[27] He, James, the brother of Jesus, as earthly intercessor for disobedient Israel, corresponded to Jesus the Son of Man as the heavenly intercessor at the right hand of God. By contrast, the Temple cult itself had lost its atoning effect.

The following objections are more difficult to answer. Here we have a traditio-historical problem. *In Aramaic-speaking Jewish Palestine, round about the year AD 30, could the notion of the universal representative atonement achieved by the death of the Messiah come into being at all?* A number of counter-arguments are advanced against this possibility.

2. *Inter alia*, these include the history of *the influence of Isa. 53,* the only Old Testament text which could have prompted the beginning of this development, as elsewhere the Old Testament tends to reject vicarious atonement or the death of a man for the sins of others (see above, p. 7). However, at this particular point one would be glad of a substantiated history of interpretation in the pre-Christian period. One would not refer, either, to the messianic interpretation of this chapter in the prophetic Targum, as this is post-Christian, and in it not only are the statements about suffering transferred to the nations and thus turned into statements about salvation for Israel, but the idea of vicarious suffering is interpreted away. I myself feel that an 'anti-Christian' interpretation is

quite probable, though there is no sure proof of this and as a result it will always be a matter for dispute.[28] The only 'remnant' to which reference could be made is the Armenian version of TestBenj 3, which contains an earlier version of the vicarious suffering of a sinless man probably without Christian interpolations. However, even here there is dispute over the messianic interpretation and the originality of the text.[29] On the other hand, however, it must be recognized that with the exception of PsSol 17 and 18, we have very few 'messianic' texts from the pre-Christian period in any case, and therefore do not know very much about Jewish messianic expectations before the Christian era. There was certainly not a fixed 'doctrine of the Messiah' before the first century AD. It would be therefore better to talk of a plurality of messianic motifs.[30] It should also be noted that the LXX translation, which already diverges strongly from the Hebrew text, represents a quite arbitrary 'interpretation', which shows that this text was not without effect in pre-Christian times. The same is true of Aquila, Theodotion, Symmachus and the Targum, even though they are post-Christian. Even rabbinic interpretation is not uninteresting, and refers the text both to the Messiah and to the innocent sufferer. There was evidently constant work on and with this refractory text.[31] Furthermore, J. Starcky has already pointed to an Aramaic text which presumably comes from a Testament of Jacob, in which there is mention of an eschatological saviour figure who 'achieves atonement for all the sons of his race', who 'teaches the will of God' and whose word 'works to the ends of the earth'. However, he comes up against resistance and enmity, 'and is involved in deceit and violence'.[32] Abbé Starcky, who kindly put this text at my disposal, also told me that in a further fragment of the same writing and perhaps even in the same column, there is mention of a persecuted person. *wmk'byn 'l* appears in the first line; *ngdy mk'bykh* is all that is left of the third. As *mak'ob*, which is relatively rare in the Old Testament, appears twice in close succession in Isa. 53.3 and 4, there could well be a reference to this chapter here. The servant of God is indeed the 'man of sorrows'. However, we cannot of course reach certainty here. Our knowledge is indeed 'in part', and we must be content with the fragment of old documents which worms and beetles have left to us. Of course this 'not know-ing' also holds for the opposite position. We cannot claim that Isa. 53 had no kind of messianic interpretation in pre-Christian Judaism.[33] It is simply the case that too few texts have come down to us from the pre-rabbinic period. Think of the treasures which the library of Qumran, with its thousand scrolls, may have con-tained, and of the tiny fragment which has come down to us! Of the Isaiah *pesharim* we sadly know only parts of the passage on Isa. 11, and nothing on Isa. 53. The fact that the first Isaiah scroll from Cave 1 read *mšhty* (i.e. *māšaḥtī*, cf. Isa. 61.1), instead of the mysterious word *mšht* (*mišhat* or *mošhat*), could equally indicate a messianic interpretation, though it probably stems from a scribal error.

So far, then, we have no clear text from pre-Christian Judaism which speaks of the vicarious suffering of the Messiah in connec-tion with Isa. 53. Of course, this does not rule out the possibility of such a tradition, and there are some indications in favour of it, but the basis provided by our sources is too restricted. At all events, a suffering Messiah did not belong to the widespread popular Messianic hope in the time of Jesus and a crucified Messiah was a real blasphemy.

On the other hand, we must ask whether at present too much weight is not being attached to the traditio-historical argument, since we must reckon with creative innovations in the earliest Christian community, which was utterly influenced by an enthusi-astic and eschatological experience of the Spirit. These revolu-tionary innovations already began, after all, with Jesus himself.

3. By contrast, it should no longer be doubted *that Isa. 53 had an influence on the origin and shaping of the earliest kerygma*. It was perhaps an understandable reaction that after long and excessive emphasis on the theme of the servant of God in the sayings of Jesus himself, to some extent as a counterblast, people should have wanted suddenly to drive the *'ebed Yahweh* out of large areas of the New Testament 'with swords and staves'. However, this can only be done by treating the texts violently.[34] Neither the formula of the 'surrender' of Jesus nor that of his representative dying 'for many' or 'for us' would have come into being without the back-

ground of this mysterious prophecy.[35] It must also be said that alongside the earliest 'messianic hymns', the Psalms, Isaiah was by far the most important prophetic text for Jesus and earliest Christianity. One cannot immediately measure the influence of an Old Testament text on early Christian traditions by the total of literal quotations from it, otherwise for example Hos. 6.2, which people are fond of using to explain the third day in I Cor. 15.4, would have no significance at all, as it is quoted for the first time in Tertullian (*adversus Iudaeos* 13,23; *adversus Marcionem* 4,43,1). Besides, a glance at the *loci citati et allegati ex vetere testamento* in the new Nestle-Aland[36] shows that the immediately demonstrable influence of this disputed text is by no means small: at any rate, there are ten literal quotations from the fifteen verses of Isa. 52. 13–53.12, and thirty-two allusions to it. As far as I can see, this is one of the best results for any Old Testament text to be found in the New Testament. Besides, even today we know of texts and quotations which are so very familiar to everyone that we have hesitations about continually quoting them, which would become tedious, and therefore content ourselves with allusions. This may also have been the case with so important a text for the New Testament kerygma as Isa. 53.

4. A further argument for a Hellenistic Jewish-Christian derivation of the conception of the representative atoning death of Jesus is seen in the fact that we seem to find pre-Christian references to the *vicarious atoning effect of the death of a martyr* only in Jewish Hellenistic texts.[37] These are only hinted at in II Macc. 7.32f., 37f.; the idea of representation is expressed more clearly in IV Maccabees, with its stronger Greek tone, decked out in the style of a Hellenistic panegyric, which probably comes from the Jewish community of the Antioch of the first (or second) century AD. That is the case in the prayer of Eleazar in 6.28f. and the closing considerations in 17.21f.[38] However, can we draw a distinction between 'Hellenistic' and 'Palestinian' Judaism so sharply? I have already tried to show on pp. 2f. above that this is no longer possible on the basis of our present knowledge of the sources. In addition, both II and IV Maccabees contain numerous 'Palestinian' traditions. Against this, too, is the fact that in writings composed in Palestine

we find at least beginnings in this direction. There is a penitential prayer which probably comes from the time of the Maccabean troubles; it was originally composed in Hebrew and inserted by an unknown author into the Greek additions to Daniel, where according to LXX it was spoken by all three men in the burning fiery furnace, whereas Theodotion puts it only in the mouth of Azariah.[39] This prayer first confesses that God has inflicted judgment on the people 'for our sins', that he has 'given us over into the hands of our lawless enemies and the hated apostates'; however, there follows the petition for mercy because of the merits of the patriarchs, i.e. Abraham, Isaac and Israel. In a similar way, according to the 'Hellenistic' LXX of Job and the 'Palestinian' Targum of Job from Cave 11, God forgives Job's friends their sins 'for Job's sake', that is, because of his intercession and the sacrifice which – in contrast to M – he offers for his friends.[40] At the end of the Prayer of Azariah it is stressed that because of the destruction of the Temple no further sacrifices can be offered 'to find mercy'. Instead, the suppliant prays that they may be accepted 'with a lowly spirit',

> like holocausts of rams and bulls,
> like ten thousand fat sheep,
> so may our sacrifice be before you today,
> to bring about atonement with you
> (καὶ ἐξιλάσαι ὄπισθέν σου LXX).[41]

In the original version of the penitential prayer, the atoning sacrifice may have referred to the prayer itself, but in the mouths of the three men in the burning fiery furnace, i.e. according to the LXX version, the martyrdom of the three men becomes an atoning sacrifice offered to God. According to Dan. 3.28 'they offered up their bodies' so as not to be able to venerate any god other than the God of Israel (see above, p. 12). Here we have the earliest account of a martyrdom, from pre-Maccabean Judaism, which, however, ends with the miracle of God's deliverance. For later rabbinic tradition, despite their miraculous deliverance, the three become prototypes of the pious martyr.

5. A further complex, the age of which is disputed, is the *'Aqēdat Yiṣḥaq*, 'the binding of Isaac for sacrifice', according to

Gen. 22.[42] In rabbinic texts from the second century it provides vicarious atonement for the sins of all Israel. However, individual traces point back to an earlier period. This is the case, *inter alia*, with the identification of Mount Moriah with Mount Zion and the dating of the sacrifice of Isaac on the feast of the passover in the book of Jubilees (18.7, 13; cf. 17.15). Later, there are many references to the sacrificing of Isaac in the Pseudo-Philonic *Liber Antiquitatum Biblicarum*, which was composed towards the end of the first century AD. It has a unique significance here. First of all Isaac compares himself with the lamb which is chosen *in oblationes domini*, viz., with the sacrificial animals which are offered *pro iniquitatibus hominum*. However, as man he is destined 'to inherit the world'. There follows a prophecy: 'But my blessedness (*beatitudo*, here in the sense of blessing?) will be over all men (or also, will come to all men?), because there will be no other (sc. sacrifice), and generations will be told about me, and through me peoples will come to know that God has thought the soul of a man worthy of sacrifice.'[43]

In another passage Jephthah's daughter, also destined to be a sacrifice as a result of her father's oversight, compares herself with Isaac. She is afraid that – in contrast to his sacrifice – the sacrifice of her life will not be well-pleasing to God because of her father's hasty vow, but God himself determines 'that her life is surrendered because of his vow (cf. 39.11) and that her death will for all time be precious in my eyes'.[44]

There is a further instance in the oracle of Balaam, where it is said of Isaac: 'And because he did not object, his sacrifice was well pleasing to me, and on the basis of his blood I chose these people.'[45] There is a clear statement here of the vicarious saving effect of the sacrifice of Isaac. The connection between the sacrifice (*oblatio*) of Isaac and his blood (*pro sanguine eius*) indicates its character as an atoning sacrifice. The blood of Isaac's sacrifice is already associated with that of the passover lamb in the Tannaitic Midrash Mekilta on Exodus.[46]

The reason why by contrast the conception of atonement for the sin of Israel still does not appear explicitly may be that here attention is focussed on the future of Israel, and its election and future greatness stand in the foreground. Among other things, the allusion in Rom. 8.32 suggests that in the first century AD the soteriological interpretation of the sacrifice of Isaac was already known in Judaism.

6. We cannot go any further here in detail into the complicated question of representative atonement in the rabbinic literature, which deserves a separate monograph. Moreover, it has been dealt with in Lohse's study, which is still a basic work.[47] We should not put too much stress on the argument that haggadic traditions about it only appear during the course of the second century, since the haggadic tradition from first-century teachers which has come down to us is relatively slim. This is already evident from a look at Bacher's *Haggadah of the Tannaites*.[48] Even more than the Halakah, the Haggadah represents a continuous broad stream in which there are constant ebbs and flows; we can see only a tiny part of this broad stream as early as the first century AD, but that certainly does not mean that the stream was not flowing then. So if a Haggadah appears for the first time in the work of a teacher from the middle of the second century, we cannot simply assert that in all probability it was not yet present in the first. In particular because of the number of political martyrs and the widespread political radicalism, even in Pharisaic circles, in the first and second centuries, the rabbinic tradition later underwent a process of strict self-censorship. In an exegesis of I Kings 20.42 and 22.34, a statement has been handed down about Shimeon b. Yohai, hostile to Rome and almost a zealot, who survived the persecution of Hadrian: 'Every drop (of blood) which flowed from that righteous man (I Kings 20.37: one of the prophet's disciples) brought about atonement for all Israel.'[49] For Shimeon b. Yohai, this was certainly not a completely new idea, but a conception which has its *Sitz im Leben* in the bloody conflict between Rome during the first century and the first half of the second. The same is true of the anonymous tradition of the Tannaitic Midrash Sifre Deut. 32.32:[50] 'the Israelites killed by the Gentiles are an expiation for the world to come' and of a whole series of statements from another Tannaitic Midrash, Mekilta Ex., e.g. on 12.1, where R. Jonathan, a contemporary of Shimeon b. Yohai, draws the further conclusion from Jonah's readiness to

sacrifice his life to save the ship (Jonah 1.12),[51] 'and so you find that
the patriarchs and prophets gave their life for Israel.' The connection between Num. 25.13 and Isa. 53.12 probably also goes back
to old zealot tradition: God's blessing on the zeal of Phinehas is
explained by Isa. 53.12: 'because he gave up his life to death'. Thus
he not only wrought atonement at that time, 'but he stands
(continually) and achieves atonement until the dead are raised.'[52]
In zeal for God Phinehas puts his life at risk, and as in the *'Aqēdat
Yiṣḥaq*, an atoning effect is ascribed to this action which goes
beyond time. The doctrine of the three or four kinds of atonement:
through penitence, through the Day of Atonement, through death
and through suffering, already mentioned above, which is to be
found in the Mishnah, Tosephta and the early Tannaitic discussion,
also presupposes a lengthy development of tradition and a very
complex doctrine of the various kinds of atonement, from which
vicarious atonement is not excluded. The popular formula 'I will
be atonement for you', which expressed solidarity with the person
or persons affected by showing a readiness to take over suffering in
cases of sorrow or disaster, certainly goes back to the time of the
Second Temple; it later became a common cliché. It occurs often
in the Mishnah and Tosephta in anecdotes which are set in a time
when the Second Temple was still standing.[53] The discussion of
rabbinic texts by Wengst is quite inadequate, and his criticism of
E. Lohse, *Märtyrer und Gottesknecht*, suffers from his inability to
cope properly with rabbinic texts.[54]

As a result, after careful consideration of all the sources indicated,
we must agree with Jeremias and Lohse that the vicarious atoning
effect of the death or even the suffering of a righteous man was not
unknown in the Palestinian Judaism of the first century AD,
independently of the question of terminology. Objections against
deriving the soteriological interpretation of the death of Jesus from
the earliest Aramaic-speaking community are therefore at any rate
unconvincing. There is nothing from a historical or traditio-
historical point of view which stands in the way of our deriving it
from the earliest community and perhaps even from Jesus himself.
This does not rule out the possibility *that the earliest Christian
message of the self-offering of the Messiah Jesus on the cross for the*

salvation of the 'many' was an unprecedentedly new and bold – and at the same time *offensive* – *statement* in the context of the tradition of both Greek-speaking and Aramaic-speaking Judaism, because of its scandalous content, its eschatological radicalism and its universal significance.

(v) The origin of the message of the atoning death of the Messiah Jesus

With some degree of probability, we can derive the message of the saving death of the Messiah Jesus of Nazareth as an 'expiatory sacrifice' for our sins from the 'basic event which gave rise to the Christian community', and which is so difficult for us to discern.

In this case, however, what is the relationship between this and the events of the resurrection, along with the confession of the resurrection to which they led? The appearances of the risen Christ gave the disciples, utterly overwhelmed and disoriented as a result of the shameful and accursed death of their messianic Master, the assurance that God himself had recognized Jesus of Nazareth, executed as a false claimant to messiahship, as the true Messiah of Israel. The earliest confession of the resurrection, 'God has raised Jesus from the dead', was constructed on the basis of this experience, probably following the divine predicates in the Eighteen Benedictions, which in the second petition address God as *meqim metim* (Staerk, 11, Palestinian Version).[55] However, this experience really meant much more than just the assurance that Jesus had now been 'accepted' by God as a prophetic martyr or an innocent sufferer in a particularly ostentatious way and had been transported into the heavenly dwellings of the righteous, along the lines of what we find, say, in the two prophets raised from death in Rev. 11.11f. or the children of Job in *Test. Iobi* 39.8–40.4.[56] For the disciples, their encounters with the risen Lord first confirmed the messianic claim of Jesus which had brought him to the cross, a confirmation given by God himself which at the same time amounted to his now public identification with the Son of Man, exalted to the right hand of God (Ps. 110.1)[57] and soon to come as judge. At the same time, through the resurrection God had proved

him to be the only innocent one, 'who knew no sin' (II Cor.
5.21).

We can hardly envisage these first days, weeks and months of the
disciples after Easter as the meditative assembly of a quietistic
group[58] with esoteric mystical experiences; rather, what they
experienced ought to be compared with the violent force of an
explosion which broke up all traditional conventions and bour-
geois assurances. Here something new and unheard-of emerged, a
new experience which radically transcended the everyday life of
Palestinian fishermen, peasants and craftsmen. To some degree
people lived with an enthusiastic assurance that the heavens
would open and the kingdom of God would dawn. It was no
accident that the appearances of the risen Jesus were connected
with the eschatological experience of the Spirit which was compared with the force of heavenly fire. At the same time that means
that the Jesus community which first took shape after Easter
understood these events as the beginning of the end of the world
and the dawn of the rule of God. The resurrection marked the
beginning of the general resurrection of the dead; in Paul Jesus
still appears as the 'firstfruits of those who have fallen asleep'
(I Cor. 15.20), and in the Colossians hymn and in Revelation as the
'firstborn from the dead' (Col. 1.18; Rev. 1.5). It was hoped that
believers would be made like him when he appeared (Rom. 8.29;
Phil. 3.21; cf. I Thess. 4.17f.).

Jesus' preaching about the coming Son of Man was now transformed in the light of the Easter experience into the kerygma of the
Lord of the community, risen, exalted to the right hand of God,
and still to come, and to some extent the rule of God and his
anointed were already present in embryo form. The disciples
understood themselves to be the eschatological remnant of Israel
and thus at the same time the nucleus of the new people of God.
They were aware that they had been sent by the risen Lord himself
to call their brothers to believe in the one who was exalted and
still to come. In all this the dynamic and creative enthusiasm of the
Spirit, as the eschatological gift of God to his renewed people, was
at work. A vision of the risen Lord along with the gift of the Spirit
formed the presupposition for the sending of the 'messengers of

the Messiah', the ἀπόστολοι Χριστοῦ. Even for Paul, his authentication as an apostle of Jesus Christ is still inseparably bound up with the vision of the Kyrios (I Cor. 9.1; 15.8ff.).

At the same time, however, we should not overlook the humanly insuperable barrier which divided the disciples from their master. Between the kingdom of God breaking in with the resurrection and exaltation of the Messiah Jesus and the former disciples and followers of Jesus was the awareness of their *utter failure and deep guilt*. Again, it is Mark's passion which depicts everyone's guilt over God's anointed in an impressive way. This solidarity in sin unites all those involved here. No one is excepted, from Pilate and the soldiers in the execution squad, through the leaders of the people and the crowd which they goaded on, to the twelve, with Judas who betrayed Jesus and Peter who denied him, indeed to the women at the tomb who fled in utter confusion and in their fear failed to obey the command of the angel (Mark 16.8). Their flight is matched by the flight of the disciples in 14.50; thus they too share in the scandal which Jesus prophesied in Mark 14.27.[59] In this way Mark brings the crucified Messiah face to face with the barriers of human guilt. Here we can really say with Paul in Rom. 3.23, 'for all have sinned and come short of the glory of God'.

However, the question of guilt and forgiveness in the face of the imminent kingdom of God goes back even further. Repentance and the forgiveness of sins through baptism in the Jordan were proclaimed to be the only way of escaping the threat of the wrath of God to come or the fiery judgment of the coming Son of man in the revival movement, aimed at penitence, led by John the Baptist, the milieu from which Jesus himself was called to messianic service (Matt. 3.11f.; Luke 3.16f. Q) and from which the first disciples also came (John 1.35ff.). Differing somewhat from the preaching of John the Baptist, by both his words and his deeds Jesus himself had proclaimed the boundless love of the Father for all who were lost, and had himself promised forgiveness to individual sinners. The forgiveness of sins had been an essential ingredient of the Lord's Prayer: the coming of the kingdom and the removal of sin were indissolubly connected.

John the Baptist apparently failed in his preaching of repentance and his baptism in the Jordan, and was executed as a martyr prophet. Jesus, too, came up against growing rejection and resistance with his message of the dawn of the kingdom of God and the overwhelming love of the Father, above all among those of his contemporaries who had influence and power. In other words, the guilt of the leaders of the people and their followers in Jerusalem, like that of the disciples, was bound up with the guilt of the whole people. They resisted the coming of the kingdom of God. This means, with the passion and the death of Jesus the question of guilt became more oppressive and more urgent than ever, and no one could avoid it: the appearances of the risen Jesus gave it new and added urgency.

Another factor makes it clear that the earliest community put at the heart of their proclamation the problem of the forgiveness of sins, which was central for both John the Baptist and for Jesus. Indeed, in this respect the original church can in some ways be regarded as the heir and instrument of the 'revival movement' which came into being with John the Baptist. Peter and the Twelve once again made baptism 'for the forgiveness of sins' binding as an 'eschatological sacrament' or as a 'sealing' for the coming kingdom of God and his Messiah, albeit now 'in the name of the Messiah Jesus' (Acts 2.38, cf. 3.19), in order to express its dedication to the guarantor of salvation. This reintroduction of baptism 'for the forgiveness of sins' during the earliest period in Palestine itself – presumably under the impulse of the Spirit – for its part presupposes the insight that the eschatological event of the death of Jesus 'for us' had atoned for past sin and created 'peace with God'. According to Mek. Ex. 20.25,[60] 'peace between the Israelites and their Father in heaven' was brought about on the altar. Now at the end of the old age and the dawn of the new, the crucified Messiah had appeared once and for all to replace this constant occurrence. At the same time this certainty answered the urgent question why the Messiah had to die an accursed death on the cross. It was in order to atone, as an innocent, for the guilty, in other words to bring about forgiveness of their sins. The assurance of forgiveness of personal guilt through the death of Jesus underlies the earlier 'surrender formula', as it does the creed of the dying of the Messiah for us.

How were the disciples able to justify this new assurance of forgiveness after Easter, beginning with the first eyewitness, Simon Peter, who denied his master, through James, who untrustingly had opposed his physical brother (cf. John 7.5), to the last of them all, Saul – Paul, who hated the Messiah and persecuted his followers? How did they know that the Son of Man had been given up *for them*? The stories of the appearances of Jesus, with their legendary elaborations, do not tell explicitly of a promise of forgiveness from the risen Lord, but they do mention the continual unbelief of the disciples and the way in which it was corrected (Matt. 28.17; Luke 24.11, 25, 38; John 20.19, 25, 29; 21.12, 16ff.). On the other hand, at least the emphatic greeting of 'Peace' from the risen Lord (Luke 24.36; John 20.19, 21, 26) is to be understood as a promise of salvation. We can hardly doubt that the question how the disciples could be sure that their secession and flight in Gethsemane (like Peter's denunciation) had been forgiven and settled must have been a decisive presupposition for their own missionary preaching about the eschatological reconciliation of sin by Christ. This can also be said about James, the formerly unbelieving brother of Jesus (John 7.5; cf. Mark 3.21 and The Gospel according to the Hebrews in Jerome, *De viris inlustribus* 2), and last but not least about the latest witness to the resurrection (I Cor. 15.8f.), Paul, the former persecutor and blasphemer of Christ (Gal. 1.13; Phil. 3.6; cf. I Cor. 15.9). The experience of forgiveness was surely of basic importance in his encounter with the risen Jesus before Damascus. This experience, that God in Jesus 'justifies the ungodly' (Rom. 4.5), made him from the very start the apostle to the Gentiles. This encounter with the risen Christ gave all witnesses the certainty that they were no longer 'still in their sins' (cf. I Cor. 15.11). As a result of the passion of Jesus, the question of guilt, which had already played a role in the preaching of John the Baptist and which was closely bound up with the conduct and the message of Jesus, was once again raised in a new and more radical fashion. In contrast to the preaching of John the Baptist, who connected forgiveness with the specific action of personal repentance and its consequences, this completely new certainty, produced by the appearances of the risen Jesus, was based on the act of the love of God through his Messiah, preceding all human action, in other words through the *extra nos* as Luther understood it, or, to use the earliest soteriological statement which we know, in the *service of the Son of Man* who gave his life as 'the ransom for many', that is, for everyone. At the same time this provides an answer to the burning question: why did the Messiah have to suffer? This assurance of forgiveness was hardly the result of a lengthy development bound up with theoretical scribal reflection, preceded by a primarily 'non-soteriological' interpretation of the death of Jesus and his resurrection; rather, as is shown by the old surrender formula which is quoted by Paul in Rom. 4.25, the death of the Messiah and his resurrection or exaltation from the dead was understood, in terms of the salvation thus given, as an indissoluble unity:

> Who was surrendered for our trespasses,
> and raised for our justification.

As a result, it is wrong to regard the two-membered credal formulae which confess the unity of Jesus' dying for us and his resurrection as secondary in theological content to the one-membered statements, say about the raising of Jesus by God. There is no clear way of pointing to a pure resurrection kerygma without a soteriological interpretation of the death of Jesus. Conversely, it was also impossible to refer only to the death of Jesus, without confessing his resurrection: 'If Christ has not been raised, your faith is futile and you are still in your sins' (I Cor. 15.17). The content of this statement of Paul's essentially applied from the beginning: through the resurrection the death of the Messiah Jesus was manifested as valid and effective representative atonement by God himself.

If in this way the kerygma of the death and resurrection of Jesus for our salvation prove to be a unity which cannot be separated in terms of content, or chronologically, even at the time of the origin of the church, a last question nevertheless remains. How did it come about that the disciples, essentially against the predominant contemporary messianic tradition now known to us, on the basis of their encounter with the risen Jesus, came to understand the crucifixion of Jesus as an eschatological saving event in the sense of the universal vicarious atoning death of the Messiah?

If the roots of this lay *only* in scribal messianic interpretation of Isaiah 53, it would have to be possible to demonstrate something like a lengthy process of development within the soteriological interpretation of the death of Jesus. However, this is improbable, as an independent unsoteriological interpretation of the death of Jesus and his resurrection cannot be shown to be the earliest tradition. Reference should not be made in this context to the hymn in Philippians or Peter's speeches in Acts, because a soteriological understanding of the death of Jesus is taken for granted in these relatively late texts.

It is also striking that the early kerygmatic formulae very soon qualify the universal 'for all' and reduce it to 'for us', meaning the community of believers. This is clear, for example, from a comparison of Mark 10.45 and I Tim. 2.6 with other surrender formulae or of Mark 14.24 with I Cor. 11.24 (cf. however, 10.17). This understandable tendency to reduce the scope of salvation to one's own community presumably already began with the events of Easter, which only affected a limited group.

Methodologically, then, we are justified, indeed compelled, to push our enquiry *back to Jesus himself.* He was certainly anything but an other-worldly fanatic, who unsuspectingly went to meet his death in Jerusalem. It should no longer be doubted that he reckoned with the possibility of his own execution, at the latest after that of John the Baptist. What later community could have had any interest in subsequently constructing such an obscure, indeed questionable saying as Luke 12.50? The Gethsemane story was also a constant cause of mockery and scorn for the anti-Christian polemicists of antiquity.[61] The temptation of Jesus in the garden completely went against any ancient ideal of martyrdom. It is more difficult to answer the question how he understood and interpreted his way to death. Within the framework of his proclamation of the dawn of the kingdom of God he must also have considered the increasingly threatening possibility of a violent death. Indeed he was one of those gifted men who are in a position to see through

situations and people. Even the most radical sceptic cannot avoid
the simple historical question how this simple wandering teacher
and his outwardly inglorious death exercised such a tremendous and
unique influence that it still remains unsurpassed.[62] Some of the
reasons for this must lie *in the person and actions of Jesus* himself,
not least in the face of the threat of his death. Here the question is
concentrated above all on Jesus' last struggle in Jerusalem. Here
too we again come up against the unique agreement of our earliest
written evidence, Paul and Mark, in their accounts of the Last
Supper.

As Joachim Jeremias has made the essential points in this
particularly controversial area,[63] and Rudolf Pesch has largely
confirmed his arguments, I need only give a brief summary. On
the night before his death, 'in which he was betrayed' (or 'delivered
up': I Cor. 11.23), Jesus celebrated the passover meal with his
disciples and in it – presumably in parallel to the traditional words
of interpretation which explained what was happening at the meal
– in a symbolic action he related the broken bread to the breaking
of his body and at the end of the meal the wine in the cup of
blessing to the pouring out of his blood, through which the new
eschatological covenant with God would be founded and atonement would be achieved for all. In this way, at the same time he
represented his imminent death as the eschatological saving event
which – in connection with Isa. 53 – in the context of the dawn of
the kingdom of God brought about reconciliation with God for all
Israel, indeed for all men, and sealed God's eschatological new
covenant with his creatures. We are probably to understand Mark
14.25, the reference to the coming meal in the kingdom of God, as
meaning that Jesus wanted to prepare the way for the coming of
the kingdom of God through his sacrificial death in the face of the
apparent supremacy of evil and sin in God's own people and all
mankind. Of course we can only put all this forward as a hypothesis,
justified though it may be. Here we come up against the ultimate
mystery of Jesus' career.

Their encounter with the risen Lord confirmed for the disciples
this legacy of Jesus, the meaning of which had been overshadowed
by the catastrophe of the sudden arrest and shameful crucifixion of

Jesus and their own failure, which immediately followed. It was not primarily their own theological reflections, but above all the interpretative sayings of Jesus at the Last Supper which showed them how to understand his death properly. As a saying of Jesus, Mark 10.45 probably also belongs in the context of that last night; it will have been used by him to elucidate his mysterious symbolic action. From Luke (22.24) and Mark (13.12) we hear independently of each other that Jesus spoke at the Last Supper about 'serving'. He will hardly have done this without including his imminent fate. The saying over the cup and the saying about ransom are connected by the universal service 'for the many', in the sense of 'for all', which is presumably to be derived from Isaiah 53. This boundlessness of the appropriation of salvation matches the freedom of the proclamation and the activity of Jesus towards all the outcast, the lost and the sinners in Israel.

As it took place at least weekly, the celebration of the eucharist after Easter could no longer bear the features of the yearly passover meal; it was probably originally understood as a Todah sacrificial meal of the risen Lord.[64] Here people thought both of his vicarious sacrifice of his life on the cross and his exaltation and hoped-for coming again. The words with which Jesus interpreted the last supper with his disciples came to occupy a central place, because in it Jesus had dedicated to the disciples, his people – and beyond them to all men – the fruits of his violent death. The saving significance of his representative dying was probably expressed primarily at the common meal, in constantly new ways – on the basis of Jesus' own words. At each Lord's Supper, the first Christians proclaimed 'the Lord's death until he comes' (I Cor. 11.26). For that reason, this meal, along with the promise of the forgiveness of sins, came to lie at the heart of early Christian liturgy.

We now return to the question which was raised at the beginning. From a formal point of view, there are a whole series of analogies between Graeco-Roman, and even more Jewish, conceptions of atonement and the primitive Christian interpretation of the death of Jesus as representative atonement. However, seen in total, the event described in the New Testament breaks through the ancient conceptual framework and even goes beyond contemporary Jewish parallels. It concerns not only the unheard-of scandal that here the Son of God died on the cross the most shameful death known to the Roman world, but also the universality of the atonement brought about by this Son, involving all men, which not only warded off the anger of a God at particular misdeeds, but blotted out all human guilt and thus – as an eschatological act in the perspective of the dawning kingdom of God – reconciled the apostate creatures with their Creator.

It was consistent with this, and indeed necessary, that the pre-Pauline Greek-speaking community should have interpreted the death of the Messiah on the cross as an event which, more than the death of a pure martyr and righteous sufferer, stemmed from God himself and therefore at the same time recognized the crucified one as the pre-existent Son of God and mediator at creation, whom the Father had sent into the world to redeem his creation (Rom. 8.3; Gal. 4.4; Phil. 2.6–11; I Cor. 8.6; Col. 1.15ff.).[65] In the last resort, in the man Jesus of Nazareth God took death upon himself (cf. II Cor. 5.18ff; John 1.1, 14; 19.30). This did not in any way diminish the 'scandal of the cross'; indeed it *accentuated it, to an unprecedented degree for the ancient world.* But that means that in essentials we can only talk about the saving significance of the death of Jesus in appropriate theological terms if we talk of him in a 'trinitarian context'. Of course this basic theological problem, which we should never lose sight of, far transcends the framework of this study, which has been deliberately restricted to the historical developments between Jesus and Paul and their religious and historical background. For Paul and John – and not only for them – the voluntary self-sacrifice of the sinless Son of God which took place once and for all was the unsurpassable expression of God's free love:

But God shows his love for us in that while we were yet sinners Christ died for us (Rom. 5.8).

In this is love, not that we loved God but that he loved us and sent his Son to be the expiation for our sins (I John 4.10).

Here we are concerned not simply with a mythical view which has now become obsolete and which could be put aside without further ado; here – we may confidently affirm – perhaps in a mythical form which at first seems strange to us,[66] we come up against the heart of the gospel which grounds and supports our faith as it did of the first witnesses. It is the prime task of theology to show what lies at this heart in the language of our own time.

Notes

Chapter One

1. M. Hengel, *Die Zeloten*, AGAJU 1, ²1976, 265f., 333, 353ff. and index 475 s.v. 'Kreuzigung'.

2. The dissertation by M.-L. Gubler, *Die frühesten Deutungen des Todes Jesu*, OBO 15, Freiburg 1977, gives an instructive account of most recent attempts at interpretation. Of course, at the same time it also shows the limitations of modern exegesis. As it discusses all recent publications, I need not give an extensive bibliography here.

3. I have tried to do some demolition work on this false alternative in *Judaism and Hellenism, Studies in their Encounter in Palestine in the Early Hellenistic Period*, London and Philadelphia 1974. Cf. *Jews, Greeks and Barbarians*, London and Philadelphia 1980. For Galilean Jewry cf. Seán Freyne, *Galilee from Alexander the Great to Hadrian, 320 BC to 153 CE*, Notre Dame 1980.

4. Klaus Wengst, *Christologische Formeln und Lieder des Urchristentums*, StNT 7, Gütersloh 1972, 70: 'The conception of the representative atoning death was developed in Hellenistic rather than Palestinian Judaism.' It was 'Hellenistic Judaism which stressed the notion of the representative atoning death, which was not current in Palestinian Judaism before Christianity and in the early Christian period. This suggests that we should also assume that the interpretation of the death of Jesus originated in the Christianity which came out of Hellenistic Judaism, i.e. in Hellenistic Jewish Christianity.' Cf. also M.-L. Gubler, op. cit., 252ff.

5. Gubler, op. cit., 34ff., 95ff., 200ff. The main treatment in a monograph of the theme of the suffering righteous man, which is so popular today, can be found in L. Ruppert, *Der leidende Gerechte*, Würzburg 1972; *Jesus als der leidende Gerechte*, SBS 59, Stuttgart 1972.

6. Apollodorus 2,7,7. Cf. the development of the hero's voluntary death in Seneca, *Hercules Oetaeus*. F. Pfister, *ARW* 34, 1937, even conjectured that a 'primal gospel' underlying all four gospels has been influenced by a 'Stoic-Cynic biography of Heracles' (59). H. J. Rose, *HTR* 31, 1938, 113–42, rightly attacked this. Among other features, Pfister (53) referred to Jesus' death-cry *tetelestai* in John 19.30 and the

threefold *peractum est* of *Herc. Oet.* 1340, 1457, 1472. However, there it is simply a matter of the hero suffering his fate: *fata se nostra explicant* (1472). On the other hand, see Rose's parallels between the ascension of Heracles and the two Lucan ascension accounts: 'There is a certain resemblance between the accounts of the two ascensions' (124). On this point see also Marcel Simon, *Hercule et le christianisme*, Paris 1955, and M. Mühl, 'Des Herakles Himmelfahrt', *RhMus* 101, 1958, 106–34. In general on the ancient ascension and transportation stories see N. Lohfink, *Die Himmelfahrt Jesu*, SANT 26, Munich 1971, 32ff.

7. *Iliad* 18,114ff., cf. 9,410ff.; in this connection Plato, *Symposium* 179d–180b makes Achilles an example of ὑπεραποθνῄσκειν or ἐπαποθνῄσκειν motivated by love, and compares him with Alcestis. For the apotheosis cf. H. Hommel, *Der Gott Achilleus*, SAH 1980, 1.

8. For his task see *Apology* 29a–31c, cf. 30a: 'For the god commands this' (ταῦτα γὰρ κελεύει ὁ θεός). For his death see *Crito*, especially the last remark, 54d: 'Well, then, Crito, let us act in this way, since it is in this way that the god leads us' (ἐπειδὴ ταύτῃ ὁ θεὸς ὑφηγεῖται); *Phaedo* 115b–118a, esp. 117b/c, his prayer to the gods before drinking the fatal draught, 'that my departure hence be a fortunate one'.

9. See the article by K. v. Fritz, 'Peregrinus (Proteus)', *PW* 19, 1, 1937, cols. 656–63.

10. N. Lohfink, op. cit., gives the best summary, 32–50.

11. L. Wächter, *Der Tod im Alten Testament*, AzTh II, 8, Stuttgart 1967; H. Gese, *Zur biblischen Theologie*, BEvTh 78, Munich 1977, 31–54: 'The Old Testament is familiar with such traditions (of heroes), but its concern for God does not allow a cult of heroes any more than it allows idolatry' (35).

12. On this see U. Kellermann, *Auferstanden in den Himmel. 2 Makkabäer 7 und die Auferstehung der Märtyrer*, SBS 95, Stuttgart 1979; following H. v. Campenhausen, *Die Idee des Martyriums in der Alten Kirche*, Göttingen ²1964, 153f., he refers to the example of the martyr philosopher (46ff.). The most recent work, T. Baumeister, *Die Anfänge der Theologie des Martyriums*, Munster 1980, pays too little attention to the Greek roots of the ideology of martyrdom. But cf. his concession on pp. 12f.: apart from Isa. 53, Israel did not have any 'theology of martyrdom' even in connection with the murder of prophets.

13. The few texts which are to some extent an exception here mostly go back to the archaic period. The Song of Deborah (Judg. 5.18) praises Zebulon as 'a people which despised its life, prepared for death' (*'am ḥerep napšō lāmūt*), and Judg. 9.17 says that Jerubbaal-Gideon 'fought for you (= Israel), hazarded his life (*wayyašlek napšō*, i.e. put his life at stake) and delivered you from the hand of Midian'. This mode of expression is quite extraordinary; its closest parallel is in Isa. 53.12:

266

The Atonement

he 'era lammawet napšō, cf. also n.19 below. We also find the formula *šīm* ('*et*) *napšō bᵉkappō*, I Sam. 19.5, cf. 28.21; Judg. 12.3; Job 13.14: take his life in his hands, risk the utmost.

14. Both Zech. 14.10ff. and 13.7ff., the saying about the death of the shepherd, could have a concealed reference to the death of a messianic figure. However, the saving significance of this figure remains cryptic, and can only be inferred indirectly from 14.10a; 13.1f. and 13.9b. On this see W. Rudolph, *Haggai-Sacharja 1–8—Sacharja 9–14—Maleachi*, KAT XII, 4, Gütersloh 1976, 211ff., who conjectures a connection with the servant of God in Isa. 53 (213f., 223f.). The text already belongs in the Hellenistic period (163, 211): the *terminus a quo* is *c*.350, the *terminus ad quem* 200. Cf. also H. Gese (op. cit., n.11), 137: 'Although . . . this figure does not appear as a bringer of salvation, but as one who has fallen in the battles of the end-time, he leads his people along the way to the new covenant.' In 12.10ff. there is also an indirect reference to the conception of the resurrection, as there is in Isa. 26.19ff., which comes from about the same time (52).

15. For details see O. H. Steck, *Israel und das gewaltsame Geschick der Propheten*, WMANT 23, Neukirchen-Vluyn 1967; of course he puts rather too much emphasis on the traditio-historical significance of the theme. Cf. M.-L. Gubler, op. cit., 34–94; T. Baumeister, op. cit., 6–13.

16. *EvTh* 26, 1966, 237.

17. Deut. 24.16. The text is quoted in two other places: II Kings 14.6; II Chron. 25.4. On this see K. Wengst, op. cit., 65f.

18. Ex. 32.30–33, cf. H. Gese, op. cit., 88: 'Moses wants to make atonement, offers himself as *kōper*, i.e. offers his existence which is written in the book of life. This is a substitute offering of his life through a total representative sacrifice.'

19. I Macc. 2.50: ζηλώσατε τῷ νόμῳ καὶ δότε τὰς ψυχὰς ὑμῶν ὑπὲρ διαθήκης πατέρων ἡμῶν. Cf. T. Baumeister, op. cit., (n.12), 138f. For the formula cf. Dan. 3.28 (see above, p. 12) and the later rabbinic terminology.

20. *Antt.* 12.281: ὥστε ἀποθανεῖν ὑπὲρ τῶν νόμων, ἂν δέῃ, cf. 267,282; cf. Aristotle, *Nicomachaean Ethics* 1169a, 18ff.: ἀληθὲς δὲ περὶ τοῦ σπουδαίου καὶ τὸ τῶν φίλων ἕνεκα πολλὰ πράττειν καὶ τῆς πάτριδος, κἂν δέῃ ὑπεραποθνῄσκειν. Cf. Epictetus, *Diss.* 2.7.3.

21. Dying for freedom: Josephus, *BJ* 3. 357; cf. *Antt.* 12.433; 13.5; for the Jewish people, *Antt.* 13.1; 6; for the Law: *BJ* 1.650; 2.6; *Antt.* 15.288; *Contra Apionem* 1.42f.; II Macc. 7.19; 8.21: ἑτοίμους ὑπὲρ τῶν νόμων καὶ τῆς πατρίδος ἀποθνῄσκειν, III Macc. 1.23; IV Macc. 6.27: διὰ τὸν νόμον; 9.1; 13.9; περὶ τοῦ νόμου; Philo, *Leg.* 215: καὶ προαποθνῄσκειν αἱρουμένους τῶν πατρίων. Cf. also *Ass. Mos.* 9.6: *et moriamur potius, quam praetereamus mandata domini dominorum . . .* cf.

M. Hengel, op. cit. (n.1); U. Kellermann, op. cit. (n.12), 20; and K. Wengst, op. cit. (n.4), 68f.; T. Baumeister, op. cit., 39–62.

22. I Macc. 6.44: ἔδωκεν ἑαυτὸν τοῦ σῶσαι τὸν λαὸν αὐτοῦ καὶ περιποιῆσαι ἑαυτῷ ὄνομα αἰώνιον. For the theme of glory among the Greeks see G. Steinkopf, *Untersuchungen zur Geschichte des Ruhmes bei den Griechen*, Diss. phil. Halle-Wittenberg 1937 (up to Thucydides). For Judaism see the praise of the fathers in Sir. 44.1; 46.2; 47.6; 49.13; 50.1. K. Wengst, op. cit. (n.4), 68 n.S8, makes the wild guess that in two texts from I Maccabees, originally written in Hebrew, 2.50f. and 6.44, 'the assumption of a Jewish-Hellenistic interpolation is inescapable', since 'these statements . . . are so isolated in the Palestinian Jewish sphere and are so little different from Greek and Hellenistic Jewish parallels'. However, this distinction in principle is extremely questionable.

23. Euripides, *Alcestis* 18, 178, 282ff., 339ff., 383, 434, 472, 524, 620, 644f., 649, 682, 684, 690, 698, 701, 710, 716, 1002f. The prepositions which express representativeness change: in addition to ὑπέρ we also find πρό and ἀντί. For Alcestis cf. also Apollodorus, *Library*, 1.9.5.

24. 968f.: αὐτός . . .
θνῄσκειν ἕτοιμος πατρίδος ἐκλυτήριον.

25. 997f. (cf. 1056, 1090: Κρέοντος παῖς ὁ γῆς ὑπερθανών).). The emphatic 'I go' may be an allusion to the resolve of Achilles (see n. 7 above).

26. *Heraclides*, 550f.: . . . τὴν ἐμὴν ψυχὴν ἐγὼ
δίδωμ' ἑκοῦσα τοῖσδ', ἀναγκασθεῖσα δ'οὔ,
cf. 501f., 509f., 530ff.: 'For this life (ψυχή) is ready, willing and ungrudging. And I proclaim that I die for my brothers and for myself. Not loving my life (μὴ φιλοψυχοῦσ' ἐγώ), I made this supreme discovery: gloriously to leave it.' For the stress on free will cf. John 10.18.

27. Cf. *Symposium* 208d (and 207b). Other examples given by Plato in addition to Alcestis are Achilles and the Athenian king Codrus (see p. 22 above). The theme of love is not of itself enough for vicarious death: it must be supplemented by the 'immortal remembrance of their *aretē*' and the hope of a 'noble reputation, for they love the immortal'. This theme appears in the New Testament in Rom. 5.6–8 and John 15.13.

28. *Iliad* 15.495–8, cf. 24.500 and 12.243, which according to Diodore 15.52.4 was quoted by Epaminondas before the battle of Leuctra (again a quotation from Hector): εἷς οἰωνὸς ἄριστος ἀμύνεσθαι περὶ πάτρης, 'One thing is the best sign, to fight for one's country.' Tyrtaeus no. 6, ed. C. Prato, Rome 1968, 27. There are further parallels there, see H. Hommel, 'Dulce et Decorum . . .', *RhMus* 111, 1968, 219–52 (236ff.). For Callinus see fr. 1.6f., ed. J. M. Edmonds, *Elegy and Iambus*, LCL 1.44.

29. Strabo 9.4.2 (425 C) = W. Peek, *Griechische Grabgedichte*, Darmstadt 1960, no. 3. Cf. also no. 9.3; 14.2; 17.4; 21.5; 32; and the private epitaphs no. 125.1; 130.3; 136.5; 173.5; 457.11f. See further on the shared death of the father and his seven-year-old son, 272.5f.: ἀντὶ χοῶν δ'ὁ πατὴρ ψυχὴν ἰδίαν ἐπέδωκεν κοινὸν ἔχειν ἐθέλων οὔνομα καὶ θάνατον, 'instead of a libation the father gave his own life. He did not want (only) to share a name (with you) but also death.' The chief prepositions are περί, ὑπέρ and πρό.

30. 237a: τὴν τελευτὴν ἀντὶ τῆς τῶν ζώντων σωτηρίας ἠλλάξαντο, cf. 243a, 246b.

31. Fragment 66, O. Werner (78, B. Snell et al.), see LCL, p. 556; Plutarch, *De Gloria Atheniensium* 7 (349c), attributes this verse to Epaminondas when he and the Thebans 'sacrificed themselves in the finest and most glorious battles for their country, its tombs and sanctuaries' (ὑπὲρ πατρίδος καὶ τάφων καὶ ἱερῶν ἐπιδιδόντες ἑαυτοὺς τοῖς καλλίστοις καὶ λαμπροτάτοις ἀγῶσιν). Athenagoras, *Apology* 19a, ascribes the verse to Pindar and stresses that it is inspired by the heroic spirit of the *Iliad*. For the sacrificial terminology cf also Euripides, *Erechtheus* fr. 79.38f.: κόρην/θῦσαι πρὸ γαίας; Plutarch, *Pelopidas* 21.2: Λεωνίδαν τε τῷ χρησμῷ τρόπον τινὰ προθυσάμενον ἑαυτὸν ὑπὲρ τῆς Ἑλλάδος.

32. 'Martyriumsparänese und Sühnetod in synoptischen und jüdischen Traditionen', in *Die Kirche des Anfangs. Festschrift für Heinz Schürmann*, Leipzig 1977, 223–46 (238).

33. Aristides 21, cf. Diodore 11.33.3 and the account by W. Burkert, *Homo necans*, 1972, 68f. For the cult of heroes and sacrifice to the dead see L. R. Farnell, *Greek Hero Cults and Ideas of Immortality*, 1921, and W. Burkert, *Griechische Religion der archäischen und klassischen Epoche*, 1977, 293ff., 313ff.

34. Fr. 5 Diels: εὐκλεὴς μὲν ἁ τύχα, καλὸς δ'ὁ πότμος, βωμὸς δ'ὁ τάφος, πρὸ χόων δὲ μνᾶστις, ὁ δ'οἶνος ἔπαινος. ἐντάφιον δὲ τοιοῦτον εὐρὼς οὔθ'ὁ πανταδαμάτωρ ἀμαυρώσει χρόνος ἀνδρῶν ἀγαθῶν, ὁ δὲ σηκὸς οἰκέταν εὐδοξίαν Ἑλλάδος εἵλετο. See H. Fränkel, *Dichtung und Philosophie des frühen Griechentums*, [3]1969, 365, cf. 366: 'Thus the fallen are declared to be effective heroes, like the great dead of mythical times, whose tombs are at the same time also sanctuaries'.

35. Cf. M. Hengel, *Jews, Greeks and Barbarians*, London and Philadelphia 1980, 55ff.

36. L. R. Farnell (n. 33), 362: 'The cult is a reward for patriotism, for a noble death against the national foe.' 363: 'Such honours for great public services may well have had a certain social value as a stimulus to effort and sacrifice; for their appeal to the vanity of the Hellene, whatever was his actual faith in these matters, must have been strongly felt.'

37. Plutarch, *Apophthegmata Lacedaimonia* (*Leonidas Ano*. 10) 225C. Cf. (no. 4) 225A; cf. the quotation from *Pelopidas* 21.2, and n. 31 above. Further Isocrates 4 (*Panegyric*) 90–92; 6 (*Archidamus*) 100; Lysias, *Epitaphios* 26; Lycurgus, *Oratio in Leocratem* 24 (104); 28 (109), etc.; Polybius 9.38.4: μὴ μόνον ⟨ὑπὲρ⟩ τῆς αὐτῶν, ἀλλὰ καὶ περὶ τῆς τῶν ἄλλων Ἑλλήνων ἐλευθερίας προκινδυνεύειν.

38. 2.43.1/2 . . . κάλλιστον δὲ ἔρανον αὐτῇ (sc. τῇ πόλει) προϊέμενοι. κοινῇ γὰρ τὰ σώματα διδόντες ἰδίᾳ τὸν ἀγήρων ἔπαινον ἐλάμβανον, cf. Isocrates 4 (*Panegyric*) 75: τοὺς τοῖς σώμασιν ὑπὲρ τῆς Ἑλλάδος προκινδυνεύσαντας. For the terminology cf. W. Popkes, *Christus Traditus*, 1967, 86f. Libanius, *Declamationes* 24.23 (ed. Foerster 6.458, line 5) which he quotes: ἀναμνήσθητε τῶν ἐν Πύλαις ὑπὲρ ἐλευθερίας τῶν Ἑλλήνων δεδωκότων τὰ σώματα is dependent on the earlier terminology of Thucydides and Isocrates.

39. *wihabū gešmᵉhōn di lā' yiplᵉḫūn* . . . LXX καὶ παρέδωκαν τὰ σώματα αὐτῶν εἰς ἐμπυρισμόν, ἵνα μὴ λατρεύσωσι . . . cf. I Cor. 13.3.

40. 4 (*Panegyric*) 77; cf. 75 (n. 38 above). The formula appears particularly frequently in the 'pan-Hellenic' Isocrates. Cf. also 4.62, 83, 95, 154; 5 (*Philip*). 55, 135: ὑπὲρ δὲ τοῦ τυχεῖν καλῆς δόξης ἀποθνήσκειν ἐν τοῖς πολέμοις ἐθέλοντας; 6 (*Archidamus*). 93f., 107; 12 (*Panathenaicus*), 185: κινδυνεύειν ὑπὲρ τῆς πατρίδος, 186: περὶ τῶν ἀλλοτρίων ἑτοίμως ἀποθνήσκειν; 20 (*Lochites*), 20: ἀποθνήσκειν ὑπὲρ τῆς πολιτείας.

41. Lysias 2 (*Epitaphios*). 68; Demosthenes, 18 (*De corona*) 205: 20 (*contra Lept.*) 83; 26 (*contra Aristogeiton II*). 23; Lycurgus, *Oratio in Leocratem* 27 (104) and often.

42. Polybius 2.30.4; Gauls: καὶ διδόντες σφᾶς αὐτοὺς ἑκουσίως ἀπέθνησκον; 9.38.4; 15,10,3; 16,34,11; Dio Chrysostom 32, 48f.; Plutarch, *Moralia* 219B; 238A; *Brutus* 40, and often.

43. *Topica* 22, 84: see also below p. 82, n. 49.

44. POx Col. I = Acta Alexandrinorum XI B lines 11ff. On this see the commentary by H. A. Musurillo, *The Acts of the Pagan Martyrs*, 1954, 215, 237.

45. For Aristotle see above p. 78 n. 20. E. Schwartz, *Ethik der Griechen*, 1951, 121. For the εὔλογος ἐξαγωή of the Stoa see von Arnim, *SVF* III, fr. 757 = Diogenes Laertius 7,130 and fr. 768, the anonymous *Excerpta philosophica*, Cod. Coislin 387, and on this E. Benz, *Das Todesproblem in der stoischen Philosophie*, 1929, 69ff. Epicurus: see H. Usener, *Epicurea* no. 590 = Diogenes Laertius 10.121, cf. on this E. Schwartz, op. cit., 191, and A. Deissmann, *Light from the Ancient East*, London ²1927, 118 n. 1, the quotation from the biography of the Epicurean Philonides and Rom. 16.4. For Epictetus see *Diss*, 2.7.3: 'To incur danger for a friend when necessary, indeed even to die for him'.

270 The Atonement

For the philosophical tradition see the commentary by R. A. Gauthier and J. Y. Jolif, *Aristote, L'Éthique à Nicomaque* II, 1959, 748ff.

46. Cf. A. Oltramare, *Les Origines de la diatribe romaine*, Thèse Gèneve 1926, 52f., 60f., 285f. See also index s.v. 'guerre', 'état', 'mort'. A later example, of an undeterred philosophical 'martyr', also cited relatively often in the Jewish and Christian tradition, was the Cynic Anaxarchos from the time of Alexander. See Diels-Kranz, *Vorsokratiker*, no. 72; Diogenes Laertius 9.59f.; Philo, *Quod omnis* 106–9; Clement of Alexandria, *Stromateis* 4.57. Cf. A. Alföldi, 'Der Philosoph als Zeuge der Wahrheit...' *Scientiis Artibusque. Collectanea Academiae Hungaricae* I, Rome 1958, 7–19 (8).

47. *Odes* 3.2.13, cf. H. Hommel, 'Dulce et decorum...' *RhMus* 111, 1968, 219–52, also *Odes* 3.12.2 and 4.9.50ff. (the description of the *recte beatus*):

> Peiusque leto flagitium timet,
> Non ille pro caris amicis
> aut patria timidus perire.

'He is afraid of evil more than of death; he is not afraid to die for dear friends or for his homeland.' For the difficult *dulce* cf. H. Usener (n. 45), 338f., 601, esp. Seneca, *Ep.* 66.18; and Pausanias 9,17,1 on Antipoinos and his two daughters: Ἀντιποίνῳ μὲν οὖν... οὐχ ἡδὺ ἦν ἀποθνήσκειν πρὸ τοῦ δήμου, ταῖς δὲ Ἀντιποίνου θυγατράσιν ἤρεσκε. ('Antipoinos did not find it sweet to die for the people, but it pleased his two daughters.')

48. Cf. Scherling, *PW* 11, 1, cols. 984ff. See Hellanikos, FGrHist 4 fr. 125: ὃς καὶ ὑπὲρ τῆς πατρίδος ἀπέθανε, or Horace 3.19.2: *Codrus pro patria non timidus mori*. The earliest extant account of the saga appears in Lycurgus, *Oratio in Leocratem* 20 (84–89): τοὺς πολεμίους ἐξαπατῶντες ἀποθνήσκειν ὑπὲρ αὐτῆς (sc. τῆς πατρίδος).

49. Cicero, *Tusculan Disputations* 1.48f., 116f.; cf. 1.37,89. On this cf. H. W. Litchfield, 'National *Exempla virtutis* in Roman Literature', *Harvard Studies in Classical Literature* 25, 1914, 1–73. For Vercingetorix see Caesar, *De bello gallico* 7.89: *et quoniam sit fortunae cedendum, ad utramque rem seillis offerre, seu morte sua Romanis satisfacere seu vivum tradere velint*.

50. Dio Cassius, *Epitome* 63.13f. For the suicides of soldiers at his death see Tacitus, *Histories* 2.49.4; *non noxa neque ob metum, sed aemulatione decoris et caritate principis*.

51. I Clement 55. 1–5.

52. Virgil, *Aeneid* 5.815. Cf. in Plutarch, *Phocion* 17.3, the reply of the politician to his enemies confronted with the demands of Alexander the Great: τὸ μὲν γὰρ αὐτὸς ὑπὲρ ὑμῶν ἁπάντων ἀποθανεῖν εὐτυχίαν ἂν ἐμαυτοῦ θείμην. Libanius, *Declaratio* 42, 46 (Foerster 7,415). For the Roman *Devotio* see Livy 5.41.2: *eos se pro patria Quiritibusque*

Romanis tradant. Cf. F. Schwenn, *Die Menschenopfer bei den Griechen und Römern,* 1915, 154ff.; Patsch, *PW* 5.1, cols. 277ff., K. Latte, *Römische Religionsgeschichte,* ²1967, see index s.v., see also p. 23 and n. 90.
53. Billerbeck 2.545f. (GenR 94,9): the advice given by R. Yehoshua b.Levi to hand over someone sought by the Roman authorities. The whole passage is in the context of the discussion of the handing over to Joab of Sheba son of Bichri: II Sam. 20.16ff., and that of Jeconiah to Nebuchadnezzar: II Kings 24.12. In Josephus, *De Bello Judaico* 6.95,103ff., Titus and Josephus asked for the leaders of the rebels to give themselves up to save the city, referring to the example of Jeconiah: αἰχμαλωσίαν ὑπέμεινεν ἐθελούσιον ὑπὲρ τοῦ μὴ παραδοῦναι ταῦτα πολεμίοις τὰ ἅγια καὶ τὸν οἶκον τοῦ θεοῦ περιιδεῖν φλεγόμενον.
54. Origen, *Contra Celsum* 2.45: οὔτε συναπέθανον οὔτε ὑπεραπέθανον αὐτοῦ.
55. Fr. 44, Diels/Kranz: I owe this reference to my colleague Eberhard Jüngel; Fr. 114; cf. also Fr. 24: 'Gods and men honour those who fall in war.' Heraclitus presupposes the high estimation of those fallen in war common among the Greeks of his time.
56. 26 (*Contra Aristogeiton* II), 23.
57. Cf. H. v. Campenhausen, *Die Idee des Martyriums in der alten Kirche,* ²1964, 153; 'The Christian martyr . . . . . . appears in the role of Socrates and explicitly refers to his example.' Cf. above pp. 4f.
58. Diogenes Laertius 5.7f. = Athenaeus 15, p. 696b–d (Aristotle, Fr. 674, 675 Rose). Cf. Theopompus, FGrHist 115 F 291, and I. Düring, 'Aristoteles', in *The Ancient Biographical Tradition,* 1957, 272ff.
59. Sirach 4.28. In Aramaic the root 'ṣ' has the meaning 'press, oppress' and in Syriac *repugnare,* see C. Brockelmann, *Lexicon Syriacum,* 1928, 539b, with a reference to hebr. Sir.4.28.
60. Philostratus, *Vita Apollonii,* 7.12 beginning; 7.13 end; 7.14 beginning and end, ET, LCL 171–91. The closing quotation from *Iliad* 18.309 relates to a saying of Hector as he goes out to meet Achilles in battle.
61. Op. cit. (n. 4), 64. For the theme, cf. A. Alföldi, op. cit. (n. 46).
62. K. Fauth, *Der kleine Pauly* 4, 309. For the Hittites see H. M. Kümmel, 'Ersatzkönig und Sündenbock', *ZAW* 80, 1968, 289–318, cf. also W. Burkert, *Structure,* 59ff.; for the sacrifice of children throughout the Semitic world see O. Kaiser, 'Den Erstgeborenen deiner Söhne sollst du mir geben', *Denkender Glaube. Festschrift C. H. Ratschow, zum 65,* Berlin 1976, 24–48 (29ff.); and on this Philo Byblius in Eusebius, *Dmonstratio Evangelica* 4, 16, 11 (FGr-Hist 790, 3b): ἀντὶ τῆςπάντων φθορᾶς τὸ ἠγαπημένον τῶν τεκνῶν τοὺς κρατοῦντας ἢ πόλεως ἢ ἔθνους εἰς σφαγὴν ἐπιδιδόναι λύτρον τοῖς τιμωροῖς δαίμοσι. Philo Byblius supports

this with a reference to the Phoenician primal king Kronos-El, who sacrificed his firstborn in a time of extreme peril during a war.

63. In the first instance I would refer here to the basic investigations by W. Burkert, 'Greek Tragedy and Sacrificial Ritual', *Greek Roman and Byzantine Studies* 7, 1966, 87ff.,; *Homo necans*, 1972; *Griechische Religion der archaischen und klassischen Epoche*, 1977, 129ff., 139ff.; *Structure and History in Greek Mythology and Ritual*, 1979, 59ff., 168ff. I am grateful to him for sending me xeroxes of proofs of the last book and for some further references. Cf. also E. von Lasaulx, *Die Sühnopfer der Griechen und Römer und ihr Verhältnis zu dem einen auf Golgotha*, Würzburg 1841, and F. Schwenn, *Die Menschenopfer bei den Griechen und Römern*, 1915, still provide usable collections of material. The brief but full study by W. Speyer, 'Religionen des griechisch-römischen Bereichs. Zorn der Gottheit, Vergeltung und Sühne,' in *Theologie und Religionswissenschaft. Der gegenwärtige Stand ihrer Forschungsergebnisse*, ed. U. Mann, 1973, 124–43, is also instructive.

64. F. Schwenn (n. 63), 112ff., 119ff., and *PW* 15.1, cols. 948ff.; U. von Wilamowitz-Moellendorff, *Der Glaube der Hellenen*, ²1959, I, 293ff. For the repudiation see e.g. Porphyry, *De abstinentia* 2.54–56; in Plutarch see H. D. Betz (ed.), *Plutarch's Theological Writings and Early Christian Literature*, 1975. Index s.v. 'Sacrifice, human', 368. W. Burkert, *Homo necans*, index s.v. 'Menschenopfer', 348.

65. Burkert, op. cit., 56, with reference to Mommsen, *Römisches Strafrecht*, 1899, 900ff. According to Dionysus of Halicarnassus, *Antt.* 2.10.3, patrons and clients who broke contracts should be killed as traitors, in accordance with a law of Romulus, ὡς θῦμα τοῦ καταχθονίου Διός. Cf. Livy 3.55.7: *qui tribunis plebis, aedilibus . . . noccuisset, eius caput Iovi sacer est.* Cf. also C. Brecht, art. '*perduellio*', *PW* 16.621f. Cf. M. Hengel, *Crucifixion*, 1977, 33ff., 86ff.

66. For Euripides, *Phoenissae* 911–1018, 1090ff., see above, p. 9. Cf. Höfer, *Roschers Lexikon* 2.2.2794f.; J. Schmitt, *Freiwilliger Opfertod bei Euripides*, 1921, index 105, s.v. *Phoenissae*, see espec. 12: 'Ares requires this human sacrifice as atonement for the slaughter of the earthborn dragon'; F. Schwenn, *Menschenopfer*, 134–7. It seems improbable that the sacrificial death of Menoeceus is an invention of Euripides. For the later influence of the sagas see Cicero, *Tusculans* 1. 48, 116. The description of Menoeceus' prayer of devotion to the gods in Statius, *Thebais* 10.768ff., is impressive:

> at Tyriis (i.e. the descendants of Cadmus in Thebes) *templa, arva,*
> domos, conubia, natos
> reddite morte mea: si vos placita hostia iuvi,
> si non attonitis vatis consulta recepi
> auribus et Thebis nondum credentibus hausi

haec Amphioniis pro me *persolvite tectis*
ac mihi deceptum, precor, exorate parentem.

As *devotus* he hurls himself down on the enemy from the walls and with
his blood sprinkles and purifies the besieged city:

> *ast illum amplexae Pietas Virtusque ferebant,*
> *leniter ad terras corpus; nam spiritus olim*
> *ante Iovem et summis apicem sibi poscit in astris.*

The expiatory sacrificial death is followed by the apotheosis of the hero.
Hyginus, *Fabulae* 68: *Menoeceus cum vidit se unum civium salutem posse*
redimere, muro se praecipitavit. Cf. also the anonymous figure in Ps.
Quintilian, *Declamationes* 326 (Ritter, 282).

67. J. Schmitt (n. 66), see index s.v. and above all 13ff. In contrast to
Aeschylus' *Agamemnon*, where 'Iphigenia is carried off to the altar as a
defenceless sacrifice' and 'her cries and laments . . . did not touch her
ambitious father', Euripides introduces the element of free will. For the
various earlier versions of the sagas see H. von Geisau, *Der kleine Pauly*,
2.1447f.

68. Euripides, *Hecuba*, 343ff., 432ff., 518ff.; Seneca, *Troades* 193ff.;
Ovid, *Metamorphoses* 13.448: *placet Achilleos mactata Polyxena manes.*
J. Schmitt (n. 66), see index 105 s.v.

69. Lycurgus, *Oratio in Leocratem* 24 (98ff.) presents Erechtheus as a
paradigm of a patriot and quotes a lengthy fragment from the lost play of
Euripides: fr. 360 Nauck, = C. Austin, *Nova Fragmenta Euripidea*,
1968, 25ff.; there is also a collection of the various ancient accounts, 22ff.
Cf. Aristides I, 19, Dindorf: τὴν θυγατέρα ὑπὲρ τῆς πόλεως ἐπιδοῦναι,
τοῦ θεοῦ χρήσαντος, Apollodorus 3.15.4. The fragment Pap. Sorb 2328,
Austin, op. cit., 33ff., contains the making of the three daughters into
heroes by Athene: line 72: εἰς αἰθερ᾽αὐτῶν πνεῦμ᾽ ἐγὼ [κ]ατῴκισα,
cf. also J. Schmitt (n. 66), 63ff. The daughter is often confused with her
sisters, for whom a similar fate was prophesied (see p. 22 above). On
this cf. Phanodemos, FGrHist 325F4 = Suidas, *Lexikon* s.v. παρθένοι:
δοῦναι ἑαυτὰς σφαγῆναι ὑπὲρ τῆς χώρας.

70. M. P. Nilsson, *Geschichte der Griechischen Religion* 2, ²1965, 771:
'With Euripides the Enlightenment, with its particular discussion of
problems, came on to the scene.' However, cf. E. R. Dodds, 'Euripides
als Irrationalist', in *Der Fortschrittsgedanke in der Antike*, 1977, 97–112
(English version *The Ancient Concept of Progress*, 1973, 97–129).

71. J. Schmitt (n. 66), 1f., cf. P. Roussel, 'Le thème du sacrifice
volontaire dans la tragédie d'Euripide', *Revue belge de philologie et
d'histoire* 1, 1922, 225–40.

72. Cf. Schmitt (n. 66), 78. The group θύειν, θυσία, θῦμα only
appears with frequency in the *Iphigenia*. Cf. also P. Stengel, *Opferbräuche der Griechen*, 1910, 92–104; W. Burkert, *Homo necans*, 16f. n. 42;

274   *The Atonement*

Greek Tragedy (n. 63), 102ff. Referring to R. K. Yerkes, *Sacrifice in Greek and Roman Religions and Early Judaism*, 1952, Burkert, op. cit., 103, stresses 'that Semitic (Phoenician and Hebrew) sacrificial rites offer the closest parallels to Greek ritual'.

73. J. Schmitt, op. cit., (n. 66), 11, 22ff., 39ff., 63ff.

74. Op. cit., (n. 71), 240, Cf. E. R. Dodds (n. 70), 108: 'What Euripides presents to us here is the incursion of the mystery behind life, of the "other which is dearer than life" (*Hippolytus* 191). Beside this other, the chorus sings, wisdom is the folly of the sophists (*Bacchae* 395).' Cf. René Girard, *La Violence et le Sacré*, 1972, 170ff.

75. Diogenes Laertius 1.110; Athenagoras 13.602c: Κρατῖνος ... ἑκὼν αὐτὸν ἐπέδωκεν ὑπὲρ τῆς θρεψαμένης· ᾧ καὶ ἐπαπέθανεν ὁ ἐραστὴς Ἀριστόδημος, λύσιν τ' ἔλαβε τὸ δεινόν, quoted from Neanthes of Cyzicus, *Peri teletōn* = FGrHist 84 F 16.

76. W. Burkert, *Structure and History* . . . 72ff.; F. Schwenn (n. 63), 154ff.; S. Eitrem, 'Die göttlichen Zwillinge bei den Griechen', *Skrifter Videnskap Kristiania* II, 1903, no. 2, 72ff.

77. *Homo necans*, 76ff.; cf. *Structure*, 74ff.

78. Metioche and Menippe, Antonius Liberalis 25, ed. M. Papathomopulos, 1968, 43f., and commentary 125ff., Ovid, *Metamorphoses* 4,1,389ff.

79. Androcleia and Alcis, daughters of Antipoinos, Pausanias 9.17.1. Cf. F. Schwenn (n. 63), 128f.

80. Aelian, *Varia historia* 12.28: ταύτας δὲ ὑπὲρ τῆς πόλεως τῆς Ἀθηναίων ἀναιρεθῆναι λόγος ἔχει, ἐπιδόντος αὐτὰς τοῦ Λεὼ ἐς τὸν χρησμὸν τὸν Δελφιόν. ἔλεγε γὰρ μὴ ἂν ἄλλως σωθῆναι τὴν πόλιν, εἰ μὴ ἐκεῖναι σφαγιασθεῖεν. Cf. also Diodore 17.15.2, the speech of Phocion, opponent of Demosthenes, who, with reference to the example of the daughters of Leo and Hyacinthus, ὠνείδιζε τῶν μὴ βουλομένων ὑπὲρ τῆς πόλεως τελευτᾶν, see also pp. 12f., n. 52.They were partly confused with the daughters of Erechtheus, see Cicero, *De natura deorum* 3.50; so the tradition, too, is uncertain, although it is a question of a sacrifice or offering by the father, see the commentary by A. S. Pease on *De natura deorum*, ad loc., cf. also F. Schwenn (n. 63), 129f., and Kock, 'Leokorion', *PW* 12.2, cols. 2000f.

81. Apollodorus 3.15.8; Hyginus, *Fabulae* 238. They, too, are sometimes identified with the daughters of Erechtheus, as in Ps. Demosthenes 60.27; Suidas, *Lexicon*, s.v. παρθένοι, cf. F. Schwenn (n. 63), 131.

82. Philochorus, FGrHist 328F 105 + 106 (Schol. Dem. 19. 303): . . . ἔχρησεν ὁ Ἀπόλλων ἀπαλλαγήσεσθαι ἐάν τις ἀνέληι ἑαυτὸν ὑπὲρ τῆς πόλεως· ἡ τοίνυν Ἄγραυλος ἑκοῦσα αὐτὴν ἐξέδωκεν εἰς θάνατον. ἔρριψε γὰρ ἑαυτὴν ἐκ τοῦ τείχους. εἶτα ἀπαλλαγέντος τοῦ πολέμου, ἱερὸν ὑπὲρ τούτου ἐστήσαντο αὐτῆι... For the oath of the ephebes see Plutarch,

Alcibiades 15.4. Cf. W. Burkert, *Homo necans*, 77f. For the complicated history of the tradition see F. Jacoby, *FGrHist* Supplement b, *A Commentary on the Ancient History of Athens*, I, 1954, 425ff., and II, 326ff.

83. Plutarch, *Theseus* 32.4: ἀφ'οὖ (=Marathos) δὲ Μαραθῶνα τὸν δῆμον, ἐπιδόντος ἑαυτὸν ἑκουσίως κατά τι λόγιον σφραγιάσασθαι πρὸ τῆς παρατάξεως. Cf. F. Schwenn (n. 52), 133.

84. J. Schmitt (n. 66), 83ff., who refers to Wilamowitz-Moellendorff; Roussel (n. 71) 229, n. 1 differs. The name, which already speaks for itself and indicates a heroizing, suggests a later formation. See also Wrede, *PW* 14.1, cols. 622f.

85. Cheiron: Apollodorus 2.5.4; 2.5.11: Χείρωνα ἀθάνατον ⟨ὄντα⟩ θνῄσκειν ἀντ'αὐτοῦ θέλοντα. For Augustus see Dio Cassius 80.20; Caligula: Suetonius, *Caligula* 27; Hadrian: *Historia Augusta* I (Spartian) 14; cf. also Suetonius, *Nero* 36; for the whole question see F. Schwenn (n. 63), 183f.

86. H. W. Parke and D. E. W. Wormell, *The Delphic Oracle*, Vol. 1, 1956, 295ff. (260): 'For the dramatic purposes of folk memory the command to offer a human sacrifice was the most thrilling answer the oracle could give.' Cf. Libanius, *Declamatio* 42.25 (7,415): οὐκ ἀκούετε τὸν Πύθιον . . .; καὶ οἱ μὲν παῖδες ἐτέθυντο.

87. Cf. e.g. the report by Caesar on the religion of the Gauls, *Bellum Gallicum* 6.16: 'The whole Gallic people is remarkably addicted to religious observances. So people suffering from severe illnesses or those who pass their lives in war and danger offer or vow to offer human sacrifices and employ Druids to perform the sacrificial rites. For they believe that unless the life of man be offered for man's life, the divine spirit cannot be propitiated (*quod pro vita hominis nisi hominis vita reddatur, non posse deorum immortalium numen placari*).' The whole account is biassed, in order to stress the barbarism of the Gauls. On the other hand, Caesar himself killed men 'as a sort of ritual observance' during a mutiny, Dio Cassius 43.24.3, see F. Schwenn, op. cit. (n. 63), 166f.

88. 8.9.4–12 (10): *Sicut caelo missus piaculum omnis deorum irae, qui pestem ab suis aversam in hostes ferret*, cf. Cicero, *De divinatione* 1.51, and the commentary by A. S. Pease, 184f.; *De finibus* 2.61; *De natura deorum* 2.10; 3.15, see above, p. 14. See also F. Schwenn, op. cit., 154ff.; W. Burkert, *Structure* (n. 63), 59–64. For the term *piaculum* see P. C. Tromp, *De Romanorum piaculis*, cf. 21.

89. Livy, 10.28.13: *datum hoc nostro generi est ut luendis periculis publicis piacula simus. iam ego mecum hostium legiones mactandas Telluri ac deis Manibus dabo.*' Cf. also Livy 8.10.12. For the frequent mention of the Decii in the Roman collections of *exempla virtutis* see H. W. Litchfield (n. 49), 48 n. 4. It extends as far as Dante, *Paradise* 6.47.

90. *Pharsalia* 2.304–9:

> *Sic eat: inmites Romana piacula divi*
> *Plena ferant, nullo fraudemus sanguine bellum.*
> *Utinam caelique deis Erebique liceret*
> *Hoc caput in cunctas damnatum exponere poenas*
> *Devotum hostiles Decium, pressere catervae*
> *Me geminae figant acies, me barbara telis*
> *Rheni turba petat, cunctis ego pervius hostis*
> *Excipiam medius totius volnera belli.*
> *Hic redimat sanguis populos, hac caede luatur*
> *Quidquid Romani meruerunt pendere mores.*

Cf. W. Speyer (n. 63), 139, who rightly points out that here 'the archaic thought pattern is ethicized'. I.e. the wrath of the gods, punishment and expiation here relate to moral guilt.

91. J. G. Frazer, *The Golden Bough*, Part VI, *The Scapegoat*, [3]1925, gives a global survey of the theme of the scapegoat; for the *pharmakos* in Greece see 253ff. Cf. also F. Schwenn (n. 63), 26ff.; V. Gebhard, *Die Pharmakoi in Ionien und die Sybakchoi in Athen*, Munich dissertation 1926; id., 'Thargelia', *PW*, 2.R., 5, 1290–1304; id., 'Pharmakos', *PW* 19, 1841f.; M. P. Nilsson (n. 70) 1, 107ff.; L. Deubner, *Attische Feste*, [2]1966 (1932), 179–88; G. Stählin, περίψημα, *TDNT* 6; W. Burkert, *Griechische Religion* (n. 63), 139ff.; *Structure* (n. 63), ch. III, 'Transformations of the Scapegoat', 59–77, 168ff. (with bibliography).

92. FGrHist 334, fr. 50 = Harpokration/Suda s.v.; cf. Helladios in Photius, *Bibliotheca*, p. 534 a3.

93. See Deubner (n. 91), 184 n. 5: Scholion Aristophanes, *Equites* 1136: λίαν ἀγεννεῖς καὶ ἀχρήστους... ἔθυον; *Ranes* 730: τοὺς γὰρ φαύλους καὶ παρὰ τῆς φύσεως ἐπιβουλευομένους.... ἔθυον. Cf. also scholion Aeschylus, *Septem contra Thebas* 680, Dindorf p. 376, 29: λιμοῦ συμβάντος παρ' Ἕλλησιν ἤ τινος ἄλλου τῶν ἀπευκτῶν, λαμβάνοντες τὸν ἀηδέστατον, καὶ παρὰ τῆς φύσεως ἐπιβεβουλευομένον πηρόν, χωλόν, τοὺς τοιούτους, τοῦτον ἔθυον εἰς ἀπαλλαγὴν τοῦ ἐνοχλοῦντος δαίμονος.

94. See Deubner (n. 91), 186 n. 3 and 186 n. 2: Petronius according to Servius on Virgil, *Aeneid* 3,57 (= *Satyricon*, ed Konrad Müller, F1, p. 185) on Massilia: '*unus se ex pauperibus offerebat ... hic postea ornatus verbenis et vestibus sacris circumducebatur per totam civitatem cum execrationibus.*' Cf. Lactantius Placitus on Statius, *Thebaid* 10,793: he calls this form 'of purifying a city by human sacrifice a Gallic custom' (*lustrare civitatem humana hostia Gallicus mos est*), presumably because of the Celtic predilection for human sacrifice (see above, p. 87 n. 87). A very poor man (*aliquis de egentissimis*) was persuaded into selling himself for a high price: for a whole year he was fed on the choicest food.

On an appointed festival he was eventually led out of the city by the whole population and stoned by the people outside the city walls (*denique certo et solemni die per totam civitatem ductus ex urbe extra pomeria saxis occidebatus a populo*).

95. Strabo 10, 2, 9, C 452; cf. Ovid, *Fasti* 5, 629f. and the commentary by F. Bömer, 2, 330.

96. *P. Ovidii Nasonis Ibis*, ed. R. Ellis, Oxford 1881, p. 81. I owe this reference to Eberhard Jüngel. Cf. also the commentary, 140f.

97. Callimachus, ed. R. Pfeiffer, Oxford ²1965, I, 97: εἶτ' ἔξω τοῦ τείχους περίεισι κύκλῳ περικαθαίρων (?) αὐτῷ τὴν πόλιν, καὶ τότε ὑπὸ τοῦ βασιλέως καὶ τῶν ἄλλων λιθοβολεῖται, ἕως ἐξελασθῇ τῶν ὁρίων.

98. *Historiarum Variarum Chiliades*, ed. T. Kiessling, Leipzig 1826, 5, 729, 731. Cf. Deubner (n. 91), 183 n. 3. The treatment of the body corresponds with the action of the Trojans over the Locrian maiden whom they had killed, see W. Leaf, *Troy. A Study in Homeric Geography*, London 1912, 126ff. (129), 392ff.

99. *Acta Sanctorum Novembris* I, 1887, chs. 2–8, 106–8 (ch. 5 p. 107). On this cf. S. Weinstock, 'Saturnalien und Neujahrsfest in den Märtyreracten', in *.·lullus, Festschrift T. Klauser*, Münster 1964, 391–400.

100. G. Stählin (n. 91).

101. J.-P. Vernant in J.-P. Vernant and P. Vidal-Naquet, *Mythe et tragédie en Grèce ancienne*, 1973, 117ff. (122): '*Roi divin-pharmakós*: telles sont donc les deux faces d'Oedipe, qui lui confèrent son aspect d'énigme en réunissant en lui, comme dans une formule à double sens, deux figures inverses l'une de l'autre. Cf. *Oedipus Rex* 1424ff.

102. *Oedipus Coloneus*, 1656–66.

103. Ibid. 1751:   ἐν οἷς γάρ
χάρις ἡ χθονία νὺξ ἀπόκειται
πενθεῖν οὐ χρή.

cf. 1720: ἀλλ' ἐπεὶ ὀλβίως γ'ἔλυσεν
τὸ τέλος, ὦ φίλαι, βίου.

104. Plutarch, *Pelopidas* 21 and 22, ET, LCL V,391ff., cf. Xenophon, *Hellenica* 6.4.7; Diodore 15.54.1–4; Pausanias 9.13.5f.: 'At that time Epaminondas sacrificed to Skedasos and his daughters and prayed that the battle should not take place to bring about the salvation of the Thebans, but to wreak vengeance on them (the Spartans).' For the development of the saga of the Leuctrides Korai see F. Pfister, 'Skedasos', *PW* 2 R. 3, cols. 465ff.

105. For early Christianity as a 'mad superstition', see M. Hengel, *Crucifixion*, London and Philadelphia 1977, 1ff.

Chapter Two

1. W. Popkes, *Christus Traditus*, 1967, makes an excellent investigation of these 'surrender formulae', though I cannot follow his results at every point.

2. Here I can refer above all to the numerous works by J. Jeremias, see e.g. *Abba*, 1966; *New Testament Theology* Vol. 1, *The Proclamation of Jesus*, ET 1971, 286ff., 295ff.; cf. L. Goppelt, *Theologie des Neuen Testaments*, 1975, 1, 243ff.

3. *Weil Ich dich liebe. Die Verkündigung Jesu und Deuterojesaja*, 1976, 231ff.

4. On Mark 10.45 see now P. Stuhlmacher, 'Existenzvertretung für die Vielen: Mk 10.45 (Matt. 20, 28)', in *Werden und Wirken des Alten Testaments, Festschrift für Claus Westermann zum 70. Geburtstag*, 1980, 412–27. He rightly derives the logion from Jesus himself, see p. 95 n.55 below.

5. On this see W. Kramer, *Christ, Lord, Son of God*, ET SBT 50, London 1966, 26ff., 133ff. This is rightly corrected by K. Wengst (see above p. 76 n.4), 78ff. The term 'dying formula' also appears there.

6. The same is true of I Peter 2.21. The fact that I Peter prefers the verb πάσχειν to ἀποθνήσκειν is connected with his paraenetic application of the death of Jesus. Possibly he replaced ἀποθνήσκειν by πάσχειν in one of the passages that he incorporated.

7. Suetonius, *Claudius*, 25; in Tacitus, *Annals* 15, 44, 21 the reading should be *Chrestiani*. Cf. K. Weiss, *TDNT* 9, 484,35ff. and A. Wlosok, *Rom und die Christen*, 1970, 8–12.

8. On this see P. Stuhlmacher and K. Haacker et al., in *Biblisch-Theologische Studien* 1, 1977, 38f.

9. For the 'apostolic council' see my *Acts and the History of Earliest Christianity*, 1979, 111ff.

10. Op. cit., 71ff.; cf. 'Zwischen Jesus und Paulus. Die "Hellenisten", die "Sieben" und Stephanus (Apg 6,1–15; 7,54–8,3)', *ZThK* 72, 1975, 151–206 (literature).

11. It is the special contribution of the great commentary by R. Pesch, *Das Markusevangelium* II, 1977, that he investigates the historical background and here comes up against the towering significance of the question of the Messiah.

12. 'Der gekreuzigte Messias', in *Der historische Jesus und der kerygmatische Christus*, ed. H. Ristow and K. Matthiae, 1961, 161.

13. M. Hengel, *ZThK* 72, 1975, 192 n. 128; so also P. Stuhlmacher, *Das Evangelium von der Versöhnung in Christus*, 1979, 25f.

14. Op. cit., 23.

15. GenR. 65.22. See above, pp. 8f. Cf. M. Hengel, *Crucifixion*, 84f.

16. *JTS* 14, 1945, 4; see now also H. Gese (n. 11), *Die Sühne*, 85–106, esp. 105; P. Stuhlmacher, 'Zur neueren Exegese von Röm 3,24–26', in *Jesus und Paulus. Festschrift W. G. Kümmel zum 70. Geburtstag*, 1975, 314–33. The Tübingen dissertation by B. Janowski, *Sühne als Heilsgeschehen. Studien zur Sühnetheologie der Priesterschrift und zur Wurzel KPR im Alten Orient und im Alten Testament*, 1979, supervised by my colleague Hartmut Gese, is now of fundamental importance for the Old Testament concept of atonement. There is an investigation of Romans 3.25 in the light of underlying tradition in Part IV, 3B (pp. 242ff.).

17. In my study *Nachfolge und Charisma*, 1968, I have attempted to show that this designation is in no way sufficient.

18. The fundamental problem of chronology has not been taken seriously enough in connection with the question of the origin of christology; see my article 'Christologie und neutestamentliche Chronologie', in *Neues Testament und Geschichte, Festschrift O. Cullmann zum 70. Geburtstag*, 1972, 43–67.

19. See the extensive collection of evidence in W. Popkes, op. cit. (n. 1), 61ff. and 56 n. 1.

20. See above, p. 90, notes 3 and 4.

21. The penetrating linguistic analyses by J. Jeremias, *The Eucharistic Words of Jesus*, ET [2]1966, 178ff., 225ff., 227 n. 5, are still of fundamental importance. The rare verbal correspondence of the two Targums points to the antiquity of this interpretation: *uzᵉraq ʿal madbᵉḥā lᵉkappārā ʿal ʿammā*. The rabbinic texts (other than the Targums) interpret Ex. 24.8 in terms of blood from circumcision, thus reducing the significance of atonement, in order to stand apart from Christianity. The two statements about atonement give the impression of being early relics.

22. Josephus, *Antt.* 20.200ff.: τὸν ἀδελφὸν Ἰησοῦ τοῦ λεγομένου Χριστοῦ, Ἰάκωβος ὄνομα αὐτῷ, καί τινας ἑτέρους, ὡς παρανομησάντων κατηγορίαν ποιησάμενος παρέδωκε λευσθησομένους. For Peter and James cf. Hengel, *Acts and the History of Earliest Christianity*, London and Philadelphia 1979, 92–98.

23. Epiphanius, *Panarion* 30, 16, 5–7: ἦλθον καταλῦσαι τὰς θυσίας, καὶ ἐὰν μὴ παύσησθε τοῦ θύειν, οὐ παύσεται ἀφ᾽ὑμῶν ἡ ὀργή. Cf. 19, 3, 6 (see A. F. J. Klijn and G. J. Reinink, *Patristic Evidence for Jewish-Christian Sects*, 1973, 182ff.).

24. *Recognitions* 1.35ff. There are further instances from the *Kerygmata Petrou* in G. Strecker, *Das Judenchristentum in den Pseudoklementinen*, 1958, 179ff. However, the criticism of sacrifice cannot be derived directly from a Jewish criticism; it is a rationalistic development of the attitude of the primitive community. In addition, we should assume Gnostic influence.

25. H. J. Schoeps, *Theologie und Geschichte des Judenchristentums* 1949, 219ff.: for the Ebionite hostility to the cult and their place in the history of religion, cf. *Das Judenchristentum*, 1964, 68ff., 95ff. Anti-Paulinism and then Gnostic influence may be responsible for the relative silence of the later Ebionite texts, since the gnostics were no longer interested in the death of Jesus. According to Jerome (*in Jes.* 31.6–9 = CC 73.404 = Klijn/Reinink, op. cit., 222f.), they took a positive attitude to God's mercy and the power of the cross, cf. also Epiphanius, *Panarion* 30.3.5, op. cit., 178, and Jerome, *Ep.* 112.13, op. cit., 200. They also had to deal with Deut. 21.23 (Jerome, *in Gal.*, MPL 26.387B = op.cit., 204).

26. Josephus, *Antt.* 18.19. On this see G. Klinzing, *Die Umdeutung des Kultus in der Qumrangemeinde und im NT*, 1971, 45ff.: 'The sending of gifts for dedication is the least binding way of honouring the Temple and does not amount to taking part in its cult.'

27. Eusebius, *HE* 2.23.6: μόνος εἰσήρχετο εἰς τὸν ναόν ... ἀεὶ κάμπτειν ἐπὶ γόνυ προσκυνοῦντα τῷ θεῷ καὶ αἰτεῖσθαι ἄφεσιν τῷ λαῷ.

28. On Isaiah 53 and the death of Jesus see the survey of research in M.-L. Gubler (p. 76, n. 2), 259–335.

29. See the well-considered verdict by W. Popkes (p. 81, n. 38), 47ff. (55): 'TestB 3,8 could be the point of connection between Isaiah 53 (attested as the LXX understands it) and the early New Testament, if it could be demonstrated that there was an interpretation of the servant songs in terms of a suffering Messiah in a group standing near to primitive Christianity. However, this cannot be taken as certain.' Only the discovery of a new text could help us out of this dilemma.

30. Cf. O. Cullmann, *Christology of the New Testament*, 111: 'We must not forget that at this time Judaism had by no means a single *fixed* concept of the Messiah' (author's italics, not reproduced in ET). He is followed by H. R. Balz, *Methodische Probleme der neutestamentlichen Christologie*, 1967, 112.

31. For LXX see K. F. Euler, *Die Verkündigung vom leidenden Gottesknecht aus Jes. 53 in der griechischen Bibel*, 1934. For the later translations and the Targum on the prophets see H. Hegermann, *Jesaja 53 in Hexapla, Targum und Peschitta*, 1954. For the rabbinate see G. Dalman, *Der leidende und der Sterbende Messias der Synagoge im ersten nachchristlichen Jahrtausend*, 1888; Billerbeck 1.481ff.; J. Jeremias, παῖς θεοῦ, *TDNT* 5, 677–700.

32. *RB* 70, 1963, 492.

33. The attack made on J. Jeremias with more vigour than critical understanding by M. Rese, 'Überprüfung einiger Thesen von J. Jeremias', *ZThK* 60, 1963, 21–41, goes to the opposite extreme, by funda-

Notes 281

mentally challenging any pre-Christian messianic interpretation. The fact that we have very few 'pre-Christian' messianic texts at all, and the problem of dating rabbinic haggadic traditions, which usually raise almost insuperable difficulties for us, is unknown to him. His interpretation of TestB 3,8 in terms of the 'death of the righteous', 24–8, is unsatisfactory. The completely sinless and perfect righteous one is the Messiah, see PsSol. 17. Unfortunately he does not go into the problem of the text of the LXX, which presents an amazing, background paraphrase.

34. A new investigation is urgently needed. The brief study by H. W. Wolff, *Jesaja 53*, ²1950, is still very well worth reading, although it shows its age. Cf. also J. Jeremias (n. 21), 191–216.

35. W. Popkes (p. 81, n. 38) goes into the relationship of the 'surrender' statements to Isa. 53, 219ff., 253ff., 258ff., but underestimates its significance.

36. *Novum Testamentum Graece*, ²⁶1979, 761.

37. For this theory by Wengst, which found a large degree of assent, see p. 3 above and M.-L. Gubler (p. 73, n. 2), 254ff., 316ff.

38. In this dating I am following E. Bickerman, *Studies in Jewish and Christian History* I, 1976, 276–81. The most recent investigation by K. Breitenstein, *Beobachtungen zu Sprache, Stil und Gedankengut des 4.Makkabäerbuchs*, 1976, follows A. Dupont-Sommer in assuming for linguistic reasons that the work was composed in the second half of the century. It is probable that IV Maccabees already presupposes the persecution of the Jews after AD 66–70, or even 115–117 and 132–136. The martyr story also found its way into the rabbinic tradition, see Gittin 57b; Lam.R. 1.50; Seder Eliyahu R. 30 (28).

39. Dan. 3.25–45. Cf. O. Plöger, 'Zusätze zu Daniel', *JSHRZ* I,1,67f.

40. Cf. Dan. 3.34 LXX with Job 42.8–10 (a) καὶ ἔλυσεν τὴν ἁμαρτίαν αὐτοῖς διὰ Ἰώβ and 11QtgJob (ed. J.P.M.v.d.Ploeg/A.S.v.d.Woude, 1971), col. 38,2f.: *wšbq lhwn ḥṭ'yhwn bdylh* (= Job). The Hebrew text mentions only Job's prayer for his friends.

41. The reading varies here between Theodotion and o¹ text καὶ ἐκτελέσαι ὄπισθέν σου is read by Theodotion and syʰ. In individual instances in LXX, ὀπίσω can stand for '*im* or *lipnē*: I Kings 1.8; I Sam. 17.31 and above all Dan. 8.4 (LXX).

42. On this see S. Spiegel, *The Last Trial*, 1963; G. Vermes, *Scripture and Tradition in Judaism*, ²1973, 193–227; R. J. Daly, 'The Soteriological Significance of the Sacrifice of Isaac', *CBQ* 39, 1977, 45–75; this is supplemented by P. R. Davies and B. D. Chilton, 'The Aqedah: A Revised Tradition History', *CBQ* 40, 1978, 514–46, though they 'underinterpret' the texts. Does the fact that haggadic parallels to the Targums first appear among the Amoreans really mean that the Targumic tradi-

tions are similarly as late? One cannot in any way conclude from the fact that we have little demonstrable 'Tannaitic Haggadah' that the Pharisaic teachers of the first and second centuries AD were relatively uninterested in the Haggadah. The Haggadah was often handed on anonymously. The wall-paintings of the synagogue of Dura Europos, for example, show how rich and living the Haggadah must have been even at the beginning of the third century AD. It goes back to earlier acknowledged traditions.

43. *LAB* 32,3 (ed. G. Kisch, p. 204): '*Erit autem mea beatitudo super omnes homines quia non erit aliud (sc. sacrificium), et in me annunciabunt generationes et per me intelligent populi, quoniam dignificavit Dominus animam hominis in sacrificium.*' For the interpretation of this difficult passage see P. R. Davies and B. D. Chilton (n. 42), 523ff.

44. 40.2–4 (G. Kisch, p. 220f.): '*Et nunc detur anima eius in peticione eius, et erit mors eius preciosa ante conspectum meum omni tempore*' (40.4). As in Euripides the voluntary nature of the sacrifice is stressed. The daughter consoles her despairing father: '*Et quis est qui contristetur moriens, videns populum liberatum?*' At the same time she points to the example of Isaac: '*et erat qui offerebatur paratus et qui offerebat gaudens.*' For the voluntary nature of the sacrifice of Isaac see e.g. GenR 56.8.

45. 18.5 (G. Kisch, p. 159): '*et filium eius petii in holocaustum et adduxit eum ut poneretur in sacrario, ego autem reddidi eum patri suo, et quia non contradixit (sc. Isaac), facta est oblatio in conspectu meo acceptabilis, et pro sanguine eius elegi istos.*' R. Le Déaut, *La nuit pascale*, 1963, 158, and Davies and Chilton are wrong in supposing that the passage can be referred to Abraham.

46. Mek. de R. Yishmael on Ex. 12.23 (Lauterbach 1,87): 'Another interpretation. "And when he (Yahweh) sees the blood." ' He sees the blood of the '*aqedat* of Isaac, as is said: 'and Abraham called the place "Yahweh will see" ' (Gen. 22.14). The anonymous interpretation points to an earlier tradition (against P. R. Davies and B. D. Chilton, 536). In the Haggadah there is no 'normative interpretation' in the strict sense, as there is in the Halachah. One cannot draw the conclusion from the introduction that this must be an early tradition. It is a traditional interpretation which has become anonymous. For the age of the Mekilta de R. Yishmael see now G. Stemberger, *Kairos* 21, 1979, 84–118.

47. *Märtyrer und Gottesknecht*, [2]1963.

48. *Die Aggada der Tannaiten* I, [2]1903, 1–72 (including the pupils of Johanan ben Zakkai). Cf. also the critical view of J. Neusner, *The Rabbinic Traditions about the Pharisees before 70*, I–III, 1971.

49. jSanh 11,7,30c, lines 29ff.: '*wth ḥṭyph šyṣ't m'wtw ṣdyq kyprh 'l kl ysr'l.*

50. §333 (ed. Finkelstein, p. 383, 6).

51. Pisḥā c.1, lines 106f. (Lauterbach 1,10): *šh'bwt whnby'ym ntnw npšm 'l ysr'l*, with reference to Moses' offer to atone in Ex. 32.32. Cf. lines 111ff. (p. 1,11).

52. Sifre Num. 25.13 §139 (Horovitz, p. 173,16f.). See M. Hengel, *Die Zeloten*, [2]1976, 161f.

53. MSanh 2.1f. par TSanh 4.1 (Zuckermandel), p. 420: TShebuot 1.4 (446 par.); Sifre Num. 35.24 §161 (Horovitz p. 222,5), cf. also MNeg 2,1.

54. Op. cit., (n.47), 63ff.

55. Text following W. Staerk, *Altjüdische liturgische Gebete*, KlT 58, [2]1930, Palestinian recension. Second petition: the twofold *meḥayyeh ham-metim* also appears alongside it. Cf. Paul (*a*) with finite verb (ἤγειρεν): Rom. 10.9; I Cor. 6:14; cf. I Thess. 1.10; I Cor. 15.14. (*b*) With the aorist participle (ἐγείρας as a predicate of God): Rom. 4.24; 8.11; II Cor. 1.9; 4.14; Gal. 1.1; Eph. 1.20; Col. 2.12; Acts only with the finite verb: 3.15; 4.10; 5.30; 13.30, 37; I Peter, aorist participle: 1.21. See also P. Stuhlmacher, 'Auferweckung Jesu und Biblische Theologie', *ZThK* 70, 1973, 365–403 (387).

56. For all its interesting observations, the main thesis of Klaus Berger, *Die Auferstehung des Propheten und die Erhöhung des Menschensohnes*, 1976, is unconvincing, despite its wealth of material and valuable insights. See the objections made by E. Schweizer, *TLZ* 103, 1978, 874–8, and my controversy with R. Pesch, who refers to Berger's theories, *ThQ* 153, 1973, 252–69.

57. The interpretation of this, the most important christological text in the Old Testament after Isa. 53 in terms of the risen Son of Man, was similarly made in the earliest community, as is shown by the prayer *mārān 'atā* (I Cor. 16.22), see my study 'Hymnus und Christologie', in *Festschrift K.H. Rengstorf zum 75. Geburtstag*, 1980, 1–23, see also D. M. Hay, *Glory at the Right Hand*, 1973, and M. Gourgues, *A la droite de Dieu*, Paris 1980.

58. Against M. Dibelius, *Studies in the Acts of the Apostles*, 1956, 124: 'A band of people had been gathered together in a common belief in Jesus Christ and in the expectation of his coming again, and were leading a quiet, and in the Jewish sense,"pious" existence in Jerusalem. It was a modest existence,and nothing but the victorious conviction of the believers betrayed the fact that from this company a movement would go out which was to change the world.' He is followed by E. Haenchen, *The Acts of the Apostles*, 1971, 189: 'It is likely, however, that in reality the Christians sought adherents for their Lord, in the earliest days, without attracting much attention . . . it was the "Hellenists" who first broke out from this reserve of the Jewish sect that believed

in Jesus.' This is to underestimate the power of eschatological enthusiasm; the first Christians did not expect less than happened later, but infinitely more, namely the complete transformation of the world by the return of the crucified Jesus. The missionary impulse which this provided is shown not least in the winning over of the Hellenists. See 'Die Ursprünge der christlichen Mission', *NTS* 18, 1971/72, 30ff.

59. M. Hengel, 'Maria Magdalena und die Frauen als Zeugen', in *Abraham Unser Vater, Festschrift O. Michel z. 60. Geburtstag*, Leiden 1963, 253.

60. Lauterbach 2,290.

61. See Walter Bauer, *Das Leben Jesu im Zeitalter der neutestamentlichen Apokryphen*, 1909 (reprinted 1967), 467, cf. *C.Cels.* 2.9, 10, 12, 18; 6.10; A. von Harnack, *Der Philosoph bei Makarius Magnes, Kritik des Neuen Testaments von einem griechischen Philosophen des 3. Jhs.*, TU 37,4, p. 34 (3,2).

62. See the fine investigation by H. Schürmann, *Jesu ureigener Tod*, ²1975.

63. *The Eucharistic Words of Jesus*, ²1966; *New Testament Theology I, The Proclamation of Jesus*, 1971, 277ff., 288ff. Cf. also, with a partly different emphasis, H. Patsch, *Abendmahl und historischer Jesus*, 1972, and L. Goppelt, *Theologie des Neuen Testaments I, Jesu Wirken in seiner theologischen Bedeutung*, 1975, 234ff., 241ff., 261ff.

64. For the eucharist as a death meal see H. Gese, *Zur biblischen Theologie*, 1977, 107–27: the origin of the Lord's Supper, which already gives this character to the last meal of Jesus with his disciples.

65. See *The Son of God*, ET 1976, 89ff. For the Philippians hymn see O. Hofius, *Der Christushymnus Philipper 2, 6–11*, 1976.

66. For the Near Eastern and Old Testament background to atonement and its different modes of theological interpretation, see the excellent dissertation by B. Janowski, *Sühne als Heilsgeschehen*, Tübingen Dissertation 1979, which will soon be published in WMANT.

Bibliography

On Chapter 1

Baumeister, T., *Die Anfänge der Theologie des Martyriums*, MBT 45, Münster 1980

Benz, E., *Das Todesproblem in der stoischen Philosophie*, TBAW 7, Stuttgart 1929

Betz, H. D. (ed.), *Plutarch's Theological Writings and Early Christian Literature*, SCHNT 3, Leiden 1975

Burkert, W., 'Greek Tragedy and Sacrificial Ritual', *GRBS* 7, 1966, 87–121

—, *Griechische Religion der archaischen und klassischen Epoche*, RM 15, Stuttgart 1977

—, *Homo necans. Interpretationen altgriechischer Opferriten und Mythen*, RVV 32, Berlin and New York 1972

—, *Structure and History in Greek Mythology and Ritual*, Berkeley 1979

Campenhausen, H. von, *Die Idee des Martyriums in der Alten Kirche*, Göttingen ²1964

Detienne, M., and Vernant, J.-P., *La cuisine du sacrifice en pays grec*, Paris 1979

Deubner, L., *Attische Feste*, Hildesheim ²1966 (reprint of 1932 edition)

—, 'Der Pharmakos von Abdera', *SIFC* NS 11, 1934, 185–92

Dodds, E. R., 'Euripides the Irrationalist', in *The Ancient Concept of Progress and Other Essays on Greek Literature and Belief*, Oxford 1973, 78–91

Eitrem, S., *Die göttlichen Zwillinge bei den Griechen*, SNVAO. HF, 1902, 2

Farnell, L. R., *Greek Hero Cults and Ideas of Immortality*, Oxford 1970 (reprint of 1921 edition)

Fraenkel, H., *Dichtung und Philosophie des frühen Griechentums*, Munich ³1969

Frazer, J. G., *The Golden Bough. A Study in Magic and Religion*. Part VI: *The Scapegoat*, London ³1925

Gebhard, V., *Die Pharmakoi in Ionien und die Sybakchoi in Athen*, Munich dissertation 1926

Gese, H., 'Der Messias', *Zur biblischen Theologie*, Munich 1977, 128–51,

—, 'Die Sühne', op. cit., 85–106

—, 'Der Tod im Alten Testament', op. cit., 31–54

Girard, R., *La violence et le sacré*, Paris 1972

Gnilka, J., 'Martyriumsparänese und Sühnetod in synoptischen und jüdischen Traditionen', in *Die Kirche des Anfangs, Festschrift H. Schürmann*, Leipzig 1977; ETS 38, Freiburg 1978, 223–46

Gubler, M-L., *Die frühesten Deutungen des Todes Jesu*, OBO 15, Fribourg and Göttingen 1977

Hengel, M., *Crucifixion in the Ancient World and the Folly of the Message of the Cross*, London and Philadelphia 1977

—, *Jews, Greeks and Barbarians*, London and Philadelphia 1980

—, *Judaism and Hellenism*, London and Philadelphia 1974

—, *Die Zeloten*, AGJU 1, Leiden ²1976

Hommel, H., 'Dulce et decorum . . .', *RhMus* 111, 1968, 219–52

Kaiser, O., 'Den Erstgeboren deiner Söhne sollst du mir geben', in *Denkender Glaube, Festschrift C.H. Ratschow zum 65*, Berlin 1976, 24–48.

Kellermann, U., *Auferstanden in den Himmel*, SBS 95, Stuttgart 1979

Koch, K., 'Sühne und Sündenvergebung um die Wende von der exilischen zur nachexilischen Zeit', *EvTh* 26, 1966, 217–39

Kümmel, H.M., 'Ersatzkönig und Sündenbock', *ZAW* 80, 1968, 289-318

Lasaulx, E. von, *Die Sühnopfer der Griechen und Römer und ihr Verhältnis zu dem Einen auf Golgatha*, Würzburg 1841

Latte, K., *Römische Religionsgeschichte*, HAW 5, 4, Munich ²1967

Litchfield, H. W., 'National *Exempla Virtutis* in Roman Literature', *HSCP* 25, 1914, 1–71

Lohfink, G., *Die Himmelfahrt Jesu*, SANT 26, Munich 1971

Muehl, M., 'Des Herakles Himmelfahrt', *RhMus* 101, 1958, 106–34

Mommsen, T., *Römisches Strafrecht*, Darmstadt 1955 (reprint of 1899 edition)

Musurillo, H. A., *The Acts of the Pagan Martyrs. Acta Alexandrinorum*, Oxford 1954

Nilsson, M. P., *Geschichte der Griechischen Religion*, HAW 5, 2, Munich I, ²1961; II, ²1965

—, *Griechische Feste von religiöser Bedeutung*, Darmstadt 1957 (reprint of 1906 edition)

Oltramare, H., *Les origines de la diatribe romaine*, Geneva 1926

Parke, H. W., and Wormell, D. E. W., *The Delphic Oracle*, Oxford 1958

Pfister, F., 'Herakles und Christus', *ARW* 34, 1937, 42–60

Popkes, W., *Christus traditus*, ATANT 49, Zurich and Stuttgart 1967

Robinson, P. A., *The Conception of Death in Judaism in the Hellenistic and Early Roman Period*, London 1980

Rose, H. J., 'Herakles and the Gospels', *HTR* 31, 1938, 113–42

Roussel, P., 'Le thème du sacrifice volontaire dans la tragédie d'Euripide', *RBPH* 1, 1922, 225–40

Ruppert, L., *Jesus als der leidende Gerechte?*, SBS 59, Stuttgart 1972

—, *Der leidende Gerechte*, Würzburg and Stuttgart 1972

Schmitt, J., *Freiwilliger Opfertod bei Euripides*, RVV 17, 2, Giessen 1921

Schwartz, E., *Ethik der Griechen*, Stuttgart 1951

Schwenn, F., *Die Menschenopfer bei den Griechen und Römern*, RVV 15, 3, Giessen 1915

Simon, M., *Hercule et le christianisme*, PFLUS, Second Series, 19, Paris 1955

Speyer, W., 'Religionen des griechisch-römischen Bereichs. Zorn der Gottheit, Vergeltung und Sühne', in *Theologie und Religionswissenschaft*, ed U. Mann, Darmstadt 1973, 124-43

Steck, O. H., *Israel und das gewaltsame Geschick der Propheten*, WMANT 23, Neukirchen-Vluyn 1967

Steinkopf, G., *Untersuchungen zur Geschichte des Ruhmes bei den Griechen*, Halle/Wittenberg dissertation 1937

Stengel, P., *Opferbräuche der Griechen*, Darmstadt 1972 (reprint of 1910 edition)

Tromp, S. P. C., *De Romanorum Piaculis*, Lugduni Batavorum dissertation 1921

Vernant, J.-P., and Vidal-Naquet, P., *Mythe et tragédie en Grèce ancienne*, Paris 1972

Waechter, L., *Der Tod im Alten Testament*, AzTh, Second Series 8, Stuttgart 1967

Wengst, L., *Christologische Formeln und Lieder des Urchristentums*, StNT 7, Gütersloh ²1973

Wilamowitz-Moellendorff, U. von, *Der Glaube der Hellenen*, Darmstadt ²1955

Yerkes, R. K., *Sacrifice in Greek and Roman Religions and Early Judaism*, New York 1952

On Chapter 2

Bacher, W., *Die Aggada der Tannaiten*, Strassburg, I, ²1903

Balz, H. R., *Methodische Probleme der neutestamentlichen Christologie*, WMANT 25, Neukirchen-Vluyn 1967

Barrett, C. K., 'The Background of Mark 10.45', in *New Testament Essays. Studies in Memory of T. W. Manson*, edited by A. J. B. Higgins, London 1959, 1–18

Bauer, W., *Das Leben Jesu im Zeitalter der neutestamentlichen Apokryphen*, Darmstadt 1967 (reprint of 1909 edition)

Baumeister, T., *Die Anfänge der Theologie des Martyriums*, MBT 45, Munster 1980

Berger, K., *Die Auferstehung des Propheten und die Erhöhung des Menschensohnes*, SUNT 13, Göttingen 1976

Bickerman, E., *Studies in Jewish and Christian History*, AGJU 9, I, Leiden 1976

Breitenstein, K., *Beobachtungen zu Sprache, Stil und Gedankengut des 4. Makkabäerbuches*, Basle and Stuttgart 1976

Conzelmann, H., 'Historie und Theologie in den synoptischen Passionsberichten', in *Zur Bedeutung des Todes Jesu*, Gütersloh 1967, 35–53

—, 'Zur Analyse der Bekenntnisformel I. Kor. 15, 3–5', *EvTh* 25, 1965, 1–11

Cullmann, O., *The Christology of the New Testament*, London and Philadelphia ²1963

Dahl, N. A., 'The Atonement – An Adequate Reward for the Akedah? (Ro 8:32)', in *Neotestamentica et Semitica, Studies in Honour of M. Black*, edited by E. Ellis and M. Wilcox, Edinburgh 1969, 15–29

—, 'Der gekreuzigte Messias', in *Der historische Jesus und der kerygmatische Christus*, edited by H. Ristow and K. Matthiae, Berlin ²1962 149–69

Dalman, G., *Der leidende und der sterbende Messias der Synagoge im ersten nachchristlichen Jahrtausend*, SIJB 4, Leipzig 1888

Daly, R. J., 'The Soteriological Significance of the Sacrifice of Isaac', *CBQ* 39, 1977, 45–75

Davies, P. R., and Chilton, B. D., 'The Aqedah: A Revised Tradition History', *CBQ* 40, 1978, 514–46

Le Déaut, R., *La nuit pascale*, AnBib 22, Rome 1963

Delling, G., *Der Kreuzestod Jesu in der urchristlichen Verkündigung*, Göttingen 1972

Dibelius, M., 'The First Christian Historian', in *Studies in the Acts of the Apostles*, London 1956

Euler, K. F., *Die Verkündigung vom leidenden Gottesknecht aus Jes. 53 in der griechischen Bibel*, BWANT 66, Fourth Series, 14, Stuttgart 1934

Gese, H., 'Die Herkunft des Herrenmahls', in *Zur biblischen Theologie*, Munich 1977, 107–27

—, 'Psalm 22 und das Neue Testament', in *Vom Sinai zum Zion*, Munich 1974, 180–201

—, 'Die Sühne', in *Zur biblischen Theologie*, Munich 1977, 85–106

Goppelt, L., *Theologie des Neuen Testaments I, Jesu Wirken in seiner theologischen Bedeutung*, edited by J. Roloff, Göttingen 1975

Gourgues, M., *A la droite de Dieu*, Paris 1978

Grimm, W., *Weil Ich dich liebe. Die Verkündigung Jesu und Deuterojesaja*, ANTJ 1, Berne and Frankfurt 1976

Gubler, M.-L., *Die frühesten Deutungen des Todes Jesu*, OBO 15, Fribourg and Göttingen 1977

Haenchen, E., *The Acts of the Apostles*, Oxford and Philadelphia 1971

Hahn, F., *Christologische Hoheitstitel*, FRLANT 83, Göttingen 1963

Harnack, A. von, *Kritik des Neuen Testaments von einem griechischen Philosophen des 3. Jhs.*, TU 37, 4, Third Series 7, Leipzig 1911

Hay, D. M., *Glory at the Right Hand*, Nashville and New York 1973

Hegermann, H., *Jesaja 53 in Hexapla, Targum und Peschitta*, BFCT Second Series 56, Gütersloh 1954

Hengel, M., 'Christologie und neutestamentliche Chronologie', in *Neues Testament und Geschichte. Festschrift for O. Cullmann*, Zurich and Tübingen 1972, 43–67

—, 'Hymnus und Christologie', in *Festschrift K. H. Rengstorf zum 75. Geburtstag*, Leiden 1980, 1–23

—, 'Ist der Osterglaube noch zu retten?', *ThQ* 153, 252–69

—, *Nachfolge und Charisma*, Berlin 1968

—, *The Son of God*, London and Philadelphia 1976

—, 'Die Ursprünge der christlichen Mission', *NTS* 18, 1971/72, 15–38

—, *Die Zeloten*, AGJU 1, Leiden ²1976

—, *Acts and the History of Earliest Christianity*, London and Philadelphia 1979

—, 'Zwischen Jesus und Paulus. Die "Hellenisten", die "Sieben" und Stephanus (Apg 6,1–15; 7,54–8,3)', *ZTK* 72, 1975, 151–206

Hofius, O., *Der Christushymnus Philipper 2,6–11*, WUNT First Series 17, Tübingen 1976

Hooker, M. D., *Jesus and the Servant*, London 1959

Janowski, B., *Sühne als Heilsgeschehen*, Diss. Tübingen 1979

Jeremias, J., *Abba*, Göttingen 1966

Jeremias, J., *The Eucharistic Words of Jesus*, London and Philadelphia ²1966

—, 'Die älteste Schicht der Menschensohn-Logien', *ZNW* 58, 1966, 159–72

—, "Ἀμνὸς τοῦ θεοῦ-παῖς θεοῦ', *ZNW* 34, 1935, 115–23

—, 'Artikelloses Χριστός. Zur Ursprache von 1. Cor. 15,3b–5', *ZNW* 57, 1966, 211–15

—, 'Das Lösegeld für Viele (Mk 10,45), in *Abba*, Göttingen 1966, 216–99

—, *New Testament Theology Vol. 1: The Proclamation of Jesus*, London and New York 1971

—, 'παῖς θεοῦ', *TDNT* 5, 654–717

—, 'παῖς(θεοῦ) im Neuen Testament', in *Abba*, Göttingen 1966, 191–216

—, 'Zum Problem der Deutung von Jesaja 53 im palästinensischen Spätjudentum', in *Aux sources de la tradition chrétienne, Mélanges M. Goguel*, Neuchâtel and Paris 1950, 113–19

Käsemann, E., 'Die Heilsbedeutung des Todes Jesu nach Paulus', in *Zur Bedeutung des Todes Jesu*, Gütersloh ²1967, 11–34

Kessler, H., *Die theologische Bedeutung des Todes Jesu*, Düsseldorf 1970

Kilian, R., *Isaaks Opferung*, SBS 44, Stuttgart 1970

Klijn, A. F. J., and Reinink, G. J., *Patristic Evidence for Jewish-Christian Sects*, NT.S 36, Leiden 1973

Klinzing, G., *Die Umdeutung des Kultus in der Qumrangemeinde und im Neuen Testament*, SUNT 7, Göttingen 1971

Kramer, W., *Christ, Lord, Son of God*, SBT 50, London 1966

Leaf, W., *Troy. A Study in Homeric Geography*, London 1912

Lehmann, K., *Auferweckt am dritten Tag nach der Schrift*, QD 38, Freiburg 1968

Levi, I., 'Le sacrifice d'Isaac et la mort de Jésus', *REJ* 64, 1912, 161–84

—, 'Encore quelques mots sur le sacrifice d'Isaac', *REJ* 65, 1913, 138–43

Lindars, B., 'Passion Apologetic', in *New Testament Apologetic*, London 1961, 75–137

Lohse, E., 'Die alttestamentlichen Bezüge im neutestamentlichen Zeugnis vom Tode Jesu', in *Zur Bedeutung des Todes Jesu*, Gütersloh [2]1967, 97–112

—, *Märtyrer und Gottesknecht*, FRLANT 64, New Series 46, Göttingen [2]1963

Manson, T. W., "ΙΛΑΣΤΗΡΙΟΝ', *JTS* 46, 1945, 1–10

Morris, L., 'The Meaning of "ΙΛΑΣΤΗΡΙΟΝ in Romans III, 25', *NTS* 2, 1955, 33–43

Nauck, W., 'Freude im Leiden', *ZNW* 46, 1955, 68–80

Neusner, J., *The Rabbinic Traditions about the Pharisees before 70*, I–III, Leiden 1971

Patsch, H., *Abendmahl und historischer Jesus*, Stuttgart 1972

—, 'Zum alttestamentlichen Hintergrund von Röm 4,25 und 1.Ptr 2,24', *ZNW* 60, 1969, 273–9

Pesch, R., *Das Abendmahl und Jesu Todesverständnis*, QD 80, Freiburg 1978

—, *Das Markusevangelium* II, HTK 2,2, Freiburg 1978

—, *Wie Jesus das Abendmahl hielt*, Freiburg, Basle and Vienna 1977

Plöger, O., 'Zusätze zu Daniel', *JSHRZ* 1, 1973, 63–86

Popkes, W., *Christus traditus*, ATANT 49, Zürich and Stuttgart 1967

Rese, M., 'Überprüfung einiger Thesen von J. Jeremias zum Thema des Gottesknechtes im Judentum', *ZTK* 60, 1963, 21–41

Robinson, P. A., *The Conception of Death in Judaism in the Hellenistic and Early Roman Period*, London 1980

Roloff, J., 'Anfänge der soteriologischen Deutung des Todes Jesu', *NTS* 19, 1972, 38–64

Ruppert, L., *Jesus als der leidende Gerechte?*, SBS 59, Stuttgart 1972

Schoeps, H. J., *Das Judenschristentum*, Berne and Munich 1964

Bibliography

—, 'Die jüdischen Prophetenmorde', in *Aus frühchristlicher Zeit. Religionsgeschichtliche Untersuchungen*, Tübingen 1950, 126–43

—, Paul. *The Theology of the Apostle in the Light of Jewish Religious History*, London 1961

—, *Theologie und Geschichte des Judenchristentums*, Tübingen 1949

Schrage, W., 'Das Verständnis des Todes Jesu Christi im NT', in *Das Kreuz Jesu Christi als Grund des Heils*, edited by F. Viering, Gütersloh ²1968, 49–89

Schürmann, H., *Der Einsetzungsbericht Lk 22, 19–20*, NTA 20,4, Münster 1955

—, *Jesu Abschiedsrede Lk 22,21–38*, NTA 20,5, Münster 1957

—, *Jesu ureigener Tod*, Freiburg, Basle and Vienna 1975

—, 'Wie hat Jesus seinen Tod bestanden und verstanden?', in *Orientierung an Jesus, Festschrift J. Schmid*, edited by P. Hoffmann, Freiburg 1973, 325–63

Schwager, R., *Brauchen wir einen Sündenbock?*, Munich 1978

Schweizer, E., 'Das Abendmahl. Eine Vergegenwärtigung des Todes Jesu oder ein eschatologisches Freudenmahl?', *TZ* 2, 1946, 81–101

—, 'Besprechung von K. Berger, *Die Auferstehung des Propheten und die Erhöhung des Menschensohnes*', *TLZ* 103, 1978, cols. 874–8

—, *Erniedrigung und Erhöhung bei Jesus und seinen Nachfolgern*, ATANT 28, Zurich ²1962

Spiegel, S., *The Last Trial. Translated from the Hebrew with an introduction by J. Goldin*, New York 1967 (original in *Alexander Marx Jubilee Volume*, New York 1950)

Staerk, W., *Altjüdische liturgische Gebete*, KIT 58, Berlin ²1930

Starcky, J., 'Les quatre étapes du messianisme à Qumrân', *RB* 70, 1963, 481–505

Strecker, G., *Das Judenchristentum in den Pseudoklementinen*, TU 70, Fifth Series 15, Berlin 1958

Stuhlmacher, P., 'Das Bekenntnis zur Auferweckung Jesu von den Toten und die Biblische Theologie', *ZTK* 70, 1973, 365–403

—, and Class, H., *Das Evangelium von der Versöhnung in Christus*, Stuttgart 1979

—, 'Existenzstellvertretung für die Vielen: Mk 10,45 (Mt 20,28)', in *Werden und Wirken des Alten Testaments, Festschrift C. Westermann*, Göttingen and Neukirchen 1980, 412–27

—, 'Zum Thema: Biblische Theologie des Neuen Testaments', in *Biblisch-theologische Studien* 1, edited by K. Haacker and others, 1977, 25–60

—, 'Zur neueren Exegese von Röm 3,24–26', *Jesus und Paulus, Festschrift W. G. Kümmel*, Göttingen 1975, 315–33

Vermes, G., 'Redemption and Genesis XXII – The Binding of Isaac

and the Sacrifice of Jesus', in *Scripture and Tradition in Judaism,*
Haggadic Studies, StPB IV, Leiden 1961, ²1973, 193-227

Vielhauer, P., 'Gottesreich und Menschensohn in der Verkündigung
Jesu', in *Festschrift Günther Dehn,* edited by W. Schneemelcher,
51-79; reprinted in *Aufsätze zum Neuen Testament,* Munich 1965,
55-91

Viering, F., *Der Kreuzestod Jesu. Interpretation eines theologischen
Gutachtens,* Gütersloh 1969

Weiss, K., χρηστός, *TDNT* 9, 483-9

—, *Der leidende Gerechte und seine Feinde,* Würzburg 1973

Wengst, K., *Christologische Formeln und Lieder des Urchristentums,*
StNT 7, Gütersloh ²1973

Whiteley, D. E. H., 'St Paul's Thoughts on the Atonement', *JTS* NS 8,
1957, 240-55

Wlosok, A., *Rom und die Christen,* Stuttgart 1970

Wolff, H. W., *Jesaja 53 im Urchristentum,* Berlin ³1952

Wood, J. E., 'Isaac Typology in the New Testament', *NTS* 14, 1967/
68, 583-9

Index of Biblical References

Index of Ancient Authors

Index of Modern Authors

Behm, J., 10
Ben-Chorim, S., 6
Benz, E., 120, 183, 269 n.45
Bentzen, A., 20
Berger, K., 29, 41, 44f., 52, 59, 61, 65, 76, 283 n.56
Bergmeier, R., 31
Bernhardt, K. H., 21
Bethe, J. A. E., 108
Bettenson, H., 29
Betz, H. D., 34, 272 n.64
Betz, O., 32, 62, 80
Beyschlag, K., 31
Bickerman, E., 56, 108, 111, 281 n.38
Bieler, L., 29
Bietenhard, H., 56
Billerbeck, P., 33, 43, 67, 280 n.31
Blank, J., 8f., 12
Blinzler, J., 117, 121, 133, 183
Bloch, E., 89
Boers, H. W., 16
Boissevain, U. P., 119
Bömer, F., 28, 277 n.95
Bonnet, R. A., 30
Boudreaux, P., 170
Bousset, W., 10, 17, 75, 78
Braaten, C. E., 16
Brandenburger, E., 57, 105, 183
Brasiello, U., 126f.
Bratke, E., 88
Braun, H., 18, 24f., 28f., 33, 35
Brecht, C., 131, 155, 272 n.65
Bréhier, E., 53
Breitenstein, K., 281 n.38
Brockelmann, C., 271 n.59
Bruckner, M., 64
Brunner, H., 21
Buber, M., 6, 68
Büchner, K., 155f.
Bultmann, R., 16f., 26f., 88
Bureth, P., 28
Burkert, W., 209, 268 n.33, 271 n.62, 272 nn.63–5, 273 n.72, 274 n.76, 275 nn.82, 88, 276 n.91
Burkhill, T. A., 185

Calhoun, G. M., 22
Camerarius, J., 101
Campenhausen, H. F. von, 11, 56, 265 n.12, 271 n.57
Cancik, H., 98, 101f.
Capocci, V., 119

Cardascia, G., 127
Carman, A. S., 50
Carmingnac, J., 2
Carter, J. B., 36
Cèbe, J.-P., 128
Chadwick, H., 22
Charlesworth, M. P., 172
Chilton, B. D., 281 n.42, 282 nn.43, 46–6
Christ, F., 73
Colpe, C., 24, 27, 31, 82
Conzelmann, H., 58
Corte, G., 133
Crusius, O., 167
Cullmann, O., 280 n.30
Cumont, F., 101, 169f.

Dahl, N. A., 60, 229
Dalman, G., 280 n.31
Daly, R. J., 281 n.42
Davies, P. R., 281 n.42, 282 nn.43, 45–6
Davies, W. D., 66
Déaut, R. Le, 282 n.45
Deichgräber, R., 74
Deissmann, A., 57, 269 n.45
Delling, G., 22
Denis, A.-M., 46
Deubner, L., 283 n.558
Dibelius, M., 1, 283 n.58
Diels, H., 270 n.46, 271 n.55
Dindorf, W., 273 n.69, 276 n.93
Dinkler, E., 111, 183
Dodds, E. R., 273 n.70, 274 n.74
Drexel, J., 169
Drexler, W., 105
Duckworth, G. E., 44
Duckrey, P., 103, 124, 163ff., 183
Dunand, F., 25, 77
Dupont-Sommer, A., 281 n.38
Düring, I., 271 n.58

Edmonds, J. M., 276 n.28
Eichholz, G., 9, 57
Eitrem, S., 274 n.76
Elfrink, M. A., 33
Ellis, R., 277 n.96
Eltester, F. W., 14, 50, 71, 73
Euler, K. F., 280 n.31

Farnell, L. R., 268 nn.33, 36
Fauth, K., 271 n.62
Fauth, W., 25

Printed in the USA
CPSIA information can be obtained
at www.ICGtesting.com
JSHW010315300724
67042JS00020B/386

9 780334 019631